Understanding U.S.–Latin American Relations

This book examines U.S.–Latin American relations from an historical, contemporary, and theoretical perspective. By drawing examples from the distant and more recent past—and interweaving history with theory—Williams illustrates the enduring principles of International Relations theory and provides students the conceptual tools to make sense of inter-American relations. It is a masterful guide for how to organize facts, think systematically about issues, weigh competing explanations, and confidently draw your own conclusions regarding the past, present, and future of international politics in the region.

Mark Eric Williams is Professor of Political Science at Middlebury College. His research interests include U.S.–Latin American Relations, International Relations, Comparative Latin American Political Economy, Venezuelan Foreign Policy, and Mexican Politics.

Map of North America

Map of South America

Understanding U.S.–Latin American Relations

Theory and History

MARK ERIC WILLIAMS

Routledge
Taylor & Francis Group

NEW YORK AND LONDON

First published 2012
by Routledge
711 Third Avenue, New York, NY 10017

Simultaneously published in the UK
by Routledge
2 Park Square, Milton Park, Abingdon, Oxon OX14 4RN

Routledge is an imprint of the Taylor & Francis Group, an informa business

Library of Congress Cataloging in Publication Data
Williams, Mark Eric, 1954–
Understanding U.S.–Latin American relations : a discourse between theory
and history / Mark Eric Williams.
p. cm.
Includes bibliographical references and index.
1. Latin America--Foreign relations--United States. 2. United States--Foreign
relations--Latin America. I. Title. II. Title: Understanding US-Latin American
relations. III. Title: Understanding United States-Latin American relations.
JZ1519.A57U6 2011
327.7308--dc23
2011022098

ISBN: 978–0–415–99314–2 (hbk)
ISBN: 978–0–415–99315–9 (pbk)
ISBN: 978–0–203–80510–7 (ebk)

Typeset in Avenir and Dante
by Keystroke, Station Road, Codsall, Wolverhampton

Acquisitions Editor: Michael Kerns
Development Editor: Felisa Salvago-Keyes
Editorial Assistant: Mary Altman
Production Editors: Siân Findlay and Alf Symons

Dedication

To the Memory of Mary Frances and Joseph Leonardo Williams, my first, ablest, and most important teachers

And for Jannine, one of the world's pure souls

Contents

Illustrations

Figures

Tables

Foreword

What is the key problem that Latin American countries have faced in the international system? The problem is easy to name but difficult to analyze. The name of the problem is the United States of America.

Consider the name. In the late eighteenth century, thirteen small former British colonies on the eastern seashore of North America sought boldly to appropriate for themselves the symbolic name of the entire American continent. The country might have been called the United States East of the Appalachians and South of the Great Lakes but, alas, it chose a name bound to confuse forevermore primary school children from Tierra del Fuego to Hudson Bay.

Consider the behavior. Only the United States has posed a credible military threat to its Latin American near-neighbors. It acquired Spanish Florida through coercive diplomacy. It invaded Mexico in 1846 and went on to annex half of the country's territory. In 1898, it conquered Puerto Rico and occupied Cuba. In the decades that followed, it repeatedly sent troops to occupy the Dominican Republic, Nicaragua, Haiti and, at times, Cuba, all of which it occupied for years, sometimes decades. It compelled Panama's secession from Colombia. It invaded Mexico yet again in 1914 and 1917. In the second half of the twentieth century, it organized military forces to overthrow the governments of Guatemala (successfully), Nicaragua (unsuccessfully), and Cuba (unsuccessfully). It invaded the Dominican Republic (1965), Grenada (1983), Panama (1989), and Haiti (1994, 2003) to overthrow their governments. From the 1940s to the 1970s, the U.S. government supported military coups near and far, across the Americas, all in the name of "protecting freedom."

U.S. capacities did not equip it to invade much further than the southern Caribbean, we now know, but South Americans did not quite know what to expect for much of the time from 1846 to the end of the 1920s when U.S. forces withdrew from occupation of several of its near-neighbors, never to return. But during that near-century of repeated military actions and especially in 1898, in response to the U.S. defeat of Spain and its seizure of Spain's remaining American colonies (Puerto Rico and Cuba), the Uruguayan José Enrique Rodó wrote the first best-selling nonfiction work to spread like wildfire across the world of the Spanish-speaking peoples. How should Latin Americans assess the United States? Why was its culture vulgar, its Protestantism designed as an arm of the criminal law to curtail the passions and shame the wicked, its military power so threatening, and yet what made it so successful and, in some respects, so admirable?

Alas, that was also a key part of the problem. To the then slaves in Brazil and Venezuela, weighted down by chains and oppression, those thrilling words in the 1776 Declaration of Independence of just thirteen of the many British colonies in the Americas had to hold appeal: "We hold these truths to be self-evident, that all men are created equal." And to their American-born white masters, other words in the same declaration were just as important: governments "derive their just powers from the consent of the governed." This is what Mark Williams in this book calls the "soft power" of the United States—the irresistible attraction of the elements of its polity, its economy, its civilization, its capacity for innovation, and its culture that elicit respect, support, emulation, cooperation, and, yes, admiration.

In this splendid book, Williams describes these seemingly incongruous attitudes as the many faces of power in addition to "soft power." In the face of relentless and repeatedly deployed U.S. military power, Latin American states had to be realistic. Their realism mandated self-help in the face of this Northern menace. The Cuban government of Fidel Castro after 1959 was, however, the only one to succeed in arming itself to such an extent that it could credibly threaten the United States with severe harm if it were to invade it. That is what Williams calls "internal balancing." And that same Cuban government sought the assistance of the Old World to redress the imbalance of power in the New World, namely, Fidel Castro's Cuban government sought the assistance of the Soviet Union and, at a key moment, Soviet nuclear weapons. That demonstrated a keen understanding of the uses of the "balance of power," as Williams explains it, and a direct application of a realist theoretical approach to the conduct of Cuba's foreign policy. To counter the United States, Cuba employed both internal and external balancing as acts of self-help in an anarchic international system.

More common was what Williams calls "bandwagoning." Too weak to challenge the United States, too repelled by Nazi Germany's racism in the 1930s and 1940s or communist ideologies in the twentieth century, most Latin American governments cooperated with the United States most of the time. Yet, it was often a rickety wagon and a dispirited band that summoned the Latin Americans to the side of the United States. Yes, from 1970 onwards, their governments had no choice but to cooperate with the U.S. "war on drugs" even if they understood that the transnational problem could never be addressed successfully given the high demand for drugs in U.S. society—and they understood even better that the "war on drugs" exported the violence to Colombia and to Bolivia and elsewhere from a United States that was unwilling and unable to address its own problems.

Just as important was the extensive practice of policies and behaviors associated with what Williams calls liberal and neoliberal policies. The United States would become for many years the leading trade and investment partner of nearly all the countries of Latin America. Matched with the much more prosperous countries of Western Europe, Latin American countries proved remarkably more important to the United States. In the early twentieth century, the United States exported more to Mexico than to the United Kingdom or Germany, more to Colombia than to Spain, more to the Dominican Republic than to Austria. Domestic elites and coalitions in Latin American countries were the pillars of inter-American cooperation because their interests in partnership with the U.S. economy were so significant. In these respects, the United States and the Latin American countries work effectively to develop their joint prosperity.

In that same spirit, Latin Americans helped to fashion international institutions in the Western Hemisphere that, in the pursuit of lofty shared values, sought in fact to constrain the brute display of U.S. power. Led since the end of the nineteenth century by Argentine jurists and diplomats, Latin Americans sought to ban the use of military force by any outside power to collect international debts or to protect expatriates. For the most part, they succeeded in enshrining these principles in international law and practice. Latin Americans also made a deal with the United States in time for the onset of the Cold War between the United States and the Soviet Union: the Latin Americans would side with the United States against the Soviet Union provided the United States refrained from interfering in the domestic affairs of Latin American countries. Neither side kept to its side of the bargain. The United States repeatedly backed the overthrow of governments in various Latin American countries, including some distant and big such as Brazil in 1964 and Chile in 1973. And especially in the 1970s, the Latin Americans freely engaged with the Soviet Union to advance policies of which the U.S. government disapproved. In the 1970s, for example, Peru purchased advanced weapons systems from the

Soviet Union; in 1980, Argentina sold grain to the Soviet Union to help it break a grain boycott that the United States had imposed to punish the Soviet invasion of Afghanistan.

Yet, inter-American institutions served the hemisphere well for other purposes. They have made inter-state war rare and, if war breaks out, generally short-lived and limited. The resolution of inter-state disputes has remained generally peaceful and successful, even if it may take many years. The varied institutions of the hemisphere and its subregions have fostered cooperation in various other ways, notably in public health.

In war as in trade, nearly all Latin American countries sided with the United States when it really mattered. The American Republics declared war on Nazi Germany, Fascist Italy, and Imperial Japan in the months that followed the Japanese attack on Pearl Harbor in 1941 (only Argentina remained neutral until nearly the end of the war in Europe). In 1962, in the face of the Soviet Union's deployment of nuclear weapons to Cuba, the American Republics rallied again to defend the Western Hemisphere from such an unacceptable breach, joining the United States to balance Soviet power in the wider international system. And on September 11, 2001, all the countries of the Americas felt that they, too, were Americans, grieving for the dead and wounded from the terrorist attacks on New York and Washington. Even Fidel Castro's Cuba, ever fearful of U.S. aggression, opened its airports to U.S. airplanes that needed to land in an emergency; and, led by Brazil, for the first time ever, the Inter-American Treaty for Reciprocal Assistance was invoked to face a threat on one of the countries of the hemisphere from outside attack.

In peace and in hope, Latin Americans, too, have aligned with the United States time and again. By the start of the twenty-first century, there was one and only one way to legitimate a ruler in a Latin American country: elections. There was clearly far more success among those Latin American countries that had shaped and fostered a market economy (Chile, Brazil, Uruguay) than among those few that had tried to shun it (Venezuela, Bolivia, Cuba). No Latin American country possessed nuclear weapons, notwithstanding the necessary technical skills and other resources in Argentina and Brazil. The architecture of inter-state territorial peace was gradually strengthened in the years that followed the end of the Cold War, especially in South America's southern cone. In these very practical respects, most countries of the Americas had come to share common values in their domestic and international behavior.

At the dawn of the third millennium, the principal Latin American complaint derived precisely from the "soft power" of the United States: live up to your own principles. Dismantle the walls of protectionism that discriminated against Brazilian steel, Dominican sugar, or Colombian textiles. Cheer the fact that the largest cement company in North America was headquartered in Mexico and that Brazilian entrepreneurs had purchased control of Burger King and Budweiser as tributes to the spread of a genuinely "American" entrepreneurial spirit. Uphold the rule of law at home and do not export the violence from the "war on drugs". Set an example: do not practice torture in the name of anti-terrorism, given the vast torture pandemic that faced much of Latin America from the 1960s to the 1980s. Be true to the words inscribed on the Statue of Liberty in New York harbor, and thus welcome "your tired, your poor, the wretched of the earth," even from Latin America. And lead the Americas—all of them—to fulfill the elusive but powerful promise of yet another of the key concepts in the 1776 Declaration of Independence, namely, "the pursuit of happiness."

Jorge I. Domínguez
Harvard University

Preface

Most Americans spend little time thinking about Latin America. Their knowledge of the region is spotty and superficial. They often are surprised at the latent (and sometimes overt) anti-Americanism exhibited across the region, and while they draw comfort to learn that the United States' government—not its people—is generally the focus of these sentiments, the sentiments nonetheless seem puzzling. Much of the puzzlement stems from a shallow comprehension of U.S.–Latin American relations.

The relationship is significant. On a range of issues, Latin America *matters* enormously to the United States and vice versa. In terms of trade, Latin America absorbs nearly 20 percent of U.S. exports, and following Africa, it is the United States' fastest growing geographical trading partner (from the mid-1990s through 2006, total U.S. exports to, and imports from, Latin America jumped 118 percent). The United States relies more on Latin America for its energy needs than it does on the Middle East, with four countries—Colombia, Ecuador, Mexico, and Venezuela—providing over a third of all U.S. oil imports. Latin America affects U.S. demographics too. Since 2000, it has accounted for nearly 59 percent of all immigrants that have come to the United States.[1] The two Americas are also linked by a durable black market: Latin America is the United States' chief supplier of illicit drugs, and Americans spend over $30 billion a year on cocaine alone (90 percent of which comes from Colombia). Finally, the United States and Latin America have shared common security concerns. Most governments in the region joined Washington to oppose fascism in World War II, and Communism during the Cold War. Most sided with Washington when the United States faced the existential threat of Soviet nuclear weapons stationed in Cuba. Most also have joined the United States in combating drug trafficking.

The significance of the U.S.–Latin American relationship is matched by its complexity. It is a relationship marked by asymmetries in influence, power, and wealth, and by two-way friendly overtures, mistrust, and mutual resentments. For two centuries, it has been characterized by cycles of cooperation and conflict, hope and disappointment. A little over a decade after Spanish colonies began to declare their independence from Madrid, the United States—through the 1823 Monroe Doctrine—went on record in support of Latin America's newly acquired independence and in opposition to European efforts to recolonize the region. Yet, just six years later, South America's preeminent liberator, Símon Bolivar—a great admirer of American democracy—proclaimed that the United States "appears to be destined by Providence to plague [the] America[s] with miseries in the name of Liberty."[2] This comment speaks to the tensions that developed early on in U.S.–Latin American relations, and which remain a strong undercurrent even today.

At first blush, the tension and complexities inherent in U.S.–Latin American relations seem paradoxical. Although historically separated by culture, ethnicity, and language, the two Americas actually have much in common. They share a common experience of colonialism, revolution, and Western orientation. In general, the people of Latin America admire the United States' democracy, much of its culture, and its economic prowess. Many governments of Latin America have been loyal allies of the United States. They have joined America in partnerships, formal alliances, informal ententes, and other U.S.-sponsored initiatives; often, they have voted as a bloc with Washington in international forums like the Organization of American States and the United Nations. However, they have differed sharply with the United States on such basic foreign policy issues as respect for sovereignty and the principle of nonintervention, the definition of and approach to security threats, and the desirability of unilateral vs. multilateral actions.

Much of the disagreement stems from what Latin American governments have perceived as a gap between the objectives, principles, and political values the United States has espoused, and the actual policies (and their consequences) it has pursued. Although America's domestic political ideals—consent, democracy, equality, liberty, and self-determination—are usually enshrined in official U.S. policy statements, they have not always been honored in practice. At different times, for example, Washington has accommodated and supported non-democratic governments in Latin America, while at other times it has confronted them and intervened in their internal affairs. At still other times, it has opposed Latin American governments that *were* democratically elected, encouraged coups that brought dictatorial regimes to power, then supported these dictatorships as they trampled consent, democracy, and individual liberty.

When the renowned Mexican author and intellectual, Carlos Fuentes, gave the Commencement Speech at Harvard University in 1983, he employed a blunt allegory to criticize these policy zigzags and inconsistencies. The United States, he said, acted like a "Dr. Jekyll and Mr. Hyde"—operating with pristine democratic values at home for its own citizens, but denying everybody else the chance to do the same. Although Fuentes' claims were no doubt an exaggeration, his critique raised important questions. Why has the United States sometimes acted so erratically toward Latin America? How have Latin American states responded to U.S. policy? Why have hemispheric relations been characterized by cycles of cooperation and conflict?

Such questions inform the writing of this book, which, in turn, draws inspiration from a course on U.S.–Latin American relations that I have taught at Middlebury College for 16 years. Teaching this course has been a satisfying experience (I have learned much from my students over the years), and at times, a challenging one too. Because the literature on international relations tends to focus on inter-state dynamics in regions other than Latin America, finding material that simultaneously provides appropriate historical examples, introduces students to the region, and exposes them to international relations theory has not always been easy.

This book seeks to fill that gap. Its goal is to introduce students to a way of thinking about U.S.–Latin American relations (and international politics more generally), by providing a set of analytic tools that will better equip them to organize facts, think systematically about issues, untangle complexity, weigh competing explanations, and have confidence in their own conclusions regarding the past, present, and future of international politics in the region. While the United States is the dominant actor in the relationship and its policies and actions bear close assessment, the book strives to avoid a pure U.S.-centric perspective. Consequently, as the analysis unfolds—and especially from Chapter 5 onward—Latin American states increasingly emerge as actors in their own right and their behavior is assessed using standard analytic tools.

Still, this book is not an exhaustive review of every aspect of U.S.–Latin American relations, nor is it a comprehensive text on the history of hemispheric diplomacy. Its objective is not simply to describe past or present relations, but rather, to explain the causes of state actions, reactions, and the patterns of cooperation and conflict that have characterized the relationship. By drawing examples from past and more contemporary periods—and interweaving history with political theory—it illustrates the utility and limitations of some of the central theories, concepts, and analytic frameworks developed to explain international relations and foreign policy making.

This text provides students a firm foundation in realist theory and concepts, then adds to this foundation an understanding of dependency and liberal approaches where they are appropriate. It presents these theories, concepts, and approaches in clear, straightforward prose that students will readily grasp, and employs ample historical and contemporary examples that are relevant to international politics in general and U.S.–Latin American relations in particular. When used in conjunction with suggested readings, the text is well suited to an undergraduate course on these topics.

Mark Eric Williams
January 2011

Acknowledgments

Writing a book is both a solitary and collaborative enterprise, and I would be remiss in failing to acknowledge the many individuals who played a direct or indirect part in bringing this project to fruition. In graduate school I was fortunate to have studied U.S.–Latin American relations under the instruction of Jorge I. Domínguez—a superb mentor and teacher—and for three years, to have served as a Teaching Fellow for Joseph S. Nye, Jr., when he taught an introductory course in International Relations at Harvard. Long before this book was ever conceived, they taught me a great deal about the subject matter and how best to present and explain it. No doubt, many of their insights have crept into my own thinking, and I am happy to acknowledge this intellectual debt. I am also grateful to other colleagues who read the manuscript or portions of it and offered constructive comments, including Michael E. Allison, University of Scranton; Terry L. McCoy, University of Florida; Scott Morgenstern, University of Pittsburgh; Chalmers Brumbaugh, Elon University; Russell Bither-Terry, University of North Carolina at Chapel Hill; Clemente Quinones, Georgia Gwinnett College; Mark A. Martinez, California State University, Bakersfield; Gastón Fernández, Indiana State University; and Mona M. Lyne, University of Missouri–Kansas City. At Middlebury College, I extend thanks to my able research assistants: John Paul Allen, Peter Coccoma, Alethea Gross, and Daniel Sheron. Special thanks also go to Brian Fung for designing the maps used in this book, and to Carolann Davis for assistance on graphics design. A Mellon Foundation Research Award provided financial assistance to help complete this project, and for which I am grateful. Finally, I'd like to thank the team at Routledge—Michael Kerns, Felisa Salvago-Keyes, Siân Findlay and Alf Symons —all of whom provided excellent assistance.

International Politics and U.S.–Latin American Relations

1

Figure 1.1 Flags of the Americas

Over the last three centuries, international politics in the Western Hemisphere have changed significantly. Formal empires have vanished and their colonies have given way to independent states; international institutions and negotiation have replaced warships and threats of force as instruments of debt collection; and states that had waged war against each other (Mexico and the United States, Argentina and Brazil) are now linked tightly together in regional trade accords. Over the last hundred years U.S.–Latin American relations have changed too. Fairly routine U.S. intervention in Latin America's internal affairs has been eclipsed by a broadly shared respect for state sovereignty throughout the hemisphere. The Cold War ideological struggles Washington waged against Communism in Latin America—which helped occasion some U.S. intervention—now constitute only historic artifacts, and today regional governments and the United States cooperate more routinely on joint initiatives in economic development, democracy promotion, anti-drug trafficking programs, and environmental protection. In short, the general relations between the United States and much of Latin America are strong and cordial.

Nevertheless, some aspects of U.S.–Latin American relations have not changed much in over a century. Latin Americans' admiration for U.S. democracy, power, and prosperity is still tempered by resentment of how the United States chooses to wield its influence. For many Latin American governments, its choice in 2002—to encourage and support a coup against Venezuela's democratically elected government—seemed reminiscent of similar choices to support coups in 1973 and 1954, against Chile and Guatemala's democratically elected governments. While most Latin American states spend little time worrying about a potential U.S. military invasion, in the early 2000s such scenarios were discussed openly in Venezuelan government circles, much as they were in other countries a hundred years ago. Latin Americans are still highly sensitive toward even the hint of U.S. intervention in their internal affairs. Across the region, suspicions remain strong regarding U.S. actions and intentions, and Venezuelan president Hugo Chávez's anti-American rhetoric echoes earlier sentiments expressed by a long list of Latin American citizens, intellectuals, and leaders. Indeed, on this point, the more some things change, the more other things stay the same. As historian Alan McPherson notes, "From the days of independence to the middle of the twentieth century, anti-U.S. sentiment touched every major social group in Latin America . . . Peasants, workers, and members of the middle class and the elite all resented being exploited or disdained by the United States at some point."[1]

To say that U.S.–Latin American relations have had their ups and downs is no exaggeration. What explains the seesaw pattern of cooperation and discord, amiability and rancor? What accounts for the relationship's underlying but enduring tensions? Are Latin American states simply jealous of America's economic and political success? Is the United States the Dr. Jekyll and Mr. Hyde that Mexican author Carlos Fuentes once described—acting democratically at home, protecting its citizens' rights to liberty and self-determination, but denying its southern neighbors an opportunity to do the same? Or are there more complex factors behind U.S. policy toward the region and the historic tensions that have colored the relationship? To understand U.S.–Latin American relations requires us to contend with the old and the new, and comprehend both the continuities and changes. By learning the traditional theories of international politics, applying them to historical cases, and adapting them to contemporary conditions, we will open a discourse between history and theory. That discourse, in turn, will provide a broader, deeper understanding of how the two Americas have related to each other and why.

This book seeks to enhance readers' understanding of both the theory and concepts of international politics, and their relevance to the study of U.S.–Latin American relations. It is not a comprehensive diplomatic history of relations between the two Americas, nor is it a pure international relations theory text. Rather than presenting the "whole story" of hemispheric relations, it aims to instruct readers in effective ways of thinking about those relations and international politics more broadly. By situating U.S.–Latin American relations within a broader intellectual and world context, it helps readers appreciate how political scientists assess hemispheric relations, and illustrates how western hemispheric states have responded not just to each other, but to events outside their region. By drawing upon both U.S. and Latin American examples from the distant and more recent past—and interweaving history with theory—it provides readers the conceptual tools required to help organize facts, think systematically about issues, weigh competing explanations, and have confidence in their conclusions regarding the dynamics of inter-American relations. Chapters 3–10 follow the arc of U.S.–Latin American relations from the nineteenth century to the present. This first chapter, the next, and parts of Chapter 3 lay the theoretical foundations for that journey.

International Politics and Foreign Policy

States adopt foreign policies to protect their interests, pursue their objectives, and interact with other states. However, what kind of environment do states exist and interact in, and how does that environment influence the type of foreign policies they might adopt? Most scholars agree that international politics take place inside what we call an *anarchic state system*, one where sovereign states exist without any higher power above them. Such a system is, by default, a self-help system, because states cannot appeal to any higher power for protection or assistance.

A good example of this kind of system is the period of New World colonialism, when Britain, France, Portugal, and Spain came to the Americas and competed against each other to establish colonies. Because these states could rely on no higher government to regulate their competition, boundary and territorial disputes produced conflicts that often were settled by force. Another example would be the post-colonial period: most of Britain's American colonies and many of Spain's too, won their independence and became separate, sovereign states. Again, wars developed within this anarchic system—some between the new Latin American states, others between the United States and Latin American states, and still others between the New World and Old World states. Since the collapse of Europe's formal New World empires in the late eighteenth and early nineteenth centuries, international politics in the Western Hemisphere has been characterized by the sovereign territorial state.

Consequently, when we study relations between the two Americas, we usually will be studying them in the context of an anarchic system of territorial states. What, then, does "anarchic" actually mean and how does this condition affect the way states behave? Anarchy does not mean complete disorder. Rather, it simply means the absence of a higher power or ruler above states that can enforce order or regulate their interactions. The implications this has for international politics and for states' behavior are significant. One crucial implication is that anarchy compels states to operate within a self-help system, where each state has to look out for itself. This situation is akin to what the British philosopher Thomas Hobbes wrote of in the seventeenth century when he talked about a *state of nature*. In this situation, individuals had to fend for themselves and survive as best they could, since there was no higher authority to appeal to for aid. For Hobbes, the state of nature was hardly a tranquil, bucolic environment. Instead, it was riddled with insecurity and potential conflict because absent a higher power to enforce order, it pitted everyone against each other. As a result, Hobbes explained, life in a state of nature could be nasty, brutish, and short.

Using Hobbes' state of nature as a template of international relations can reveal a great deal about world politics and how it differs from domestic politics, particularly with respect to the role played by law and force. In democratic and non-democratic societies alike, for example, most domestic laws are obeyed, and if they are broken, the police and courts can enforce compliance and punish violators. International law, however, is a different story. Not only is it less developed and less coherent than domestic law, but international law also lacks an effective enforcement mechanism. U.S. President Theodore Roosevelt—who had a major impact on the course of U.S.–Latin American relations—believed that the problems and wars that international anarchy helped generate could not be solved readily through international law, due to the lack of an effective enforcement mechanism at the international level. Comparing the domestic to the international realms, he found "no analogy" between international and domestic law "because there is no sanction of force for the former while there is for the latter."[2] Roosevelt's insight captured a fundamental distinction between how the law works at the domestic and international levels.

Like law, force also plays a role in domestic and international politics, but that role is fundamentally different in each realm. Whether democratic or not, in well-run states it is the government—that common ruler above society—which has a monopoly on the legitimate use of force. By contrast, in the international realm no state holds a monopoly on force. The anarchic, self-help nature of international politics means strong states can employ force against weaker ones (and have), and there is always a danger that one state might aggress against another. As a result, anarchy leads states to harbor suspicion and mistrust toward each other, because it "permits" some states to use force against others, and it diminishes the capacity of international law to regulate inter-state relations.

Realism, Liberalism, Marxism, and Dependency

While the absence a higher government above sovereign states is unquestionable, the intensity of international anarchy is open to debate. In the state of nature, anarchy is stark and its problems are intense—everyone is for himself or herself, and it is kill or be killed. Drawing on Hobbes' state of nature, political scientists developed one of the central theories of international relations, *realism*. Realist theory suggests that in the context of anarchy, states are the primary actors in international politics, and issues of security, force, and survival occupy center stage in states' political calculations. Some examples of modern realist scholars include Hans Morgenthau, Kenneth Waltz, John Mearsheimer, and T.V. Paul. Some examples of modern realist practitioners include presidents Theodore Roosevelt, Richard Nixon, Ronald Reagan, former secretary of state Henry Kissinger, and former defense secretary Donald Rumsfeld.

One way to appreciate the realist concept of international politics is to visualize states as something akin to pool balls that are isolated from each other and bounce off each other as they try to protect their security by balancing each other's power. History offers examples of such balancing dynamics. In the 1880s, Brazil and Chile developed an entente to balance the power of Argentina, Bolivia, and Peru.[3] In 1962, Havana accepted Moscow's suggestion that Soviet nuclear missiles be installed in Cuba to help balance U.S. power and stave off an American invasion. In the early twentieth century, the United States took over the national customs houses of the Dominican Republic, Haiti, and Nicaragua to ensure orderly repayment of their debts to European powers, keep the Europeans from sending their militaries to collect debts by force, and thus, prevent the Europeans from establishing a military presence in the region that could tip the balance of power against the United States.

These examples indicate how realists might explain the way states act under certain conditions. Consequently, the more clearly we understand realist theory, the more effectively we can apply it to specific cases. Having said that, however, it is important to note that political theories have limits and that some level of uncertainty is inherent in any theory we use; individuals, after all, actually lead states and human behavior can vary widely.

Although international relations theory owes an intellectual debt to Thomas Hobbes, other political philosophers saw things differently. Both John Locke and Immanuel Kant, for example, accepted anarchy; but they also believed that people could still develop ties with each other, and Kant, especially, believed that states could forge international institutions to help bring them closer together, engender cooperation, and preserve peace. From these insights sprang a second approach to international relations, *liberalism*—a school of thought that should not be confused with the "liberal" label of progressive or left-of-center politics fashionable in U.S. domestic politics. Liberals believe that economic interdependence, international institutions, international trade, transnational contacts, and other dynamics can help bridge the gap between individual states, and thereby mitigate the intensity of anarchy. Some examples of liberal theorists include Hedley Bull, Michael Doyle, Robert Keohane, Stanley Hoffmann, and G. John Ikenberry. Modern liberal practitioners would include Woodrow Wilson, Jimmy Carter, Óscar Arias, Bill Clinton, and (yes) Hugo Chávez.

Liberal theorists believe that realists exaggerate the intensity and problems of anarchy, and overlook critical aspects of international politics as a result. Liberals stress the factors that help link states together, and the way these linkages mollify friction, dampen security threats, and moderate the use of force. International institutions, for example, serve as forums in which states can communicate, deliberate, and resolve conflicts peacefully. Unlike realists, liberals also contend that states are not the only significant actors in international politics. The Organization of American States (OAS)—an international institution—is an important non-state actor in the Western Hemisphere. When Venezuelan president Hugo Chávez was briefly deposed in 2002, the OAS refused to recognize the government led by businessman Pedro Carmona that assumed power as a result of the coup. In this case, the OAS acted to defend the Western Hemisphere's norm of constitutional rule, and its action deprived the Carmona government of an important source of international legitimacy.

Finally, because of the various ways that financial flows, institutions, trade, and other factors can link states together, liberals also see the possibility for a community of states to develop. Such a supranational entity would not constitute a common sovereign above the individual states, but liberals contend it could still develop norms and principles that affect states' behavior, promote cooperation, and help regulate their interaction. For example, the "Bolivarian Alternative for the Americas" developed by the Chávez government in Venezuela, is an integration project whose norms of cooperation, reciprocity, and solidarity link Venezuela with other states such as Argentina, Bolivia, Cuba, and Nicaragua. Through a series of trade accords (People's Trade Agreements) these states endeavor to cooperate and facilitate each other's national development. They can exchange goods (energy and agricultural products) for services (education, health care, technical assistance), and finance oil purchases from Venezuela in hard currencies or "trade in kind." Another example is the North American Free Trade Agreement, or NAFTA—a tri-national arrangement in which Canada, Mexico, and the United States comprise an economic community of trading partners. Its norms of free trade, reciprocity, and transparency govern their economic interactions, while its environmental side-agreements address threats to each state's environmental wellbeing that expanded trade might create. By integrating these three states' economies, NAFTA links the economic fortunes of one to all and creates powerful incentives to cooperate and support one another in times of need (as when the United States rushed to supply Mexico with a $50 billion loan during the 1994–95 peso crisis).

By contrast, realists discount the moderating effects of trade or institutions. They point out that the explosive growth of international trade in the early twentieth century did not prevent World War I between states that traded extensively with each other. Nor did the United Nations (or the Organization of American States for that matter) prevent the 1982 Falkland Islands War between Argentina and Great Britain. Moreover, the very fact of anarchy fuels security concerns that compel states to maintain standing armies even in peacetime. Such examples, realists believe, demonstrate that despite the liberals' more optimistic vision, the "reality" of international politics remains centered on security, force, and survival. In response, liberals point out that today, the vast majority of politics among states actually have little to do with military security or armed inter-state conflict. In the Western Hemisphere, for example, the big states (Argentina, Brazil, Chile, Colombia, Canada, Mexico, Venezuela, and the United States) have not fought each other in over 150 years.

They do, however, maintain strong trade and economic relations through arrangements that tie their economies ever more closely together; they cooperate on issues of material interest (drug trafficking, the environment, supporting democracy); and they pursue a host of other collaborative endeavors. Does it make sense, liberals ask, to define and study international politics in a way that fails to capture such a broad range of activities?

Liberals and realists view international politics quite differently, and the debate between these two schools of thought is an important one that will not be resolved soon. Neither theoretical approach holds a monopoly on explanatory power. As we shall see, each can explain some aspects of hemispheric relations the other cannot, and despite being dominant theoretical perspectives in the field, neither has gone unchallenged.

Beginning in the nineteenth century, for example, *Marxism* began to attract a significant following. Based on the writings of Karl Marx and Friedrich Engels (and developed further by others), Marxism stressed the importance that domestic economic factors and class structures have for the development of capitalist states and their foreign policies. In states with capitalist economic systems, a minority of citizens (the *bourgeoisie*) exploits the majority (the workers or *proletariat*) for private gain, by controlling society's means of production. Because capitalist systems excel at manufacturing vast quantities of products—but an exploited majority lacks the means to consume them—domestic under-consumption, a lack of investment opportunities, and periodic recessions plague capitalist countries. Marxists argued these factors led capitalist states to adopt imperialist foreign policies that could expand foreign investment opportunities, open new trade markets, secure access to raw materials, and ensure continued capitalist expansion. In the end, economic imperatives would drive capitalist states to be highly aggressive—both toward countries with large resource endowments, and other capitalist states too—while relations between non-capitalist states that lack these imperatives would be more peaceful.

History suggests, however, that foreign policy output is more than a function of countries' economic systems, and Marxist explanations of international politics encounter real problems. One of the biggest is that by restricting states' interests chiefly to economic matters, Marxist theory completely ignores the ubiquitous security concerns states face under international anarchy that influence their behavior. Another problem is how real-world relations between states often confound Marxist predictions. For example, states with some variant of capitalist economics have certainly aggressed against non-capitalist states and each other (witness the two world wars), but after World War II, capitalist states have enjoyed an extended period of peaceful relations, while Marxist states have clashed (Cambodia vs. Vietnam in 1978,

China vs. Vietnam in 1979, or China vs. the USSR in 1969). A Marxist view of international politics has difficulty explaining such outcomes.

Dependency theory is a variant of Marxism, and enjoyed broad appeal in the 1960s and 1970s. As defined by Brazilian economist Theotonio Dos Santos, dependency exists when "the economy of certain countries is conditioned by the development and expansion of another economy to which the former is subjected . . . [such that] some countries (the dominant ones) can expand and can be self-sustaining, while other countries (the dependent ones) can do this only as a reflection of that expansion."[4] How wealthy and underdeveloped countries are situated, function, and inter-relate in the capitalist global marketplace promotes the concentration of wealth in the former, and impedes development in the latter. Respecting international politics, dependency theorists argued that advanced, wealthy capitalist states (the "center") would dominate and exploit countries in the world's poorer regions (the "periphery"), and adopt foreign policies—including intervention—designed to perpetuate this exploitation. In turn, underdeveloped countries could only progress by severing their linkages to wealthy "center" states and international capitalism—often through revolution—and thereby, acquire the independence to develop more autonomously.

Dependency theory cast a bright light on aspects of global capitalism that helped induce economic inequality between different countries. It aptly captured elements of early twentieth-century relationships between the United States and some of its neighbors, and some U.S. policies that sought to advance and defend American economic interests. Its logic also appealed powerfully to Latin American intellectuals and political leaders, who found in it exogenous reasons for their countries' economic and political disadvantages. In the 1950s, for example, Argentine economist Raúl Prebisch helped popularize the Prebisch–Singer thesis which argued that over time, the terms of trade between advanced and developing countries (who exchanged commodities for manu-factured goods) would evolve in ways that advantaged the former at the latter's expense. This thesis became a cornerstone of dependency theory, and Prebisch later helped formulate economic prescriptions he hoped could help Latin American states break their economic dependence. Similarly, in the 1970s Brazilian sociologist Fernando Henrique Cardoso co-authored a major treatise on dependency theory and became one of the region's leading dependency theorists.

The logic of dependency arguments sheds light on what motivated some Latin American states to adopt policies that might increase their economic or political autonomy. However, as a robust, predictive theory, dependency encountered problems. In the Western Hemisphere, for example, sometimes

U.S. policy did seek to promote and protect American economic interests to the disadvantage of weaker "dependent" Latin American states. But as we shall see in Chapters 5 and 7, at other times U.S. policy prioritized larger political goals over American economic interests (as in the Good Neighbor Policy and early Alliance for Progress), and did so even when U.S. economic interests were at stake. By the 1980s, dependency theory had become widely discredited due to its inability to explain why East Asian peripheral countries like South Korea or Singapore realized stronger economic performance by embracing aspects of global capitalism instead of avoiding it. By the 1990s, even Cardoso (then, President of Brazil) had abandoned dependency's policy prescriptions in favor of more liberal, capitalist- and market-oriented ones, while realist and liberal views of international politics retained much of their utility.

Why Do We Need Theory?

If states adopt foreign policies in the realm of a self-help, anarchic system, what is the best way to study U.S.–Latin American relations? Some historians might recommend a close reading of diplomatic history, while some political scientists may stress the value of a theoretical understanding of states' behavior over historical analysis. However, neither history nor theory alone will suffice. An approach more conducive to deep comprehension is to meld history with political theory, so that the latter helps illuminate the former.

Some might question this approach. Why bother with theory at all? Why not just focus on what particular states have done or how the U.S. and Latin American governments have related to each other at different times or respecting different issues? The answer is that good analysis transcends merely learning "the facts" of a case, and without theory, the study of U.S.–Latin American relations would devolve into a simple chronicling of events—a description of who did what to whom. If we want our efforts to yield a deep understanding of why particular events unfolded the way they did, we need some way to organize facts and explain outcomes systematically, and for this, theories are crucial. As political scientist Robert Keohane suggests, if we ignore theory in our analysis, we are, in essence, choosing to be "guided by an unexamined jumble of prejudices, yielding conclusions that may not logically follow from the assumptions."[5] Keohane makes an apt point. We can always look up the facts respecting some aspect of U.S.–Latin American relations, or consult an encyclopedia to learn about the Cuban Missile Crisis or the Alliance for Progress. What we will not always find in this source, though, is a good, satisfying explanation for why the Cuban Missile Crisis occurred, why the U.S.

government adopted the Alliance, why this policy took the form that it did, or why it ultimately failed to achieve its goals. Because theory enables us to organize facts and systematically weigh competing explanations, it can help us derive the most persuasive account for why events developed the way they did, and in the process, make U.S.–Latin American relations more intelligible.

Using theory is important, but what exactly does this term mean? For political scientists, "theory" refers to a causal explanation of an event or outcome that is based on certain prior conditions or occurrences. The standard formulation of a causal theory is: "If A, then B," or "Whenever A is present, then B can be expected to follow." We can move from this abstract formulation to one that is more concrete, and which can be tested against real-world facts: "The more states respect each other's sovereignty, the fewer international conflicts there will be." This proposition has real-world utility precisely because most violations of sovereignty lead to inter-state friction, and sometimes war. The 1846–48 Mexican-American War, for example, started in part from a perceived violation of sovereignty, as did the 1982 Falkland Islands War between Argentina and Great Britain.

Violations of sovereignty occur when one state intervenes in another's territory or internal affairs. Since these actions can lead to conflict, the question arises as to why states intervene in the first place. There are many possible explanations. Perhaps it is because there is no world government to enforce the rules, settle disputes, and keep the peace. This explanation puts the blame for interventions on the kind of international anarchy that realists stress, since under anarchic conditions there is really nothing to *stop* a state from intervening. Yet, anarchy alone cannot fully account for violations of sovereignty; otherwise, many states would intervene much more routinely. States also intervene from a desire to spread their own ideology. The Soviet Union, for example, intervened in Eastern Europe to spread Communism (as did Cuba in some neighboring states), while the United States intervened in Latin America to spread democracy. Sometimes states intervene for humanitarian reasons too (as with the 1994 U.S. intervention in Haiti), or because they perceive an external threat coming from another state. This is what the United Sates seemed to do when it trained and financed a group of Cuban exiles to invade communist Cuba in 1961.

Given that many different factors might cause one state to violate another's sovereignty, how can we determine which factor was most important? Simply hazarding a guess will not do. A better approach is to employ theory to help us organize our facts, systematize our thinking, and weigh competing causal arguments.

Constructing Good Theoretical Explanations

To construct a good theoretical explanation of foreign policy output or of the dynamics of U.S.–Latin American relations, we first need to clarify our units of analysis and their modes of operation. Who are the principal actors in international politics? What are their primary goals and what instruments do they use to obtain these goals? To what extent does the traditional realist view of international politics on these matters capture how each may have changed over time?

From the tradition of realist theory, states are the only significant actors in international politics, and it is the strong states that matter most. For example, suppose we considered the 1823 Monroe Doctrine (which marked the beginning of explicit U.S. policy toward Latin America) from a realist perspective. What we would see is that James Monroe directed this policy toward strong sovereign states like Britain, France, and Spain (whose power had waned) that might act to re-colonize the territories in the Western Hemisphere. By contrast, the weak states of Latin America—Argentina, Colombia, Haiti, Mexico, Peru, and so on—did not factor in as *actors* at all. They were neither the principal targets of this U.S. policy, nor did they play any role (or have any say) in its promulgation. Traditional realist theory, then, identifies strong states as the primary actors, and only strong states are significant.

Yet, this situation is changing. In modern times, some Latin American states whose military power is dwarfed by that of industrial states in North America or Western Europe have developed foreign policies with regional aspirations that rival Washington's. Cuba in the 1960s and 1970s, and Brazil and Venezuela today, exemplify this. Another important change has been the emergence of non-state actors. Multinational corporations (MNCs) play critical roles in the U.S. and Latin American economies, and in the past, U.S. firms like the United Fruit Company, or Anaconda and Kennecott Copper, mattered a great deal to the economic (and political) fortunes of countries like Guatemala and Chile. In Chile's case, for example, depending on the year, the two copper firms' total production accounted for 7–20 percent of Chile's Gross Domestic Product, financed 10–40 percent of its federal budget, and generated 30–80 percent of its hard currency earnings. As political scientist Theodore Moran observed in 1974: "All of *Fortune's* 500 largest U.S. corporations combined do not play nearly the role in the economy of the United States or pay more than a fraction of the percentage of U.S. taxes that Anaconda and Kennecott alone supplied in Chile."[6]

Although MNCs lack the military power that states possess, some have economic resources that surpass those of many states in the region (Tables 1.1 and 1.2). Chile and Peru's GDP, for example, is smaller than sales of firms like

Shell and Exxon-Mobile, while Colombia's and Venezuela's GDPs are smaller than Wal-Mart's sales. Other non-state actors include international institutions like the Organization of American States, the Inter-American Development Bank, World Bank, and International Monetary Fund (in the 1980s and 1990s the last two wielded enormous influence in the remaking and marketization of many Latin American economic development models). They also include nongovernmental organizations such as Amnesty International and Americas Watch, and of course, transnational crime and drug-running networks that operate throughout the hemisphere and threaten the interests of states large and small. While states remain the most important actors in hemispheric affairs, the role of non-state actors cannot be overlooked.

The goals pursued in international politics have changed too. The realist perspective asserts that in an anarchic system, a state's most important goal is military security. Yet, many states also care deeply about issues besides security. Today, economic development, greater prosperity, environmental degradation, food scarcity, and the spread of deadly viruses all compete with security to form a more complex agenda.

Table 1.1 Gross Domestic Product Estimate of Select Countries ($ in Purchasing Power Parity), 2009

United States	14.1 trillion
China	8.8 trillion
Japan	4.1 trillion
Germany	2.8 trillion
United Kingdom	2.1 trillion
Brazil	2 trillion
Mexico	1.4 trillion
Argentina	568.2 billion
Colombia	407.5 billion
Venezuela	348.8 billion
Peru	251.0 billion
Chile	243.2 billion
Cuba	110.8 billion
Ecuador	110.4 billion
Costa Rica	48.8 billion
Bolivia	45.5 billion
Nicaragua	16.6 billion
Haiti	11.9 billion

Source: Central Intelligence Agency, *CIA World Factbook 2010*

Table 1.2 Annual Sales of Select, Private-Sector Multinational Corporations ($), 2010

Wal-Mart (US)	408.2 billion
Royal Dutch Shell (Netherlands)	285.1 billion
Exxon Mobil (US)	284.6 billion
BP (Britain)	246.1 billion
Toyota (Japan) '	204.1 billion
General Electric (US)	156.7 billion
Volkswagen (Germany)	146.2 billion
AT&T (US)	123.0 billion
Carrefour (France)	121.4 billion
Nippon Telegraph & Telephone (Japan)	109.6 billion
Samsung Electronics (South Korea)	108.9 billion
General Motors (US)	104.5 billion
Siemens (Germany)	103.6 billion
Nestlé (Switzerland)	99.1 billion
Hitachi (Japan)	96.5 billion
IBM (US)	95.7 billion
Honda Motors (Japan)	92.4 billion
Vodafone (Britain)	70.8 billion
BASF (Germany)	70.4 billion
Peugeot (France)	67.2 billion
PepsiCo (US)	43.2 billion

Source: *Fortune Global 500, 2010,* http://money.cnn.com/magazines/fortune/global 500/2010/full_list, accessed January 6, 2011

What about the tools states use to pursue their objectives? Here too, the situation has been dynamic, not static. Traditional realist theory sees military force as the instrument of choice, since hard power can deter an attack or repel it (thus preserving security), as well as help a strong state advance its non-security interests too. In the *Federalist Papers*, Alexander Hamilton argued that one of the main goals the new United States *had* to pursue was to construct a strong navy that could defend the country, and influence the balance of power in the Caribbean where European powers struggled over colonial possessions and influence. Today, states in the Western Hemisphere still employ military force on occasion, but more often, they utilize other tools to achieve their goals. Diplomacy, foreign aid, information technology, international institutions, and trade agreements are some examples of alternative tools that are widely used today.

Several factors have undercut the utility of military force in modern hemispheric relations. Some issues are simply less amenable to hard power (economic prosperity, the spread of AIDS or Avian Flu, drug and immigrant smuggling, trade disputes, transnational pollution flows). Domestic politics can also work against the routine use of force. In the 1980s, for example, American public opinion opposed direct U.S. military intervention in Nicaragua, despite the Reagan administration's contention that the Sandinista government represented a clear threat to U.S. national security. And since the mid-twentieth century, Inter-American peacekeeping arrangements (through the OAS and third-party arbitration efforts) have also helped minimize the use of force. All this is not to say that military power has become obsolete as a tool of international politics, but rather, that in today's world it can be more costly to use and often less effective in various contexts than other tools.

Identifying the actors, goals, and tools is the first step toward analyzing international politics from a theoretical perspective. The next step is to understand how theory and analytic concepts shed light on foreign policy decisions and key political events. In 1962, the relations between the United States and Cuba—a tiny Latin American/Caribbean state—almost triggered a global thermonuclear war. The Cuban Missile Crisis has been the subject of intense scrutiny. The actors involved, the goals they pursued, and the tools they used in many respects bore the hallmarks of realist theory. In Chapter 7, we will study this dramatic crisis in detail; but for now, even a brief review will illustrate and affirm the value that a discourse between history and theory provides, and which we will encounter throughout much of this book.

The Cuban Missile Crisis: Summarizing a Complex Story

For the first half of the twentieth century the United States and Cuba maintained close political and economic relations. In 1898, U.S. forces intervened in Cuba's war of independence and helped defeat its colonial master, Spain. Thereafter, Cuba struggled to develop a robust democracy, yet relations between Havana and Washington remained close, and stayed that way even when Cuba fell into dictatorship. In 1958, however, Fidel Castro's guerrilla army ousted Cuba's dictator, Fulgencio Batista. Castro took over the government as the leader of a nationalist movement, and a short time later, declared he was a socialist. From this point onward, the relations between the United States and Cuba soured, then turned hostile. In 1960, Cuba formally allied itself with the United States' mortal Cold War enemy, the Soviet Union; the United States restricted trade with Cuba and the Cuban government nationalized $1 billion in American assets. U.S.-Cuban relations had collapsed.

Then in 1961 President John Kennedy authorized a covert invasion of Cuba by U.S.-trained Cuban exiles to remove Castro from power. Although the

Central Intelligence Agency had promised Kennedy that the invasion would be a sure thing, it was just the opposite—a complete disaster that ended in the absolute defeat of the Cuban exiles. After repelling this invasion, Castro expected the United Sates to launch a full-scale assault by uniformed U.S. troops, and he had no illusions that Cuba could defend itself against such a force. It was in this context of tension, hostility, and insecurity that the Soviet Union suggested that nuclear missiles be installed in Cuba to defend against a U.S. attack. The Cuban government accepted its ally's suggestion and made a formal diplomatic request for the missiles. The Soviets obliged, shipping, then installing the missiles covertly. Once the United States discovered the missiles in October 1962, the Cuban Missile Crisis began; with it, came the possibility of nuclear exchanges between Soviet and U.S. naval vessels around Cuba, nuclear strikes against the United States, U.S. bases in the Caribbean, along the Gulf of Mexico, and Europe, and nuclear strikes against the Soviet Union.

Stunned by the Soviets' audacity, mindful that he risked impeachment without a strong American response, and dreading the consequences of making the wrong move, Kennedy reluctantly told the world that any missile launched from Cuba against any state in the Western Hemisphere would be considered an attack by the Soviet Union on the United States and would be met with a full retaliatory nuclear response. The missile crisis had produced a situation of appalling magnitude. It threatened Cuba, the United States, the Soviet Union—and the world—with the specter of nuclear destruction. Besides promising a retaliatory nuclear strike, the Americans also elected to blockade Cuba to stop any more missile shipments and, through the OAS, Latin American states threw their support behind this initiative. Eventually, the Soviets turned their ships around and promised to dismantle the missile sites. Further promises were made by both sides: the Soviets would never reintroduce offensive nuclear weapons into Cuba; the United States, meanwhile, would never invade the island and would also remove similar missiles it had stationed close to the Soviet border in Turkey. As the threat of nuclear war receded, the world breathed easier.

Ironically, at first blush the missile crisis itself might seem counter-intuitive. Throughout the Cold War the United States had worked to contain the spread of Communism. It had established a network of alliances to surround the Soviet Union in Western Europe, Japan, Turkey, and Greece. It counted all of Latin America as its zone of influence and had established a mutual defense treaty with Latin American states to defend against a Soviet attack. It also built a ring of military bases around the Soviet state itself, many with nuclear missiles set to deliver their payloads inside Soviet territory.

The United States had taken these actions to protect its security in an anarchic international system, and to protect the security of its friends. Yet, even with all its defensive efforts, in 1962 the United States still was not secure (nor were the Soviet Union and Cuba), and the world teetered on the brink of nuclear war. How did the United States wind up less secure despite its many precautions? Given the enormous U.S. military might surrounding it, why would the Soviet Union risk provoking the United States to use those weapons by installing nuclear missiles in Cuba? Even though Havana's quest for greater security and defense might seem quite understandable, how did the two superpowers nearly experience what no one really wanted—a nuclear holocaust?

One possibility is that the Soviets acted irrationally when they decided to install missiles in Cuba. Perhaps they were angry with U.S. attempts to overthrow their new ally and fellow socialist state. Maybe this anger—combined with jealousy over America's technological prowess—made them act from emotion rather than reason. Since decisions made in the heat of emotion are often irrational, this might explain the actions that nearly led to nuclear war. Another possibility, however, is that the Soviets really did act rationally, and what caused the nuclear crisis was a *security dilemma*.

The Security and Prisoner's Dilemma

Security dilemmas are generated by one of the basic features of international politics, namely anarchy, or the absence of a common ruler above individual states. Within an anarchic environment, one state's actions to make itself more secure can paradoxically make it and other states more insecure. If state A takes steps to increase its strength and ensure another state cannot harm it, state B may see A becoming stronger, and take steps to protect itself from A. The result is a type of ratcheting effect through which each state's independent actions to make itself stronger and more secure, ultimately leave both states more insecure. Since taking precautions in the face of a threat is reasonable, both states acted rationally. Security dilemmas are a major dynamic in international politics and a paradoxical one too, in that absent a common sovereign, each state's rational actions to make itself more secure may ultimately make it more insecure instead.

In 1962, Soviet Premier Nikita Khrushchev wrote to President Kennedy and explained his country's actions in words that uncannily exemplify the security dilemma. Khrushchev told the president that he understood his concern for the security of the United States, "because this is the first duty of the president"; but he reminded Kennedy that as Chairman of the Soviet Union he also faced the "same duties" for his state, and that Cuba had security concerns too.

"You want to relieve your country from danger and this is understandable. However, Cuba also wants this. [Moreover] you have surrounded
the Soviet Union with military bases, surrounded our allies with military
bases, set up military bases literally around our country, and stationed
your rocket weapons at them . . . in Britain and in Italy . . . Your rockets
are [also] stationed in Turkey. You say that [Cuba] worries you because
it lies at a distance of ninety miles across the sea from the shores of the
United States. However, Turkey lies next to us . . ."[7]

Considering the United States' dramatic defensive posture—its encirclement
of the Soviet Union by U.S. military bases and nuclear weapons—Moscow's
decision to install nuclear missiles in Cuba to balance U.S. power and defend
an ally against a potential attack seems less emotionally driven and less
irrational than it might initially appear. Khrushchev's letter to Kennedy made
this very point. Yet, as we have seen, the rational decision to go this route left
all states much less secure.

How might states avoid getting caught in a security dilemma? One possibility would be to cooperate and reach an agreement that neither will increase
its strength and defenses to the detriment of the other. Such cooperation seems
like common sense, yet effective cooperation under anarchy is actually quite
difficult; after all, if it truly were easy, the Soviet Union, United States, and Cuba
would have avoided the whole missile crisis. We can understand why cooperation is hard by considering a theoretical game called the "Prisoner's
Dilemma." Think of what might happen if the police stopped a car for a traffic
violation and found two male occupants with several thousand dollars cash,
who fit the description of two bank robbers. While the police run the driver's
license and vehicle registration, the two men jointly pledge to remain silent.
Since the cash on hand can be traced to the crime, the men are arrested on
suspicion of bank robbery; but without direct evidence of the crime itself, they
can only be convicted of receiving stolen goods, which carries a one-year jail
term. However, if the police can get one suspect to testify that the other is a
bank robber, a conviction would carry a 30-year term. So the police offer the
prisoners this proposition: whoever testifies against the other goes scot-free,
and if they both testify against each other their sentence will be 10 years.

After proposing the deal, the police place each prisoner in separate isolation
cells where they cannot talk to each other, and each one contemplates his
situation. If he squeals, he can preserve his liberty, go back to his life, and send
the other guy to jail for 30 years. If he keeps quiet he can be out of jail in a year.
However, if they each squeal, they are each looking at a 10-year jail term. The
dilemma each prisoner faces becomes even clearer as he thinks through his

options and the possible outcomes. Individually, the best outcome is for one fellow to cheat on his buddy—to squeal, go free, and send the other guy to jail for 30 years. The second best outcome is for both to remain silent, spend only a year in jail, then go free. A third outcome (much less appealing) would result if they both testified and spent the next 10 years in the clinker. The worst individual outcome would be to wind up a "sucker"—to stay quiet while the other fellow rats you out, and to spend the next 30 years in jail while he goes free. Figure 1.2 illustrates these different payoffs.

These different outcomes highlight the paradox of rational, independent action because if each prisoner proceeds rationally and acts independently of the other, and if he does what is best for himself—which is to squeal—they both wind up with a bad outcome. Of course, the prisoners might escape this dilemma and obtain the best payoff by coordinating their actions with each other. If they could find some way to communicate they might decide to hold to their pledge and keep silent, spend a year in jail, then go home. However, their isolation from each other precludes this remedy, and even if they found some way to exchange information and coordinate plans, could either one truly trust the other to keep his word? "If I agree to keep quiet and help him out,"

	Prisoner "A" **Squeal?**	
	No	Yes
Prisoner "B" **Squeal?** No	A = 1 B = 1	A = 0 B = 30
Yes	A = 30 B = 0	A = 10 B = 10

Figure 1.2 The Prisoner's Dilemma

we can imagine each prisoner thinking, "how can I be sure he won't stab me in the back to get the better deal?" Fear of a double-cross can minimize the potential benefits of communication; it also might tempt one or both to try to get the best deal for himself by squealing. States sometimes can get into the same kind of predicament as these prisoners. Even if one state tells the other "my arms are only meant for defense, not offense, so you don't need to worry," the other state might find it quite difficult to trust its counterpart's claims.

If we go back to the Cuban Missile Crisis, we see how the prisoner's dilemma came into play. Both the United States and Soviet Union had distinct political cultures and policy processes: one reflected pluralism, checks and balances, and openness; the other reflected centralized control and secrecy. Both states had diametrically opposed ideologies—liberal democracy and Communism—which emphasized different sets of values and priorities, and by default, defined the other side as an enemy. Both states also had their own spheres of influence. These factors not only locked the Americans and Soviets into distinct, separate "cells," but made it hard for them to communicate effectively and especially hard for one to trust the other. Thus, in October 1962, the Soviet Union and United States appear trapped in a prisoner's dilemma—their fate and that of Cuba's hung in the balance. The best individual outcome for each superpower would be to "cheat" by striking the other first, removing its opponent's capacity for a nuclear response, and enjoying enhanced security from any nuclear strike in the future. The second best outcome would simply be to live uneasily with the threat of swift destruction posed by the presence of nuclear weapons stationed close to each state's borders. A third outcome would be a limited nuclear exchange that would penalize both states significantly, but (hopefully) not escalate into global nuclear war. The worst outcome would be to do nothing, and become a "sucker" as the other side launched a massive, devastating nuclear attack.

Fortunately, despite the momentum of events pulling the world toward catastrophe, in the end a nuclear holocaust was avoided. How come? One reason is a good deal of luck, as we shall see in Chapter 7. Another reason, however, is because the Americans and Soviets managed to communicate and coordinate their actions through a series of letters exchanged by President Kennedy and Premier Khrushchev. These letters helped dramatize the effects of "cheating" (nuclear destruction) and convinced the U.S. and Soviet leadership that each side was rational and genuinely desired to avoid war. They also provided the basis on which each side could trust the other's promises to dismantle the Soviet missiles in Cuba and not reintroduce them, to remove the American missiles in Turkey, and not invade Cuba itself. In reaching this understanding, Washington and Moscow essentially cut Havana out of these negotiations, much to Castro's consternation. But with communication and coordinated actions, Kennedy and Khrushchev managed to back away from the nuclear threshold, and as a result the United States, Soviet Union, and Cuba became more secure.

Neither the Cuban Missile Crisis, the Cuban Revolution that brought Castro to power, nor Cuba's break with the United States and subsequent alliance with the Soviet Union occurred in a vacuum. Rather, they occurred within the context of an anarchic international system and Cuba's historic relations with the United States. According to Harvard political scientist and Cuba expert, Jorge Domínguez, "Castro's vision, ambition, and beliefs led him and his comrades to break with the United States. Their understanding of the past, and their analysis of the international system's structure at that juncture, led them to form a close alliance with the Soviet Union."[8] These actions, in turn, eventually helped lead to the Cuban Missile Crisis.

Just as the international system and the relations between states affected the options, perceived constraints, and foreign policy decisions of Cuba's leaders in the mid-twentieth century, so they have exerted a similar influence on other states at other times. As we study U.S.–Latin American relations, and international politics of the Western Hemisphere more broadly, we will encounter many examples of this dynamic. The balance of power, the search for security in an anarchic system, the problems of achieving cooperation and of replacing suspicion with trust, will also emerge again and again. The historical and contemporary examples that we study will demonstrate the utility, relevance, and limitations of different international relations theories, illustrate how the actors, goals, and instruments that actors use to achieve them may have changed over time, and underscore why pursuing a discourse between history and theory is essential to sound analysis.

Study Questions

1. What do political scientists mean by the term "theory"? Why are theories useful in the study and understanding of inter-state relations?
2. What type of theory of international politics is implicit in Philip Brenner's account of the Cuban Missile Crisis? From a theoretical perspective, was the crisis easily avoidable or was it hardwired into the nature of international politics?

Selected Readings

Brenner, Philip. "Thirteen Months: Cuba's Perspective on the Missile Crisis." In *The Cuban Missile Crisis Revisited*, edited by James A. Nathan, 187–217. New York: St Martin's Press, 1992.

U.S.–Latin American Relations and Political Theory

2

Figure 2.1
The Western Hemisphere

Realism and Liberalism: A Closer Look

Realism and liberalism are the two dominant theoretical perspectives of international politics, and each can be useful in the study of U.S.–Latin American relations. The theory of realism has a long pedigree. Its intellectual roots stretch back to the ancient Greek and Chinese civilizations. Both Thucydides and Sun

Tzu, who authored the *History of the Peloponnesian War* and *The Art of War* respectively, wrote of international politics from a realist perspective. In the sixteenth century, the Italian philosopher Niccolo Machiavelli also wrote of statecraft from a realist perspective with emphasis on alliances, counter-alliances, balances of power, and the imperative of state survival. In Machiavelli's world, the Italian peninsula was populated by separate city-states, each striving for security in the absence of a common ruler above them. This same kind of anarchic environment characterized Thucydides' world of ancient Greek city-states.

Not surprisingly, therefore, anarchy plays a dominant role in realist theory and realists perceive international politics as characterized by conflict, struggle, and competition between states without a higher sovereign above them. The realist view of world politics is not particularly optimistic. Even though realists may personally desire peace, justice, or stability, their understanding of how world politics actually work leads them to view inter-state relations more pessimistically. For realists, the "high politics" of security and survival are the overarching concerns states must grapple with, and they can engage in the "low politics" of trade, commerce, and socio-economic development only to the extent that their survival is guaranteed. Preserving security is so imperative that in order to survive, states sometimes must resort to war, expansion, or as Machiavelli wrote, commit what in a domestic setting could be considered an unjust act. Since states' very survival can be at stake, realists do not believe that ethics and morality should (or even can) play a significant role in how they formulate their foreign policies. As we shall see in later chapters, many dynamics surrounding U.S.–Latin American relations bear the hallmarks of realist principles and concerns.

Realism, however, is more than just a pessimistic view of world politics. It is also a theory that rests on a set of underlying assumptions. We might summarize these assumptions as follows: (1) states are the main actors and act rationally in pursuit of their national interest; (2) they exist in an anarchic, self-help international system; (3) military security is their highest priority; and (4) power and force are their tools of choice. These assumptions can help us predict how states might act. Because their logical inter-linkage stems from the basic premise of international anarchy, it is useful to consider the effects of anarchy a bit more deeply.

Sometimes I use an example from *Star Trek* to help my students grasp the predictive power of international anarchy. I begin by asking them to imagine that I possessed one of those marvelous teleportation devices found on the *Star Ship Enterprise* (which can disassemble a person at the molecular level, then transport and reassemble her at a more distant location). I then ask them to imagine that I used this device to transport them into the middle of the

Caribbean Sea or South Pacific. Finally, I ask: "What's the first thing you'd do once you re-materialized on the water's surface and discovered there was no land in sight?" Invariably, my students tell me they would respond by floating or trying to swim. "Why?" I probe. "In order to survive," they respond. "Why aren't you floating or swimming now?" I ask again. The answer, of course, is so obvious that they hesitate to voice it: "Because we don't need to in the classroom." The relevance of the exercise is readily apparent. Just as the aquatic environment that I might teleport them into would provide powerful incentives to act in certain—and in fact, predictable—ways in order to survive, so the anarchic environment in which states exist exerts a similar influence over their behavior and for similar reasons. Although realist theory has limitations, it also has great utility, and when analyzing U.S.–Latin American relations from this perspective, we must remember to give anarchy its due.

Like realism, the theory of liberalism also has deep roots. Its precursors lie in the works of seventeenth-, eighteenth-, and nineteenth-century political philosophers and economists, whose primary focus was domestic, not international affairs. The writings of John Locke, Jeremy Bentham, Adam Smith, and David Ricardo are some of liberalism's early intellectual foundations. To varying degrees, these classical liberals focused on the individual as a basic unit of analysis. Locke made the case for how individuals could best exercise their rights in the context of a minimalist state or limited government; Bentham's utilitarian philosophy stressed that rational individuals could determine what was best for themselves without much government tutelage; Smith and Ricardo, meanwhile, spoke of the role of individual entrepreneurs who worked and prospered, unimpeded by a meddling state. A common thread among classical liberal thinkers was the belief in an underlying harmony of interests between individuals, which—even absent intense state involvement—could facilitate cooperation and make economic, political, and social progress possible.

These views on domestic affairs carried over into how liberals conceive of international politics. Liberals agree with realists that anarchy foments mistrust and impedes cooperation among states, and they agree that power plays an important role in international affairs. However, they disagree that international politics is inevitably zero-sum (your gain is, by default, my loss); they suggest that states can devise foreign policies that reflect at least a modicum of ethics and morality; and they argue that realists overstate the intensity of anarchy and the centrality of conflict and power politics. Just as a harmony of interests can facilitate cooperation and a degree of ethical behavior among individuals within a specific state, similar dynamics are possible among states themselves, provided that state leaders take steps to capitalize upon and nurture that harmony.

Classical liberalism, therefore, made several broad claims regarding international politics. First, all nations could gain—and more important, preserve peace—by pursuing trade and interstate commerce; after all, war is quite costly and bad for business. Second, expanding democracy domestically among various states would expand peace internationally between different democratic states (since leaders accountable to a domestic electorate would not embrace war on a whim). Finally, international institutions could dampen the effects of anarchy and facilitate collective action, cooperation, and some measure of ethical behavior between states. These claims are among the propositions advanced by the German philosopher, Immanuel Kant, in his essay *Perpetual Peace*. They also influenced Woodrow Wilson's worldview and the foreign policy the United States adopted in the early twentieth century toward Latin America and beyond. During the Wilson administrations, the United States proposed a Pan-American Pact to facilitate peace and commerce among the American republics, expanded trade with Europe and Latin America, sought to promote democracy in the Dominican Republic and Mexico, and pushed for the creation of the League of Nations after World War I to help prevent future wars.

Contemporary *neoliberal* theory retains some aspects of the classical variety, but it is less deterministic and more refined. For today's neoliberals, trade *per se* does not prevent states from aggressing; however, it does help states perceive their interests in ways that might curb conflicts and make war less appealing. Here, the neoliberals' argument is that expanding trade provides the means by which states can upgrade their stature and position in the international system without having to seize another state's territory or engage in aggression. One example of this dynamic that neoliberals cite is Japan, which in the 1930s, sought to increase its international position by conquering its neighbors and compelling them into a Japanese-led trade arrangement (the Greater East Asia Co-prosperity Sphere). After its defeat in World War II, Japan changed tactics, focused solely on trade, and today ranks among the world's top economies.

In Latin America, Brazil's experience illustrates the same point. In the nineteenth century, Brazil fought two wars for prominence and territory with Argentina—its chief rival for regional influence. Neither conflict did much to increase Brazil's stature. By the 1920s, Brazil was a large but incredibly poor country that envied the growth and prosperity of its competitor. As late as the 1970s, its relations with Argentina remained tense and marked by mutually shrill denunciations, protestations, and even atomic rivalry (clandestine nuclear research carried out contrary to their obligations under the Nuclear Non-proliferation Treaty). Since the mid-1980s, though, Brazil has focused principally on trade, economic expansion, and economic diversification. In 1986, it signed an economic integration pact with Argentina; in 1991, it helped found the South American Common Market, MERCOSUR; and since 2000 it has expanded trade relations with other dynamic economies, including China's. In the process, Brazil transformed its international position significantly: according to a World Bank study, in 2007 it boasted the largest economy in South America and the sixth largest economy worldwide.

Another thread of neoliberal theory suggests that various factors associated with "globalization"—an integrated world market, expanding transnational contacts and networks, and the rapid advancement of global communications technology that facilitates international finance—have shifted the hierarchy of interests that concern states away from the traditional realist ranking. Because of globalization, many states find that military security no longer tops the list. Instead, economic and social welfare issues have assumed greater prominence, and have prompted states to eschew conflict in order to pursue these objectives. According to neoliberal political scientists Robert Keohane and Joseph Nye, one reason most Latin American states now settle their remaining territorial disputes peacefully, is that the incentives generated by "economic and social globalism" have dampened tendencies to use force, mainly from fear of "being distracted from tasks of economic and social development and of scaring away needed investment capital."[1]

Today's neoliberals also stress the importance of international institutions and organizations, both as actors in their own right that can affect international politics along with states, and as mechanisms that facilitate communication, cooperation, and problem-solving among states. In August 1982, international financial institutions like the International Monetary Fund and World Bank helped carry Mexico through a harrowing financial crisis that threatened its financial solvency, as well as the international financial system. Large, private commercial banks were instrumental in helping Mexico and other debt-laden Latin American states work through the "lost decade" of the 1980s and recover their credit-worthiness. In the 1990s, the hemisphere's quintessential international institution, the Organization of American States (OAS), moved vigorously to defend democratic governance in the Americas against military coups as occurred in Haiti (1991), and against so-called "self-coups"—in which presidents closed down legislatures and supreme courts in order to rule by decree—as occurred in Guatemala (1993), Paraguay (1996), and Peru (1992). In each case the OAS Permanent Council passed stiff resolutions that condemned the democratic set-backs, demanded rectification, warned of punitive action, and in some cases, imposed actual sanctions.[2]

Neoliberals contend that organizations like the OAS and other international institutions create a context that enhances the prospects of cooperation and problem-solving. By linking states together in an otherwise anarchic system, they help foster shared norms such as support for democratic governance, provide forums to negotiate the resolution of conflicts, and create the semblance of a broader global community.

Liberalism and realism offer opposing views of world politics. Realism tends to stress the continuities of international politics, the difficulties of cooperating under anarchic conditions, and the zero-sum nature of inter-state relations (an increase in your power is, by default, a decrease in my security and survival chances). Its strengths lie in explaining the causes of conflict between states, why peace often eludes national leaders, and the reasons why states sometimes adopt foreign policies that seem unjust to other states. In light of these continuities, realist political scientist Robert Gilpin asserts that "the nature of international relations has not changed fundamentally over the millennia."[3] By contrast, Liberalism stresses salient changes in international politics, and it focuses on elements and dynamics that realist theory fails to capture: the rise of important non-state actors, the possibilities of progress, and the emergence of critical issues beyond a state's need to ensure its security. Its strengths are in explaining the causes of inter-state cooperation, problem-solving, and tendencies toward peace.

Box 2.1 Have International Politics Really Changed? A Skeptic's View

The assumption of continuity in the affairs of states has been challenged by much recent scholarship in the field of international relations. Contemporary changes in technology, economics, and human consciousness are said to have transformed the very nature of international relations. International actors, foreign-policy goals, and the means to achieve goals are said to have experienced decisive and benign changes; it is said that the nation-state has receded in importance, that welfare goals have displaced security goals as the highest priority of societies, and that force has declined as an effective instrument of foreign policy . . . Although this vision that technological, economic, and other developments have transformed the nature of international relations is appealing, it is not convincing. [Even though] modern science, technology, and economics have changed the world, there is little evidence to suggest that the human race has solved the problems associated with international political change, especially the problem of war.

Robert Gilpin, *War and Change in World Politics*
(Cambridge: Cambridge University Press, 1981), 211, 213

International politics would be transformed completely if individual states were eliminated, or a world government above the states were created. Neither development, however, seems remotely likely in the near to mid future. States prize their independence and peoples around the globe value the sense of shared community, protection, and citizenship rights that they derive from belonging to an independent, sovereign state. Consequently, despite realism's pessimistic prognosis, as long as sovereign states endure, its focus on states and the problems they face in an anarchic setting remains relevant. A realist perspective can offer instructive insights into the tensions that surround U.S.– Latin American relations. Later chapters will draw generously on this theory, and employ liberal approaches in instances where realist explanations prove inadequate.

Power

Earlier we noted that anarchy plays a critical role in realist theory. Power does too. Although realists and liberals disagree about the centrality of power in international affairs—as well as its utility and how routinely states employ it to achieve their goals—they both agree that power *matters* in international politics. Much of the ill will that has characterized Latin America's views of the United States is often blamed on how America has used its power to its neighbors' disadvantage: stark power differentials between the two Americas have made some Latin American states the objects of U.S. saber rattling, gunboat diplomacy, covert interventions, and outright military invasions. To appreciate how power affects states' behavior, their foreign policy decisions, and international politics more generally, we need to know exactly what "power" is.

States seek power to ensure their survival, protect their security, extend their influence, and pursue their objectives. Power varies widely from state to state, and throughout modern history, only a relatively small number of states have commanded most of the world's power resources. Oddly enough, however, the concept of power can be difficult to define, and its effects hard to analyze. Many analysts might be comfortable defining power as "the ability to make others do something they would not otherwise do." A standard international relations textbook defines power as "the ability to prevail in conflict and overcome obstacles."[4] Both definitions view power in what we might call "capacity outcome" terms, wherein the evidence that power has been exercised is seen either in the changed behavior of others, victory in conflict, or triumph over hindrances. Both definitions are correct, yet they are analytically problematic. One problem is that changed behavior is not always the best way to measure power. How can we be certain that what a state is doing now, is not something it would have done anyway? There are other analytic problems too. Sometimes, for example, states prevail in conflicts not because of their power alone, but simply because their opponents make mistakes. Are such instances accurate measurements of a victorious state's power? And if we measure power in terms of the ability to triumph over obstacles, we become entangled in circular logic: power explains triumph over hindrances and the triumph itself is the measure of power.

Thomas Hobbes' view of power can help avoid these analytic problems. Hobbes saw power as the present means to obtain some future apparent good. This definition alludes to what political analysts call *power resources*, or the tangible assets a state might employ to realize its goals. There are many different types of power resources: a country's population, its territory and natural resource base, its relative political stability, its technology, the size and strength of its economy, and of course, its military. Measuring power in terms of power resources offers analytical advantages; on the one hand, tangible assets are more discrete and easier to measure; on the other, conceiving of power in these terms does not entrap us in circular logic. Because states with many power resources can be expected to act differently than those with fewer resources, analyzing power resources can help us predict or understand states' behavior. Given their significant power differentials, for example, it is not surprising that the United States has intervened more frequently and dramatically in the affairs of Latin American states than vice versa.

Most states actively seek to expand their base of power resources. In the nineteenth century, both territory and population were important power resources, and as we might expect, weak states in the Western Hemisphere sought ways to expand their territory and increase their populations. In the War of the Pacific (1879–1883), for example, Chile acquired mineral-rich territories from Bolivia and Peru, and in the Mexican-American War (1846–1848), the United States acquired Arizona, California, New Mexico, and parts of Utah from Mexico; it also managed to purchase Florida from France (along with a vast swath of what is now the American Midwest), and Alaska from Russia. Many states also courted European immigrants to increase their populations. In 1853, Argentina adopted a constitutional mandate (Article 25) designed to liberalize European immigration, and eventually saw its demographics transformed as a result; in the late 1880s, Brazil, Chile, and Uruguay also attracted their share of Europeans;[5] and the United States, of course, accepted large waves of immigrants through most of the nineteenth century.

States can exercise their power directly or indirectly. When one state brings tangible assets to bear on another in order to change its behavior by force (or fear), it is exercising its power directly. The same holds true when one state extends "carrots"—offers of aid, assistance, and support—that are contingent upon another state changing its behavior. By contrast, when one state can get others to desire the same things it wants, and to change their behavior accordingly, it is exercising its power and international influence more indirectly. Political scientists call such indirect influence *soft power.* Professor Joseph Nye of Harvard has written extensively about soft power, and defines it as "the ability to attract others by the legitimacy of [a state's national] policies and the values that underlie them."[6]

Soft power resources include a state's cultural appeal, ideology, political values, and its leverage in international institutions. They are less tangible than traditional "hard power" resources, but they can still get results. The United States, for example, has used the appeal of its consumer society, economic prosperity, and democratic culture to showcase the benefits of political democracy, free markets, and free trade, and to induce other states to follow America's lead in pursuing these objectives. Similarly, under President Hugo Chávez, Venezuela has used the appeal of its anti-imperialist ideology and populist policies to attract followers among several Latin American states. Both states also have used their leverage in international institutions to set the political agenda, influence the preferences other states hold, and thus influence their behavior. Traditionally, the United States has had success in institutions such as the United Nations, World Bank, and International Monetary Fund, while Venezuela recently has had similar success in the Organization of Petroleum Exporting Countries and the Organization of American States.

Soft power and hard power can interact and they are related. Triumphs in war, for example, or national achievements in economic performance, industry, science, and technology can all burnish the appeal of a state's ideology or its cultural and political values. But soft power is distinct from hard power and can be exercised effectively in its absence, as the Venezuelan case illustrates. Venezuela not only lacks the force projection capabilities of more advanced states, but also lacks the indigenous elements of effective hard power—advanced aeronautic, computer, nuclear, and satellite technology—that developing states like Brazil possess. Yet, Venezuela has more influence within Latin America and beyond, than other states of comparable military and economic capacity.

Power resources are not static. As contexts change over time, power resources do too. In the sixteenth century, gold bullion (seized from the civilizations and mines of the New World) made Spain the richest, most powerful state in the world; by the eighteenth century, a large population and large, citizen-based army transformed France into the leading state, just as industry, finance, and a strong navy would do for Britain in the nineteenth century. By the mid-twentieth century, the scale of the United States' economy, its industrial and scientific advancements, the alliance networks it had developed, and the application of technology to its large military forces had transformed America into a superpower.

The quantity of power resources states possess is not the end of the story. Not all states can convert their power resources into effective influence as well as others. Throughout the nineteenth and twentieth centuries, Brazil—like the United States—possessed an enormous territory with a vast base of natural resources. But unlike the United States, Brazil was unable to transform its assets into actual power as easily. The upshot has been a considerable gulf between the power commanded by the United States and Brazil. Gregory Treverton and Seth Jones, political scientists at the RAND Corporation, suggest that today, the United States holds nearly 20 percent of total global power (based on its GDP, population, defense spending, and capacity for technological innovation). By contrast, Brazil represents Latin America's largest economy and the Western Hemisphere's third largest territorial state, but holds only 2 percent of total global power.[7]

The problem of *power conversion*, therefore, can make the difference between which states will likely wield more influence, best advance and protect their interests, prevail in war, or realize their preferred outcomes. Historically, geography created power conversion problems for Latin American states and accounts for at least some of the disparities in power between them and the United States. Vast mountain ranges and dense tropical jungles hindered national integration, impeded transportation, and made it difficult to exploit economic opportunities and natural resources. Besides geography, however, other factors mattered too.

States that are politically stable can harness their resources and focus their energies more consistently on foreign policy matters than states that are not. The United States has enjoyed substantially more stability (despite the Civil War) than its Latin American counterparts. Similarly, innovation in agriculture, business, finance, science, and technology permits states to exploit their power resources more readily; social capital (especially investment in a broadly educated population) helps stimulate knowledge production, and the capacity to leverage the knowledge generated more effectively; and efficient market frameworks spur capital accumulation and compound economic growth that can be converted into political and military power. Historically, the United States devoted more energy to each of these processes and displayed more skill at manipulating them than its Latin American counterparts. Consequently, while the United States faced its own power conversion problems, its ability to address them left a widening gap between America's power and influence and that of its neighbors. In time, this trend solidified into a marked power asymmetry.

Balance of Power

Power asymmetries are related to an important concept of international politics, the balance of power. This concept is found in much of the academic literature on international relations, and it is used in different contexts for different purposes: political scientists use the balance of power concept to predict and better understand states' behavior; strategists use the concept to analyze security threats and plan appropriate responses; and states use the balance of power to inform their foreign policy decisions. International relations scholars have noticed that states often strive to maintain a balance of power between them. They pay close attention to how power is distributed among individual states in the international system (or its sub-units), and they are sensitive to developments that might alter the status quo. The examples abound.

In the 1820s, the United States was concerned that European encroachment into the Americas could upset the international balance of power and threaten U.S. security. It would be "impossible," President James Monroe had said, for European states to "extend their political system to any portion" of the Western Hemisphere "without endangering our own peace . . ."[8] By the 1860s, France had become concerned with the increase in U.S. power and how it might affect French interests in the New World: "We have an interest in the republic of the United States being powerful and prosperous," exclaimed Napoleon III, "but not that she should take possession of the whole of the Gulf of Mexico, thence command the Antilles as well as South America . . ."[9] In the 1880s, Mexico had serious concerns over Guatemala's foreign policy ambitions. Led by President Justo Rufino Barrios, Guatemala (then the strongest state in Central America) hoped to unite Costa Rica, El Salvador, Honduras, and Nicaragua into a new Central American Union under Guatemalan control. Mexico feared that a Guatemala-led Central American Union would create a powerful neighbor and tip the regional balance of power against Mexico City;[10] consequently, it opposed Guatemala's unionist plans and worked to torpedo them by discouraging Costa Rica and Nicaragua's participation. Similar dynamics occur on the global level. After the 1959 Cuban Revolution, American leaders grew alarmed by Cuba's transition from a U.S. to a Soviet ally, because it threatened to alter the global balance of power between communist and noncommunist forces.

The incentives international anarchy generates and the dangers it poses, give the balance of power concept useful predictive properties. Under anarchic conditions, states often strive consciously to balance power in order to preserve their independence and security. States can seek to balance against a more powerful state either unilaterally or multilaterally. Some states, for example, may choose to build up their own power resources, defensive capabilities, and military might. Such unilateral measures are termed "internal hard balancing" and tend to be taken when states face powerful, hostile opponents. The Venezuelan government of Hugo Chávez illustrates this dynamic. When U.S.-Venezuelan relations deteriorated sharply in the early 2000s, Venezuela voiced fears of a U.S. invasion (a scenario that American leaders repeatedly denied). To balance U.S. power and defend against this possibility, Caracas began to modernize its military by purchasing arms and helicopter gunships from Russia, and by creating a large citizen militia. States also might seek to balance a stronger power by forming alliances with other states; such multilateral efforts are termed "external hard balancing." In the 1880s, for example, Brazil and Chile developed an entente to balance Argentina, Bolivia, and Peru;[11] and in 1908, Guatemala sought an alliance with Europe (which never materialized) in order to balance U.S. power and deter a possible U.S. military intervention under provisions of the Roosevelt Corollary.[12]

For centuries, states have employed both types of hard balancing strategies to counter a stronger power. More recently, though, as the global distribution of hard power has shifted decisively toward the United States, some states have adopted *soft balancing* tactics to counter America's influence, and to preserve their own independence. Soft balancing involves the use of nonmilitary means to raise the political costs a strong state incurs when using its hard power, and to limit its ability to realize preferred outcomes. The recent advent of this practice reflects one of the stark realities of contemporary international politics: U.S. military power now exceeds that of any other state by orders of magnitude, which in turn, renders effective hard balancing against America impractical. Thus, instead of trying to match the United States weapon-for-weapon, or forging formal military alliances in a futile attempt to balance American might, some states have begun to coordinate their policies in more subtle ways—working through informal ententes and international institutions—to make it more difficult for Washington to exercise unfettered hegemonic power.[13]

One tactic states have followed is to impede U.S. action by ensnaring the United States within the constraining procedures of international institutions. In 2002 and 2003, for example, Chile, France, Germany, Mexico, and Russia used the United Nations institutional procedures to forestall U.S. military action against Iraq, and then to deny the American-led invasion the official support of the UN Security Council. The invasion still proceeded, but at the cost of an enormous loss of international legitimacy and prestige for the United States. In 2005, a number of Latin American states used a similar "entangling" strategy in the Organization of American States to derail what they claimed was a thinly disguised U.S. effort to isolate Venezuela, intervene in its domestic affairs, and curtail its independence. In this case, Washington had proposed creating a mechanism within the OAS to monitor whether member states were governing democratically, and to hold to account those that did not. Because the proposal came at a time Venezuelan-U.S. relations were at an historic low (and after the United States had encouraged, then supported, a failed coup against Venezuelan president Hugo Chávez), Caracas saw the initiative as a direct threat to its independence, and many other OAS members agreed. In the end, over 80 percent of the membership voted down the proposal.

Balance of power theory has great predictive power, even in cases that at first blush might seem counter-intuitive. For example, when World War II began, it was hard to imagine Western powers would join the Soviet Union in an alliance against Germany. Why? Because the Western powers were democracies while the communist Soviet Union was decidedly undemocratic. Yet, this alliance of strange bedfellows still developed, due to the Allies' shared desire to balance German power, and ultimately prevent Hitler's Germany from obtaining hegemony. Similarly, after the United States downgraded its relationship with Argentina's anti-communist, but brutal military dictatorship in the late 1970s, a close relationship between Washington and Buenos Aires was hard to imagine. Yet, by the early 1980s the United States was working closely with the dictatorship to train guerrilla forces fighting what Washington considered to be a communist government in Nicaragua (Nicaraguan President Daniel Ortega never claimed the communist label). One factor that united this dictatorship and democracy was a shared desire to tilt the balance of power decidedly against communist forces in the Western Hemisphere. These examples demonstrate how balance of power theory can explain states' foreign policies, even when they have significant ideological— or domestic-level—differences.

Despite the constraints of international anarchy, however, states do not always engage in balancing behavior, so we must be careful how we use balance of power theory. One factor that limits the theory's predictive power is the way different states perceive threats. During the late 1940s and early 1950s, for instance, a strict application of balance of power theory would have predicted that Latin American states would join the Soviet Union to balance U.S. power during the Cold War. After all, the United States emerged from World War II as one of the world's two superpowers; for several years it had a monopoly on nuclear weapons; and, of course, it was the strongest state in the Western Hemisphere. Yet, such balancing did not occur: most Latin American states joined their North American neighbor, not the communists. That is, they *bandwagoned* with the stronger state rather than tried to balance it. One reason this happened is that after the Soviet Union began taking over East European states—and especially after its Cuban ally tried to topple several Latin American states—most governments in Latin America perceived the communists as more aggressive, dangerous, and threatening than the United States.

The perception of threat can be triggered by many factors including the power of another state, its actions, cultural dissimilarities and ideology, or even its proximity. In fact, proximity plays a very predictable role, in that the proximity of a particular threat tends to enhance a state's perception of it. Consider how the United States reacted in the 1980s to events in Central America, where countries like El Salvador and Nicaragua had either experienced a socialist revolution or seemed vulnerable to one. These developments propelled Central America to near the top of the U.S. foreign policy agenda, and led U.S. Secretary of State, Alexander Haig, to proclaim that the United States had to draw the line against communist intrusion in Central America. These developments, though, were not a function simply of the power these particular states possessed. Even if both had become socialist, they did not possess sufficient power to threaten U.S. security. What made the difference for American policymakers was the combination of a threatening ideology and especially their location: their proximity to the United States enhanced the perception of threat Washington felt.

Like realism and liberalism, balance of power theory can help us understand states' behavior, and important dynamics of U.S.–Latin American relations. As we examine the relationship more closely, though, we also will encounter several other concepts, strategies, and recurring themes: isolationism, democracy-promotion, intervention, unilateralism, multilateralism, and sovereignty. Assessing these issues from a theoretical standpoint can reveal some of the strengths and limitations of our theories, and advance our ability to analyze U.S.–Latin American relations accordingly.

Isolationism

Realists suggest that anarchy compels states to prioritize their security, plan their foreign policies strategically, and rely on force and power in order to survive. Yet, because realism focuses on large, strong states—and most states fall outside this category—it does not always help us understand the behavior of small or weak states that might act contrary to realist expectations. Rather than employing force to achieve their security goals, states sometimes adopt a policy of isolationism to protect themselves. An isolationist foreign policy rests on the notion that a state's national interest is best served by withdrawing from the political entanglements of the international community, and avoiding involvement in political or military affairs outside its borders. The eighteenth-century philosopher Jean Rousseau was an early proponent of this doctrine. Rousseau argued that for weak states especially, isolationism was the best source of security because it would not provoke the hostility of stronger powers. States that pursue this strategy seldom cut off *all* their ties to the outside world. Typically, they still preserve commercial contacts with other states; however, they will not form military alliances or take on external political commitments. Notable examples of isolationist policy include Switzerland and, in the past, China. In the early stages of World War II, Canada, Latin American countries, and the United States all adopted isolationist policies to some degree, and during the Cold War, some states in the developing world refused to align with either the Eastern bloc led by the Soviet Union, or the Western bloc led by the United States.

Isolationism, however, does not serve all states equally well, and several factors can enhance or impinge on its efficacy. To the extent that a state's geography helps insulate it from potential enemies—for instance, the mountains of Switzerland or the oceans surrounding North America—then isolationism is more practical. But the advance of technology can limit the benefits states derive from isolationism. The United States, for example, remained isolationist in World War I until Germany's advances in submarine warfare made American ships vulnerable to attack; and with today's intercontinental missiles, hiding from the world through isolationism probably would not give some states much real security at all.

The United States adopted an isolationist foreign policy very early on, with presidents Washington, Jefferson, and Monroe all affirming the United States as an isolationist power. Under the 1823 Monroe Doctrine, the United States declared it would not involve itself in either Europe's political affairs or its military conflicts. The United States maintained an isolationist stance toward Europe through the early twentieth century; however, it was much less isolationist in the Western Hemisphere despite the Monroe Doctrine. Proximity, power, economic interests, expansionist ideology, and a desire to spread democracy all contributed to this apparent policy inconsistency.

States typically have stronger interests in regions close to their own borders, and they are more sensitive to potential threats that are close at hand. Given its proximity to Mexico, the Caribbean, and Central America, the United States was more inclined to pursue and protect its economic and strategic interests in these regions. Also, while the early power disparities between Europe and the United States clearly influenced America's initial decision to embrace an isolationist foreign policy toward Europe, the power of Latin American states did not command the same level of respect as the Europeans', and thus, did not provide the United States sufficient incentives to follow a strict isolationist path in the region. As we shall see in Chapter 3, in the mid- and late nineteenth century, the ideology of *manifest destiny* influenced U.S. expansionism into northern Mexico, and U.S. interventions in the Caribbean and Central America. Finally, America's desire to spread its democratic values worked against U.S. isolationism in the Western Hemisphere too, especially in the twentieth century. In 1914 Woodrow Wilson sent U.S. forces into Mexico and justified the invasion, in part, to promote constitutional democracy; in the 1980s Ronald Reagan waged proxy war against the Sandinista government of Nicaragua to safeguard democracy; and in 1994 Bill Clinton sent U.S. forces to Haiti to restore the deposed, but democratically elected, president, Jean Bertrand Aristide.

Democracy-Promotion

Examples like the ones cited above have led some to see the spread of democracy as an overriding U.S. foreign policy concern. To illustrate, professor Tony Smith of Tufts University has suggested that promoting democracy was "the central ambition of American foreign policy during the twentieth century."[14] Not everyone accepts this view, especially those in Latin America. Chilean diplomat Heraldo Muñoz, for example, notes that "U.S. foreign policy has often expressed a genuine humanitarian concern for freedom, democracy, and the well-being of Latin American nations, and sometimes it has acted on those concerns." But Muñoz also points out that periodically, promoting democracy took a back seat to America's perceived security needs; as a result, "Washington repeatedly has ended up on the side of dictatorial regimes, or else has kept silent while 'friendly regimes' murdered, tortured, and exiled thousands of dissidents."[15] Similarly, writing of Mexico before its 2000 democratic transition, historian Lorenzo Meyer observed that except in the early years of Woodrow Wilson's first administration, U.S. policy toward Mexico stressed political stability over promoting democracy, and that historically, "the nondemocratic nature" of Mexico's political system was never "a significant factor in Mexican-U.S. relations."[16]

Both the North and Latin American analysts' viewpoints have merit. It is true that in modern times, democracy-promotion has been a key theme in

U.S. foreign policy. Yet, even a brief review of U.S. policy toward Latin America suggests the notion that promoting democracy was an overriding policy goal is debatable. In the second half of the twentieth century, for example, Washington aligned itself with brutal, repressive, and highly undemocratic governments in Latin America (as in Argentina, Brazil, and Chile); it supported a counterinsurgency that badly damaged basic human and democratic rights of most Nicaraguans; and it engineered or supported coups that toppled governments that had been democratically elected (in Guatemala and Chile). Such inconsistencies tarnished America's image in Latin America and exposed the United States to charges of hypocrisy: Washington, Latin Americans exclaimed, was much less concerned with spreading democracy than it was in advancing its own interests.

Realist theory offers one way to explain America's drive to spread democracy and the policy inconsistencies it exhibited. From this perspective, U.S. efforts to promote its ideology are hardly unique. The Soviet Union promoted Communism in its satellites; Cuba sought to promote communist ideology in Latin America; and today, the Venezuelan government of Hugo Chávez seeks to promote the ideology of its Bolivarian Revolution. States often try to spread their ideology, realists suggest, because of security: countries with similar ideologies are generally friendly toward each other. Hence, the more one state can get others to adopt its ideology, the more likely it can transform potential enemies into friends (or even allies). Some people who are realists also would assert that post-1945, U.S. policy inconsistencies were products of benefit/cost analysis, calculated within a Cold War, anarchic context. Although Washington preferred to see democratic regimes develop in the region, if faced with the trade-off between embracing a rightwing, anti-communist dictatorship or enduring a (sometimes perceived) communist state—even one whose government was democratically elected—security dictated the former.[17] Realist explanations, therefore, account for U.S. policy zigzags by stressing the constraints and incentives generated by an anarchic, international system.

Liberalism provides a different take on why the United States often promotes democracy, but has more difficulty explaining America's policy inconsistencies. Liberals suggest that expanding the number of democratic states will also expand the scope of peace (liberal democracies tend to resolve their disputes with each other through peaceful means rather than war) and offer the greatest potential for human development. But unlike realists, liberals also believe that domestic-level factors account for America's penchant to spread democracy—specifically, congressional, constituent, and interest-group pressures on the executive to promote democracy abroad, and the influence America's own deeply held democratic values exert on the outlook policymakers bring to bear in foreign policy matters.[18] The importance of these domestic factors is recognized even by liberal Latin American analysts. As Chilean diplomat Heraldo Muñoz observed,

> The United States is exceptionally reliant on certain ideological tenets in order to preserve a sense of national identity. Liberalism, both economic and political, constitutes the core of this national ideology and explains why promoting democracy . . . remains sufficiently resilient in the U.S. national consciousness so as to contain policymakers when they stray too far for too long.[19]

Liberal theory, however, has little to say regarding why the United States has opposed some democratic governments in Latin America, cozied up with undemocratic, authoritarian regimes, or at times, adopted other illiberal foreign policies.

Intervention and Sovereignty

Often, U.S. efforts to promote democracy have entailed intervention in the affairs of Latin American states. Intervention is an important concept in international politics and a recurring theme of U.S.–Latin American relations. Broadly defined, intervention refers to any external actions that influence the internal affairs of another sovereign state. Such actions transcend simple military invasions; they can also include efforts by one state to influence another's domestic affairs through clandestine measures, economic aid, electoral manipulation, or the media. There are many examples of non-military intervention. In the 1960s and 1970s, the United States financed political parties and campaigns in Chile to influence its domestic elections. In 1983, it created Radio Martí—a powerful radio station in Miami—that beamed pro-U.S. and anti-Castro messages to Cuba, in order to influence Cuba's domestic politics. Small states have intervened in U.S. affairs as well. In 1976, South Korea tried to influence U.S. foreign policy toward the Korean Peninsula by bribing American lawmakers (several of whom resigned as a result of the subsequent scandal). And in more recent years, the Chávez government in Venezuela has provided subsidized heating fuel to low-income families in the Northeast and Midwest United States (and widely publicized the program) to promote popular goodwill that, in turn, might lead to a more cordial policy posture toward Venezuela.

Today, nonintervention in other states' internal affairs is a cardinal norm of international law, enshrined in the Charter of the United Nations. The principle of nonintervention stipulates that because states have legal sovereignty over their territories and inherent rights to self-determination, interference in their internal affairs by another state is prohibited. In terms of international politics, the nonintervention norm has enormous practical utility. Even in an anarchic world, states can enjoy more security and stability if they adhere to the norm of nonintervention (and, generally, the reverse is also true).

However, the principle of nonintervention was less accepted in the nineteenth and early twentieth centuries, and in fact, was a sharp point of contention between Latin American governments and the United States. During the early twentieth century, the United States intervened militarily in the Dominican Republic, Haiti, Mexico, and Nicaragua—ostensibly to promote democracy, sometimes simply to ensure its preferred candidate assumed power. Other interventions (El Salvador, Guatemala, Honduras, Panama) occurred in the context of domestic revolts, disputed elections, or threats to U.S. investments. To weak, ostensibly "sovereign" Latin American states, these violations of sovereignty were particularly galling. These states were perfectly willing to let America run its own affairs (and never had the capacity to interfere in U.S. domestic matters anyway), but resented the fact that the United States—which *did* have the power to intervene dramatically—succumbed so often to the temptation.

Consequently, throughout much of this period Latin American states sought to protect their sovereignty and security, not through force and power as realism would expect, but through the more liberal approach of appealing to international law. Repeatedly, they proposed that the principle of nonintervention become a basic legal norm of hemispheric relations, and in international conferences they badgered the United States to accept this principle and craft its policies accordingly. In 1936, Washington finally agreed to foreswear intervention and signed an international treaty to that effect; in 1948, it made a similar promise and signed the Charter of the Organization of American States, which categorically barred intervention. As we shall see, these developments increased goodwill toward the United States and vented some of the tension in U.S.–Latin American relations. However, U.S. backsliding on this promise in the 1950s, 1960s, 1970s, and 1980s would rekindle the old resentments.

Both intervention and nonintervention are closely related to state sovereignty, a status that confers on states legal supremacy within their territory. Ever since the 1648 Peace of Westphalia established territorial states as the basic unit of international organization, states have been considered sovereign, and under international law, all states are equally sovereign. Sovereignty, therefore, is a legal concept; but it is also a political one, subject to political realities and limitations. Despite their sovereign status, states are not always able to exercise absolute control over their territory. For much of the 1990s, for example, the Revolutionary Armed Forces of Colombia, or FARC—a guerrilla insurgency that opposes the Colombian government—controlled a swath of Colombian territory the size of Switzerland. The FARC has lost ground in recent years, but the Colombian state still has not regained control over all its territory.

Other factors like international economic interdependence and drug trafficking can also encroach on a state's ability to control what goes on inside its borders. Consider the events of December 1994, when the Mexican government tried to devalue its national currency, the peso, by about 15 percent. The government quickly discovered that Mexico's economy had become so interdependent with the U.S. and Canadian economies (in part, thanks to the recently finalized North American Free Trade Agreement and other economic policy reforms), that when it tried to adjust its currency's value, foreign investors fled in droves. In less than two weeks foreign investors pulled more than $8 billion out of Mexico, its foreign reserves dwindled to almost nothing, and the peso's value plunged nearly 50 percent. Interdependence did not curtail the Mexican state's legal sovereignty, but did limit the control it had over its own currency policy. Similarly, drug trafficking has reduced the control that many states have over their borders and what takes place within them. In the United States, where borders remain porous and easily penetrated, the flow of drugs has created a variety of criminal and social problems. In Colombia, Central America, and Mexico, the challenges that drug trafficking poses to state sovereignty—militarized and armed confrontations, struggles over political power and territory, spectacular corruption episodes—are even more intense.

Both realists and liberals agree that sovereignty is important. They disagree, however, over the value of yielding some measure of state sovereignty in the interests of peace and international order. Liberals see international institutions, norms, and laws as effective means to achieve both. To illustrate, the United Nations, European Union, and Organization of American States help unite states of widely varied interests, power, and status, and offer institutional frameworks to negotiate disputes, resolve conflicts, and regulate state interactions. However, because international institutions are composed of sovereign states, their strength and efficacy often are determined by the extent of sovereignty individual states are willing to cede to the larger collective. Similarly, adherence to international law and norms of behavior requires states to relinquish some measure of their sovereignty in order to realize the collective benefits of more orderly international relations, and security from outside intervention. Liberals believe that states can enjoy real gains by structuring their relations on firm legal and normative bases, and can sacrifice some sovereignty to international institutions and be better off for it. By contrast, because realists stress the primacy of states and power, they typically put less stock in international institutions as a way to maintain order, promote peace, or pursue joint gains. And while realists do not dismiss the significance of law or norms out of hand, they tend to view power as the more reliable guarantor of a state's security in an anarchic world, and often a more effective means to advance its interests.

Although Latin American states pursued realist policies toward each other in the nineteenth century (through wars, ententes, and balance of power strategies), in the twentieth century they generally embraced a more liberal approach in their relations with the United States. To safeguard their sovereignty against U.S. interference, they pushed to establish nonintervention as the norm of inter-state behavior and sought to codify that norm in legally binding treaties. In the early twentieth century especially, much of the tension between the Americas would turn on Latin Americans' insistence that the United States accept this norm and behave accordingly, and Washington's reluctance to do so. In contrast, through most of the nineteenth and early twentieth centuries, U.S. policy toward Latin American states was typically more realist. By mid-century, however, both Americas embraced the liberal approach in creating the Organization of American States, and in an ironic twist, Latin American states proved less willing to cede as much sovereignty to the OAS as Washington periodically suggested: they consistently resisted calls to invest the OAS with a permanent or independent military capacity (out of fear the United States might invoke it against them).

Relations between the United States and Latin America display the full range of theoretical perspectives, concepts, and themes presented in this chapter. Power and balance of power, democracy-promotion, intervention and sovereignty, are all issues that have helped shape U.S.–Latin American relations. They have done so, however, in different ways, at different times.

Study Questions

1. What is Realism? How does it perceive the motives behind state actions and the relations among states? In what ways does it differ from a Liberal or a Dependency perspective?
2. What do analysts mean by the "balance of power"? What role does it play in international politics and how does it influence states' actions and foreign policy calculations?

Selected Readings

Burr, Robert N. "The Balance of Power in Nineteenth Century South America: An Exploratory Essay." *Hispanic American Historical Review* 35 (1955): 36–60.

Doyle, Michael W. "Liberalism and World Politics." *The American Political Science Review* 80 (1986): 1151–1169.

Jackson, Robert and George Sorensen. *Introduction to International Relations: Theories and Approaches*, 96–108. New York: Oxford University Press, 2007.

Keohane, Robert O. "Realism, Neorealism and the Study of World Politics." In *Neorealism and Its Critics*, edited by Robert O. Keohane, 1–13. New York: Columbia University Press, 1986.

Machiavelli, Niccolo. "On Princes and the Security of their States." In *International Relations Theory: Realism, Pluralism, Globalism*, edited by Paul R. Viotti and Mark V. Kauppi, 85–88. New York: Macmillan, 1987.

Mearsheimer, John. "Anarchy and the Struggle for Power." In *International Politics*, ninth edition, edited by Robert J. Art and Robert Jervis, 50–60. New York: Pearson, 2009.

Morgenthau, Hans. *Politics Among Nations*, ch. 1. New York: Knopf, 1989.

Paul, T. V. "Introduction: The Enduring Axioms of Balance of Power Theory and Their Contemporary Relevance." In *Balance of Power: Theory and Practice in the 21st Century*, edited by T. V. Paul, James J. Wirtz, and Michel Fortmann, 1–12. Stanford, CA: Stanford University Press, 2004.

Further Readings

Baldwin, David. *Neorealism and Neoliberalism: The Contemporary Debate*. New York: Columbia University Press, 1993.

Bull, Headly. *The Anarchical Society: A Study of Order in World Politics*. New York: Columbia University Press, 1977.

Caporaso, James A. "Dependence and Dependency in the Global System." *International Organization* 32 (Winter 1978): 13–43.

Cardoso, Fernando Henrique and Enzo Faletto. *Dependency and Development in Latin America*. Berkeley: University of California Press, 1979.

Keohane, Robert O. (ed.). *Neo-Realism and Its Critics*. New York: Columbia University Press, 1986.

Waltz, Kenneth N. *Theory of International Relations*. Reading: Addison-Wesley, 1979.

Foreign Policy Fundamentals: International Systems and Levels of Analysis

3

Figure 3.1
James Monroe

International Systems

Scholars of international politics often stress the importance of the *international system*, a term that refers to the overall patterns of behavior among sovereign states. Just as the planets in our solar system rotate on their axes in predictable rhythms and orbit in predictable patterns, so states can display predictable patterns of behavior vis-à-vis each other that are characteristic of a system. Systems transcend their individual parts and produce outcomes that reflect the contribution of their individual units. Take the human digestive system, for example. In different ways, the mouth, esophagus, stomach, small and large intestines, liver, and so on, each contributes to the body's ability to utilize the energy contained in food. But no single organ of the digestive system can accomplish this alone; it is the system itself that ultimately produces this health-benefiting outcome.

Systems also can influence their individual parts. Gravitational forces within the solar system keep the planets aligned and prevent their orbits from producing planetary collisions. Just like the digestive or solar systems, the international political system can influence its members, the states. For example, in 1794, the United States was forced to sign the humiliating "Jay Treaty" with Britain (then at war with France) that granted Britain many concessions but kept the United States out of the conflict between its former motherland and revolutionary ally. When President George Washington finished his second term in 1796, he established America's foreign policy of isolationism. Thomas Jefferson picked up the isolationist policy in 1803, and Secretary of State John Quincy Adams reiterated it in 1821. The United States, Adams explained, had "without a single exception, respected the independence of other nations while asserting and maintaining her own . . . [and had] abstained from interference in the concerns of others."[1] Two years later, the 1823 Monroe Doctrine reaffirmed U.S. isolationism as official state policy.

Yet, despite its leaders' intentions, despite its geography and the oceans that kept it isolated, the United States soon discovered that it was not an isolated entity at all, but rather, was part of a larger international system. This system, in turn, began to affect how the United States government behaved. By 1848—just 25 years after announcing the Monroe Doctrine—the United States had gone outside its borders, made war with Mexico, and acquired half of Mexico's national territory in the process. Then in 1898, the United States went to war with Spain over an issue the Spanish Crown considered an internal matter: how to deal with an insurrection in its colony, Cuba. As a result of this war the United States acquired non-continental territories from Spain that stretched from the Caribbean to Asia, just like Britain, France, and other imperial powers possessed. These examples illustrate that despite its early intentions to remain isolationist, in time the United States began to behave like other states did. A major factor behind this development was the United States' inclusion within a larger system of sovereign states, where states competed, strove to survive, and were compelled to look out for themselves.

Political scientists focus on the international system because the more we understand its characteristics, the better positioned we are to explain why states act the way they do or adopt specific types of foreign policy. As we have seen, the international system's fundamental characteristic is anarchy, which diffuses power among the various states rather than concentrating it in a higher, common ruler above them. By studying the dispersal of power among states, we can hypothesize how they might behave, given their power levels, proximity, and relations to each other. We might predict, for example, that when one state feels threatened by another, there is a high probability it will act on its sense of insecurity and take measures to protect itself. A weak state might build up its own defenses for self-protection, seek the aid of a stronger state, or search for safety in isolationism. A stronger state may contemplate war against the state that threatens it. There are many examples of such behavior.

In 1904, for example, Venezuela defaulted on international debts owed to Britain and Germany, then faced the prospects of a joint British-German naval bombardment to compel repayment. Completely out-gunned, the Venezuelan state sought protection by asking the United States to mediate the dispute and stave off a naval assault. In the late eighteenth century the United States was a small, weak country clustered along the eastern North American seaboard, surrounded and threatened by more powerful, predatory states: Britain in the North and South (Canada and the Caribbean), France to the South (the Caribbean), and Spain to the South and West (Florida, Louisiana, the Caribbean, the Midwest, Arizona, California, Mexico, Texas, Utah). In this context, the United States chose to become isolationist. However, as U.S. power increased, America's response to threats changed accordingly. When the United States again felt threatened in the mid-nineteenth century by French designs to acquire and rule Mexico through a puppet emperor, Ferdinand Maximilian, Washington protested and pressured Paris to withdraw. Eventually it deployed 50,000 troops to the Rio Grande in a show of force (Mexican forces ultimately executed Maximilian without direct U.S. intervention). The United States took these actions, not because it was overly belligerent, but rather, because it perceived a threat from the encroachment of a strong power next door. These examples illustrate how the dispersal of power within an anarchic international system can affect states' behavior: when the balance of power seems tilted against them, we can expect most to respond with steps to protect their security.

Levels of Analysis

One way to gain even more leverage on states' behavior and the dynamics of hemispheric relations is to employ a different set of analytic tools. Most textbooks on international relations devote some time to discussing levels of analysis, drawing on the work of political scientists such as J. David Singer and Kenneth Waltz.[2] Scholars use these levels of analysis to understand policy output and the factors that motivate states' behavior.

The first level of analysis is that of the individual. Here, the focus is on the actions of specific individuals, their skills and weaknesses, personality traits, and beliefs or ambitions. What we seek at the first level is to assess how individuals might affect the course of events or influence foreign policy output. The first level encompasses not only individual state leaders; it also includes those who might advise a national leader or exercise significant influence in shaping policy preferences and goals from outside the government (e.g., in banking, business, or journalism). How did Mexico's president, Carlos Salinas de Gortari, influence the creation of the North American Free Trade Agreement between Mexico, the United States, and Canada? Was President James Monroe the most important individual force behind the Monroe Doctrine, or did others play important roles as well? Did President William McKinley really matter to the outbreak of the Spanish-American War, or did his Assistant Secretary of the Navy, Theodore Roosevelt, carry more weight? Was Fidel Castro the driving force behind the U.S.-Cuban estrangement? Different people might answer these questions in different ways, as we shall see. However, caution is warranted: it is hard to explain international politics completely if we only consider individuals. By default, international politics entails interaction between separate states, and by focusing only on what any one individual did, we may overlook other factors that affect individual actions to begin with.

Take the case of U.S. isolationism. By focusing only on Washington or Adams' intentions to keep the United States an isolationist power, we may not notice how the anarchic international system influenced America to embrace policies similar to those of other states. Yet, it remains the case that sometimes individuals *do* matter. Washington made a significant contribution to the course of U.S. foreign policy. The fact that Monroe and McKinley selected Adams and Roosevelt for positions of authority, had real consequences for the Monroe Doctrine and Spanish-American War (Roosevelt's personality, in particular, was critical in charting the United States' path to war, and the expansionist policy it followed thereafter). However, neither the Doctrine nor the war can be explained solely on an individual basis; and while Castro had the final say on

Cuba's foreign policy, the Cuban-U.S. standoff itself had many roots. Individuals do not act in a vacuum, and major events between states have multiple causes. While the first level of analysis can be useful, it rarely tells us all we need to know about a state's foreign policy.

Other casual factors can be found in the domestic setting in which national leaders operate, or the second level of analysis. Like individuals, states have distinct characteristics that can influence their policy choice and political outcomes. Is the state's political regime democratic or authoritarian? Is its economic system capitalist or socialist? Is its economy large or small, industrial or agrarian? What about its ideology? Does it embrace liberal democracy, Communism, economic nationalism, Islamic fundamentalism, or some other "ism"? Understanding the fundamental characteristics of states or societies can shed light on the forces that shape a state's perception of its interests and help drive its foreign policy.

If a state's political regime is democratic, for example, then factors such as public opinion or domestic pressure groups can influence its foreign policy—or constrain its leaders—more than if the regime were authoritarian. Under a capitalist economic system, certain groups or economic sectors will likely have greater influence with government leaders, and can translate their preferences into state policy more easily at certain times or in certain issue areas. If the ideology that animates the state is expansionist—Communism or manifest destiny, for instance—this can influence how the state perceives its interest and the type of policies it crafts to pursue and protect them. Ideologies are sets of ideas that offer a comprehensive vision or normative worldview of what society or the world *should* look like, and are based on assumptions that typically go largely unexamined. Two assumptions central to communist ideology, for example, are a belief in the inevitable overthrow of the capitalist class, and the inherent enmity between capitalist and communist systems. On this basis, we would expect states that have communist ideologies to fear or be hostile to their capitalist counterparts, and to support political movements that seek to overthrow capitalism. Cuba's foreign policy in the 1960s—which endeavored to export revolutions to Venezuela, Panama, and Guatemala—illustrates this dynamic.

Another example would be the U.S. ideology of manifest destiny. Among its assumptions were that America's society and political system were exceptional and uniquely virtuous compared to others, that its racial stock (Anglo-Saxon) was naturally superior to other ethnic groups, and that it was divinely predestined to increase in stature, prestige, and territory. In the mid-1800s, this expansionist ideology helped justify U.S. aggression against Mexico during the Mexican-American War, which cost Mexico roughly half its territory. A third example is the United States' domestic, democratic ideology, which emphasizes core values like individual liberty and self-determination. When America first announced the Monroe Doctrine in 1823, and at various times thereafter, U.S. policy toward Latin America did reflect a desire to extend and preserve such democratic principles.

Box 3.1 Manifest Destiny and the Mexican-American War

In 1845, journalist John O'Sullivan coined the term "manifest destiny" to describe his vision of America's mission. The United States, he asserted, was destined "to overspread the continent allotted to us by Providence for the free development of our yearly multiplying millions." The general idea of such a national mission preceded O'Sullivan by many decades. An early manifestation surfaced in the generation of the Founders (Thomas Jefferson's discourse on the rising "Empire of Liberty"), and subsequent iterations grew steadily among intellectual circles thereafter. By the mid-nineteenth century, the mission's parameters were widely accepted across American society and O'Sullivan's terminology caught on.

Neither an explicit doctrine nor a strategic policy, manifest destiny was instead an ideology, and a powerful one at that. Precisely because it was not an explicit policy, manifest destiny could mean different things to different people, at different times. Early on, some Americans saw it as expansionist but inwardly oriented: the United States was destined to extend its territory, but only for the benefit of American citizens who would settle unused land, and prosper in liberty as a yeoman class of small farmers. Later, others saw it as expansionist and outwardly oriented: America's mission was to extend civilization, liberty, and prosperity not only to its own people, but also to regions far beyond its (expanded) borders. As one of O'Sullivan's contemporaries, U.S. Congressman John Wentworth, put it, in the march of history the United States was "the great center from which civilization, religion, and liberty should radiate and radiate until the whole continent shall bask in their blessing."[a]

Manifest destiny played an important, though not necessarily causal, role in the Mexican-American War—an event that secured significant territory for the United States, created a deeply humiliated southern neighbor, perennially suspicious of U.S. motives, and has been described by Octavio Paz, Mexico's Nobel laureate in literature, as "one of the most unjust wars in the history of imperialist expansionism."[b]

The raw materials of the war—U.S. interest in acquiring Mexican territory and Mexico's disinterest in accommodating the United States—developed shortly after Mexico achieved its independence from Spain in 1821. With the overthrow of Spanish authority, the United States hoped to acquire portions of Mexican territory, and in fact, tried to purchase Texas in 1825. Northern Mexico (Arizona, California, New Mexico, Texas, parts of Utah) was sparsely populated and isolated from the central political authority in Mexico City. From the U.S. perspective, not only was much of Mexico's northern region "unused," but its economic potential was virtually untapped, its few inhabitants were of distinctly different racial stock, and their political values, practices, and institutions were decidedly undemocratic—an ideal setting for American expansion. Manifest destiny did not mandate a policy of war against Mexico to facilitate U.S. expansion; it did, however, set the ideological context that justified expansion into Mexican territory by means peaceful, or otherwise.

The war's focal point was Texas, which essentially served as a buffer between Mexico and the more powerful United States. Unable to stem the steady flow of American settlers into Texas, in 1823 Mexico sought to regularize the process by granting the *Norteamericanos* permission to settle under Mexican sovereignty. In time, Anglos outnumbered Mexicans, and the settlers then looked to secede from Mexico and create an independent state. Mexico, however, viewed these efforts as products of a renegade province; it never recognized the legitimacy of secession, and indeed, fought against it (remember the Alamo!). But ultimately, Mexico could not hold on to Texas: secession occurred, then annexation by the United States. In response, Mexico broke diplomatic relations with the United States, and when President James Polk deployed U.S. troops into a region of Texas that Mexico still claimed—hoping to precipitate a Mexican response—the outcome was not unexpected. On April 24, 1846, Mexico defended its territorial claims against U.S. forces, firing on U.S. troops, and the war was on.

The war lasted two years, much longer than Polk had expected, and was a divisive issue in the United States. In 1846, for example, Congressman Abraham Lincoln denounced Polk's engineering and explanations of the war as the "sheerest deception."[c] In 1848, the House of Representatives also criticized "Polk's War": in a bill praising General Zachary Taylor's leadership in the conflict, Whig lawmakers attached an amendment that described the war as "unnecessarily and unconstitutionally begun by the President of the United States."

The war's outcome—the Treaty of Guadalupe Hidalgo—compelled Mexico to cede much of its territory to the United States (for which the United States paid Mexico $15 million). This outcome dramatically altered the development potential and trajectory of both countries, tipping the scales decidedly toward the North. In 1824, Mexico and the United States were roughly equivalent in population and size: Mexico consisted of 1.7 million square miles and 6 million people; the United States consisted of 1.8 million square miles and 9.6 million people. By 1853 (after the Gadsden Purchase of southern Arizona and New Mexico), the United States consisted of 2.8 million square miles and 23 million people (thanks to immigration), while Mexico was reduced to 760,000 square miles and a population of 8 million—nearly three times smaller than its neighbor. Not surprisingly, Mexico viewed its humiliating defeat as a national disgrace and decried the war's outcome as patently unjust. Some prominent Americans agreed. In his 1885 memoirs, former U.S. President Ulysses S. Grant—who had served in the war as a young officer, and had opposed the U.S. annexation of Texas—labeled the war "one of the most unjust ever waged by a stronger against a weaker nation."

For most U.S. citizens today, the war is an historical artifact devoid of any tangible meaning. For most Mexican citizens, it remains a symbol of national humiliation. According to Piero Gleijeses, a political scientist at the Johns Hopkins School of Advanced International Studies, in the run-up to the war, Mexico searched for a way to avoid armed conflict with America but came up empty handed. In the end, it found itself caught in a self-help situation characteristic of international politics. If war came, Mexico would be forced to "stand alone against the United States: Spain was too weak to help, France was not interested, and England had decided not to interfere."[d] Consequently, for political scientists the war offers vivid examples of how ideologies can influence a state's foreign policy, and of the stakes and consequences that can arise when weak states face stronger ones inside an anarchic international system.

[a] Quoted in Timothy J. Henderson, *A Glorious Defeat: Mexico and its War with the United States* (New York: Hill & Wang, 2007), 32.

[b] Octavio Paz, *The Labyrinth of Solitude* (New York: Grove Press, Inc., 1961), 124.

[c] "Abraham Lincoln to Congress, January 12, 1848." American Memory Project, http://memory.loc.gov/cgi-bin/query/r?ammem/mal:@field(DOCID+@lit(d0007 400)), accessed January 23, 2011.

[d] Piero Gleijeses, "A Brush with Mexico," *Diplomatic History* 29 (April 2005): 228.

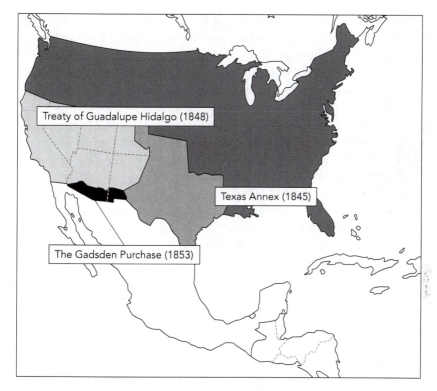

Figure 3.2 Mexican Territory Lost to the United States: 1845–1853

Still, we must take care how we use domestic, second-level analysis. As we shall discover, despite its democratic ideology, over time U.S. leaders reinterpreted the Monroe Doctrine in ways that actually worked against self-determination for Latin American states. Mexico, Cuba, the Dominican Republic, and other states in the Caribbean and Central America all bore the brunt of this development. Moreover, the United States adopted confrontational policies against some governments in Latin American that had been elected democratically, and whose tenure in power was an expression of self-determination by voters (Chile, Guatemala). These outcomes suggest that while the nature of a given state or society can tell us much about how that state might act, it is not always an accurate predictor. Factors beyond the individual and domestic levels influence states' political calculations too, and thus, their foreign policies and interactions with other states.

The international system constitutes the third level of analysis, and reflects the mirror opposite of the second. Whereas the latter explains outcomes by way of a state's internal features, the former does so by way of its external setting. One question we might ask here, is how the incentives and constraints the anarchic international system generates might affect the behavior of individual states. Perhaps the most important incentive that emanates from the international system is a powerful self-help motivation. One of the system's most important constraints is the way the balance of power in the system affects state actions. Each is consequential.

As we study U.S.–Latin American relations we will discover compelling explanations of state behavior often involve interplay between the various levels, but we should not assume that all three levels are always of equivalent weight. It is not simply the case that "everything matters." Sometimes domestic, level-two factors may carry more weight than international, level-three factors; sometimes it may be the reverse; and sometimes, individual factors rise to the fore in combination with the other two. Our task in studying the dynamics and U.S.–Latin American relations is to use levels of analysis in conjunction with other analytic tools and theories, to construct persuasive causal explanations of international politics in the Western Hemisphere. A good causal explanation may be complex, but should also be parsimonious—that is, it should stress the most significant causal factors while weeding out unnecessary details. Systemic third-level explanations typically are quite parsimonious because they have the fewest "moving parts"; they may not, however, sufficiently address the complex issues we hope to explain. When we encounter such complexity, therefore, a wise approach is to begin with the third level, then move to the second and first, until step by step, we construct a tight, comprehensive explanation of a particular case.

Systemic Structures and Rules

Earlier we saw how the dispersal of power among states in the international system can influence their behavior. Power dispersal patterns also affect the structure of the international system itself. As realist theorist Kenneth Waltz observed, when the distribution of power among states changes, the system's structure changes too.[3] When power is concentrated in one large state, for example, the system has one center of power and takes on a *unipolar* structure; when power is clustered in two strong states or alliance networks, the system exhibits a *bipolar* structure; and when three or more centers of power exist, the system assumes a *multipolar* structure. Systemic structure is not static. It can, and has, changed over time in response to changes in the distribution of power among states. In the ancient Western world, Rome illustrated a unipolar system par excellence; in nineteenth-century Europe, the Concert of Europe encompassed five great powers and constituted a regional multipolar system; in the second half of the twentieth century, the U.S. and Soviet alliance networks exemplified a rigid, global bipolar system.

Structure constitutes a critical dimension of international systems that merits close scrutiny, because different structures influence the way individual states relate to one another. In a unipolar system, one state acquires a preponderance of power and by virtue of its strength, can "milk" the system to its benefit. Rome, for example, required subordinate regions to pay tribute. Subordinate states may tow the hegemon's line for a while, but if their own capabilities grow, they are likely to seek greater independence, if necessary through force. In a bipolar system, each strong state or alliance will work to balance the other's power. The system may attain some stability through balancing, but suspicion and mutual insecurities will color each side's view of the other. Should alliances collide within a bipolar structure, the conflict can be large and devastating. In a multipolar system, states also will balance each other's power—individually or through flexible alliances. Smaller conflicts are not uncommon in multipolar systems.

A second dimension of the international system that warrants attention is what we might call its systemic rules. Most systems have rules (or even laws) that govern the interaction of their respective units. In our solar system, for example, the law of gravity governs the actions of its units, the planets. Sports systems and economic systems—comprised of sports teams and firms—also have rules that govern how their constituent parts inter-relate. Similarly, there are rules within international systems regarding the interaction of their units, the states. During the nineteenth-century Concert of Europe, the great powers adhered to certain rules of behavior. They agreed to recognize monarchies as the legitimate form of government, take steps to balance power and power resources among them, permit small wars but prohibit large ones, and hold periodic meetings to discuss issues of concern, assess the balance of power, and make adjustments if needed. Systemic rules can be devised multilaterally by several leading states (as with the Concert of Europe) or unilaterally by a powerful state. Because multilaterally derived rules are also mutually acceptable, the major powers quickly become stakeholders in the system with incentives to support it and act within prescribed parameters. By contrast, when a state gains sufficient power to establish rules unilaterally, absent a war that might impose these rules on others, major powers must be pressured (or threatened) to accept them and behave accordingly.

The Structure and Rules of Hemispheric Relations: 1700s–1900

Modern U.S.–Latin American relations have been conditioned in important ways by basic changes in the structure and rules of the Western Hemispheric international system. Since the eighteenth century, three different structures have evolved. The colonial era witnessed a multipolar structure with four major powers: Britain, France, Portugal, and Spain (Figure 3.3). Through most of the nineteenth century, this multipolar structure endured, but the number and

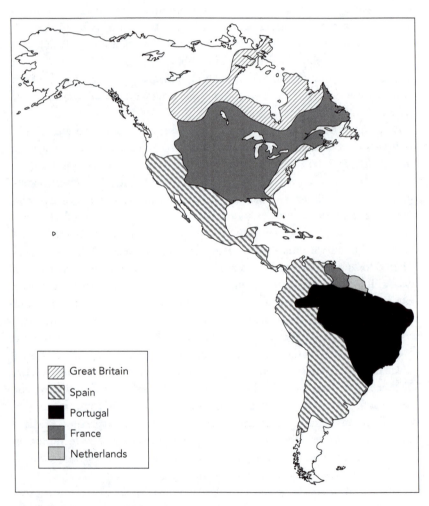

Figure 3.3 European Colonial Possessions in the New World, c.1763

composition of major powers changed. Britain and France remained important hemispheric actors, but the United States displaced Portugal (which lost its colony in Brazil) and Spain (which lost most of its New World possessions). Once the American Civil War ended, and especially from the 1890s onward, the structure grew increasingly unipolar due to a major change in the distribution of power. U.S. economic, military, and political power expanded greatly, Latin American states failed to develop equivalent capabilities, and Washington squeezed European states out of the Western Hemisphere, leaving U.S.–Latin American relations to play out within a unipolar, highly asymmetrical context.

Box 3.2 Structural Change in the Western Hemisphere

1700–1823
Multipolarity: Britain, France, Portugal, Spain

1823–1895
Multipolarity: Britain, France, United States

1895 onward
Unipolarity: United States

Major rule changes accompanied the system's changing structure, as old rules established between Europe's major powers gave way to new ones developed unilaterally by the rising United States. During the colonial period, competition between Europeans for New World colonies was the norm. In the post-colonial era, European powers that retained some New World possessions enjoyed the right to settle border disputes directly with the relevant Latin American state, and to collect debts from Latin American states by force of arms. The American and Latin American wars of independence challenged the legitimacy of colonialism in the New World. Later, the United States sought to vitiate that rule completely through the Monroe Doctrine, but lacked the power to do so. However, once the United States acquired the capability to enforce the Doctrine, it did so decisively. In the 1890s, it challenged Britain's involvement in a border dispute between Venezuela and London's British Guyana, and in 1902, it threatened Germany with war if it endeavored to acquire any Venezuelan territory during its dispute over unpaid loans.

Britain's acceptance of the Monroe Doctrine in 1896, and Germany's reluctant acquiescence to it in the early 1900s, placed the Americas out of bounds for imperial quests (at least by Europeans), and ended the practice of negotiating directly with Latin American states over contested borders. Thereafter, any border dispute involving Europeans would first pass through the interlocutor between European and Latin American governments, the United States. As we shall see in Chapter 4, the 1905 Roosevelt Corollary to the Monroe Doctrine laid to rest the European practice of collecting debts by force, thereby negating the possibility of any future European military presence in the Americas. Finally, the broad acceptance of the Monroe Doctrine provided the United States a regional zone of influence that established an additional, if implicit rule: Latin American governments must defer to the United States on matters of strategic significance and show fidelity to U.S. regional leadership.

International Structure and Modern U.S.–Latin American Relations

From the late nineteenth century onward, unipolarity within the Western Hemisphere and the American unilaterally derived rules, became "constants" of U.S.–Latin American relations. With other major powers excluded from the region and Latin American states at a decided power disadvantage, the United States was able to "milk" the system to serve its national interest as structural theory would predict, by employing its political and military capacity to extend its political reach, and expanding trade and economic opportunities accordingly.

Politically, the United States took over customs houses in the Dominican Republic, Guatemala, Haiti, and Nicaragua, and at times, placed these states under military occupation. It intervened politically and militarily in Mexico's revolution. It also prised Panama away from Colombia, constructed the Panama Canal, and established a series of protectorates in Central America and the Caribbean to extend its influence, protect its interests, and enhance its commercial opportunities. The upshot was a zone of influence that spanned Mexico and Central America, stretched down into the northern Andean region, and expanded U.S. commercial enterprise.

As a result, both the United States' share of Latin America's exports and its percentage of total direct investment in the region grew substantially. In just 32 years (1897–1929), U.S. investment in Latin America grew from $308 million to $5.2 billion.[4] America became the largest export market for Mexican, Central American, and many Caribbean products and commodities, the largest asset-holder in these countries' economies, and it developed significant trade and investment relations with Venezuela. The U.S. government aggressively backed American investors who competed with European counterparts for the region's markets. The petroleum sector is a good example. Believing that any oil concessions in proximity to the Panama Canal should be held only by Americans, the U.S. State Department pressured governments in Mexico and the Caribbean to grant concessions to American, rather than European oil companies. This tactic paid handsome dividends: in 1912, U.S. firms produced less than 50 percent of all crude oil pumped in the Western Hemisphere (excluding crude pumped from wells on American territory); by 1922, the U.S. share had jumped to over 76 percent, with the increase coming largely at the expense of Anglo-Dutch competitors.[5]

In the twentieth century, challenges to the Western Hemisphere's unipolar order generated intense international confrontations, and at times, had severe repercussions for the Latin American countries involved. These challenges stemmed from the direct (or perceived) encroachment of a strong, extra-hemispheric power, the Soviet Union. The Cuban-Soviet alliance of the 1960s introduced an external, anti-U.S. military presence into the region and brought the world to the brink of nuclear war. In other instances, the extra-hemispheric element of the challenge was more tenuous (and often inflated), but the U.S. response was firm: the 1950 election of a leftist, reform-minded government in Guatemala led to a CIA-sponsored military coup and subsequent military regimes; the 1970 election of a socialist government in Chile with ideological leanings toward Cuba and Moscow led to U.S. support of a military coup that installed a brutal dictatorship in 1973; the 1979 socialist revolution in Nicaragua led to 10 years of U.S.-supported guerrilla insurgency against the Sandinista government; and ideological ties between the Soviet Union and the small Caribbean state, Grenada, led to a full U.S. military invasion in 1983.

Because of the interventionist means Washington employed to enforce systemic rules and protect the unipolar order, because unipolarity positioned the United States to derive economic and political benefits, and because America availed itself of those opportunities, it is not surprising that Latin American states grew wary of U.S. power and developed deep anti-U.S. sentiments. Structural analysis, therefore, can tell us a great deal about why U.S.–Latin American relations took on the tension-filled, admiration/resentment dynamics that observers in both Americas often lament. Yet, a pure structural explanation is incomplete and in fact, overly deterministic, because it leaves many critical questions unanswered. Why, for example, did U.S. power begin to grow disproportionately to that of Latin American states? Why didn't the strong European states try to prevent the rise of American power or resist enforcement of the Monroe Doctrine? If Britain had refused to accept the Doctrine's sanctions against European meddling in the Americas, Germany most likely would have followed suit. The hemispheric system would then have retained a more multipolar structure, where the influence of other strong states might have balanced America's power and perhaps tempered its interventionist tendencies. This counterfactual outcome would certainly have changed the tenor and overall trajectory of U.S.–Latin American relations. Why, then, did political outcomes unfold as they did? These are questions that structural analysis alone cannot answer.

A structural explanation also fails to account for human agency in the development of unipolarity and baggage-laden U.S.–Latin American relations. Powerful personalities sometimes occupied the corridors of power in late nineteenth-century Washington. Theodore Roosevelt and Senator Henry Cabot Lodge were especially important. Both had long desired to drive Europeans completely out of the New World, leaving the United States as the hemisphere's preeminent power. Both also favored an expansionist foreign policy and had sought a war with Spain (which was too weak to pose a threat to U.S. security when the 1898 war occurred). Roosevelt in particular took deliberate steps as Assistant Secretary of the Navy to prepare for and help engineer a war, then as president, pursued a unipolar strategy thereafter. A pure structural explanation does not allow for these individual contributions; rather, it makes the expansion of U.S. power, the way the United States exercised its power in and against Latin American states, and the tension-filled relationship that developed, seem inevitable. To make sense of these issues we must remember the importance of human agency. We also must consider the contributions made by domestic factors in the United States and Latin America, along with Europe's broader balance of power considerations.

In the early nineteenth century, U.S. weakness rendered the Monroe Doctrine null and the object of European contempt. The United States possessed abundant resources but could not convert them into actual power that was sufficient to confront the stronger European states. Moreover, instability and domestic politics—especially the Civil War and the destruction, national polarization, and reconstruction that followed—kept the United States internally focused. By contrast, the second half of the nineteenth century brought the end of Reconstruction, rapid economic growth, and advancements in industrial and transportation technology, all of which helped America solve its power conversion problem and begin to enforce the Monroe Doctrine. In Latin America, meanwhile, chronic political instability and warfare plagued the newly independent states. Their labor-intensive agrarian and extractive-based economies had little need for technical innovation. Unlike their northern neighbor, they failed to develop the kind of institutional arrangements (effective constitutions and market frameworks) that compelled political elites to compromise, and channeled profits and surplus back into economic enterprise (and more economic growth).[6] As a result, struggles for power—inside states and between them—drained national treasuries, destroyed infrastructure, discouraged investment, and retarded development, leaving the United States to surge ahead dramatically.

Both Europe's failure to prevent the United States' ascension and its ultimate acceptance of the Monroe Doctrine can be linked to balance of power struggles on the European continent. By the time U.S. power began to surge, the Concert of Europe had collapsed, wars in Africa, Asia, and Europe drew the attention and sapped the treasury of Europe's great powers, and toward the end of the nineteenth century, Germany began to challenge Britain for naval supremacy. The naval arms race that followed heightened London's own security concerns, leading it to see friendly relations with the United States as a means to help balance rising German power. Thus, by the 1890s, rather than insist on its right to determine the Venezuelan-British Guyanan border directly with Venezuela, Britain accepted America's insistence to arbitrate the dispute under auspices of the Monroe Doctrine. In the process, London accepted the Doctrine itself. This led the way for other powers to follow suit, which in turn, helped guarantee Western Hemispheric unipolarity.

As we see, unipolarity in the Western Hemisphere helped give modern U.S.–Latin American relations their peculiar properties. It conditioned Latin American states to defer to U.S. influence, seek and accept U.S. assistance, admire U.S. economic and political progress, resent U.S. behavior, and suspect U.S. intentions. It conditioned the United States to expect deference, exercise its power sometimes unrestrained by Latin American interests or sensitivities, and to protect its unipolar position with vigor. The system's unipolar structure itself, however, emerged through a long, complex process. In explaining its development and the type of relations it helped produce, we began with a simple, parsimonious structural account but found it inadequate; we then layered increasing complexity into our analysis to explain key issues that a structural approach alone, could not.

Understanding the international system's structure and rules can tell us a great deal about how international politics developed in the Western Hemisphere and the general framework in which U.S.–Latin American relations evolved. We can gain even greater insights into these developments by understanding the contributions of specific U.S. foreign policies, the Latin American response to them, the concerns and policy visions of early U.S. leaders, and by viewing this historical period through the lens of our theories and analytic concepts.

Box 3.3 Looking Toward the Future: What Type of Structure will International Politics in the Western Hemisphere Assume?

In modern times, unipolarity has been a key structural feature of international politics in the Western Hemisphere. Europe's remaining territorial possessions in the region are more famous for their beaches and resorts, than their geostrategic significance. No state in Latin America has appreciable hard power projection capabilities, and no state in the region—or combination of states—can match the United States in military, political or broad economic power. Will this same structure endure throughout the twenty-first century?

As political scientist Kenneth Waltz observed, systemic structure changes in response to changes in the distribution of power among states. The questions, then, are whether power dispersal patterns are changing, and if so, are they changing enough to recast the system's structure. The answers are yes, and we don't know; it's too early to tell. The probability is high that the United States will retain a commanding edge over Latin American states in hard military power, economic capacity, and industrial and information resources. However, several Latin American states have found ways to challenge U.S. influence in soft power terms. These challengers—in the Andean Ridge, Central America, and Southern Cone—have established transnational communication systems (Telesur), political arrangements (UNASUR), and multilateral lending institutions (Bancosur) that may increasingly contest America's near monopoly on disseminating satellite broadcast news (or what the challengers call U.S. "informational hegemony"), and the political leverage it traditionally has wielded through regional institutions like the Organization of American States and Inter-American Development Bank. By pursuing these "soft balancing" tactics, the challengers seek to create an alternative power center, eliminate unipolarity, and provide space for states to pursue their development and policy objectives outside of the institutions where America holds sway.

Will soft balancing succeed in ending unipolarity? Since the unipolar system itself took a century to develop, only time will tell. Another possibility, however—and one that concerns some U.S. officials—is China's growing economic and financial presence in the region. Since 1990, China's overall trade with Latin America has skyrocketed, and in just seven years (2000–2007) it jumped from $10 billion to $100 billion. Presently, however, Beijing does not display any interest in establishing political (and certainly not military) influence in Latin America. Whether it will do so in the future remains to be seen.

Early U.S. Foreign Policy Toward Latin America and Beyond

At the time of U.S. independence from Britain, Latin America remained colonized by European powers. The United States' earliest foreign policy interests, therefore, concerned Europe, but were closely connected to activities, contingencies, events, and power struggles between European states in Latin America, particularly in the Caribbean.

Early American leaders well understood the balance of power. Even before the U.S. Constitution was ratified in 1789, Alexander Hamilton contemplated how the United States might influence the balance of power in the Western Hemisphere. "We may hope, erelong," he wrote in *Federalist No. 11*, "to become the arbiter of Europe in America, and to be able to incline the balance of European competitions in this part of the world as our interest may dictate."[7] As Hamilton saw it, the key to success in this respect was first, Union of the original 13 states, followed by the construction of a U.S. Navy whose ships could weigh in on European struggles in the Caribbean, favoring the British, French, or Spanish according to America's own national interests. "There can be no doubt," he believed, that a Union of the 13 original states would permit creating a navy "which, if it could not vie with those of the great maritime powers, would at least be of respectable weight if thrown into the scale of either of the two contending parties."[8]

Yet, Hamilton was not content merely to see the United States become one of several powers jostling for position and protection in the New World. His global view was somewhat larger. In the late 1780s, Hamilton saw a world dominated by strong, imperial, predatory powers, one in which a weak United States would be vulnerable. But he also foresaw a future in which a strong United States might actually determine not just the outcome of a particular Caribbean naval battle between European forces, but the extent that—and procedures under which—Europe would be permitted to interact with the Western Hemisphere. His thoughts on these subjects are worth quoting at length.

The world may politically, as well as geographically, be divided into four parts, each having a distinct set of interests. Unhappily for the other three, Europe, by her arms and by her negotiations, by force and by fraud, has in different degrees extended her dominion over them all. Africa, Asia, and America have successively felt her domination. The superiority she has long maintained has tempted her to plume herself as the mistress of the world, and to consider the rest of mankind as created for her benefit . . . Let Americans disdain to be the instruments of European greatness! Let the thirteen States, bound together in a strict and indissoluble Union, concur in erecting one great American system superior to the control of all transatlantic force or influence and able to dictate the terms of the connection between the old and the new world![9]

Here is a mind given to geostrategic concerns of the first order. Hamilton not only perceived the need for power and the stark reality of power politics, but also the vulnerability of his country in an anarchic world, and the possibility of altering the balance of power in ways that would protect its security and advance its national interests. In the following decades, however, the United Sates displayed little more than an intellectual and rhetorical interest in Latin America. It did not provide Latin Americans much support in their struggles for independence, and it was slow to recognize those Latin American states that had severed their ties to Spain, granting official recognition to Argentina, Chile, Colombia, Mexico, and Peru only in 1821—well after most had already won de-facto independence. However, two centuries after Hamilton penned *Federalist No. 11*, his vision of a unipolar Western Hemisphere would be realized. The path toward this outcome began with the Monroe Doctrine.

The Monroe Doctrine

The Monroe Doctrine constitutes the historical cornerstone of official U.S. policy toward Latin America. It enjoyed deeper popular support, broader public acclaim, and greater longevity than any other U.S. foreign policy doctrine (such as the Bush, Carter, Reagan, and Truman doctrines), and it provided American policymakers greater political utility too. In essence, the Doctrine proclaimed the Western Hemisphere off limits to further European colonization and intervention. It drew a sharp distinction between the political systems of the Old World and the New—that is, between monarchies, aristocracies, and subjects on the one hand, and republics, popular sovereignty, and citizens on the other. It warned Europeans that any attempt to extend "their system" to any part of the New World would jeopardize U.S. security, that any attempt to oppress or control the destiny of Latin American states would be viewed as an "unfriendly disposition" toward the United States; and it promised that in return for Europe leaving the Americas to the Americans, the United States would remain neutral in all European military and political affairs.

Box 3.4 The Monroe Doctrine (1823)

[T]he American continents, by the free and independent condition which they have assumed and maintain, are henceforth not to be considered as subjects for future colonization by any European powers . . . In the wars of the European powers, in matters relating to themselves, we have never taken any part, nor does it comport with our policy to do so . . . With the movements in this hemisphere, we are, of necessity, more immediately connected, and by causes which must be obvious to all enlightened and impartial observers. The political system of the allied powers is essentially different, in this respect, from that of America. This difference proceeds from that which exists in their respective governments. And to the defence of our own, which has been achieved by the loss of so much blood and treasure, and matured by the wisdom of their most enlightened citizens, and under which we have enjoyed unexampled felicity, this whole nation is devoted. We owe it, therefore, to candor, and to the amicable relations existing between the United States and those powers, to declare, that we should consider any attempt on their part to extend their system to any portion of this hemisphere, as dangerous to our peace and safety. With the existing colonies or dependencies of any European power we have not interfered, and shall not interfere. But with the governments who have declared their independence, and maintained it, and whose independence we have, on great consideration, and on just principles, acknowledged, we could not view any interposition for the purpose of oppressing them, or controlling, in any other manner, their destiny, by any European power in any other light than as the manifestation of an unfriendly disposition towards the United States. In the war between those new governments and Spain we declared our neutrality at the time of their recognition, and to this we have adhered, and shall continue to adhere, provided no change shall occur, which, in the judgment of the competent authorities of this government, shall make a corresponding change, on the part of the United States, indispensable to their security . . .

> Our policy, in regard to Europe, which was adopted at an early stage of the wars which have so long agitated that quarter of the globe, nevertheless remains the same, which is, not to interfere in the internal concerns of any of its powers; to consider the government *de facto* as the legitimate government for us; to cultivate friendly relations with it, and to preserve those relations by a frank, firm, and manly policy; meeting, in all instances, the just claims of every power; submitting to injuries from none. But, in regard to these continents, circumstances are eminently and conspicuously different. It is impossible that the allied powers should extend their political system to any portion of either continent, without endangering our peace and happiness: nor can any one believe that our Southern Brethren, if left to themselves, would adopt it of their own accord. It is equally impossible, therefore, that we should behold such interposition, in any form, with indifference. If we look to the comparative strength and resources of Spain and those new governments, and their distance from each other, it must be obvious that she can never subdue them. It is still the true policy of the United States to leave the parties to themselves, in the hope that other powers will pursue the same course.
>
> James Monroe

In general, the Monroe Doctrine was well received by U.S. neighbors, whose new governments appreciated its warning against European attempts to re-colonize the region. Writing to U.S. Secretary of State John Quincy Adams, for example, Colombia's vice president, Francisco Santander y Omaña explained: "My Government has received [President Monroe's doctrine] with the greatest pleasure." The Colombian government, he said, also had Monroe's message translated into Spanish and then circulated in Peru and Chile. Further south in what would become Argentina (then, the United Provinces of Rio de la Plata), the national congress hailed the Doctrine's intent "to prevent any foreign assistance from being introduced to the aid of our rival [Spain]." Governments in Chile and Central America were also well disposed to U.S. policy.[10] For some in Latin America, the Monroe Doctrine conjured up images of hemispheric solidarity (or even a military alliance) vis-à-vis Europe—a united front of New World states determined to develop their own political systems and exercise their right of self-determination free of European meddling.

Yet, the Monroe Doctrine did not lead to hemispheric solidarity, and for decades, it did not prevent European intervention. Moreover, eventually it was applied in ways that denied Latin American states important features of self-determination, and was reinterpreted by Washington in ways that justified U.S. intervention in Latin America's internal affairs. Such outcomes were scarcely imaginable when the United States first announced the Doctrine. How might they be explained? Realism, balance of power issues, and levels of analysis all offer useful insights.

The United States promulgated the Monroe Doctrine in response to changes in the global balance of power, political turmoil in Spanish America, and Russia's foreign policy ambitions. The wars of independence in Spanish America unfolded in the context of larger balance of power issues in Europe during the Napoleonic Wars (1803–1815). Napoleon sought to subordinate other European powers to French domination, but was defeated at Waterloo in 1815 by Austria, Britain, Prussia, and Russia (the Quadruple Alliance). Across the Atlantic, however, Napoleon's exploits had far reaching consequences. On the one hand, France's 1807 incursion into the Iberian Peninsula precipitated the armed revolt of Spain's colonies from the mother country, and Brazil's more gradual and peaceful separation from Portugal. On the other hand, France's hegemonic aspirations aroused Europe's great power monarchies to the dangers posed by liberalism and democratic revolutions. To preserve the legitimacy of monarchical systems, leaders from Austria, Prussia, post-Napoleonic France, and Russia met in 1820 at the Congress of Troppau. There, they agreed to contain the spread of republicanism and crush anti-monarchical insurrections wherever they sprang up. The following year, Austrian forces took action against revolts in Italy; the next year French forces suppressed an uprising in Spain; monarchist powers also intervened against an uprising in Greece.

In the United States, these developments raised the question of whether Europe's great powers would confine their "containment" strategies toward republican political aspirations to the Old World, or extend them to the New, and seek to reactivate Spain's American Empire. Since Britain refused to join in suppressing anti-monarchical insurrections—and only France had naval forces sufficient for a joint European campaign against the New World uprisings—rumors swirled that Spain would compensate France for its assistance by transferring some of its possessions in the Western Hemisphere to French control.

Around the same time, U.S. leaders grew concerned over imperial Russia. In 1821, Czar Alexander claimed the entire northwest coast of North America for Russia. This claim conflicted with American and British counter-claims in the Oregon Territory, and its aim was to keep all commerce and fishing along the west coast and Alaska in Russian hands. Toward this end, Alexander threatened to confiscate any foreign ships that came within 100 miles of the region. The Czar's proclamation raised the specter of a possible Russian colony in North America, and eventually, perhaps even Russian troops.

Having opted out of the Europeans' anti-republican enterprise, Britain's primary interest was to maintain a balance of power among the European states. It had remained neutral in Spain's fight to retain its colonies, hoping that Madrid would make political concessions that would keep its American colonies within a reformed, imperial framework (London had long carried on clandestine trade with Spanish colonies which it did not want to see jeopardized). By 1823, however, Britain was resigned to the loss of Spanish control in the Americas, yet equally determined to oppose efforts by any other European state (especially France) to acquire territories from the remnants of Spain's New World empire. In August 1823, Britain's Foreign Secretary, George Canning, floated the idea of a joint Anglo-American protest against further European intervention in the Americas to Richard Rush, U.S. Minister to Great Britain. Canning also suggested the two governments should mutually renounce any intent to acquire more territory themselves. Rush, in turn, transmitted the proposal to President James Monroe.

Monroe saw light in the British offer and was inclined to accept it. He was further disposed to do so after consulting former presidents Jefferson and Madison, both of whom also approved. History, however, does not record any such bilateral Anglo-American statement, but instead, an official, unilateral U.S. policy: the Monroe Doctrine. Ironically, Monroe himself was not the driving force behind the policy that bears his name. His Secretary of State, John Quincy Adams, played the more decisive role. After consulting Jefferson and Madison, Monroe submitted the proposal to his cabinet, every member of which save Adams favored the bilateral approach. Adams was as much concerned over Russian aspirations on the west coast, as with potential French territorial acquisitions in Latin America. He also smelled a trap: he suspected that Britain's call to mutually disclaim new territory was really designed to prevent further U.S. expansion into Spanish America (he had eyes on Cuba and the Mexican province of Texas). Adams, therefore, argued forcefully against bilateral action based on reasons of national interest, prestige, and security. "It would be more candid, as well as more dignified, to avow our principles explicitly to Russia and France," he felt, "than to come in as a cockboat in the wake of the British man-of-war." Remarkably, Adams managed to persuade the president to reject his own initial position and his cabinet's: the United States would follow a unilateral approach. Thus, in the end, while third-level, security, and balance of power factors set the context for a U.S. policy toward Latin America, individual, first-level factors determined the exact form that policy would take.

A TOOTHLESS DOCTRINE

To say that the new U.S. policy failed to impress European states is an understatement. Many openly ridiculed it. Russia's foreign minister said that most European leaders paid more attention to what London said, than anything that Washington might. For his part, Czar Alexander heaped scorn on the Doctrine as an object worthy of "only the most profound contempt." Austria's foreign minister, Klemens von Metternich, agreed, adding that it was nothing more than a set of "indecent declarations." France's foreign minister, Francois Rene de Chateaubriand, believed the Doctrine should be "resisted by all the powers having commercial or territorial interests in the hemisphere." He also pointed out the obvious disparity between the Doctrine's prohibitions against European intervention and the United States' naval capacity to enforce them.[11]

Chateaubriand made a good point. By any realistic assessment, the United States lacked the power to enforce the Monroe Doctrine. Washington knew this; the Europeans did too. The Monroe Doctrine simply had no teeth. Consequently, over the next few decades, Europeans continued to intervene in the Western Hemisphere and the United States did little to stop them; sometimes it did not even protest. In 1833, for example, Britain seized the Falkland Islands from Argentina and expanded the borders of British Honduras in Central America; in 1841, London created a protectorate over the Miskito Indians' territory in Nicaragua; in 1838, Britain and France intervened militarily in Argentina; in 1843, France imposed a naval blockade against Argentina. All these incursions occurred without any appreciable U.S. response. The most dramatic and flagrant violation of the Monroe Doctrine, however, occurred in the 1860s, and in the United States' virtual backyard: Mexico.

In 1862, Britain, France, and Spain launched a joint military expedition to Veracruz to collect debts owed by the Mexican government. Eventually, the British and Spanish withdrew; the French, however, did not. Instead, with 30,000 troops in Mexico, France became intoxicated with the idea of extending its empire in the New World. In 1864, it took steps to rule Mexico through a puppet emperor, Ferdinand Maximilian of Austria. Second-level factors had provided France a window of opportunity to test the Monroe Doctrine, and good reasons to believe its enterprise would succeed. Mexico was weak and internally divided, with conservative monarchists locked in battle against liberal reformers led by President Benito Juárez. The United States, meanwhile, was completely preoccupied with its own domestic matters: the Civil War.

Consequently, while the United States *did* protest this particular European incursion, it lacked the power to repel it. However, the closer the war drew to a conclusion, the more "teeth" the United States began putting into its protests.

For example, initially, U.S. Secretary of State, William Seward, wrote France only mild notes of concern about its activities: establishing a monarchy in Mexico, he told Paris, would not be easy or preferable. But as the Civil War wound down, the tone of Seward's letters changed: a permanent French presence in Mexico would put friendly U.S.-French relations at serious risk, he explained. Even before the Civil War ended, the United States began to make threatening growls based on the Monroe Doctrine. On April 4, 1864, the U.S. Congress unanimously resolved to oppose the establishment of a monarchy in Mexico. Once the war ended in 1865, the French intervention received Washington's full attention. Fifty thousand American troops were dispatched to the United States–Mexico border where U.S. forces engaged in maneuvers that visibly threatened intervention against the French. By February 1866, Washington had stepped up the pressure even more and demanded that France withdraw from Mexico under threat of war; in May, Napoleon III finally agreed.

Unfortunately for Maximilian, he did not follow Napoleon's lead, choosing instead to remain in Mexico in hopes of defeating the liberals. In 1867, Juárez's forces captured Maximilian, tried the emperor, and sentenced him to death by firing squad. Many of Europe's crowned heads dispatched telegrams and letters to Mexico begging Juárez to commute the death sentence and spare Maximilian's life. Juárez, however, refused to yield. Maximilian's execution sent a strong signal that Mexicans would not permit their sovereignty to be compromised by any government imposed by outside powers.

France's test of the Monroe Doctrine underscores several points of theoretical relevance. First, it reminds us how changes in the balance of power between states can affect their political calculations and behavior. France was keenly aware that a war-torn, internally preoccupied United States could not oppose it effectively, even when the challenge it posed stood at America's doorstep. Second, as we noted before, it also highlights the role that proximity plays in international politics. Despite America's weakened state, establishing a French puppet monarchy on the U.S. border enhanced Washington's perception of threat, and as soon as it could the United States responded with a show of force. Third, it demonstrates how proximity and balance of power concerns cut both ways. Besides enhancing the U.S. perception of threat, proximity tilted the local balance of power in ways that favored the Americans in any military contest that might have developed with France, after the Civil War ended. In that event, unlike their French counterparts, U.S. forces would have been operating close to their principal sources of manpower and weapons. In fact, by 1866 U.S. military leaders already had drawn up a plan whereby the Union's fleet would attack and sink the French fleet stationed off Veracruz (to cut off a possible French retreat), while the Union Army swooped down through Texas into Mexico to engage French forces on the ground. In short, had Mexico become a theater of French-U.S. military conflict, the deck would have been stacked in America's favor. This factor played an important part in France's decision to quit its imperial experiment in Mexico.

Although the French incursion strengthened U.S. commitment to the Monroe Doctrine, enforcing the Doctrine effectively in regions far removed from the U.S. border required significantly more power than America possessed in 1865. Over the next 35 years, the United States would acquire the capacity to enforce the Doctrine virtually wherever it pleased.

After France withdrew from Mexico, Latin America receded somewhat from the U.S. foreign policy agenda. Over the next three decades, the United States turned largely inward and started converting some of its latent power resources into effective political leverage. It put its own house in order through Reconstruction, worked to complete the Transcontinental Railroad, secured the West (by defeating Native Americans), accepted large waves of European immigrants, experienced a second Industrial Revolution and significant technical innovation (agricultural machinery, electric lighting and power, manufacturing, steel production), developed new modes of communication (telegraph, tele-phone), and expanded its economic output dramatically. The dynamism it exhibited worked in mutually reinforcing ways. Technological innovation spurred industrialization; industrial output jumped thanks to the influx of immigrant workers; and advancements in communications and transportation connected the country, its economy, and population as never before.

The aggregate effects of this dynamism were impressive. Between 1860 and 1900, America's gross national product tripled; its exports surged from $400 million to nearly $1.5 billion; its population rose from 31.4 million to nearly 76 million (and in the process, its rural population doubled while its urban population quadrupled); and it laid 172,000 miles of new rail tracks. Although it acquired no new territory (save non-contiguous Alaska), the completion of the Transcontinental Railroad (1869) opened the way to settle millions of acres of land in the West: 430 million acres were settled between 1870 and 1900, and 225 million were cultivated. As farming expanded, wheat production grew nearly threefold (from 211 million to 599 million bushels). Similarly, as industry expanded, steel production did too. By 1900, therefore, the United States accounted for a quarter of the world's steel production,[12] boasted the world's largest economy, and had begun to apply some of its dynamism to defense and security: between 1880 and 1900 its military grew more than threefold (from about 38,000 to nearly 126,000 troops) and its warship tonnage nearly doubled (from 169,000 to 333,000 tons).[13] Just 35 years after the Civil War, America had been transformed from a divided, largely agrarian nation whose southern regions had been decimated by war, into an industrial nation whose power dwarfed its Latin American neighbors and rivaled its European counterparts. From this position, the United States could, if it chose to, enforce the Monroe Doctrine more broadly and exercise political influence effectively throughout much of the Western Hemisphere.

THE DOCTRINE ENFORCED

After the French incursion in Mexico, the Monroe Doctrine would not be tested as rigorously again until the 1890s. In this case, the test would come much further from the U.S. border: the encroaching European power would be Britain, and the target state, Venezuela. For 50 years, London and Caracas had disputed the boundaries separating British Guyana and Venezuela. The dispute began in 1841, and the contested territory—land near the mouth of the Orinoco River—had both strategic and economic value (thanks to the later discovery of gold). For decades, Venezuela's efforts to negotiate a settlement with Britain went nowhere, while its periodic requests for U.S. arbitration (under auspices of the Monroe Doctrine) fared no better. By the 1880s, Britain had expanded its land claims by 33,000 square miles, and in 1889, British Guyana proclaimed its sovereignty over the entire mouth of the Orinoco River. From 1890 onward, therefore, Venezuela stepped up its pressure for American assistance. Through its ambassador to Washington, it warned then Secretary of State, James Blaine, that only the United States could protect its interests vis-à-vis the stronger Britain; it also hired America's former ambassador to Venezuela, William Scruggs, to publicize its plight and lobby Washington on its behalf. Scruggs did: his 1894 manuscript, "British Aggressions in Venezuela, or the Monroe Doctrine on Trial," became wildly popular, going through four editions.

When the United States finally responded to Venezuela's appeals, it did so not just by invoking the Monroe Doctrine, but also with a breathtaking claim of political authority across the Western Hemisphere. In 1895, Secretary of State Richard Olney issued a strongly worded memorandum to the British government. The Olney Corollary to the Monroe Doctrine blamed the border troubles largely on Britain, explained America's national interests in the Western Hemisphere based on the Monroe Doctrine, and proposed that the British-Venezuelan standoff be settled through arbitration. Under the Monroe Doctrine, Olney insisted, "no European power or combination of European powers" could "forcibly deprive an American state of the right and power of self-government and of shaping for itself its own political fortunes and destiny." Britain should understand, he explained, that America took great interest in the border dispute and in British actions, since "Today the United States is practically sovereign on this continent, and its fiat is law upon the subjects to which it confines its interposition." Thus, the only peaceful way to resolve the conflict was through U.S.-assisted arbitration.

Britain's response seemed emphatic. It rejected out of hand, both America's interpretation of the situation and its call for arbitration; it also dismissed the Monroe Doctrine as having no basis in international law. In turn, the United States showed no signs of retreat. President James Cleveland asked Congress to create and fund a fact-finding commission to get to the bottom of Venezuela's border issues. The president asserted that British encroachments against Venezuela smacked of "willful aggression"; he also told lawmakers it was imperative that the United States (not Britain) determine Venezuela's true boundaries, since to do otherwise was to submit to "wrong and injustice, and the consequent loss of national self-respect and honor." Finally, in a nod to the possible implications of his request—war—he assured Congress that he fully realized "all the consequences that may follow."[14]

Many signs now pointed toward an American-Anglo war, an outcome that neither Britain nor the United States actually wanted. Yet, war did not come. Instead, in 1896 Britain backed down. It appeased America, agreed to arbitration, and in the end, it received much of the territory it had claimed (Venezuela still retained the entire Orinoco Delta region).

How might we account for London's de facto acceptance of the Monroe Doctrine and the absence of war between Britain and the United States? A realist explanation would emphasize two factors: Britain's growing appreciation of American power, and its perceptions that Germany's rising power constituted a more proximate threat to British interests than America's invocation of the Monroe Doctrine. Although the United States had surpassed Britain as the world's largest economy by 1895, Britain's navy remained considerably larger and more powerful; the chances of a British victory, therefore, were good, but the costs of fighting a war on America's side of the Atlantic would have been high. Germany, meanwhile, had begun to challenge Britain in a naval arms race, and just as the French presence in Mexico had agitated the United States, so Germany's proximity to Britain enhanced its perception of threat. Given the trade-offs between a high-cost victory over the United States on the one hand (and losing ships in the process), and conserving its naval forces to face rising German power on the other, appeasing the United States over Venezuela's borders was a prudent course of action. By contrast, a liberal account would explain Britain's actions differently by drawing upon democratic peace theory. Yes, both Britain and America had interests in the Venezuela border dispute; however, both states were also liberal democracies. Because democracies believe that wars against people who have constitutional rights are illegitimate, Britain chose to resolve the dispute peacefully.

This episode also tells us something about *appeasement* as a tool of statecraft. Today, conventional wisdom views appeasement as a sign of weakness, of giving into the demands of a bully or aggressor in order to avoid conflict, rather than drawing a sharp line past which an adversary will not be permitted to go. According to diplomatic historian Paul Kennedy, however, appeasement is a "policy of settling international quarrels by admitting and satisfying grievances through rational negotiation and compromise"; so long as an opponent's demands are reasonable, appeasement can avoid "the resort to an armed conflict which would be expensive, bloody and possibly dangerous."[15] Appeasement earned a bad reputation in the late 1930s when Britain—hoping to satisfy Hitler's appetite for new territory—permitted Germany to seize parts of Central Europe. However, Hitler's appetite was not satiated; Germany went on to expand across Western Europe, and World War II was the result. Nonetheless, states sometimes have used appeasement successfully to avoid war. In 2008, the United States accommodated North Korea's security concerns, granting Pyongyang material benefits and political concessions in exchange for a full disclosure of its nuclear weaponry program; in 1896, Britain accommodated America's interests in Latin America. Both states made reasonable concessions and avoided armed conflict in the process.

Although Britain never officially recognized the Monroe Doctrine, its decision to arbitrate in the face of American insistence conveyed essentially the same message. By virtue of being the world's strongest naval power, Britain's actions carried weight and spoke to a changed political reality: the era of European states intervening at will in the Americas was coming to an end, the United States had become the interlocutor between Europe and Latin America, and the systemic structure of the Western Hemisphere was moving toward unipolarity.

Study Questions

1. What do international relations scholars mean by the "three levels of analysis"? How might these levels interact and why are they useful in explaining states' foreign policies and international politics? Can you think of some recent events that illustrate each level?
2. What is the difference between the structure of an international system and the system's "rules"? Why does each matter in inter-state relations?

Figure 3.4 Accepting the Monroe Doctrine: John Bull concedes that Uncle Sam is custodian of the Western Hemisphere. Cartoon by Homer Davenport, *Review of Reviews*, January 1902

3. What was the Monroe Doctrine and what motivated its adoption? How did Latin American and European states initially respond to the Doctrine and why?
4. Given his views on U.S. interests in the Caribbean, Latin America, and the world, would Hamilton embrace the realist perspective of world politics?
5. What were the characteristics of the Western Hemisphere's international system from the late nineteenth century onward? How did they differ from those of the eighteenth century?

6. How did ideology influence U.S.-Mexican relations in the nineteenth century and the development of the Mexican-American War?

Selected Readings

Gilderhus, Mark T. "The Monroe Doctrine: Meanings and Implications." *Presidential Studies Quarterly* 36 (March 2006): 5-16.

Hamilton, Alexander. "Federalist #11." In *The Federalist Papers: Hamilton, Madison, Jay*, edited by Clinton Rossiter, 84–91. New York: Penguin, 1964.

North, Douglass C., William Summerhill, and Barry R. Weingast. "Order, Disorder, and Economic Change: Latin America versus North America." In *Governing for Prosperity*, edited by Bruce Bueno de Mesquita and Hilton L. Root, 17–56. New Haven: Yale University Press, 2000.

Waltz, Kenneth N. *Man, the State and War*, 1–15. New York: Columbia University Press, 1959.

Washington, George. "Farewell Address." Senate Document No. 106–21. Washington, DC: United States Government Printing Office, 2000. http://www.access.gpo.gov/congress/senate/farewell/sd106-21.pdf.

Further Readings

Singer, J. David. "The Level-of-Analysis Problem in International Relations." In *The International System: Theoretical Essays*, edited by Klaus Knorr and Sidney Verba, 77–92. Princeton: Princeton University Press, 1961.

Waltz, Kenneth N. *Man, the State and War*. New York: Columbia University Press, 1959.

Chronology: Hemispheric Relations in the Nineteenth Century

1810–1822	Spanish colonies secure independence from Madrid
1823	Monroe Doctrine proclaimed
1836	Texas declares independence from Mexico (which Mexico City disputes)
1846-1848	Mexican-American War; Mexico loses half its national territory
1860–1880s	U.S. experiences Second Industrial Revolution; U.S. power grows
1861–1865	U.S. Civil War
1862	Britain, France, and Spain occupy Mexico
1864	France installs Ferdinand Maximilian as puppet emperor of Mexico
1865	U.S. protests French intervention in Mexico
1866	French troops withdraw; Maximilian stays on
1867	Mexican forces led by Benito Juárez capture and execute Maximilian
1869	U.S. completes Transcontinental Railroad
1895	Venezuelan-British border dispute; U.S. declares itself "practically sovereign on this continent," demands that London arbitrate the dispute and ultimately, secures London's indirect acceptance of Monroe Doctrine
1905	U.S. establishes protectorate over Dominican Republic
1911	U.S. establishes protectorate over Nicaragua
1915	U.S. establishes protectorate over Haiti

The Expansion of American Power

4

Figure 4.1
Theodore Roosevelt, 1903

Historians and political scientists alike suggest that the end of the nineteenth century marked the beginning of U.S. imperialist policies toward Latin America, increased hegemony over the region, and dominance over states near the U.S. border. Since much of the tension in U.S.–Latin American relations is rooted in this period of history, it bears close scrutiny. An *imperialist* policy is one that reflects a systematic attempt by one state to establish an empire—a geopolitical arrangement whereby one state extends dominion over populations beyond its borders that are culturally and ethnically distinct from its own. Beginning in 1898, notes historian Lester Langley, the United States adopted policies toward the Caribbean and Central America, plus Hawaii and the Philippines that would "define the political, economic, and even legal basis of an insular empire that stretched from the Caribbean to the western Pacific."[1]

Hegemony refers to a situation in which one state acquires a preponderance of power, such that it can largely determine the policies of other states. Hegemonic states sometimes employ force against lesser powers, but generally prefer to wield their influence through other means. According to political scientist Peter Smith, through its showdown with Britain over the border dispute between Venezuela and British Guyana, the United States had taken steps toward realizing "de facto hegemony in the Americas" as early as 1895.[2] *Dominance*, meanwhile, also entails a state's acquisition of military, economic, and political superiority, but unlike hegemony, it yields policies marked by habitual and uninhibited military intervention, and a routine disregard for lesser powers' sovereignty. Political scientist Hedley Bull suggests that from the late nineteenth century through roughly 1933 (the advent of the Good Neighbor Policy), U.S. policy toward Central American and Caribbean nations reflected such dominance, expressed in routine "military intervention in the internal affairs and external relations of local states . . . and in failure to pay more than lip service" to their sovereignty.[3]

While scholars disagree on the exact cut-off point of U.S. imperialist designs, the general consensus is that the United States maintained an imperialist stance toward Latin America from the late 1890s through the 1920s. But not all analysts agree with these interpretations of U.S. policy toward Latin America. Professor Paul Kennedy of Yale, for example, has characterized these years simply as a period of "more assertive diplomacy" by the United States. Moreover, rather than imperialist ambitions alone driving the new diplomacy, it was a more complex set of factors: America's growing industrial power and foreign trade, its presumed "special moral endowment" (which translated into a foreign policy it perceived as morally superior to any European state's), domestic calls to fulfill its manifest destiny, and pressure from agricultural and industrial groups to expand overseas markets. By the turn of the century, this mix of domestic factors, Kennedy suggests, provoked the United States to pursue "a much more activist diplomacy—which under the administrations of McKinley and (especially) Theodore Roosevelt, was exactly what took place."[4]

There is no question that U.S. power grew substantially during the nineteenth century, that the international system within the Western Hemisphere took on a unipolar structure reflective of that growth, or that the United States began to exercise a degree of economic, military, and political influence in the region that was unparalleled by any other state. But if all we can say is that America's foreign policy "went imperialistic" for several decades, we have not said very much. Nor is an explanation of U.S. policy that stresses only domestic-level factors sufficient. Although the Western Hemisphere had become uni-polar, the United States was still part of a larger international system. The policies it fashioned toward Latin America reflected developments beyond the Western Hemisphere, and were as much a response to dynamics at the global level as they were to those in Latin America or the U.S. domestic scene.

Outside the Western Hemisphere, for example, the nineteenth century brought dramatic changes to international politics. Fueled by industrialization and significant transportation and communication advances, the world economy grew rapidly. European states competed for power, position, and prestige. Under Chancellor Otto von Bismarck, Germany unified, creating a powerful, ambitious actor in the center of Europe. Bismarck's network of secret alliances helped maintain a wobbly balance of power on the European continent. However, once Kaiser Wilhelm II fired Bismarck in 1890, those alliances began to fray: tensions spiked between the European powers, imperial competition for African colonies grew more tense, and Germany's navy began to challenge Britain's for global supremacy.

It is within this broader context that U.S. foreign policy and the projection of American power should be viewed. After developing the capacity to enforce the Monroe Doctrine, the United States burst upon the scene as a global military power. In 1898, it waged war against Spain, and thereafter, the scope of its power expanded dramatically in the Western Hemisphere and beyond.

The Spanish-American War

On April 25, 1898, the United States and Spain went to war over Cuba. A week later (and 8,000 miles away), the U.S. Navy defeated its Spanish counterpart in the Philippines at Manila Bay; and in less than two months America took possession of another Spanish Pacific island, Guam (and annexed Hawaii on July 7). In August, it wrested control of Puerto Rico from Spain. In December, Washington and Madrid signed the Treaty of Paris: Spain relinquished Guam, the Philippines, and Puerto Rico to the United States; Cuba, meanwhile, became a U.S. protectorate. Along with its de facto control of Cuba, America's new Caribbean possessions provided the United States an offshore "first-line of defense," while its new Pacific possessions opened the door to greater economic, military, and political influence in Asia. By November 1903, Washington had signed a treaty with newly created Panama that granted the United States the right to construct, operate, and maintain a canal that would connect the Atlantic and Pacific oceans, link America's holdings in each, and facilitate their protection by a two-ocean Navy.

The Spanish-American War was the milestone event that marked U.S. ascendancy. Although little studied today, this war is significant on many fronts. It changed the United States' position in the international system, its relationship with Latin America, and with the world. It effectively ended U.S. isolationism, and in the process, transformed the United States into a world player. Although European powers still clearly mattered (and Washington still sought to avoid European political entanglements), the war changed the balance of power so that the axis of world politics began a gradual shift—away from Europe to the New World. Subsequent world wars greatly accelerated this trend. The war also illustrates a wide range of factors that can drive a state's foreign policy, and demonstrates that policy output is not always determined solely by the security-related factors conventional international relations theory suggests.

The Spanish-American War also set a profound, disturbing precedent: for the first time the United States acquired territories beyond North America, and did so without any real intention of making the people who lived in these territories U.S. citizens. Neither the Filipinos and Puerto Ricans, nor the people of Guam and Cuba had much say about their own fate. Because this outcome ran contrary to the principle of self-determination enshrined in the U.S. Declaration of Independence, the war also marked a change in how ordinary Americans and their leaders perceived U.S. foreign policy. Whereas before, most U.S. leaders used foreign policy to protect national security, and usually tried to craft policies in line with America's core political values—democracy, equality, liberty, and self-determination—the Spanish-American War saw U.S. policy adopt a sharp imperialist edge, that in turn, fueled tensions between the two Americas. Why this policy shift occurred is a mystery we need to unravel. Part of the answer lies with events in Cuba.

The Cuban War of Independence

Between 1895 and 1898, Cuban society was in turmoil. Cuba's war for independence began in 1895 and the insurgents' struggle against Spanish forces exacted a heavy price in blood, property damage, and human misery. Widespread violence and political disorder prevailed. Led by General Máximo Gómez, the insurgents were of mixed background (Spanish, African, Indian). They were mobilized, organized, and infused with nationalism—and Spain found them to be a surprisingly effective force. Besides political independence from Madrid, the insurgents' political platform called for a fundamental restructuring of colonial social relations: by breaking up Cuba's large, elite-controlled estates and redistributing land to the patriots (with legal title), the rebels hoped to replace the colonial landlord/peon social system with a new society of small to medium-sized farmers. Gómez struck at Spain's economic jugular in 1895 when he declared a moratorium on all economic activity: no planting, harvesting, grinding, or marketing of sugar would be permitted. Any estate caught violating this ban would be torched and its owner tried for treason; any worker caught helping a sugar operation would be considered an enemy of *Cuba Libre* and executed.

The planters—mostly Spanish immigrants who had prospered in the sugar industry—had different goals. They understood that a Spanish defeat by the insurgents meant a death sentence for their class (and lifestyle), and that their security lay in Spain's ability to retain control of the island. While planters had long desired to have more say in local government and resented the political monopoly Spanish nationals exercised on the island, they knew that an independent Cuba controlled by the insurgents would devastate their interests. Hence, their chief political objective was simply to reform the colonial system, not abolish it. The insurgents' strategy, meanwhile, had put the planters in a bind. Ignoring the economic moratorium would run the risk of being burned out, yet suspending operations would court financial ruin. To avoid becoming targets of Spanish reprisals themselves, the planters denounced the uprising as the product of criminal elements, declared their allegiance to Spain, and created a political party—the Autonomists—to press peacefully for local autonomy and a degree of political liberalization.

Unfortunately for the planters, Spain did not distinguish between the rebels seeking outright separation, and the planters hoping to remain under Spanish rule. To crush the revolt, in 1896 Spain appointed General Valeriano Weyler to lead the campaign, committed over 200,000 troops, and moved against insurgents and planters alike. Weyler adopted the stance of war without quarter and became notorious for his scorched earth policy: to deprive insurgents of their support base in rural communities, he instituted the *reconcentrado* policy that depopulated the countryside, herded rural Cubans into concentration camps, and demolished their farms, homes, and livestock. Starvation, epidemics, and hundreds of thousands of deaths followed. Victory, however, did not. Instead, peasants who had been neutral or passive developed nationalist sentiments and joined the insurgents' ranks. Spanish forces also targeted the planters' Autonomist political party: their political meetings were banned, their newspapers closed, and their members were arrested, beaten, and deported.

By eliminating the political force that wanted Spain to retain control of Cuba, yet strengthening the force fighting for independence, Spain's tactics backfired. They prolonged the conflict and deepened Cuba's travails; they reduced the island to misery and captured American sympathies, the headlines of American newspapers, and the minds of American policymakers; finally, they ensured Cuba a special place on the U.S. foreign policy agenda. With an eye toward protecting American investments in Cuba, the United States officially demanded that Spain grant Cubans greater autonomy and restore order on the island. Spanish military power, however, was unable to prevail over a population mobilized by nationalist sentiments; thus, the conflict continued.

On February 15, 1898, events took an unexpected twist that exacerbated U.S.-Spanish tensions, when the battleship U.S.S. *Maine* exploded in Havana harbor, killing 266 U.S. sailors. In America, the explosion conjured up visions of Spanish sabotage, unleashed a torrent of negative press stories, and inspired even greater war fever in the United States ("Remember the *Maine*, to hell with Spain!"). At the time, most Americans blamed the *Maine*'s destruction on a mine, presumably laid by Spanish operatives (in 1976, however, a Navy investigation concluded that an internal explosion had destroyed the vessel). After the *Maine*'s demise, Spain began to make concessions to America and agreed to grant the insurgents autonomy, but President William McKinley faced ever greater domestic pressures to take military action. In April 1898, the president finally asked Congress for authority to expel the Spanish from Cuba and bring the conflict to an end. On April 20, Congress complied, but tacked on to its authorization the *Teller Amendment*, which prohibited McKinley from annexing Cuba to the United States: "[The] United States hereby disclaims any disposition or intention to exercise sovereignty, jurisdiction, or control over [Cuba] except for the pacification thereof, and asserts its determination, when that is accomplished, to leave the government and control of the Island to its people." Spain's political concessions had failed to stall the flow of events, and on April 21, 1898, the United States and Spain went to war.

One of the major oddities about the Spanish-American War is that President McKinley did not want it to happen. In fact, during his 1897 inaugural address McKinley pledged to avoid war. "We want no wars of conquest," the President had said; "peace is preferable to war in almost every contingency." Yet just one year later, the United States did go to war with Spain; the United States did acquire territories by conquest; and McKinley seemed powerless to stop this from happening.

Three Levels of Analysis

If President McKinley did not want a war of conquest, why did U.S. policy still take this course? One way we might answer this question is to use the three levels of analysis. Useful explanations can be found at all three levels; however, the third level is a good place to begin as it provides a tight, parsimonious account.

One possible systemic explanation is that within the context of international anarchy, the United States saw an opportunity to expand at Spain's expense and took it. This explanation rests on the premise that war between potential belligerents is more likely when one state's offensive capacities are superior to its opponents' defensive capabilities. Under these conditions, the prospects of victory are bright while the costs are limited. Such situations, notes political scientist Stephen Van Evera, make war "more alluring" and can invite "opportunistic expansion even by temperate powers."[5] In 1898, the United States enjoyed clear offensive advantages over Spain. Not only was its navy larger than Spain's, but its forces could operate close to their principal supply bases while Spain's were located across the Atlantic; this situation offered an opportunity for quick victory and relatively easy U.S. aggrandizement. Given America's penchant for avoiding conflicts with stronger powers, there may be something to this argument. However, since it tells us very little about why the United States came to enjoy a favorable power advantage in the first place, an explanation based solely on superior offensive ability is incomplete.

Balance of power offers another systemic explanation. In terms of the balance of power that existed between Spain and the United States in 1898, two factors stand out: the dramatic decline of Spain, and the equally dramatic rise in American power. The decline of Spanish power was striking. In 1570—50 years before the Pilgrims landed at Plymouth Rock—Spain completed the conquest of Latin America and took possession of an immense, resource-rich empire: enormous gold, silver, and copper mines, vast expanses of fertile land, and a population of virtual slaves to work the land and mines. The wealth that Madrid extracted from its possessions helped maintain its naval fleet and for a time, made Spain the richest, most powerful state in the world. Outside the Western Hemisphere Spain also seized territories in Asia and the Pacific, and incorporated the Philippines, Guam, and other territories into its empire.

Yet, Madrid managed its empire poorly and squandered its resources on Europe's seemingly endless wars. When Napoleon Bonaparte invaded Spain in 1807, toppled King Charles IV, and installed his brother Joseph, Latin American colonies seized the opportunity to revolt. The wars of independence that followed cost Spain most of its New World possessions, and by the time

Cuba and the Philippines launched their own struggles for independence in the 1890s, the Spanish Empire was a ghost of its former glory. While other states had expanded their empires, Spain had lost many territories; while others had begun to industrialize, Spain lagged well behind. By 1898, Spain was profoundly weak. It had fought Cuban insurgents for three years without success, and its weakness created a power vacuum in the Caribbean, centered on Cuba, that invited the attention of stronger powers, including the United States.

By contrast, if Spain was weak in 1898, the United States had grown much stronger. In 1869, the Americans completed the Transcontinental Railroad, a stunning feat of engineering that connected the country's western and eastern halves. After the Civil War, the second industrial revolution set in, transforming U.S. productive capacities in the process. By the 1890s the United States had surpassed Britain as the world's largest economy (U.S. exports jumped from $392 million to over $1.3 billion per year between 1870 and 1890). The United States also began transforming some of its industrial might into military power—in particular its naval forces—and the more the U.S. economy surged, the more some Americans thought the United States needed to play a larger role on the world stage. That stage was already crowded with strong European states jockeying for influence, possessions, and power. Beginning in 1880, the "scramble for Africa" saw European states carve nearly 9 million square miles of new colonial possessions out of the continent, and their search for opportunities outside of Africa continued. Should the Cuban insurgents ultimately defeat Spain, a weak, war-wracked, and independent Cuba would be a ripe target. The possibility of annexing Cuba had long enthralled some in the U.S. government, and for security's sake, Washington believed it could not afford to let any European power fill the void created by Spain's decline. Thus, in terms of third-level factors, changes in the global balance of power, the dominance of U.S. offensive capacities over Spanish defensive capabilities, and the struggle for colonial possessions all contributed to the outbreak of the Spanish-American War.

The second level of analysis provides additional insight into the domestic economic, political, and social forces that helped shape America's policies on war and expansion. Four factors were especially important: the ideologies that cropped up inside the United States, the economic interests and rationales that clamored for war, the pressure for war exerted by the media and public opinion, and the domestic political issues that made these policies appealing.

The ideology that most influenced U.S. foreign policy in 1898 was not liberal democracy, but rather, *manifest destiny*. At the heart of this ideology was the notion that the United States had a God-given, preordained destiny to expand and progress. Manifest destiny influenced American foreign policy in the 1840s when the United States acquired largely unpopulated regions of Mexico in the Mexican-American War. Back then, the concept meant expanding U.S. territory to provide more Americans and small family farmers the chance to prosper in freedom and dignity. By the 1890s, however, manifest destiny had come to mean something very different: since democracy had made America the world's shining light, whether by conversion or conquest the United States was divinely obligated to expand the blessings of its civilization into territories and peoples far outside its borders.

Manifest destiny was a close cousin of *social Darwinism*, another ideology that gained currency at this time. Developed by British intellectuals like Herbert Spencer, Thomas Malthus, and Francis Galton, social Darwinism was a take-off on Charles Darwin's notions of natural selection and survival of the fittest among animal species. These thinkers extended Darwin's concepts to countries, ethnic groups, and human societies. Just as some species had evolved through competition and survival of the fittest, so human societies had evolved too—from a stage of barbarism to civilization. Anglos and North Europeans, of course, were deemed the most civilized, as their industrial advances, sophisticated political systems, and technological innovations demonstrated. Couched in high-sounding, self-flattering tones, social Darwinism argued that civilized societies had a moral obligation to help the less evolved reach a higher state of being. In practice, this meant expanding into the territories of backward peoples to provide economic progress, political order, and other trappings of civilization. Following the British lead, U.S. intellectuals like John Burgess and John Fiske popularized these concepts in the United States.

At the extreme, social Darwinism could border on racism, for it implied that by virtue of their higher evolutionary status, some societies or racial groups were destined to dominate the world. In the United States, these ideas took root. For example, the American minister, Josiah Strong (General Secretary of the Evangelical Alliance of the United States), argued that the Protestant, American Anglo-Saxon had "unequaled energy," a "genius for colonizing," and was "divinely commissioned to be . . . his brother's keeper." America's God-given destiny, Strong said, was nothing less than "to impress its institutions upon all mankind . . . and spread itself over the earth." Many educated and influential Americans accepted aspects of social Darwinism, and the combination of this ideology and manifest destiny was a potent mixture. Once these ideologies captured the minds of U.S. leaders and opinion makers, it became much easier to rationalize war with the inferior (and Catholic) Spaniards, and to adopt policies toward the people of former Spanish colonies that contradicted basic American values of consent, democracy, equality, and self-determination.

Besides ideologies, economic factors offer another second-level explanation for America's intervention in Cuba against Spain, and its adoption of an expansionist foreign policy. With $50 million already invested in Cuban sugar and mining operations—now threatened by the Cubans' conflict with Spain—U.S. investors were anxious for Washington to move against Madrid and bring the war to an end. Beyond Cuba, American investors also saw vast opportunities in Asia (particularly China), and military action against Spain's position in the Philippines could open the door to an enormous, untapped market. Concerns over the domestic economy, meanwhile, influenced how Americans viewed their foreign policy options too.

Between 1893 and 1897 the American economy suffered a deep depression, which some analysts blamed on an over-accumulation of capital and lack of domestic investment opportunities. To escape the depression, they argued, the United States had to find investment opportunities abroad through an imperialist foreign policy. One strong advocate of this idea was Charles Conant. An economist, banker, and advisor to American policymakers, Conant began publishing journal articles on the topic in 1896. His classic statement on this issue was the 1898 essay, "The Economic Basis of Imperialism,"[6] in which he argued the United States had only two options to avoid another depression. One was to seize colonies from some declining power to administer, modernize, and invest in—that is, old-fashioned, "hard imperialism." The other option was to develop markets and investment outlets in states that were nominally independent, but actually controlled through U.S. military pressure—that is, "soft imperialism." These ideas affected how politically and economically influential Americans thought about the economy and its relation to foreign policy, and provided policymakers an economic rationale to expand abroad via war.

Along with economic factors, the media and public opinion also influenced America's decision to go to war. The mid- to late 1890s saw yellow journalism flourish, and competition between the Joseph Pulitzer and William Randolph Hearst newspapers was fierce: each tended to sensationalize news coverage to spike sales. While the death, misery, and destruction from Cuba's struggle with Spain offered ample fodder to these outlets to increase sales, Pulitzer and Hearst embellished news stories even more. Hearst, in particular, ran features designed to antagonize and outrage American readers (such as a front-page political cartoon depicting male Spanish officials strip searching an American female tourist for messages from Cuban rebels). His lurid and notoriously exaggerated articles whipped up anti-Spanish feelings and clamored for war. With policymakers fixated upon Cuba's fate and various calamities, potent anti-Spanish sentiments and war hysteria swept the country. Yellow journalism had helped forge a political sledgehammer—public opinion—and when President McKinley resisted calls to go to war, he was booed in public in some locations and hanged in effigy in others.

Box 4.1 Yellow Journalism in the Twenty-first Century?

The term *yellow journalism* came into vogue in the 1890s. It described a type of reporting that typically was lax on accuracy and professional standards, and emphasized sensationalized news accounts and exposés of corruption, scandals, or other forms of malfeasance. Such journalism dominated the New York newspapers of America's two leading publishers—Joseph Pulitzer and William Randolph Hearst—who competed fiercely for readers and employed yellow journalism to increase sales. Both Pulitzer's *New York World* and Hearst's *New York Journal* published highly sensationalized accounts of Spain's alleged war atrocities in Cuba and whipped up anti-Spanish sentiments that clamored for war. Is such media impact on states' foreign policy an historical artifact, or does it persist? Some social science research suggests that in the run-up to the 2003 Iraq War, Fox News may have played a similar role to yellow journalists of old, and thus represents the high-tech, twenty-first-century equivalent of this nineteenth-century media practice. Is this true?

In late 2002 and early 2003, American officials began to advance the case for war with Iraq. That case included claims that war was necessary because the government of Saddam Hussein (1) possessed weapons of mass destruction (biological, chemical, and nuclear) and planned to use them against the United States, and (2) had close ties to, and a working relationship with, the *al Qaeda* terrorist network that launched the September 11, 2001 attacks on New York and Washington. Many leading U.S. officials advanced these propositions directly and by insinuation, including Defense Secretary Donald Rumsfeld, Deputy Defense Secretary Paul Wolfowitz, National Security Advisor Condoleezza Rice, Vice President Dick Cheney, and even President George W. Bush. Like all news outlets, Fox News reported the administration's claims (although perhaps with greater enthusiasm). It also mixed its reporting with a heavy dose of patriotism and nationalistic appeals, and unlike some other news sources, Fox was more reticent to report developments that contradicted or questioned administration claims. War reporting bolstered Fox's ratings, and as more Americans tuned in, Fox dethroned CNN as the most-watched news outlet for war coverage (a position CNN had held since the 1991 Gulf War against Iraq).

The Iraq War began on March 20, 2003. U.S. forces quickly toppled Saddam's government and occupied the country. On May 1, 2003, President Bush declared an end to "major combat operations" in Iraq, and a systematic search for weapons of mass destruction began. None, however, were found, and in September 2003, the president acknowledged that there was no evidence linking Saddam Hussein to al Qaeda's 9/11 terrorist attacks. These developments undercut some of the principal rationales on which many Americans had based their support for the war.

In October 2003, the University of Maryland's Program on International Policy Attitudes released a study (based on national public opinion surveys) conducted in conjunction with the polling firm, Knowledge Networks. Its findings suggest that like the yellow journalists of old, Fox News may have played an important role in generating and sustaining public support for the invasion of Iraq.

> In the run-up to the war with Iraq and in the postwar period, a significant portion of the American public has held a number of misperceptions *that have played a key role in generating and maintaining approval for the decision to go to war* [emphasis added]. Significant portions of the public have believed that Iraq was directly involved in the September 11 attacks [on the United States] and that evidence of links between Iraq and al-Qaeda have been found, [and] that weapons of mass destruction were found in Iraq after the war . . . The extent of Americans' misperceptions varies significantly depending on their source of news . . . Fox News was the news source whose viewers had the most misperceptions. [a]

In fact, researchers discovered that 80 percent of Fox News viewers held at least one of these misperceptions (contrasted with 23 percent of Americans who consumed news from National Public Radio or the Corporation for Public Broadcasting).

After the invasion of Iraq, a consensus developed that overall, the media's pre- and post-war coverage was quite poor: news outlets failed to meet basic professional standards of accuracy, objectivity, and verification of the government's pre-war claims. Given that nearly all news sources fell short in these respects, the question is whether Fox News—whose broadcasts were the most widely watched—went further, and deliberately slanted its reporting to build up and sustain public support for the war. A definitive answer to this question will not likely come soon. However, in January 2007, Rupert Murdoch, Chief Executive Officer of News Corp., the parent company of Fox News, was asked if his media firms had worked to influence the agenda in the run-up to the U.S. conflict with Iraq. "We tried," Murdoch conceded; "We basically supported the Bush policy in the Middle East."

[a] Steven Kull, *Misperceptions, the Media and the Iraq War* (College Park, MD and Menlo Park, CA: Program on International Policy Attitudes and Knowledge/Networks, October 2, 2003), 2, 12. http://www.worldpublicopinion.org/pipa/pdf/oct03/IraqMedia_Oct03_rpt.pdf, accessed January 23, 2011.

Still another causal factor at the domestic level lies in the United States' social and political situation. The Civil War had left American society polarized. By the 1890s, waves of German, French, Irish, Italian, Russian, Catholic, and Jewish immigrants had transformed U.S. demographics. No longer was America just a nation of Protestant, Anglo-Saxon stock. The social tensions this produced (along with those remaining from the Civil War and Reconstruction) made national unity a priority. The upshot was a quest for unity that found expression through nationalism, patriotism, martial music (e.g., John Phillip Sousa's 1896 "Stars and Stripes Forever"), and an outlet for enhanced U.S. military prowess. These second-level factors do not explain U.S. policy entirely, but they do tell us much about the domestic context that made war and an expansionist, imperial foreign policy appealing options.

Second-level factors outside the United States mattered too. As tensions rose between Washington and Madrid, Spain's chief of naval operations, Admiral Pascual Cervera y Topete, could foresee defeat. He knew full well that a war with the United States "would be disastrous . . . since we are reduced, absolutely penniless, and they are rich."[7] Why then did the monarchy not avert the disaster through diplomacy? Simply put, domestic politics had paralyzed the decision-making process in Madrid, leaving the government unable to negotiate its way out of war. With the king deceased, queen regent Maria Cristina's overriding objective was to ensure that her 12-year-old son, Alfonso XIII, would inherit the throne. Besieged from the left by Liberals who hoped to replace the monarchy with a republic, and from the right by conservative Carlists who wanted to seat a separate line of Bourbons on the throne (descended from Carlos V), Cristina feared that any concessions Spain made on Cuba—either to the insurgents or the United States—could spell the end. Consequently, Madrid failed to act on several overtures McKinley made to resolve the Cuban problems diplomatically and avoid war, and by the time Spain did begin making concessions, McKinley faced a domestic situation that made accepting them nearly impossible.

What about the first level of analysis? Did the actions, ideas, and personalities of specific individuals have a meaningful effect on the course of events? What really stands out at level one is the impact of different leaders' personalities. Some were particularly forceful and ambitious. Others were weak and seemingly unable to set and maintain a firm course or exert control over American policy. Take President McKinley for instance. By all accounts, he was a decent and religious man. He was not, however, a particularly strong or decisive leader, and he knew very little about foreign policy. Constantly buffeted by the expansionist pressures that swirled across the country, McKinley was easily influenced by more powerful personalities or manipulated by more ambitious people under him. His indecision and pliability would prove consequential. Against his own reservations, in 1897 McKinley let Senator Henry Cabot Lodge persuade him to appoint Lodge's friend, Theodore Roosevelt, the Assistant Secretary of the Navy. At the time, Roosevelt was merely the New York City police commissioner, but in his new position he would wield influence on a national, hemispheric, and even global scale.

Roosevelt was McKinley's mirror opposite. Decisive, opinionated, and constantly preoccupied with squeezing the Old World out of the New World, he devoted enormous intellectual energy to foreign policy. As historian Stanley Karnow notes, Roosevelt was "a complex, contradictory and sometimes confusing figure who even today still inspires respect and ridicule, praise and censure, adulation and disdain. He was, and he remains in memory, a colossus, disproportionately larger than life."[8] Roosevelt believed strongly that the capacity to wage and prevail in war separated great civilizations and states from lesser ones, that the United States needed a large, powerful navy, and that it should employ all its military muscle to protect and advance its national interest. Roosevelt also believed in America's inherent goodness and morality; thus, any policy the United States pursued or war it engaged in was, by default, a moral cause, and anyone who opposed the United States was reprobate. He also was a racialist, though not a racist (an important distinction). This is to say, that he firmly believed in ethnic group superiority, specifically the Anglos, and in their destiny to lead the charge of global civilization; yet he could still greatly admire individual Asians, Africans, or Latin Americans. When wedded to a position of authority, these character traits could have real consequence.

Well before he joined the McKinley administration, Roosevelt had strategized war plans regarding Cuba and the Philippines with friends and lawmakers who shared his views. Among this circle was Senator Lodge himself, an ardent expansionist who longed for the United States to displace Spain in Cuba (and annex Hawaii), and Alfred T. Mahan, a naval officer and the intellectual architect of plans to develop a large U.S. Navy. All three believed strongly in the United States' manifest destiny and its moral obligation to extend the blessings of its civilization. Mahan's 1890 masterpiece, *The Influence of Sea Power upon History, 1660–1783*, became required reading at Annapolis (and at naval academies in Britain and Germany). It held that, to become great a state had to become a strong sea power, and that true national greatness would elude America until it acquired sufficient naval strength to extend its commerce and project its power, a canal that could provide passage between the Atlantic and Pacific oceans, and the logistical capacity to maintain its vessels at sea. Echoing Alexander Hamilton's early insights on the importance of naval power, Mahan's analysis offered much greater strategic and analytic clarity. Because the United States was bound to the North American continent with no military bases or colonies abroad (Mahan preferred Hawaii and the Philippines), its true naval potential could never be realized and its war vessels would forever remain as "land birds, unable to fly far from their own shores."[9]

Mahan's arguments impressed Roosevelt deeply, and once he became Assistant Secretary, Roosevelt exercised more influence over policy outcomes than his boss, Navy Secretary John D. Long. He played a major role in preparing the United States militarily for war with Spain, and in pushing the United States into that war once those preparations were finished. He kept up regular correspondence with Mahan and vowed to press his friend's strategic ideas within the government.[10] Going behind Secretary Long's back, he pulled strings to get "his man," George Dewey, appointed commander of the U.S. fleet in Asia, and positioned to attack Spain's fleet in the Philippines should war come in Cuba (once the fighting commenced in Cuba, Dewey quickly followed through). One incident on February 25, 1898, offers a glimpse of the dynamism Roosevelt brought to his Navy position. Secretary Long had taken the afternoon off and left Roosevelt in charge as Acting Secretary. Seizing the opportunity, Roosevelt placed the entire U.S. Navy on war status, ordered all commanders to stock their ships with coal, and cabled Admiral Dewey to attack the Philippines if war broke out in Cuba. Writing in his diary, Long grumbled that Roosevelt had "gone at things like a bull in a china shop . . . He immediately began to launch peremptory orders: distributing ships; ordering ammunition . . . sending messages to Congress for immediate legislation, [and] authorizing the enlistment of an unlimited number of seamen . . ." Deeply shaken by Roosevelt's burst of activity, Long never left him in charge again.

Individuals did make a difference. In different ways, key leaders made important contributions to the war with Spain and to America's decision to adopt an expansionist, imperial foreign policy. Along with his friends Lodge and Mahan, Roosevelt, in particular, played a critical role. It was a different role than President McKinley's, but just as important. Former U.S. Ambassador, Warren Zimmerman, tells us that: "The role of powerful personalities working in opposition and in concert is often as important as that of impersonal forces in shaping world historical developments."[11] To this, we might add that sometimes, weak personalities in positions of power matter too. Figure 4.2 displays some of the linkages between causal factors that emanated from the international, domestic, and individual levels of analysis which helped produce the Spanish-American War.

Over the course of their war for independence, Cuban nationalists had fought Spain so vigorously that they may well have prevailed without America's help. Although they initially welcomed U.S. intervention, their elation was short-lived. The intervention did more than just rout Spain from Cuban soil. From the Cuban nationalists' perspective, it turned everything on its head. First, the *Americans* claimed victory in the conflict, downplaying all the contributions that Cubans had made to the war effort over the last three years. Then, as the war's sole victor, the United States cut Cubans completely out of the peace process, and dictated its terms in unilateral fashion directly to Spain. The Paris Peace Treaty of 1898 compelled Spain to relinquish control of Cuba, but instead of creating an independent Cuban state, it established a U.S. Protectorate under military occupation. One reason for this was U.S. fears that an independent Cuba would become a security risk—too weak to defend itself, and thus, a territorial temptation that European states might find irresistible. Consequently, the United States would not countenance national independence; American commanders in Cuba routinely denounced those who advocated independence and worked hard to quell their nationalist sentiments. Cuban patriots, meanwhile, chafed under the military occupation and the many slights U.S. military officials dispensed their way. "None of us," explained the insurgents' leader, Máximo Gómez, "thought that [the U.S. intervention] would be followed by a military occupation of the country by our allies, who treat us as a people incapable of acting for ourselves, and who have reduced us to obedience, to submission, and to a tutelage imposed by force of circumstance. This cannot be our ultimate fate after years of struggle."[12]

Despite U.S. efforts to dampen Cubans' yearnings for independence, those dreams died hard. In 1900, for example, when Washington scheduled elections

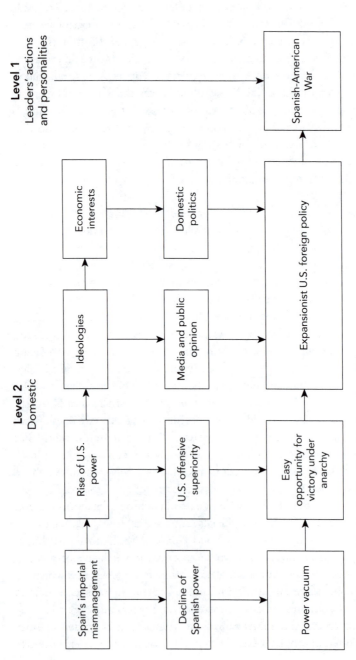

Figure 4.2 Levels of Analysis: The Spanish-American War

for municipal governments and a national assembly, it restricted suffrage to 10 percent of the population (excluding the vast majority of those who had fought the Spanish). Nevertheless, the pro-independence Cuban National Party still captured the municipal elections (while the pro-annexation Democracy Union Party failed to win even a single city), and *independentistas* also won a majority in the constituent assembly. Moreover, pro-independence sentiments continued to run strong in the 1901 convention that drafted Cuba's new Constitution. These outcomes deeply dismayed U.S. officials. Unable to annex Cuba (thanks to the Teller Amendment) yet unwilling to brook independence, Washington ultimately devised a means to exercise legal hegemony over Cuba without actual legal sovereignty.

The Platt Amendment

Four years after Spain's defeat, Cuba finally gained independence in 1902 when Tomás Estrada Palma was elected its first president. Nevertheless, Cuba did not become a sovereign state. Instead, what emerged was a state with clear limitations on its national sovereignty. The source of these limitations was the U.S.-imposed Platt Amendment. Drafted by Senator Orville Platt (as a rider to an Army appropriations bill), approved by the U.S. Congress, and signed into law by President McKinley, the Platt Amendment guaranteed U.S. hegemony over Cuba and, at Washington's insistence, became part of its new Constitution (it would remain in force for 32 years). The Amendment's third Article imposed the most obvious limitation on Cuban sovereignty: "The government of Cuba *consents* that the United States may intervene for the preservation of Cuban independence, and the maintenance of a government adequate for the protection of life, property and individual liberty" (emphasis added). Other restrictions limited Cuba's ability to make international treaties with other states, incur national debts, or grant other states access to Cuban territory. Finally, the Platt Amendment obligated Cuba to sell or lease land to the United States suitable for a military installation (a stipulation that produced the U.S. naval base at Guantánamo Bay).

One day after the American Congress approved the Platt Amendment (March 1, 1901), protests and anti-U.S. demonstrations erupted throughout Cuba. Over 15,000 people marched to the U.S. military governor's mansion and denounced the Amendment, then moved to the Constitutional Convention site to demand that delegates reject it. On April 6, convention delegates did just that, voting down the Amendment 24 to 2. On April 12 they rejected it again by 18 to 10. Washington, however, refused to yield: in order to end the U.S.

Box 4.2 The Platt Amendment's Key Articles (1903)

Article I. The Government of Cuba shall never enter into any treaty or other compact with any foreign power or powers which will impair or tend to impair the independence of Cuba, nor in any manner authorize or permit any foreign power or powers to obtain by colonization or for military or naval purposes, or otherwise, lodgment in or control over any portion of said island.

Article II. The Government of Cuba shall not assume or contract any public debt to pay the interest upon which, and to make reasonable sinking-fund provision for the ultimate discharge of which, the ordinary revenues of the Island of Cuba, after defraying the current expenses of the Government, shall be inadequate.

Article III. The Government of Cuba consents that the United States may exercise the right to intervene for the preservation of Cuban independence, the maintenance of a government adequate for the protection of life, property, and individual liberty, and for discharging the obligations with respect to Cuba imposed by the Treaty of Paris on the United States, now to be assumed and undertaken by the Government of Cuba . . .

Article V. The Government of Cuba will execute, and, as far as necessary, extend the plans already devised, or other plans to be mutually agreed upon, for the sanitation of the cities of the island, to the end that a recurrence of epidemic and infectious diseases may be prevented, thereby assuring protection to the people and commerce of Cuba, as well as to the commerce of the Southern ports of the United States and the people residing therein . . .

Article VII. To enable the United States to maintain the independence of Cuba, and to protect the people thereof, as well as for its own defense, the Government of Cuba will sell or lease to the United States lands necessary for coaling or naval stations, at certain specified points, to be agreed upon with the President of the United States.

military occupation, Platt must become part of the new Constitution. Faced with the prospect of perpetual occupation, a majority of delegates finally relented; they accepted Cuba's position as a U.S. Protectorate without national sovereignty and on June 12, passed the Amendment 16 to 11.

The Platt Amendment did not give the United States legal sovereignty over Cuba. It did, however, give Washington a preponderance of power over Cuban affairs, that is, hegemony. That hegemony, in turn, came only through the coerced "consent" of the constitutional delegates and ran contrary to the desires of the vast majority of Cuban nationals. Why would the United States adopt a policy toward Cuba that so clearly violated America's core political values?

One explanation is that the United States simply chose to behave hypocritically. American disdain toward Cuba's struggle for self-determination certainly displayed a striking level of hypocrisy. Yet, the fact remains that most U.S. officials—their attitudes colored by social Darwinian ideology, and for some, plain racism—genuinely believed that Cubans were not yet capable of self-government and independence. Adopting a policy that denied immediate independence was, therefore, also a practical, realistic decision, not just a hypocritical one.

Another explanation is that the United States grew intoxicated with the idea of economic imperialism, and fashioned a policy to ensure America could exploit Cuba's continued dependence. Cuba's protectorate status did, in fact, make it easier to protect U.S. investments and create new, safer investment opportunities on the island. By 1905 American citizens or corporations had acquired 60 percent of all rural properties in Cuba, including a string of estates in the tens and often, hundreds of thousands of acres (by contrast, Cubans owned only 25 percent of rural properties, while resident Spaniards owned the remaining 15 percent).[13] Moreover, between 1906 and 1928, U.S. investment in Cuba's sugar industry jumped dramatically (from just 15 percent of all sugar production to 75 percent of all sugar production) and large-scale American investments flowed into the railroad, shipping, utilities, and mining sectors too. This outcome is precisely what dependency theorists would predict and what Charles Conant had called for in his famous 1898 essay, "The Economic Basis of Imperialism."

There are, however, reasons to discount an explanation based solely on dependency logic and economic imperialism. Perhaps most important, it overlooks how American policy as embodied in the Platt Amendment actually conformed to the constraints of U.S. domestic politics and the requirements of an anarchic, international system. Given the congressional prohibition on annexation, the Platt Amendment's primary objectives were geo-strategic: to ensure that Cuba would relate to the outside world as would the United States (which is to say, that its foreign policy would parallel Washington's), and that no power save the United States would ever gain a military foothold on the island from which it could project power or threaten U.S. security. By exerting hegemony over Cuba via Platt, the United States pursued the tactic of strategic denial, and eliminated one more area where a potential enemy power might find a haven.

Imposing the Platt Amendment proved consequential for Cuba and the United States alike. It prevented the consolidation of political authority inside the new Cuban government, essentially by dividing the task of governing between Havana and Washington, DC. This was a recipe for government failure, and in fact, the first Republic failed quickly: challenged by political opponents, President Estrada Palma (and his cabinet) resigned in 1906 and requested U.S. intervention to preserve financial, legal, and political order. Thus, a second military occupation followed (1906–1909) and more interventions after that (1917 and 1919). The Amendment's provisions for U.S. intervention also created incentive structures that distorted Cuba's political development and stunted its political maturation. Cuba's politicians, parties, and economic interests became experts at manipulating Platt to their own advantage, deliberately creating unstable conditions that might trigger a U.S. intervention and eliminate an unwanted incumbent. Thus over time, instead of looking to Cuban voters for approval, politicians began looking to the United States; instead of learning to solve their own political problems, Cubans grew dependent on the United States to bail them out.

Perhaps most important, the Platt Amendment both frustrated and fueled the strong nationalist sentiments that had animated most Cubans since the late nineteenth century, and fostered deep resentment toward the United States in the process. By the 1930s, the amendment had outlived its political usefulness. It was a visible symbol and provocative manifestation of U.S. tutelage, and a constant reminder of Cuba's stunted sovereignty. Nothing served to arouse Cubans' national indignation more than Platt. Even after Washington abrogated the Amendment in 1934, its legacies remained. Cuba experienced well-meaning, but too often weak, inefficient, and corrupt governments that always seemed to be in Washington's pocket. As these governments' legitimacy declined, democracy lost force, and dictatorship followed. When Cuban society finally rose up to compel political change in the late 1950s, Fidel Castro would be waiting in the wings.

Projecting Power: The Panama Canal and the Roosevelt Corollary

If the Spanish-American War marked the expansion of American power, the construction of the Panama Canal and the Roosevelt Corollary to the Monroe Doctrine helped solidify the United States' new status in the Western Hemisphere, and ensure its capacity to project power. Both initiatives reflected a broader, more muscular U.S. foreign policy and world role, and as the United States developed the capacity to impose its will on other states, the power relations between it and Latin American states grew ever more asymmetrical. Even in the twenty-first century, no other Latin American state has ever come close to the capacity to project power that, by virtue of these initiatives, the United States already had achieved in the first decades of the twentieth.

The term "power projection" refers to a state's ability to extend its influence via modern weaponry and to provide tactical support for ground troops in distant theaters of operation. Today, the firepower of strong states typically includes a navy and air force (and for exceptionally strong states, inter-continental ballistic missiles); however, at the close of the nineteenth century it meant, above all, naval power. U.S. leaders realized that the projection of American power required more than a growing economy, offshore territories, or a large navy to reach and protect these distant assets. It also required a water passage that would connect the Atlantic and Pacific oceans, permit the United States to deploy its naval forces more rapidly, sustain and re-supply them more reliably, and thereby deter or repel threats. The principal architects of America's more expansive foreign policy—Alfred Mahan, Henry Cabot Lodge, and Theodore Roosevelt—had dreamed of acquiring such a passage, and when Roosevelt became president in 1901, he seized the opportunity to realize this dream.

The Panama Canal

As the shortest route between the Atlantic and Pacific oceans, the isthmus of Central America had long held a strong commercial appeal. As early as the 1830s and 1840s, British, French, and American interests had proposed projects to expedite transit across Panama (then part of Colombia) via roads, railroads, or canals to facilitate commerce; and in 1849, a U.S. firm won a contract to construct a railroad across Panama, which it completed in 1855. Alongside such commercial interests, of course, were strategic ones. A canal through Central America could shave two-thirds off the time it took to sail a war ship from San

Francisco to the Caribbean (as when the USS *Oregon* was ordered to replace the ill-fated USS *Maine* in Havana Harbor in 1898). By contrast, if a rival power established such a canal, it could facilitate an assault on the U.S. coast or sea-lanes.

Americans, British, and French all competed to realize a transoceanic canal. Initially, Washington and London hoped to construct a water passage through Nicaragua. France, meanwhile, settled on Panama where its construction efforts began in 1876, cost nearly $400 million, and thanks to malaria, yellow fever, 20,000 deaths, and engineering difficulties, ultimately ended in failure. This, in turn, provided the United States a fresh opportunity to achieve its objective.

In 1901, Roosevelt reached an agreement to buy out the French canal firm for $40 million; in 1903, he negotiated the Hay–Herrán Treaty with Colombia, under which the United States would pay Colombia $10 million, take over the French project, and complete the canal. Colombia's Senate, however, rejected the treaty. This angered Panamanian separatists (who supported the canal plans and had sought independence from Colombia since the 1830s); it also provided Roosevelt space to maneuver. He quickly signaled Washington's support of the separatists and dispatched naval vessels to the region. Events followed rapidly that would culminate in a U.S.-controlled canal: on November 3, 1903, Panama declared its independence; American ships prevented Colombian forces from interceding; two days later the United States recognized the new Panamanian government; and on November 18, Washington signed the Hay–Bunau-Varilla Treaty. Under this treaty, the United States secured all the rights it had sought from Colombia and then some. In a very sweet deal, it obtained the rights to take over and complete the French canal project, and to establish a protectorate over Panama and guarantee its independence. It also obtained a 10-mile wide Canal Zone in perpetuity, over which it could govern as "if it were the sovereign"—all this in exchange for $10 million cash, and annual payments of $250,000. Colombia protested America's recognition of Panama but to no avail. Without the muscle to counter U.S. military might (now pledged to protect Panama), Bogotá never regained possession of its former territory.

Years after the fact, Theodore Roosevelt quipped that he "took the Canal Zone" from Colombia. Given the preexisting separatist sentiments he skillfully exploited (rather than created), this may be an overstatement. Yet there is no question that Washington had supported the breakup of another sovereign state to advance its own interests, and had used the threat of force to ensure its preferred outcome. This action heightened Latin Americans' suspicions of their northern neighbor. Why would the United States impose its will on a smaller power in so dramatic a fashion?

One possibility is that national economic interest drove U.S. policy. A transoceanic canal promised to multiply trade opportunities by orders of magnitude, and a canal controlled by the United States could, theoretically, be open to American commercial interests but closed to their foreign competitors. However, the Hay–Bunau-Varilla Treaty guaranteed that the canal would be neutral in perpetuity and open to all. Nor is an explanation based on dependency and economic imperialism completely satisfying either. While the canal certainly lowered transaction costs on U.S. exports and imports, and helped U.S. firms extend their reach into foreign markets, the Canal Zone and Panama itself never became the type of colonial investment opportunity economic imperialists like Charles Conant envisioned. In 1913, a year before the canal opened, U.S. investment in Panama stood at $5 million, and had only risen to $36.3 million by the time of the 1929 Great Depression. By contrast, during the same time period, U.S. investment in America's preeminent protectorate, Cuba, grew from $220 million to $1.59 billion. In the end, then, U.S. policies toward Colombia and Panama appear to have been driven primarily by realist, geo-strategic factors. Roosevelt, especially, believed that the rise of a powerful navy in Germany (and Japan) threatened the United States' national economic and strategic interests, as well as the defense of weak Latin American states. For security's sake, these balance of power considerations argued for the enhanced U.S. power projection capabilities a canal would provide.

The Roosevelt Corollary

Panama's secession from Colombia, its quick recognition by the United States, and the subsequent construction of a transoceanic canal would permanently

Table 4.1   United States Investments in American Protectorates ($ millions), 1913–1929

Country	1913	1929
Cuba	220.0	1,059.0
Dominican Republic	4.0	23.9
Haiti	4.0	30.7
Nicaragua	3.0	24.0
Panama	5.0	36.3

Source: Max Winkler, *Investments of United States Capital in Latin America* (Boston: World Peace Foundation, 1929), 275, 278

alter the balance of power in the Western Hemisphere. One year after clinching the canal deal with Panama, the United States announced a new policy to protect it. Named after its architect, the Roosevelt Corollary to the Monroe Doctrine had three main goals. Like the Monroe Doctrine, it sought to keep European powers out of the Americas. Unlike the Doctrine, it was designed expressly to project U.S. power, create an extended infrastructure of influence, and defend the canal project and the shipping lanes it served. The general security thrust of the Corollary was imminently practical. As then-Secretary of War Elihu Root explained in 1905, "the inevitable effect of our building the Canal must be to require us to police the surrounding premises. In the nature of things, trade and control, and the obligation to keep order which goes with them, must come our way."[14]

Under the Roosevelt Corollary, the United States assumed an international "police power" that self-authorized direct intervention in the internal affairs of other Western Hemispheric states, and later, would establish formal and informal protectorates in the Dominican Republic, Haiti, and Nicaragua to complement those already in force in Cuba and Panama. The Corollary's obvious imperial impulse led to decades of resentment by Latin American governments toward the United States. Yet, imperial ambitions are not the only—or even the best—explanation for this dramatic new policy. Again, realist concerns for security in an anarchic environment offer a more comprehensive, satisfying account.

Given their commitment to construct the Panama Canal, American leaders understood that maintaining its security was imperative. Should it fall into an adversary's hands, the canal would easily expose the United States to a military attack. However, they also understood that the only practical way to defend the canal was by keeping strong powers out of the Caribbean, where weak states and financial and political instability seemed to invite European encroachment. For example, Venezuela's revolution (1898–1900) and subsequent failure to make good on its international debts led Britain, Germany, and Italy to launch a naval blockade in 1902, and bombard its coasts to compel debt collection. Venezuela asked the United States to arbitrate the dispute, and eventually arbitration resolved it. In 1904, however, Europeans again threatened to collect debts by force, this time in the Dominican Republic. Washington saw a troubling future: with Caribbean states unable to meet their financial obligations, the routine use of force to compel repayment opened the possibility of territorial compensation in lieu of money. Even a temporary occupation could have long-term military and balance of power implications, and U.S. leaders were especially wary of German intentions on this front. In the 1902 episode, for example, both Britain and Germany had reassured Roosevelt that they sought no Venezuelan territory,

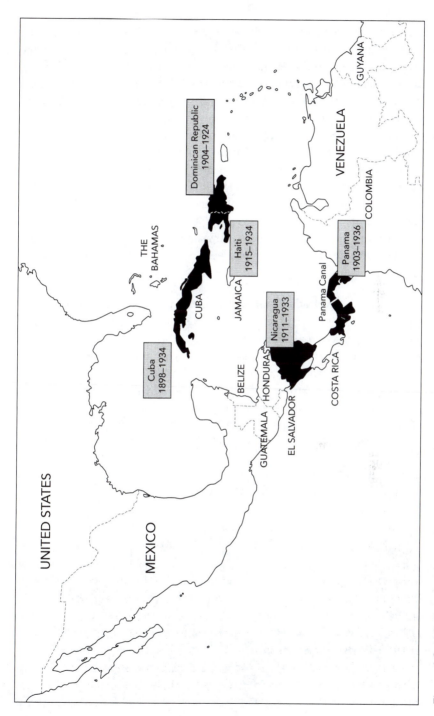

Figure 4.3 U.S. Protectorates, 1898–1934

only payment of Venezuela's debts. However, as part of its commitment to the British-led blockade, Berlin also had promised London that it was open to "the temporary occupation" of Venezuelan harbors, and Roosevelt—recalling how Germany's 1898 "temporary" acquisition of Kiaochow in China had morphed into a 99-year lease—was not anxious to see similar developments in the Western Hemisphere.

To preempt this possibility, in December 1904 Roosevelt announced his Corollary to the Monroe Doctrine. Its basic philosophy was simple. While the Monroe Doctrine guaranteed Latin American states their sovereignty and freedom from foreign domination, it also implied that they had a responsibility to exercise sovereignty effectively and safeguard their own liberty. This meant keeping their finances in order, maintaining domestic political order, and paying their debts on time; most important, it meant not creating the conditions that might provoke the Europeans to intervene in the first place. Thus, Roosevelt exclaimed:

> If a nation shows that it knows how to act with decency in industrial and political matters, if it keeps order and pays its obligations, then it need fear no interference from the United States . . . [But] chronic wrong-doing, or an impotence which results in a general loosening of the ties of civilized society, may finally require intervention by some civilized nation, and in the Western Hemisphere the adherence of the United States to the Monroe Doctrine may force the United States . . . in flagrant cases of wrongdoing, or impotence, to the exercise of an international police power.

In short, if Latin American states would not, or could not, put their houses in order, the United States would do it for them.

BOX 4.3 The Roosevelt Corollary (1904)

It is not true that the United States feels any land hunger or entertains any projects as regards the other nations of the Western Hemisphere save such as are for their welfare. All that this country desires is to see the neighboring countries stable, orderly, and prosperous. Any country whose people conduct themselves well can count upon our hearty friendship. If a nation shows that it knows how to act with reasonable efficiency and decency in social and political matters, if it keeps order and pays its obligations, it need fear no interference from the United States. Chronic wrongdoing, or an impotence which results in a general loosening of the ties of civilized society, may in America, as elsewhere, ultimately require intervention by some civilized nation, and in the Western Hemisphere the adherence of the United States to the Monroe Doctrine may force the United States, however reluctantly, in flagrant cases of such wrongdoing or impotence, to the exercise of an international police power. If every country washed by the Caribbean Sea would show the progress in stable and just civilization which with the aid of the Platt Amendment Cuba has shown since our troops left the island, and which so many of the republics in both Americas are constantly and brilliantly showing, all question of interference by this Nation with their affairs would be at an end. Our interests and those of our southern neighbors are in reality identical. They have great natural riches, and if within their borders the reign of law and justice obtains, prosperity is sure to come to them. While they thus obey the primary laws of civilized society they may rest assured that they will be treated by us in a spirit of cordial and helpful sympathy. We would interfere with them only in the last resort, and then only if it became evident that their inability or unwillingness to do justice at home and abroad had violated the rights of the United States or had invited foreign aggression to the detriment of the entire body of American nations. It is a mere truism to say that every nation, whether in America or anywhere else, which desires to maintain its freedom, its independence, must ultimately realize that the right of such independence can not be separated from the responsibility of making good use of it.

In asserting the Monroe Doctrine, in taking such steps as we have taken in regard to Cuba [and] Panama . . . we have acted in our own interest as well as in the interest of humanity at large. There are, however, cases in which, while our own interests are not greatly involved, strong appeal is made to our sympathies. Ordinarily it is very much wiser and more useful for us to concern ourselves with striving for our own moral and material betterment here at home than to concern ourselves with trying to better the condition of things in other nations. We have plenty of sins of our own to war against, and under ordinary circumstances we can do more for the general uplifting of humanity by striving with heart and soul to put a stop to civic corruption, to brutal lawlessness and violent race prejudices here at home than by passing resolutions and wrongdoing elsewhere. Nevertheless there are occasional crimes committed on so vast a scale and of such peculiar horror as to make us doubt whether it is not our manifest duty to endeavor at least to show our disapproval of the deed and our sympathy with those who have suffered by it. The cases must be extreme in which such a course is justifiable. There must be no effort made to remove the mote from our brother's eye if we refuse to remove the beam from our own. But in extreme cases action may be justifiable and proper. What form the action shall take must depend upon the circumstances of the case; that is, upon the degree of the atrocity and upon our power to remedy it. The cases in which we could interfere by force of arms as we interfered to put a stop to intolerable conditions in Cuba are necessarily very few.

Theodore Roosevelt

Although Roosevelt's words carried a strong whiff of social Darwinism (civilized vs. uncivilized nations), the policy itself reflected realist preoccupations with security in an anarchic environment, and a concern for what today might be called *failed states*. Failed states are those whose political, economic, and social institutions have deteriorated severely or collapsed; consequently, they demonstrate a marked incapacity to perform the classic functions of sovereign states with respect to maintaining law and order, exercising effective sovereignty over the national territory, providing security and defense, or meeting legal and financial obligations. At different times the Dominican Republic, Guatemala, Haiti, Nicaragua, Panama, and even Cuba all exhibited some traits of a failed state. In Roosevelt's eyes, the "impotence" of such states posed a direct threat to themselves (from European powers), and thus an indirect threat to others in the region, including the United States. Roosevelt believed that until "some kind of international police power" could be developed and wielded by a larger international institution (something he proposed in 1910),[15] strong regional powers would need to fill that void in their sphere of influence.

With the Dominican Republic in arrears on a $32 million debt, and Belgium, France, Germany, Italy, and Spain clamoring for repayment, the United States quickly put its new policy into operation. At Roosevelt's urging, in January 1905 the Dominican Republic and United States signed a protocol under which U.S. officials would take over Dominican customs houses (the chief source of national revenue), administer the collection of customs duties, and supervise repayment of Dominican debt. The protocol operated initially through an executive agreement between the U.S. and Dominican presidents, and after 1907, as a bilateral treaty between the two states. In economic terms, it put the Dominican Republic into receivership and helped restore the country's financial solvency. In political terms, it kept European creditors at bay, but cost the Dominican Republic its sovereignty by reducing it to the status of a U.S. protectorate. It also pulled the United States more deeply into Dominican internal affairs. Domestic uprisings, assassinations, political instability, and threats against the customs houses led to repeated U.S. interventions to restore order, and finally, to a full-scale U.S. military occupation. In 1916, American marines landed, restored order under military rule, and did not leave until 1924. In the interim, U.S. Navy Captain H. S. Knapp and military officers under his command assumed direct control of governmental functions.

The Dominican case became a model for the American policy of *Dollar Diplomacy*, adopted by Roosevelt's successor, William Howard Taft. Like the Roosevelt Corollary, Dollar Diplomacy's strategic purpose was to shore up financial and political stability in the region surrounding the Panama Canal (and prevent European incursions into it), by encouraging private American banks to loan money to Caribbean and Central American states. The loans would go toward servicing the debt these states owed to European creditors and to various public works projects. In turn, financial oversight by U.S. operatives—patterned after the Customs House treaty between the United States and Dominican Republic—would guarantee their timely repayment. By 1917, Washington had established such financial advisory structures in Cuba, Haiti, Nicaragua, and Panama, and as with the Dominican Republic, these arrangements opened the door for greater U.S. involvement in these countries' internal affairs. The result was a string of formal and informal American protectorates around the Caribbean, in which political order was (sometimes) maintained by the presence of U.S. troops, U.S.-sponsored elections, and U.S.-written legislation, but in which European powers were reluctant to intervene.

Under the Roosevelt Corollary and Dollar Diplomacy, American economic and financial interests expanded into the Caribbean and Central America, in tandem with U.S. political influence. During this period, the United States surpassed Britain as Latin America's most important trading partner, and New York replaced London as the center of international finance. U.S. capital began pouring into the Caribbean/Central American region; American investors began to acquire an ever-larger share of stock in firms operating there relative to their European counterparts; and regional governments began to borrow increasingly from American (as opposed to British) lenders.[16] Although closer economic links to America did little to promote robust development or economic diversification among borrowing states (whose national economies remained focused on exporting primary products), they did foster the policy objectives of Dollar Diplomacy. Typically, small states that borrowed from American lenders were obliged to sign Customs House treaties and submit to U.S. control of their revenues (greater American political influence followed), and European powers did not intervene. Although economic and political dependence were not the primary goals of the Roosevelt Corollary or Dollar Diplomacy, the working out of these policies left economies and governments of Caribbean and Central American states increasingly dependent on their northern neighbor. An extreme form of dependence developed in Guatemala, where American corporate, financial, and political interests converged and a single U.S. firm acquired a preeminent position in the national economy (see Box 4.4).

Box 4.4 Dependency and the United Fruit Company in Guatemala

Although dependency theory primarily concerns economic relations and the causes of underdevelopment, its logic can have profound political implications. As political scientist Robert Gilpin notes: "Dependency theory . . . substitutes economic for political means of subordination; whereas Lenin believed that political control was the principal feature of capitalist imperialism, dependency theory replaces formal political colonialism with economic neocolonialism and informal control."[a] The greater the foreign penetration of a national economy, therefore, the more dependent that economy (and the government) becomes, and the more informal political influence foreign investors gain in the process.

In the literature on U.S.–Latin American relations, the United Fruit Company's (UFCO) operations in Guatemala came to symbolize dependency *par excellence*. Formed in 1899, United Fruit developed a thriving banana business in Guatemala and elsewhere. Through Guatemala's need of foreign investment, as well as corporate payoffs, shrewd business deals, and political pressure (supported at times, by the U.S. State Department), UFCO acquired lucrative land deals, tax breaks, concessions in Guatemala's communications and transportation sectors, and limited (if any) government regulation.

Aside from its banana plantations, UFCO owned or controlled subsidiaries in the railroad sector (the International Railways of Central America), shipping (the Great White Fleet of steamships), and telegraph service (the Tropical Radio and Telegraph Company); it even operated Guatemala's postal service after 1930. United Fruit did not establish the dictatorships that ruled Guatemala's government; it did, however, work closely with and support them. According to historian Paul Dosal, "By doing business with dictators, United grew into *el pulpo* (the octopus), a vast enterprise with tentacles extending far beyond the coastal plantations from which it extracted bananas."[b] By 1944, United Fruit controlled 690 miles of the 719 miles of railroad in Guatemala, and had become both the country's largest private landowner (566,000 acres) and employer (15,000 people in banana production, 5,000 more in its railroad company). Its product—bananas—became Guatemala's second largest export crop behind coffee. By controlling large swaths of Guatemala's land, communications, and transportation systems, the company occupied a privileged position in Guatemala's economy and exercised great political influence in its domestic affairs. Meanwhile, the Guatemalan economy and government were heavily dependent on UFCO operations, and state leaders were especially sensitive to the company's needs and preferences.

United Fruit was not a large enterprise by American standards. In tiny Guatemala, however, and indeed, across Central America, it was a giant. In popular Latin American culture it came to symbolize the United States more than did the U.S. government, and in the writings of some of Latin America's most prominent intellectuals—including Pablo Neruda of Chile and Miguel Ángel Asturias of Guatemala—it was portrayed as a manifestation of "U.S. imperialism" in action.[c]

[a] Robert Gilpin, *The Political Economy of International Relations* (Princeton: Princeton University Press, 1987), 284.
[b] Paul J. Dosal, *Doing Business with the Dictators: A Political History of United Fruit in Guatemala, 1899–1944* (Wilmington, DE: Scholarly Resources, Inc., 1993), 3.
[c] Miguel Ángel Asturias, *The Green Pope* (New York: De la Carte Press, 1971), 3–22; and Pablo Neruda, "La United Fruit Co.," in *Canto General*, 50th Anniversary Edition (Berkeley: University of California Press, 2000), 179.

The expansion and projection of American power helped transform U.S.–Latin American relations and strengthen the United States' competitive posture vis-à-vis European states. The foreign policies adopted under the McKinley, Roosevelt, and Taft administrations served America's short-term objectives by preventing European incursions and protecting the Panama Canal region; they also served its long-term strategic and economic interests by "roping off" the Caribbean and Central America as an exclusive U.S. zone of influence. States within this zone, meanwhile, realized some clear material benefits: U.S. military engineers and personnel made substantial improvements to the infrastructure of American protectorates (drainage and irrigation systems, ports, roads), and the local economies saw an influx of foreign capital. Nevertheless, there is little question that beginning in 1898, and for several decades thereafter, Washington pursued imperialist policies toward and exercised dominion over the Caribbean and Central America. As historians Emily and Norman Rosenberg note concerning Cuba, the Dominican Republic, Haiti, Nicaragua, and Panama: "If imperialism is a process by which one state assumes sovereign powers over another, setting up a dependent relationship, relations between the United States and all of these countries can be included under the term."[17] This shift toward imperialism was the product not only of domestic second-level factors, but of systemic, third-level factors and contributions by key individuals too.

By virtue of its power projection and imperialist policies, the United States exercised dominance over the Caribbean and Central America, and actions taken in Washington could make or break regional governments. Realist concerns helped fuel Washington's imperialist project. As one U.S. State Department official explained in 1927: "Our ministers in the five Central American republics . . . have been advisers whose advice has been accepted virtually as law in the capitals where they serve . . . We do control the destinies of Central America and we do so for the simple reason that the national interest absolutely dictates such a course."[18]

American dominance had important political consequences for Caribbean and Central American states; some were better than others. It provided these states security from European military intervention and freed them from ever facing a *security dilemma* vis-à-vis each other. It did not, however, provide security from American intervention, or any real prospects of escaping from the U.S. zone of influence. Consequently, most states resigned themselves to the political benefits and constraints of U.S. dominance—trading security from each other and Europeans in exchange for nominal independence, conducting their affairs within the parameters the United States had established, and being subject to U.S. tutelage when their voluntary "good conduct" sometimes lapsed.

Moreover, the interventions that helped sustain America's preeminent position had debilitating effects on the stability and political maturation of the region's domestic political systems, and pernicious consequences for human rights. As occurred with Cuba under the Platt Amendment, many governments (and politicians) that came within the American zone of influence came to rely on the United States to solve their political problems, instead of on themselves and their voters. The result was a vicious cycle wherein U.S. intervention stymied political maturation and helped create dependent, dysfunctional governments, which in turn, provoked more interventions, and led to greater dependence. Consequently, when Washington began to dismantle its protectorates and withdraw its troops from the late 1920s onward, it sought some means to maintain political order in their absence. Its solution was to replace American forces with U.S.-trained national constabularies, militias, or police. In Cuba, the Dominican Republic, Haiti, and Nicaragua, these forces eventually became the personal armies of dictators, who—lacking any external threats from other states in the region or from Europe—periodically deployed their militaries against domestic opponents. The repression and human rights abuses that followed under these dictatorships helped stimulate various political upheavals (civil wars, insurgencies, revolutions) that U.S. policymakers would be forced to grapple with from the 1960s through the early 1990s.

Finally, American dominance established a clear hierarchical ranking of states in the region, but not harmonious relations between these weaker powers and the United States. Instead, inter-state tension and the potential for conflict were hardwired into the system itself. Washington expected states in its zone of influence to defer on matters of strategic significance and to privilege American goals and U.S. national interests over their own. When this failed to occur, tensions flared, U.S. intervention sometimes followed, and resentment toward the United States grew. Thus, the resentment Latin American states came to harbor toward America was not merely a function of past U.S. slights and transgressions, but rather, part of an ongoing process replicated within the inter-state political order itself. The longer the United States maintained the imperialist policies that rationalized American intervention and underpinned its dominance—the Platt Amendment, Roosevelt Corollary, Dollar Diplomacy, and Customs House treaties—the more intense the resentment would grow.

The expansion of American power and achievement of U.S. dominance played out within the context of an anarchic system that saw the United States act in a manner consistent with realist theory. Concerned over the global balance of power, it sought security in the face of perceived threats from European states. By the second decade of the twentieth century, the United States had fulfilled Alexander Hamilton's eighteenth-century vision. Through effective enforcement of the Monroe Doctrine, and the development and projection of American power, Washington could set the terms by which European powers were permitted to interact with the New World. The path toward this outcome began with the Monroe Doctrine, which had touted Latin America's self-determination and argued that Europe's tradition of "lording it over" weaker countries and controlling their destinies, had no place in the

Western Hemisphere. Ironically, it ended with a string of policies that contradicted the Doctrine's original intent, and denied self-determination to some of the very states the Monroe Doctrine had sought to protect. These outcomes so marred America's image and its relationship with its southern neighbors, that it would require Washington to adopt an entirely new foreign policy approach to begin effective repairs.

Study Questions

1. What caused the Spanish-American War? How might you apply the three levels of analysis to explain it?
2. What effects did the expansion of U.S. power have on American foreign policy and U.S.–Latin American relations at the end of the nineteenth century? Why were U.S. officials concerned about the decline of Spanish power at this time?
3. What factors do you believe best account for why the United States adopted the Roosevelt Corollary?
   (a) Ideology (Social Darwinism and Manifest Destiny)
   (b) Economic imperialism
   (c) Realist security concerns
   (d) Failed state dynamics
   (e) Lack of an effective supranational institution to govern inter-state relations
   (f) The weakness of international law.
4. Which set of factors—first level, second level, or third level—played a more prominent role in the expansion of American power (1860s and beyond)?

Selected Readings

Beale, Howard K. *Theodore Roosevelt and the Rise of America to World Power*, 31–84. Baltimore: Johns Hopkins University Press, 1965.

Karnow, Stanley. *In Our Image: America's Empire in the Philippines*, 78–105. New York: Random House, 1989.

Kennan, George F. *American Diplomacy*, 3–20. Chicago: University of Chicago Press, 1984.

Peceny, Mark. *Democracy at the Point of Bayonets*, ch. 3. University Park: Pennsylvania State University Press, 1999.

Pérez, Louis. *The War of 1898: The United States and Cuba in History and Historiography*, ch. 3. Chapel Hill: University of North Carolina Press, 1998.

Rosenberg, Emily S. and Norman L. Rosenberg. "From Colonialism to Professionalism: The

Public-Private Dynamic in United States Foreign Financial Advising, 1898–1929." *Journal of American History* 74 (June 1987): 59–82.

Schirmer, Daniel B. and Stephen Rosskamm Shalom (eds). *The Philippines Reader: A History of Colonialism, Neocolonialism, Dictatorship, and Resistance*, 5–11, 22–31. Boston: South End Press, 1987.

Sparrow, Bartholomew H. "Strategic Adjustment and the U.S. Navy: The Spanish-American War, the Yellow Press, and the 1990s." In *The Politics of Strategic Adjustment: Ideas, Institutions, and Interests*, edited by Peter Trubowitz, Emily O. Goldman, and Edward Rhodes, 139–175. New York: Columbia University Press, 1999.

Further Readings

Bemis, Samuel Flagg. "Development of the Panama Policy in the Caribbean and Central America (1982–1936)." In *Neighborly Adversaries: Readings in U.S.–Latin American Relations*, edited by Michael LaRosa and Frank O. Mora, 95–99. Lanham, MD: Rowman & Littlefield, 1999.

Gilpin, Robert. *The Political Economy of International Relations*, 281–290. Princeton: Princeton University Press, 1987.

Hood, Miram. *Gunboat Diplomacy 1895–1905: Great Power Pressure in Venezuela*, chs 1–3, 10–11. Boston: George Allen & Unwin, 1983.

Huntington, Samuel P. "American Ideals versus American Institutions." *Political Science Quarterly* 97 (Spring 1982): 1–37.

Tilchin, William. "Power and Principle: The Statecraft of Theodore Roosevelt." In *Ethics and Statecraft*, edited by Cathal Nolan, 97–115. New York: Praeger, 2004.

Zimmermann, Warren. "Jingoes, Goo-Goos, and the Rise of America's Empire." *The Wilson Quarterly* 22 (1998): 42–64.

Chronology: The Expansion of American Power

1895–1898	Cuban War of Independence from Spain
1898	Spanish-American War; U.S. acquires Puerto Rico, Guam, Philippines
1898	U.S. puts Cuba under military occupation
1902	Platt Amendment imposed on Cuba, transforming it into U.S. Protectorate
1902	Britain, Germany, and Italy bombard Venezuela's coastline to compel repayment of international debts
1903	U.S. encourages Panama's separation from Colombia, recognizes new state of Panama, and signs accord to construct Panama Canal
1904	Europeans threaten force against Dominican Republic to collect debts
1905	U.S. adopts Roosevelt Corollary to Monroe Doctrine, assumes right to intervene in domestic affairs of Latin American states
1905	Dominican Republic becomes U.S. Protectorate
1911	Nicaragua becomes U.S. Protectorate
1915	Haiti becomes U.S. Protectorate

Hemispheric Relations through World War II

5

Figure 5.1 Organization of American States, Washington, DC, 2008

Achieving Mutual Security and Inter-State Cooperation

During the first half of the twentieth century, hemispheric relations evolved significantly. Latin American states worked diligently—through international law, diplomacy and treaties, and international institutions—to reclaim their sovereignty, establish their juridical equality, and promote multilateralism as the core principle of inter-American relations. The United States, meanwhile, gradually shifted from exercising dominance over its immediate neighbors to simple hegemony: incrementally, it edged away from a rather routine disregard of its neighbors' sovereignty, and in the process, U.S. "gunboat diplomacy" eventually gave way to the era of the Good Neighbor, and a welcome period of inter-state cooperation ensued.

This decades-long evolution offers a unique perspective on international politics and further illustrates the array of instruments states can use when seeking to advance their interests. The period began with the United States clearly ascendant: European states had largely been squeezed out of the hemisphere, and dramatic power asymmetries separated the two Americas. As realist theorists might expect, in this context the United States could (and did) act on realist concerns and principles to advance and protect its interests, often at its neighbors' expense. The Platt Amendment, Roosevelt Corollary, and Dollar Diplomacy led to repeated U.S. interventions, which violated the sovereignty of Latin American states and the juridical equality they enjoyed under international law.

Not surprisingly, these interventions bred increasingly strong anti-American sentiment across the region. "[T]he United States today controls Cuba, Porto Rico, [and] Panama," lamented *La Prensa* of Lima, Peru, on September 13, 1913. "Tomorrow it is going to control Central America. It has commenced to control Mexico. Who says that it will not continue further?"[1] Under these circumstances, the prospects of developing genuinely cooperative hemispheric relations seemed remote. In a unipolar system, the United States could act with dispatch, while Latin American states lacked the power to protect their sovereignty, advance their interests, or engage the United States on realist terms. Nonetheless, from the late 1920s through the late 1940s, this situation changed dramatically: U.S. military interventions ceased and military occupations came to an end; U.S. Protectorates were dismantled; Central American and Caribbean states regained their sovereignty; multilateral consultations replaced unilateral U.S. actions; collaborative defense and security measures developed; and resentment toward the United States declined.

Although power asymmetries did not disappear, by mid-century both nonintervention and the legal equality of states had become prevailing and widely accepted norms, and a more cooperative relationship had developed between the two Americas. Ultimately, these trends culminated in the establishment of a regional body—the Organization of American States—that was part of a broader political and security-oriented Inter-American System. This system was designed to guarantee states' sovereignty, territorial integrity, and juridical equality, provide a forum where they could settle disputes peacefully, and address security concerns on a multilateral, collective basis.

International politics involves more than simply a struggle for power and security. It also entails efforts to achieve effective cooperation between sovereign states. Cooperation not only helps states realize a range of common economic, diplomatic, political, or strategic objectives, but also avoid some of anarchy's worst by-products: armed conflict, military interventions, and pronounced insecurity. Yet, while the benefits of cooperation seem obvious, effective cooperation often proves elusive. One reason is that international anarchy both impels states to compete, and induces mistrust and insecurity among states as they pursue their interests. The development of more co-operative U.S.–Latin American relations, therefore, did not come easy or quickly; rather, it followed a zigzag path of fits and starts, trial and error, good intentions and missed opportunities. Why, within an anarchic, unipolar environment, did cooperation eventually develop among the American republics? There are different ways to answer this question. One explanation lies in America's—and perhaps more important, Latin America's—increasing reliance on liberal principles and instruments of international politics to reorder hemispheric relations.

Early Liberal Efforts at Cooperative Relations

Unlike *realpolitik*, a liberal approach to international politics looks to protect states' security in ways that transcend hard balance of power techniques, and puts less stress on military power as a state's tool of choice. States that embrace a more liberal approach sometimes seek to leverage shared norms and principles, inter-state trade, international law, and international institutions to achieve their goals, avoid conflicts, and cooperate in common pursuits. However, early twentieth-century efforts to put liberal principles and practices in the service of more cooperative hemispheric affairs faced an uphill climb.

Wilsonianism

In 1912, Woodrow Wilson succeeded William Howard Taft as President of the United States. A complex, even contradictory man, Wilson was the product of a religious upbringing and held deep moral convictions. He was a political scientist by training and a southerner with Southern racial prejudices. He believed in manifest destiny, social Darwinism, and such liberal values as constitutionalism, self-determination, and the rule of law. However, he also believed in intervention, which contradicts self-determination, and that military force could be used to spread democratic governance abroad. Wilson had roundly condemned his predecessor's "Dollar Diplomacy" interventions that often had promoted U.S. economic interests; yet as president, he practiced intervention toward Latin America on a much grander scale.

Rather than base foreign policy solely on U.S. economic or strategic interests, Wilson sought to make America's liberal political values—democracy and democratic institutions, constitutionalism, self-determination, and the rule of law—the bedrock of U.S. foreign policy. The centering of foreign policy around such liberal values forged the concept of *Wilsonianism*. Students of international politics rightly identify the liberal-democratic aspects of Wilsonianism with U.S. policy toward Europe in the aftermath of World War I. There, Wilson advocated strongly for the creation of the League of Nations to help states settle their disputes peacefully, even democratically. Sometimes

Figure 5.2 Woodrow Wilson, 1919

overlooked, however, is the Janus-faced nature of Wilsonianism; namely, the awkward liberal-realist hybrid foreign policy that Wilsonianism exhibited toward Latin America. There, Wilson often tried to promote liberal democracy through force projection—an approach captured by the president's famous assertion that he would use American power to "teach the Mexicans [and by extension, Latin Americans] how to elect good men."

Shortly after taking office, Wilson announced his intention to seek a new direction in U.S.–Latin American relations. "One of the chief objects of my administration," he explained, "will be to cultivate the friendship and deserve the confidence of our sister republics of Central and South America, and to promote in every proper and honorable way the interests which are common to the peoples of the two continents. I earnestly desire the most cordial understanding and cooperation between the peoples and leaders of America."[2] These statements suggested the possibility of a new chapter in hemispheric relations, and sparked interest among many Latin American governments. To realize their promise, the Wilson administration began making overtures to Latin America. One example was the negotiation of a treaty with Colombia that addressed Bogotá's deep grievances against Washington for supporting the Panamanian separatist movement in 1903, and subsequently recognizing the new Panamanian state. In April 1914, the United States signed the Treaty of Bogotá, which expressed America's "sincere regret" for what had happened, and awarded Colombia $25 million in compensation for its lost province. Although the U.S. Senate refused to ratify the treaty (it did so in 1921 after Wilson left office), the apology, proposed indemnity, and expression of regret won acclaim across the region. Another example was Wilson's proposal to create a "Pan-American pact" that would generate closer economic and diplomatic relations throughout the hemisphere, promote arms control, collective defense, the arbitration of disputes, and guarantee the political independence, territorial integrity, and republican governments of the various states.

This proposal was a very liberal concept, which if realized, could address important realist concerns, advance U.S. and Latin American interests, and in historian Sidney Bell's words, "establish a pattern of cooperation."[3] A multilateral commitment to republican governments could enhance domestic stability across the region and substitute for unilateral U.S. intervention against governments Washington believed were unrepresentative or experiencing domestic turmoil. A collective security arrangement (whereby all states would guarantee the defense of any one state under attack) would dampen security concerns for all. The arbitration of disputes would preserve inter-state peace via democratic procedures (consent to the arbitration rules). And an effective multilateral pact might even diminish the resentment Latin American states held against the United States for unilateral actions taken under the Roosevelt Corollary.[4]

This liberal, regional initiative foreshadowed Wilson's more global League of Nations project after World War I. As would be the case with the League, the Pan-American pact's success turned on getting other states to accept and buy into the idea. Toward this end, U.S. officials first approached the ABC states (Argentina, Brazil, and Chile) to secure their unofficial commitment, with plans to unveil the proposal to the rest of Latin America for its consideration once the ABCs were on board. To Washington's dismay, however, these states were less than enthusiastic. Some suspected the pact was simply a way to mask and justify U.S. intervention under the Roosevelt Corollary and institutionalize U.S. economic influence. For its part, Chile—which had an ongoing border dispute with Peru—rejected the idea outright (why guarantee states' territorial integrity when border disputes remained outstanding?). In the end, Wilson's liberal proposal went nowhere and the American republics missed an opportunity to develop a more institutionalized, cooperative relationship.

Other factors that impeded better relations and worked against U.S. overtures came from the interventionist policies Wilson himself pursued toward the region, especially in Nicaragua, Haiti, the Dominican Republic, and Mexico. Under Wilson's direction, the United States sought to promote stability and democratic governance through military occupation in Nicaragua (1914), Haiti (1915), and the Dominican Republic (1916). These occupations outlasted Wilson's own administration by many years (until 1933, 1934, and 1928 respectively), and in each case, they failed to establish stable, democratic rule. They did, however, badly damage America's image across the region, hinder development of more cooperative relations, and heighten Latin American security concerns vis-à-vis the United States. In Mexico, Wilson authorized two direct interventions during that country's revolution, and while neither led to lasting military occupations (or genuine democratic governance), they proved equally damaging to America's image there and beyond.

The Mexican Revolution began in 1911 and lasted a decade. It toppled longtime dictator Porfirio Díaz, brought democrat Francisco Madero to the presidency in 1912, and unleashed violent conflict between competing revolutionary factions for the next decade. The violence also threatened U.S. investments, citizens, and American-owned properties. U.S. intervention in Mexico's revolutionary affairs actually preceded Wilson's tenure. While President William Howard Taft had concerns regarding the revolution's impact on U.S. investments, he accepted the new Madero administration. However, Taft's ambassador to Mexico—Henry Lane Wilson—did not, and actively conspired with General Victoriano Huerta to engineer Madero's downfall. In February

1913, Huerta seized power unconstitutionally after orchestrating Madero's murder. One month later, Woodrow Wilson assumed power, learned of the ambassador's complicity in the plot and replaced him, then dispatched an emissary to Mexico to size up Huerta and Mexico's political landscape.

The political situation was far from stable. Other military leaders—Venustiano Carranza, Francisco "Pancho" Villa, and Emiliano Zapata—opposed Huerta's coup and were fighting to remove the regime. Huerta's bloody power grab also offended Wilson's sense of morality and the value he placed on democracy and constitutionalism. Consequently, Washington refused to recognize the new government, and announced that henceforth, the United States would only recognize governments that had come to power through constitutional, democratic means. Wilson applied his new policy to Mexico and other Latin American states. Because "just governments rest always on the consent of the governed," he explained, the United States would "look to make these principles the basis of mutual intercourse, respect, and helpfulness between our sister republics and ourselves." The new non-recognition policy underscored Wilsonianism's commitment to democracy and the rule of law, yet drew the United States deeper into Mexico's affairs as Wilson sought to influence the revolution, shape political outcomes, protect U.S. interests, and ensure democracy would emerge from the conflict.

After urging Huerta to step down and permit new elections (which he refused to do), Wilson worked to oust him. This effort entailed permitting U.S. arms to flow to those who opposed Huerta, and occupying Veracruz to deprive him of a shipment of German arms (and retaliate for Mexico's brief detainment of U.S. sailors at Tampico who had wandered into a restricted area but were quickly released). It also entailed choosing sides among the various revolutionary leaders to make sure an acceptable "democrat" came to power. In 1915, Huerta fled Mexico for Europe; Wilson extended recognition to Carranza (which angered Villa), yet continued to intervene indirectly by pressuring Carranza not to implement aspects of Mexico's new Constitution pertaining to land reform and national ownership of natural resources.

Direct U.S. military intervention in Mexico occurred on two occasions. The first was in 1914 during the Veracruz occupation. The second was between 1916 and 1917 when General John Pershing's forces scoured northern Mexico in a futile attempt to capture Pancho Villa (who had retaliated against Wilson's recognition of Carranza with a raid on Columbus, New Mexico that killed 11 Americans). Wilson finally withdrew Pershing's forces in large part, due to German meddling in Mexico's political affairs (the "Zimmermann Telegram") and his concern for World War I—a much larger conflict with far greater implications for U.S. interests. In Mexico, as in other Latin American states, using hard power did little to advance Wilsonian liberal aims; however, it did help undermine efforts to establish more cooperative hemispheric relations, and formed part of the context that scuttled the president's notion of a Pan-American pact.

Box 5.1 Mexico, World War I, and the Zimmermann Telegram

Anticipating that the United States would side with Britain in the Great War, in January 1917, German foreign minister Arthur Zimmermann telegrammed Germany's representatives in Mexico with instructions to seek a military alliance: in exchange for joining Germany in war against the United States, Germany would help Mexico regain the territories it lost to America in the 1840s. The basic objective of Germany's offer was to preempt U.S. entry into the European war by entangling the United States in an armed conflict close to home. It was an offer that Mexican President Venustiano Carranza wisely rejected. British intelligence intercepted the famous "Zimmermann Telegram" and relayed it to Washington. Its contents helped build domestic support for war with Germany and became part of the context in which the United States joined the Allies' war effort against the Axis powers.

> We intend to begin unrestricted submarine warfare. In spite of this, it is our intention to endeavor to keep the United States of America neutral. In the event of this not succeeding, we propose an alliance on the following basis with Mexico: That we shall make war together and make peace together. We shall give generous financial support, and an understanding on our part that Mexico is to reconquer the lost territory in New Mexico, Texas, and Arizona. The details of settlement are left to you. You are instructed to inform the President [of Mexico] of the above in the greatest confidence as soon as it is certain that there will be an outbreak of war with the United States and suggest that the President, on his own initiative, invite Japan to immediate adherence with this plan; at the same time, offer to mediate between Japan and ourselves. Please call to the attention of the President that the ruthless employment of our submarines now offers the prospect of compelling England to make peace in a few months.
>
> Arthur Zimmermann

If early U.S. attempts to establish hemispheric relations on a more liberal foundation met with little success, similar efforts by Latin American states fared no better. Lacking the power to contend with their northern neighbor on realist terms, Latin American states pursued a range of liberal tactics to protect their security and sovereignty, including international law, international institutions, diplomacy, and treaties.

International Law

The legal approach—typified by the *Calvo Clause* and *Drago Doctrine*—aimed to establish the juridical equality of states and codify the principle of non-intervention within international law as a hedge against foreign incursions. Developed by Argentine jurist Carlos Calvo, the Calvo Clause challenged the European and American position that their nationals whose investments in Latin America suffered injury from domestic disturbance or civil war, could call upon their own governments to settle any claims they may have against the host state, rather than adjudicate them under domestic laws and courts. Calvo's chief legal assertions were straightforward: since all states enjoyed juridical equality and inviolable sovereignty, external intervention to enforce pecuniary claims had no basis in international law. Domestic law and courts, therefore, held sway over both foreigners and host country citizens alike. Latin American states embraced Calvo's principles (first published in 1868) and through the early 1900s, repeatedly urged their incorporation into international law; European powers and the United States, meanwhile, opposed these efforts. Although many Latin American states implemented Calvo's principles unilaterally (by amending their constitutions to reflect them and inserting them into contracts between foreign investors and host Latin American states), the lack of international consensus kept the Calvo Clause outside the canons of international law.

The Drago Doctrine grew out of the 1902 Venezuelan crisis, in which Britain, Germany, and Italy employed military force to compel Caracas to honor its debts. While this crisis led the United States to preempt further European intervention via the Roosevelt Corollary (a realist approach to Latin America's debt problems), it led Latin Americans to pursue a legal approach to achieve similar goals, based on the arguments of Luis Drago, Argentina's ambassador to the United States. In a famous legal memo, Drago acknowledged that states were obligated to meet their international financial commitments, but asserted that international law provided no authority to use force as a means to collect public—that is, state-owed—debt. Such actions, he maintained, violated the equality and sovereignty of states, which constituted "fundamental principles of public international law." Like the Calvo Clause, the Drago Doctrine gained little international traction. European powers and the United States basically ignored it, and when Latin American delegates petitioned the international court at The Hague to accept the Doctrine as part of international law, the Court ruled against the petitioners, finding that force could be used legitimately to collect debts if arbitration efforts had failed.

International Institutions

Besides international law, Latin American states also sought to protect their sovereignty via international institutions, specifically, the League of Nations. Ten months before World War I ended, Woodrow Wilson issued his famous 14-points in January 1918, which outlined the reasons why the United States had entered the conflict. Wilson's 14th point was the most memorable. It called for creating a world body of states which would guarantee that the territory and political independence of all states—the weak and the strong—would be preserved. This world body would have a specific organization, norms, and rules to facilitate the implementation of treaties, resolve inter-state disputes, and eliminate the self-help nature of international politics via "collective security" (in which an attack against one state is an attack against all, producing a common defensive response). Wilson's proposal became the League of Nations, which began operating in 1919 and grew out of the Paris Peace Conference and Versailles Treaty that ended World War I.

Although the U.S. President had been the League's chief advocate, the United States refused to join. By contrast, many Latin American states did. Three factors led the United States to opt out of the League. First, many U.S. lawmakers believed that the League's collective security arrangement would surrender U.S. war-making authority to an international body and commit America to entering distant wars in which it had no interest. Second, some feared that an influx of small, Latin American states into the League—with equal voting power in the League Assembly—would unsettle the Western Hemisphere's natural hierarchical ranking of states in which the United States enjoyed preeminence.[5] Finally, many U.S. leaders feared that the protections of state sovereignty enshrined in the League Covenant would impinge on Washington's ability to exert regional influence under the Monroe Doctrine.

To overcome U.S. reservations, Article 21 of the League Covenant explicitly recognized the Monroe Doctrine's legitimacy. The U.S. Senate, however, remained unsatisfied and refused to ratify both the Covenant and the Versailles

Treaty (instead, Washington signed the Treaty of Berlin, a separate peace treaty with Germany that gave the United States all "rights, privileges, indemnities, reparations or advantages" of the Versailles Treaty without mentioning the League). To further clarify the official U.S. stance regarding the League and Monroe Doctrine, the Senate also passed a strongly worded reservation against the League Covenant asserting America's right to maintain, interpret, and invoke the Doctrine.

Box 5.2 U.S. Reservations Concerning the League of Nations and the Monroe Doctrine

The United States will not submit to arbitration or to inquiry by the assembly or by the Council of the League of Nations, provided for in said treaty of peace, any questions which in the judgment of the United States depend upon or relate to its long established policy commonly known as the Monroe Doctrine; said doctrine is to be interpreted by the United Sates alone and is hereby declared to be wholly outside the jurisdiction of said League of Nations and entirely unaffected by any provision contained in the said treaty of peace with Germany.

United States Senate Resolution, June 28, 1919
quoted in Gordon Connel-Smith, *The Inter-American System*
(New York: Oxford University Press, 1966), 56–57

While America stayed outside of the institution that its president had worked to create, some of the very factors that led Washington to opt out—the legal equality of states, guarantees of state sovereignty, and potential limitations on the Monroe Doctrine and U.S. influence—led Latin American states to opt in. Their position was perhaps best captured by Nicaragua's president, Emiliano Chamorro. In December 1919, Chamorro lauded the League's potential to promote international justice "through the recognition of identical rights to each and every [nation], without smallness mitigating against any one enjoying its full sovereignty." By protecting the small from the great, he proclaimed, the League brought "just hope [to] all weak nations."[6]

Despite their initial enthusiasm, many Latin American states remained displeased over the League's recognition of the Monroe Doctrine, and Argentina was especially annoyed. At the first League Assembly, the Argentine delegation proposed a resolution to excise any mention of the Doctrine from

Box 5.3 League of Nations and Latin American Membership

Original Members of the League of Nations as of January 10, 1920

Argentina	El Salvador	Paraguay
Bolivia	Guatemala	Peru
Brazil	Haiti	Uruguay
Chile	Honduras	Venezuela
Colombia	Nicaragua	
Cuba	Panama	

Subsequent Accession to and Withdrawal from the League

1920	Costa Rica is admitted to the League
1924	Dominican Republic is admitted to the League
1925	Costa Rica withdraws
1926	Brazil withdraws
1931	Mexico is admitted to the League
1934	Ecuador is admitted to the League
1935	Paraguay withdraws
1936	Guatemala, Honduras, and Nicaragua withdraw
1937	El Salvador withdraws
1938	Chile and Venezuela withdraw
1942	Haiti withdraws

the League Covenant, and when the amendment was set aside, Argentina stopped participating actively in the League until 1933. Once the League began operating, Latin American states experienced other disappointments and discovered that some benefits they had expected League membership to generate failed to appear. For example, the League's tendency to seek consensus among the great powers and to defer to strong regional states on issues of regional concern, diminished the effect of Latin Americans' "voice" in League operations, but did little to diminish U.S. influence in the Americas. In time, many regional powers withdrew from the League. Great powers like Germany and Japan did too, and when the League proved unable to prevent the outbreak of World War II, Wilson's vision of a liberal, peace-preserving global institution died a quiet death.

Diplomacy, International Conferences, and International Treaties

A third way Latin American states sought to protect their sovereignty and recast hemispheric relations along more liberal lines, was through international treaties and diplomacy in hemispheric conferences. Between 1889 and 1954, Latin American states participated in 10 inter-American conferences and other more specialized convocations with their northern neighbor. Initially, these meetings were convened to address such issues as closer trade and smoother political relations, and to establish frameworks for the peaceful settlement of disputes. Ultimately, they became forums in which Latin American states increasingly expressed their displeasure with unilateral U.S. intervention, and urged the negotiation of multilateral treaties that would prohibit intervention, protect their sovereignty, guarantee their political equality, and provide for mutual security.

Box 5.4 Primary Inter-American Conferences, 1889–1954

Inter-American Conferences

Conference	Location	Select multilateral issues discussed and discussion outcomes
First, 1889–1890	Washington	Nonintervention and codification of "Calvo Clause" to prevent coercive foreign debt collection: U.S. refuses
Second, 1901–1902	Mexico City	Nonintervention and codification of "Calvo Clause" to prevent coercive foreign debt collection: U.S. refuses
Third, 1906	Rio de Janeiro	Nonintervention and codification of "Drago Doctrine" to prevent coercive foreign debt collection: U.S. refuses
Fourth, 1910	Buenos Aires	Pan-American Union created
Fifth, 1923	Santiago	Nonintervention and a proposal to create an American League of Nations: U.S. refuses

Conference	Location	Select multilateral issues discussed and discussion outcomes
Sixth, 1928	Havana	Codification of nonintervention principle: U.S. refuses
Seventh, 1933	Montevideo	Legal equality of states and codification of nonintervention principle in the Convention on the Rights and Duties of States: U.S. accepts former and agrees to latter with caveats
Eighth, 1938	Lima	Hemispheric unity in the face of possible external European threats: a vaguely worded "Declaration of Lima" that reaffirmed states' solidarity and sovereignty
Ninth, 1948	Bogotá	Organization of American States created; Latin American states seek economic development program: U.S. refuses
Tenth, 1954	Caracas	OAS declaration proclaiming Communism an external threat and permitting multilateral intervention against Guatemala: Latin American states refuse to authorize intervention against Guatemala

Special Conferences

Conference for the Maintenance of Peace, 1936	Buenos Aires	Codification of nonintervention principle in the Protocol on Nonintervention: U.S. accepts without caveats

Special Conferences		
Chapultepec Conference, 1945	Mexico City	World War II- and post-war-related security issues; the role of regional organizations in the new United Nations: general agreement to develop hemispheric security frameworks and ensure regional arrangements conformed to UN

At both the first and second conferences in Washington(1889–1890) and Mexico City (1901–1902), Latin American delegates tried but failed to persuade the United States to negotiate a treaty—based on the Calvo Clause—that would deny foreign investors special treatment not extended to a state's own citizens, and prohibit external intervention by any state to settle their nationals' commercial claims. Between the second and third conference, the United States had begun to exercise the interventionist "police power" articulated in the Roosevelt Corollary. Accordingly, at the third conference in Rio de Janeiro (1906), Latin American states pushed for—but again, failed to achieve—a multilateral treaty that recognized the Drago Doctrine's prohibition of armed intervention to enforce repayment of public debts.

By the time the fifth and sixth conferences convened in Santiago (1923) and Havana (1928), Latin American insecurities vis-à-vis the United States had grown dramatically, thanks largely to the interventionist policies of Woodrow Wilson, the ongoing U.S. occupations of Haiti and Nicaragua, and the continuation of Cuba's protectorate status under the Platt Amendment. Given their frustrations with the new League of Nations' inability to limit U.S. intervention, Latin American states came to the 1923 conference with a plan to replace unilateral U.S. intervention with a framework that could sanction multilateral intervention. Led by Uruguayan president Baltasar Brum, they proposed creating an "American League of Nations" that would multilateralize the Monroe Doctrine. As conceived by Brum, each republic would commit itself to intervene to aid an American state in the event of an extra-hemispheric attack, thereby transforming the Monroe Doctrine from a purely North American commitment against external threats into a multilateral one. Not surprisingly, Washington flatly rejected this proposal, preferring to retain exclusive rights to invoke and interpret the Doctrine.

The issue of nonintervention loomed especially large at the 1928 Havana conference, and was hotly debated (so hotly, in fact, that one observer noted it generated such "ill feeling and bad language that the minutes of the meeting had to be re-written").[7] The proposition that no state could intervene legitimately in the internal affairs of another enjoyed broad appeal among Latin American delegations, and 13 states supported a categorical declaration against intervention; the United States, however, did not, and the conference ended without a definitive, multilateral agreement on the matter.

The intervention issue returned again at the seventh inter-American conference in Montevideo (1933), and at a time when U.S. actions in Cuba were politically embarrassing for the United States. In 1933, Sergeant Fulgencio Batista led an army mutiny that deposed Cuban president Carlos Manuel de Céspedes, and brought Dr. Ramón Grau San Martín to power. Grau's legitimacy and political stability, however, were shaky; the island remained politically unstable and Grau was not without domestic opponents. With Cuba still under the Platt Amendment, Washington dispatched battleships into the vicinity to signal its concerns, and in other ways short of actually landing troops, worked to ease Grau from power and restore order. These actions, plus the continued U.S. occupation of Nicaragua sparked an outpouring of complaints at Montevideo against the United States. Referring to events in Cuba, one Cuban delegate declared to wide applause: "if it is not intervention to surround the defenseless island with an awe inspiring fleet and try to impose upon it a Government, to which we do not want to consent . . . then Gentlemen, there is no intervention in America!" Another Cuban delegate asserted that "Intervention is not only the 'curse of America,' but . . . it is the 'curse of curses' of my country, the cause of all the evils of the Cuban Republic."[8] A Haitian delegate, meanwhile, strongly denounced the Monroe Doctrine, contending that its "abusive interpretation has caused the smaller nations of this hemisphere to shed so many tears and so much blood."

These charges affected the American delegation deeply. Writing in his memoirs, Secretary of State Cordell Hull noted that the outbursts had so stunned one U.S. delegate that he "almost exploded"; Hull himself had found the experience extremely uncomfortable and disagreeable.[9]

In the end, the Montevideo conference generated a treaty (the Convention on the Rights and Duties of States) that spoke to several issues of long-standing concern to Latin American states. Article 4 recognized the legal equality of states regardless of their size or strength, while Article 8 prohibited intervention by one state in the internal or external affairs of another. The United States signed the Convention, yet reserved the right to intervene under provisions of international law, i.e., to protect the lives and property of U.S. citizens, and for reasons of self-defense. In light of these caveats, Latin American states kept pressing for a more binding commitment, and at a special 1936 inter-American peace conference held in Buenos Aires, the United States signed a multilateral Protocol on Nonintervention without reservations, thereby renouncing the right to intervene; it also signed a Consultative Pact which called for multilateral consultations to work out and adopt "methods of peaceful cooperation."

The Era of the Good Neighbor

While Latin American diplomats worked hard (and often unsuccessfully) to shift U.S. policy, from the late 1920s onward, the United States itself had begun to adjust its interactions with Latin America in ways that addressed some of the region's concerns. Gradually, and initially with little diminution in anti-American sentiments, U.S. policy shifted from a realist to a much more liberal approach that culminated in the Good Neighbor Policy. In 1928, President-elect Herbert Hoover made a goodwill tour through the region to shore up the sagging U.S. image; delivering 25 speeches across 10 countries, he promised to reduce the level of U.S. political and military interference. As president, Hoover took a series of conciliatory steps aimed at tamping down the region's rampant anti-Americanism. He abandoned Woodrow Wilson's non-recognition policy, which Latin American states saw as a form of indirect intervention, and repudiated the Roosevelt Corollary by publicizing the Clark Memorandum— an internal State Department study that determined the Corollary and the intervention it supported were damaging to U.S. interests. He also signed a treaty with Haiti to withdraw U.S. troops by 1935, and refused to intervene in Cuba and Nicaragua despite rising political instability that seemed to threaten U.S. investments and citizens.

However, Hoover never enunciated an explicit, comprehensive policy toward Latin America, and he failed to receive full credit for taking U.S. policy in a new direction. The effects of his conciliatory efforts were diminished in Latin America first, by his support for high tariffs under the Smoot–Hawley Act of 1930 (which harmed Latin American exports to the U.S. market), and by his association with the party of such prominent interventionists as Theodore Roosevelt, William Howard Taft, and William McKinley. Still, his efforts set the stage for Franklin Delano Roosevelt (FDR) to formulate a new policy that broke sharply with past U.S. practices toward Latin America.

Even before he took office, FDR was on record in opposition to U.S. interventionist policies. In a 1928 article published in the journal *Foreign Affairs*, he had sharply criticized unilateral U.S. intervention in Latin America (or what he termed "the arbitrary intervention in the home matters of our neighbors"). In lieu of a regional order maintained through unilateral U.S. military force, Roosevelt envisioned a more liberal community of nations in which shared values, mutual respect, and a harmony of interests could foster cooperation and preserve order. "Single handed intervention by us in the internal affairs of other nations must end," he argued; "with the cooperation of others we shall have more order in the hemisphere and less dislike." In his March 4, 1933 inaugural address, FDR laid out the fundamental principle of his administration's foreign policy, vowing to "dedicate this nation to the policy of the Good Neighbor . . . who respects himself [and] the rights of others." A month later, on Pan American Day (April 12), he applied the good neighbor principle explicitly to Latin America. "The essential qualities of a true Pan Americanism," he insisted, "must be the same as those which constitute a good neighbor, namely, mutual understanding, and through such understanding, a sympathetic appreciation of the others' point of view. It is only in this manner that we can hope to build up a system of which confidence, friendship and good will are the cornerstones."

Throughout FDR's first term, the United States took steps to square its actions with the president's rhetoric. At the 1933 Montevideo conference, it signed the Convention on the Rights and Duties of States, thereby renouncing intervention (but with caveats); it also began to dismantle the protectorates that had denied sovereignty to various states. In 1933, Washington withdrew its military forces from Nicaragua. In 1934, it abolished the Platt Amendment, giving Cuba its sovereignty, and accelerated the timetable to withdraw U.S. troops from Haiti; in 1936, it signed a new treaty with Panama that ended its protectorate status, plus the Consultative Pact and the Protocol on Nonintervention at the Buenos Aires conference, under which it renounced intervention without caveats. The United States also worked collaboratively with the ABC powers, Peru, and Uruguay to help end the Chaco War between Bolivia and Paraguay. Finally, it signed a series of reciprocal trade agreements with Brazil, Colombia, Cuba, and the Central American states that expanded cooperative economic relations within the "neighborhood."

Most analysts view the era of the Good Neighbor Policy as one of the most productive, successful periods of inter-American relations in history. Indeed, Latin American states warmed to the new U.S. policy. Many embraced the concept of a community of states, which seemed to offer a "new order" of hemispheric relations—characterized by multilateralism, respect for state sovereignty, and the legal equality of states—in place of the "old order" characterized by U.S. unilateralism, and the denial of weaker states' sovereignty and juridical equality. This new order did not eliminate friction or disputes between Latin American states and their neighbor, but it did produce an extended period of cooperation in which both Americas realized some important goals. The Good Neighbor Policy was an important part of this new order, but its ultimate success was more than the product of U.S. policy alone.

Box 5.5 The Good Neighbor Policy and International Relations Theory

Where does the Good Neighbor Policy fit into the standard categories of international relations theory? Was it truly a liberal approach to hemispheric relations or actually a realist project to enhance U.S. hegemony, masked by liberal trappings? Scholars disagree. According to Gregory Weeks, a political scientist at the University of North Carolina in Charlotte, "The Good Neighbor Policy poses a challenge to a realist perspective" of international politics.[a] By contrast, UCSD political scientist Peter Smith suggests that "FDR's stance reflected a hardheaded sense of *realpolitik* that promoted and protected the long-standing U.S. quest for hegemony throughout the hemisphere"; consequently, "the Good Neighbor policy can be seen not as a departure from past practices but as the *culmination* of trends in U.S. policy toward the region" (emphasis in original).[b]

Each position has some merit. It's certainly true that the Good Neighbor Policy helped perpetuate U.S. influence in the region, and that it served U.S. interests against the backdrop of rising security concerns over events in Europe. But it's equally true that the Good Neighbor Policy broke sharply with past U.S. practices of unilateralism and military intervention, and that it displayed a number of features at variance with a realist perspective. Realism views military security as a state's highest priority, and power and force as its tools of choice. Yet, the initial thrust behind Roosevelt's policy in 1933 was to repair the U.S. regional image, not erect a bulwark against a European conflict whose development was still years in the future; and under the Good Neighbor Policy, the United States eschewed the use of hard power in favor of diplomacy, communication, and compromise. Finally, the liberal concept at the heart of the policy—a community of nations where shared norms, principles, and diplomacy, not military force, might advance and protect states' interests—stands at odds with the autonomous, isolated collection of states that helps form a pure realist view of international politics. On balance, then, viewing the Good Neighbor Policy as primarily a realist construct can be theoretically misleading.

[a] Gregory Weeks, *U.S. and Latin American Relations* (New York: Pearson, Longman, 2008), 90.
[b] Peter H. Smith, *Talons of the Eagle* (New York: Oxford University Press, 1996), 65.

International Regimes and the Good Neighbor Policy

A useful way to understand this new order is the concept of an *international regime*. Political scientist Stephen Krasner defines a regime as a set of "implicit or explicit principles, norms, rules, and decision-making procedures around which actors' expectations converge in a given area of international relations."[10] In simpler terms, an international regime is a "way of doing things" based on norms, principles, and procedures that govern the relations of sovereign states. Its principal functions are to reduce uncertainty among nations, provide a set of mutually acceptable standards of action, promote orderly relations in an anarchic world, and provide a context where conflicts can be avoided or resolved peacefully. International regimes can be formal or informal arrangements. In modern times, states have devised numerous regimes to cover issues ranging from security (the Nuclear Nonproliferation Treaty) to trade (the General Agreement on Tariffs and Trade), and conservation (the International Agreement on the Conservation of Polar Bears) to natural resources (the International Convention for the Regulation of Whaling).

Regimes can be useful in international politics because they help regularize behavior between states so that countries have an understanding of their mutual rights and obligations. Once a regime has been established, states are less uncertain about what another state might do, because the norms and principles that comprise it define international behavior in mutually acceptable terms. This enables states to anticipate the actions of one another and fashion their own actions accordingly. Since international regimes mitigate the intensity of anarchy but don't eliminate it, they don't guarantee that relations will be harmonious. The potential for disagreements and tensions, therefore, remains. The important point is that when states agree to let a given set of norms and procedures govern their behavior, a regime helps them avoid situations where disagreement becomes conflict, and force is used to solve international problems.

In important ways, the Good Neighbor Policy eventually took on the properties of an informal international regime, built around the norms, principles, and procedures of nonintervention, reciprocity, multilateralism, and consultation. In exchange for its pledge of nonintervention, the United States expected Latin American governments to reciprocate with policies that guaranteed fair treatment for U.S. citizens, property, and investments in their countries. FDR did not see his policy as a one-way street in which the United States renounced intervention and received nothing in return; he also believed that in time, Latin American states would come to share his view that the new order must be "multilateral and that the fair dealing which it implies must be reciprocated."[11] Consultation and multilateral decision-making grew out of the 1936 Consultative Pact signed in Buenos Aires. This pact obligated Washington to consult with Latin American governments on hemispheric issues rather than act unilaterally, and to avoid confusion, it clarified the conditions that would trigger such consultation: (1) when peace in the Western Hemisphere was threatened by any source, (2) in the event of war or near-war between two American republics, and (3) if an external war threatened peace in the Americas. In combination, these norms, principles, and procedures established new rules to govern hemispheric relations that ended the unilateral, superior-inferior dichotomy of the old order, while offering incentives to cooperate and compromise when tensions rose.

Phases of the Good Neighbor Regime

The era of the Good Neighbor regime can be divided into two phases. The first ran from 1933 to 1939, during which the regime helped facilitate smoother relations concerning regional political and economic issues. The second phase lasted from 1939 to 1945, during which it helped address the military and security issues generated by World War II.

PHASE I: 1933–1939

During his first term in office, reestablishing cordial relations between the United States and its southern neighbors was high on FDR's agenda. The President was especially keen to transform the United States' image in Latin America from that of a "bully" to a good neighbor, and toward this end, he renounced intervention in speeches and embraced international treaties to this effect. During Roosevelt's second term, this commitment to nonintervention was put to the test against the backdrop of rising economic nationalism in Latin American states, and deteriorating political conditions in Europe.

The first big test came in 1937, when the Bolivian government nationalized the facilities and property owned by the Standard Oil Company. Bolivia charged that Standard had defrauded the government by failing to pay taxes, and alleged the company had helped promote the Chaco War—a territorial conflict between Bolivia and Paraguay. In response, the Bolivian state canceled the company's oil concession and expropriated its facilities and property. Roosevelt was not pleased at the loss of American assets, and in the past, such action could well have triggered a strong military response to protect U.S. investments. Now, however, Washington declined to use force on Standard's behalf. Instead, the State Department acknowledged Bolivia's sovereign right to expropriate the firm's assets, advised Standard to negotiate directly with the Bolivians regarding a settlement, and insisted that Bolivia "reciprocate" and compensate the company for the property it seized. In the midst of the Great Depression, the Bolivian treasury was hardly flush; but to encourage good faith reciprocity, Washington pressured Bolivia diplomatically and postponed technical assistance and loans until a compensation accord was reached (however, wartime pressures did lead it to extend Bolivia economic assistance in 1941). In 1942, Bolivia and Standard Oil agreed to a cash payment of $1.5 million; in the meantime, official relations between Washington and La Paz had remained stable if not cordial, and the principle of nonintervention passed its first real test.

A second major test occurred in Mexico in 1938, and it too concerned the expropriation of foreign oil companies. In March 1938, the Mexican government nationalized the properties of American, British, and Dutch oil companies. These expropriations grew out of a dispute between the Mexican government, Mexican workers, and foreign investors over such issues as wages, unionization, taxes, and repatriated profits. The wage and union dispute between Mexican oil workers and the foreign companies eventually came before Mexico's Supreme Court, which ruled against the companies. When they refused to comply, Mexico nationalized their assets. Again, the U.S. response was nonmilitary and followed a pattern similar to that in Bolivia. The State Department accepted Mexico's right to nationalize the foreign companies, insisted that just compensation be paid to the former owners, resisted calls by American oil executives for military protection, and encouraged the companies to reach an agreement with Mexico on their own (a suggestion most firms ignored). As with Bolivia, Washington encouraged reciprocity by withholding loans to Mexico until a settlement was reached, and suspended a 1936 agreement to buy Mexican silver.

The dispute between U.S. oil firms and the Mexican state lasted five years. Eventually, Mexico proposed (and FDR accepted) the creation of a small, bilateral commission to evaluate the seized assets' net worth and determine an appropriate compensation payment. Mexico's ability to effect compensation was compromised by the same factors that Bolivia confronted, but in the end, it agreed to pay the American companies $42 million. The joint commission recommended that Mexico draw down its debt through routine payments in annual installments, and by 1949, all outstanding liabilities had been retired. The only U.S. firm that heeded Washington's suggestion to negotiate directly with Mexico was Sinclair Oil, which received $8.5 million—ironically, an amount larger than that received by any company that had refused direct negotiations with the Mexican state.

The actions taken by Bolivia and Mexico could have ruptured their bilateral relations with the United States or precipitated a downward spiral of events leading to armed U.S. intervention. There is no doubt that each state factored Washington's nonintervention pledge into its calculations before proceeding to nationalize American-owned assets, and that later, each required U.S. "encouragement" to display appropriate reciprocity. Despite the tensions, though, the norms of nonintervention and reciprocity embedded in the Good Neighbor regime helped resolve these conflicts peacefully. Moreover, in declining to intervene militarily, Washington signaled its acceptance of these states' sovereignty, which went a long way toward meeting FDR's goal of changing the U.S. image in the region.

PHASE II: 1939–1945

By the late 1930s, international conditions had changed dramatically and events outside the Americas began to reorient a key aspect of the Good Neighbor regime. War had come to Europe and war clouds hung over the Western Hemisphere. Increasingly preoccupied with the likelihood of war, Roosevelt looked to unite both continents against possible threats from the Axis Powers. Security and defense concerns overshadowed inter-American economic issues, and the principle of reciprocity evolved from a focus on policies of economic fairness, to those of diplomatic, political, and material support against Nazi Germany and its allies.

The expanding conflict in Europe ushered in the Good Neighbor regime's second phase. Since the mid-1930s, the American republics had sought to stay neutral toward Europe's war. In 1935, for example, the U.S. Congress adopted the Neutrality Act; most Latin American states hoped to avoid war too, and joined Washington in issuing a multilateral General Declaration of Neutrality. But acts of war off the coasts of South American and Caribbean states—coupled with Germany's blitzkriegs of Poland and other North European states— threatened to expand the conflict across the Atlantic. In 1939, naval battles erupted between British, French, and German ships off the coast of Uruguay. In 1940, similar incidents occurred off the coast of Brazil and the Dominican Republic. Latin American states protested these actions as violations of their neutral zone, but to no avail: Britain, France, and Germany insisted they were not bound to honor this zone. Meanwhile, Hitler's easy conquest of Poland, Denmark, the Netherlands, other North European states, and finally France, raised the specter of Germany occupying their Caribbean territories, thereby transforming the Western Hemisphere into a new military theater.

In 1940, the U.S. Congress resolved that the United States would not tolerate attempts to transfer territory in the Western Hemisphere from one non-American power to another, and that should such an attempt be made, it would (besides taking other measures) consult with regional powers to determine a common response. The resolution's target audience was Germany, of course, but Latin America too, since the implicit threat beneath it—to invoke the Monroe Doctrine in consultation with U.S. neighbors, not unilaterally—signaled an evolution in U.S. thinking on hemispheric relations. More concrete, collaborative security-oriented initiatives followed, including a joint Montevideo–Washington effort to thwart a Nazi plot to seize control of Uruguay, and the provision of basing rights to U.S. forces from over a dozen Latin American states.

Securing these basing rights did not come easy. For one thing, many Latin American governments believed Washington's growing preoccupation with Germany jeopardized the region's stated neutrality; moreover, Latin American states had an historic and understandable apprehension regarding U.S. military forces. Yet ultimately, delicate negotiations, a more benign U.S. image, and the good will Washington had built up over the years yielded positive results. To protect the Panama Canal—and if need be, fight the Axis Powers—governments from the Caribbean to the Southern Cone offered the use of their territory. In the process, the substance of "reciprocity" shifted from policies of economic fairness to those of diplomatic, material, and security support against external threats. Absent the Good Neighbor regime, such cooperation would have been scarcely imaginable. But as Britain's Foreign Office concluded in 1941, the framework of cooperation the Americas had developed during Roosevelt's tenure, coupled with Washington's own self-restraint, had given Latin Americans "a new faith in the United States"; this in turn, had "gone far to liquidate the legacy and suspicion left by a quarter of a century of intervention diplomacy."[12] Once the United States formally entered World War II, trade with Latin America provided a steady supply of natural resources toward the war effort, including manganese, oil, rubber, tungsten, and zinc; many Latin American states declared war on the Axis Powers after Japan's attack on Pearl Harbor, and all had done so by the war's end.

The Inter-American System

The devastation caused by the Second World War led statesmen to devote enormous energy toward constructing international institutions and other mechanisms that would preserve the peace. The United Nations, World Bank, International Monetary Fund (IMF), and General Agreement on Tariffs and Trade (which later became the World Trade Organization) were global instruments designed to address states' political differences and security concerns, fund post-war reconstruction and development projects, lend money to countries with balance of payment problems, and prevent the trade wars of the 1930s by facilitating a more open, liberal world economy. Two of these institution—the IMF and World Bank—would play critical roles in the 1980s and 1990s in helping Latin American states weather an international debt crisis and reshape their economic development policies. The post-war institution building efforts continued a pattern in international politics whereby at the conclusion of great, multi-state wars, major powers engineered significant changes in international order: Europe's Thirty Years' war produced the Peace of Westphalia and established the nation-state as the preeminent unit of international organization; the Napoleonic Wars produced the balance of power Concert of Europe system; and World War I led to the League of Nations.

Building upon the momentum and achievements generated by the inter-American conferences, Pan-American sentiments, and the Good Neighbor Policy, states in the Western Hemisphere developed their own regional cooperative arrangements too. The Rio Treaty of Reciprocal Assistance (1947) aimed to deter or repel external aggression by obligating each American state to assist another that had come under attack (this collective defense arrangement became the template for the North Atlantic Treaty Organization, NATO). The Treaty on Peaceful Settlements (1948) committed its signatories to resolve their disputes through arbitration or international law, not force. The Organization of American States, or OAS (1948), guaranteed its members' sovereignty, territorial integrity, and legal equality, and provided a forum for multilateral negotiations on matters of mutual concern. These three mechanisms constituted the Inter-American System. U.S. support was critical to its development, but in some respects, the role of Latin American states was even more important.

Even before World War II ended, post-war planning had begun. Yet, Washington officials were of two minds regarding where U.S.–Latin American relations might fit into a new world order, and within the State Department a cleavage emerged between those with a regionalist perspective, and those with a more universalist one. Under Secretary of State Sumner Welles suggested that a strong, liberal institutionalized inter-American system of cooperation "should be a cornerstone in the world structure of the future,"[13] while Secretary of State Cordell Hull believed it was imperative to create a powerful, global security institution to which any regional security arrangements would be subordinate. Welles' 1943 resignation (for personal reasons) fueled speculation that the universalist perspective had prevailed, and in 1944, the United States, Britain, China, France, and the Soviet Union met at Dumbarton Oaks and drew up preliminary plans for a global organization that seemed to bear this out: their proposal would permit regional arrangements, but deny them any autonomous enforcement powers. This option did not sit well with Latin American states. In their view, a better approach was to fashion autonomous, regional arrangements that—while compatible with a new world body—could secure their interests more effectively, promote hemispheric cooperation, and perpetuate the type of neighborly behavior by the regional hegemon they had come to value. Consequently, at the 1945 founding conference of the United Nations, Latin American delegations made their case, and with backing from the United States, ensured that Article 51 of the UN Charter would accommodate such arrangements.

Box 5.6 The Organization of American States and the UN Charter

As World War II wound down, Latin American states insisted on establishing a regional, multilateral organization to help govern hemispheric relations that would be recognized by—and made compatible with—the new United Nations. With Washington's support, the result was Article 51 of the UN Charter, which sanctioned creation of defensive, regional frameworks like the Organization of American States, and accorded them international legitimacy. Latin Americans consistently viewed the OAS as complementary, not contrary, to UN purposes, and they defended the organization against such charges.

> Nothing in the present Charter shall impair the inherent right of individual or collective self-defence if an armed attack occurs against a Member of the United Nations, until the Security Council has taken measures necessary to maintain international peace and security.

Measures taken by Members in the exercise of this right of self-defence shall be immediately reported to the Security Council and shall not in any way affect the authority and responsibility of the Security Council under the present Charter to take at any time such action as it deems necessary in order to maintain or restore international peace and security.

Article 51, UN Charter

If there is a United Nations, to which the twenty-one American republics belong, why keep in Washington an Organization of American States? This question sounds reasonable, at least superficially. It is asked mostly by people who know something about the U.N., but very little about the O.A.S.

There is nothing . . . in the provisions of the O.A.S. that is opposed to the theory or the practice of a universal order. And . . . there is nothing in the U.N. Charter which opposes regional arrangements.

"Within the United Nations, the Organization of American States is a regional agency:" So reads part of the very first article of the [OAS] Charter of Bogotá. It defines the position of the regional organization, within the framework of the U.N. It is brief, clear and sincere. There is nothing in the regional Charter which in any way might contravene the spirit or the letter of the U.N. Charter. The two juridical instruments usefully complement each other in the realization of their common work.

Luis Quintanilla (Mexican Ambassador to the OAS),
"The O.A.S. and the U.N.," *World Affairs* 115 (Fall, 1952): 81

The Rio Treaty, Treaty on Peaceful Settlements, and OAS formalized the Inter-American System. Although Latin American states lobbied hard for the inclusion of an economic development component—something akin to the Marshall Plan established for Europe's post-war reconstruction—formal economic programs would not come until the late 1950s and early 1960s, when the Inter-American Development Bank was created, and the Alliance for Progress was established to help finance the region's broader development needs. Despite the lack of an economic development component, by mid-century, the American republics had formalized a set of institutions to govern their relations, address the security needs of each state, provide machinery to resolve disputes peacefully, facilitate the multilateral pursuit of collective goals, and reaffirm that future hemispheric relations would be predicated on more liberal norms.

The Role of Individuals

What role did individuals play in the transformation of hemispheric relations? Individual leaders were important causal agents, although clearly less so in the early years. Woodrow Wilson may have had good intentions, but his moral certitude and conflicting beliefs led him to take actions that impeded the development of more cooperative relations. His non-recognition policy, for example, expanded the scope of U.S. intervention, since he often deployed U.S. forces to countries that he believed lacked a "legitimate" government able to safeguard U.S. citizens and investments. His missionary zeal to "redeem" U.S. neighbors by promoting democracy through realist means also denied Latin American states self-determination, diminished the prospects for a Pan-American pact, and wound up exacerbating anti-American sentiments.

Herbert Hoover actually did take U.S. policy in a new direction—something he seldom gets credit for. Unlike Wilson, Hoover had some prior experience with Latin America, both as U.S. Secretary of Commerce and as chairman of the Inter-American High Commission (a multilateral office created in 1915 to oversee development of uniform commercial regulations). Besides repudiating the Roosevelt Corollary and Woodrow Wilson's non-recognition policy, he laid plans to lift the military occupation of Haiti and refused to intervene in other locales—Cuba, the Dominican Republic, Nicaragua, Panama—that suffered economic and political instability. But Hoover worked under multiple constraints. His credibility in the region was tarnished by his partisan affiliation. He also failed to articulate an overarching policy that might capture the imagination of Latin American leaders, unite the continents, and induce greater regional cooperation.

Franklin Roosevelt formalized and built upon policies begun by his predecessor, thereby moving U.S. policy further away from its realist past. He resisted the temptation of direct military intervention in Bolivia and Mexico, despite pressure from some U.S. business interests, and it was Roosevelt who actually proposed the special 1936 Buenos Aires conference that produced the Protocol on Nonintervention and Consultative Pact. While each leader played an important, but different role in the gradual evolution of hemispheric affairs, factors beyond the individual level mattered too.

Systemic and Domestic Causes

Three systemic factors helped shift the course of hemispheric relations: the dramatic changes in the global balance of power produced by World War I, the failure of the post-war League of Nations system, and the growing ideological and strategic contests which produced the Cold War. First, World War I changed the global distribution of power in ways that undermined the logic for security-oriented interventions. Basically, it weakened the European powers significantly—which enhanced unipolarity within the Western Hemisphere— and thus reduced the need to "preempt" European encroachments in Latin America via U.S. intervention.

A second systemic cause for improved U.S.–Latin American relations was the League of Nations' failure to ensure security and curtail expansion by the Axis powers prior to World War II. In 1931, imperial Japan invaded Manchuria, a province of League member China, and established a puppet regime (Manchukuo) to rule by proxy. In 1935, Italy attacked and eventually took over Ethiopia (a League member), and in 1936, Hitler threatened the security of France (another League member) by remilitarizing the Rhineland in violation of the Versailles Treaty; the year before, he announced that Germany would no longer adhere to the Treaty's arms limitations, and would increase its army threefold to 300,000, plus construct an air force. These developments heightened tensions and fueled security concerns among many states. The League's inability to protect its members' security and curtail Axis expansion generated strong incentives for the United States to mend fences in Latin America, avoid the distractions of further regional intervention, and nurture a friendly neighborhood to enhance U.S. (and hemispheric) security.

A third systemic cause of more cooperative hemispheric relations was the growing U.S.-Soviet estrangement that became the Cold War—a topic we will examine more closely in Chapters 6, 7, and 8. With the end of World War II, the U.S.-Soviet alliance forged to defeat Hitler began to unravel. By 1947, intense hostility had developed between the communist Soviet Union and the capitalist-democratic United States, due to mutual mistrust, sharp ideological cleavages, Soviet expansion into Eastern Europe, and perceived communist advances in Greece. In March 1947, President Harry Truman vowed to "contain" the spread of Communism and protect weak states around the world from communist subversion. The brewing struggle between East and West held little interest for Latin American states in the late 1940s, but it was an important factor behind Washington's support for multilateral mechanisms like the Rio Treaty and Organization of American States, that could preserve hemispheric security in the face of potential communist encroachment and institutionalize inter-American cooperation.

Beyond the systemic level, there were domestic causes too. In large part, these stemmed from the deep economic problems generated by the Great Depression. The Depression itself was systemic: it undermined the global economy and affected all states within the international system. However, it also produced powerful domestic economic disturbances during the inter-war period that made U.S. intervention less practical politically and financially, and eventually drew the United States and many Latin American neighbors into closer economic relations. In the United States, the Depression curtailed public support for interventionist ventures and limited the government's financial resources to conduct them. More broadly, it focused U.S. leaders' attention squarely on their domestic problems: both Hoover and Roosevelt's preoccupation with domestic matters helped keep U.S. foreign policy on a short leash (in fact, in 1932 Hoover told Secretary of State Henry Stimson that he was "so absorbed with the domestic situation that [he could not] think very much now of foreign affairs").[14] Finally, the need for economic recovery led leaders in both Latin America and the United States to enter into reciprocal trade agreements that tightened economic relations between them.

Lessons

What lessons does the evolution of U.S.–Latin American relations provide? One that is important to both students and practitioners of international politics is that inter-state cooperation can be difficult to achieve under international anarchy, but it is not impossible. Because anarchy generates incentives for states to compete, mistrust, and suspect each other's motives, it constrains their willingness to cooperate. States, therefore, must *learn* to cooperate and one way to do so is by interacting repeatedly around a given set of policy issues or goals. The more they interact, the more opportunity there is to learn that the payoffs derived from mutual cooperation can be greater than from non-cooperation. The inter-American Conferences that began in 1889 gave Latin American states and their northern neighbor multiple opportunities to interact over issues like intervention, security, and respect for sovereignty. Initially, the gap between the two Americas on these subjects was wide, yet over time it narrowed, and by the mid-1930s, it finally closed. The pattern of cooperation that emerged under the Good Neighbor regime continued through the creation of the Inter-American System, and in the process, both Americas achieved important political objectives and realized joint gains. Although learning to cooperate can be hard, the benefits of cooperation are real.

A second lesson is that the development of more cooperative relations was not inevitable. It took diplomacy, hard work, innovation, and patience from both Americas—and at times, self-restraint by the United States—to live down the past, overcome suspicions, establish trust, and develop the informal and formal frameworks that could protect states' interests and facilitate even greater cooperation. A third lesson, then, is that persistence *matters* in international diplomacy. However, we should not equate diplomatic persistence with obstinacy. States that simply hold fast to their positions are unlikely to resolve their disputes no matter how long their diplomatic negotiations run. But when states pursue their goals persistently, yet display flexibility and compromise in how they are achieved, diplomacy stands a better chance of yielding mutually acceptable solutions to many common challenges.

A fourth lesson we can draw is a greater appreciation for the range of tools states have to advance their interests. Contrary to a pure realist perspective, force is not always the tool of choice. Sometimes states can achieve their goals more effectively by relying on such liberal instruments as international law, international institutions, and international regimes. Both circumstances and states' capabilities determine which tools are appropriate. Strong states that fear for their security are more likely to behave in a realist fashion, but less likely to do so when their security is more assured; U.S. policy toward Latin America exhibited each tendency before and after World War I changed the global distribution of power. By contrast, weak states that perceive threats from much stronger ones may be more inclined to adopt a liberal approach precisely because they lack the power to pursue an effective realist policy; throughout the evolution of hemispheric relations, Latin American's foreign policy toward the United States displayed this tendency.

Of the three components that comprised the Inter-American System, the Treaty on Peaceful Settlements proved to be the weakest link, and quickly became something of a relic. Although it called for the peaceful settlement of inter-state disputes, many Caribbean states never signed the pact; many other states signed with reservations (stipulating portions of the document they would and would not abide by); and seven states that signed the covenant never ratified it, including Argentina and the United States. Nevertheless, the framework of cooperation that was established by the mid-twentieth century reflected an important evolution in hemispheric relations. Although it did not eliminate all sources of tension or resolve all outstanding disputes, the American republics rightly celebrated this achievement. But once the Cold War set in, the Inter-American System did not always function as expected. The

Cold War introduced greater discord between the United States and Latin American governments regarding the nature of domestic political developments in the hemisphere and the degree to which they might reflect external communist threats. As we shall see in succeeding chapters, this was particularly true with respect to events in Guatemala, the Dominican Republic, Chile, Nicaragua, El Salvador, and Grenada. The lack of consensus on how to define or address these problems led to a decline in multilateralism, the return of U.S. unilateralism, and the resurgence of anti-American sentiments.

Study Questions

1. In the first decades of the twentieth century, how did Latin American states' approach to ordering hemispheric relations differ from that of the United States, and how would you explain this difference?
2. Despite its obvious advantages, inter-state cooperation can be difficult to achieve. Why? How would realists account for the relative lack of co-operative relations between the two Americas in the early twentieth century? How would liberals explain the eventual development of more cooperative relations?
3. Why did Latin American states strongly support the League of Nations while the United States did not? Why did the League eventually disappoint Latin American governments?
4. What was the Good Neighbor Policy and why was it adopted? How did it affect U.S.–Latin American relations, and in what ways, if any, did it differ from earlier U.S. policies toward Latin America?
5. What is an "international regime"? Why can regimes be useful in international politics? On what basis might the Good Neighbor Policy be considered an international regime?
6. What were the main components and chief objectives of the Inter-American System? In creating the Inter-American System, to what extent did the United States and its neighbors hold similar or competing objectives?
7. What insights do realist, liberal, and dependency perspectives offer into the evolution of inter-American relations in the first half of the twentieth century?
8. What are some lessons from the history of inter-American relations in the early twentieth century that might help the two Americas strengthen hemispheric relations today?

Selected Readings

Keohane, Robert O. *After Hegemony*, 56–63. Princeton: Princeton University Press, 1984.

Kurth, James R. "The Rise and Decline of the Inter-American System: A US View." In *Alternative to Intervention*, edited by Richard J. Bloomfield and Gregory F. Treverton, 27–46. Boulder: Lynne Rienner, 1990.

Mecham, J. Lloyd. *A Survey of United States-Latin American Relations*, 110–130, 156–176. New York: Houghton Mifflin, 1965.

Smith, Tony. "Woodrow Wilson and Democracy in Latin America." In Tony Smith, *America's Mission: The United States and the Worldwide Struggle for Democracy in the Twentieth Century*, 60–83. Princeton: Princeton University Press, 1994.

Wood, Bryce. "The Making of the Good Neighbor Policy." In *Neighborly Adversaries: Readings in U.S.–Latin American Relations*, edited by Michael LaRosa and Frank O. Mora, 105–112. Lanham, MD: Rowman & Littlefield, 1999.

Further Readings

Connell-Smith, Gordon. *The Inter-American System*. New York: Oxford University Press, 1966.

Desch, Michael C. *When the Third World Matters: Latin America and United States Grand Strategy*, ch. 2. Baltimore: Johns Hopkins University Press, 1993.

Quintanilla, Luis. "The O.A.S. and the U.N." *World Affairs* 115 (Fall, 1952): 81–83.

Tuchman, Barbara W. *The Zimmermann Telegram*. New York: Ballantine Books, 1985.

Wilson, Woodrow. "An Address to Congress on the Mexican Crisis (April 20, 1914)." In *Neighborly Adversaries: Readings in U.S.–Latin American Relations*, edited by Michael LaRosa and Frank O. Mora, 101–104. Lanham, MD: Rowman & Littlefield, 1999.

Wood, Bryce. *The Making of the Good Neighbor Policy*. New York: W. W. Norton, 1967.

Young, Oran R. *International Cooperation: Building Regimes for Natural Resources and the Environment*, 11–23. Ithaca: Cornell University Press, 1989.

Chronology: Hemispheric Relations through World War II

1902	Latin American states promote Drago Doctrine
1910–1917	Mexican Revolution
1911	Mexican dictator Porfirio Díaz falls
1912	Francisco Madero elected Mexican president; U.S. ambassador Henry Lane Wilson helps engineer Madero's downfall
1912	Woodrow Wilson elected U.S. president
1913	Madero assassinated; Victoriano Huerta assumes power
1914	U.S. signs Treaty of Bogotá, expresses regret for supporting Panama's secession from Colombia; U.S. occupies Veracruz and intervenes in Nicaragua
1914–1918	World War I
1915	U.S. intervenes in Haiti; Wilson proposes Pan-American pact
1916–1917	U.S. forces led by General John Pershing intervene in northern Mexico
1916	U.S. intervenes in Dominican Republic
1917	Germany seeks military alliance with Mexico via Zimmermann Telegram
1919	League of Nations created
1929	Stock market crash; Great Depression begins
1929–1932	Hoover administration begins gradual shift away from realist policies
1930	U.S. renounces Roosevelt Corollary via the Clark Memorandum
1932–1935	Chaco War between Bolivia and Paraguay
1932	FDR elected U.S. president; Good Neighbor Policy begins
1933	U.S. withdraws troops from Nicaragua; Washington signs Convention on the Rights and Duties of States, renouncing intervention by with caveats
1933–1945	Good Neighbor regime

1934	U.S. abrogates the Platt Amendment; Cuba obtains sovereignty
1936	U.S. signs (1) treaty with Panama, ending its protectorate status, (2) Protocol on Nonintervention, renouncing intervention without caveats, and (3) Consultative Pact
1937	Bolivia nationalizes assets of U.S. firm, Standard Oil
1938	Mexico nationalizes assets of British, Dutch, and U.S. oil firms
1939–1945	World War II
1947	Rio Treaty of Reciprocal Assistance signed; Treaty of Peaceful Settlements signed
1948	Organization of American States created

The Cold War, Part I   6

Figure 6.1 Cold War Standoff: U.S. and USSR Flags

With the end of World War II, the anti-Nazi alliance between the Soviet Union and the United States began to fray. By the time the American republics had created the Inter-American System in 1947–1948, intense hostilities had surfaced and a Cold War had developed between the world's two most powerful states. It was fueled by changes in the international structure and global distribution of power produced by World War II, Soviet expansion into Eastern Europe, ideological conflicts, misunderstandings, mutual suspicions, and security threats. Throughout the conflict, each superpower sought to protect itself against the other, developed powerful alliance systems for self-defense (NATO and the Warsaw Pact), and amassed formidable conventional and nuclear arsenals to preserve their security. The Cold War lasted four decades. It ended when Soviet hegemony over Eastern Europe collapsed in 1989, the Berlin Wall was torn down, and the division of Europe ceased. Initially, the Cold War carried less urgency for Latin American states than their northern neighbor, but in time, some Latin American governments displayed much greater concerns for communist, if not Soviet, expansion.

Because of its complexity, duration, and scope, over the next three chapters we will examine the Cold War's origins, manifestations, consequences, and effects on hemispheric relations from a number of angles. This chapter approaches the case more analytically than chronologically. Spanning multiple decades, it explores the causes of this prolonged conflict, the reasons why it stimulated renewed U.S. intervention, the ethical issues generated by interventionist policies, and the consequences intervention had for the Organization of American States. Chapters 7 and 8 adopt a more chronological approach. Chapter 7 examines Cold War milestones of the 1960s, including the Cuban Revolution, Cuban Missile Crisis, and Alliance for Progress. Chapter 8, meanwhile, covers a range of non-violent and violent Cold War challenges to U.S. hegemony that emerged from the late 1960s through the 1980s, and the corresponding American response. These challenges included a broad, diplomatic offensive mounted by regional powers, the socialist presidency of Chile's Salvador Allende, and the revolutions and revolutionary movements that erupted in Central America and the Caribbean.

In his 1961 inaugural address, John F. Kennedy described the Cold War—then 14 years old—as a long, twilight struggle between two powerful opponents. The description was apt, since throughout its duration the superpowers never engaged each other in direct military conflict, but instead, waged proxy battles in areas well beyond their borders. Like Africa, Asia, and the Middle East, Latin America became a setting for Cold War competition. The Cold War is significant to students of international and U.S.–Latin American relations on several fronts. While unipolarity still reigned within the Western Hemisphere, at the global level the Cold War created a rigid, bipolar international system composed of the Soviet Union and its allies and clients, and the United States and its allies and dependents. Cooperation between the two poles declined as mutual antagonisms and suspicions rose. The Cold War, therefore, brought the realist nature of international politics back into sharp focus. Its dynamics impeded collaboration on security issues within the Inter-American System, undermined the utility of the Organization of American States, revived U.S. intervention practices (which raised troubling political and ethical issues), and reinvigorated anti-American sentiments throughout the region.

Origins and Causes

To appreciate why the Cold War had such profound effects on U.S.–Latin American relations, we need to understand its origins, nature, and impact on strategic thinking. In terms of causality, factors at all three levels of analysis are relevant. At the systemic level, World War II dramatically altered the global distribution of power. It destroyed much of the war-making capacity and industrial infrastructure of the traditional great powers in Europe and Asia (Britain, France, Germany, Japan), and at the global level, created a bipolar system anchored by two powerful and mutually antagonistic states. Europe's devastation also produced a power vacuum that each state sought to fill to protect its interests, and in time, U.S.-Soviet competition spilled outside of Europe and affected international politics around the globe.

At the domestic level, the stark contrasts between a command economy and a capitalist one, a communist ideology and a democratic one, and a centralized, totalitarian political system and a pluralist, republican one both confused and appeared threatening to the "other side." Because of its closed society and state-controlled press, Soviet foreign policymaking was a highly secretive process that occurred within an opaque arena. Because of its open, pluralistic society and free press, U.S. foreign policymaking was much less secretive, more vulnerable to domestic political dynamics, and openly discussed or reported on in the media. Both the Soviet Union and United States found it hard to understand the other's system or accurately interpret its policy moves. The fact that each state's ideology defined the other as an enemy by default, made effective communication and mutual understanding even more difficult. These domestic-level differences helped aggravate the natural suspicions states harbor against each other under anarchic conditions, and promoted the type of dynamics common to a prisoner's dilemma.

At the individual level, leaders on both sides contributed to the breakdown of relations. Soviet Premiere Josef Stalin was a paranoid, ruthless dictator whose insecurities nurtured deep-seated mistrust of others, at home and abroad. The result was severe domestic repression, and a foreign policy that saw most Western states as enemies, distrusted the United Nations as a U.S. tool, and viewed many weak states close to Soviet borders as opportunities for expansion. Harry Truman was a straight talking, mid-western domestic politician who, after Franklin Roosevelt's death, assumed the presidency with little understanding of international relations and virtually no knowledge of the inner workings of FDR's foreign policy. As a foreign affairs novice, he readily accepted the cautions and anti-Soviet counsel of advisors like Admiral William Leahy (who, historian Daniel Yergin notes, was himself "suspicious of all foreigners"), and Ambassador Averell Harriman (who, Yergin observes, saw the Soviet Union as "a bully" on the world scene).[1] As the Democratic Party's new leader, Truman moved his party to the right and after his 1948 reelection, appointed strong anti-communists to high positions (Dean Acheson as Secretary of State; James Forrestal as Secretary of Defense). As president, he found it difficult to understand the Soviet Union's genuine security concerns or differentiate between such concerns and Moscow's more opportunistic expansionist ventures.

In short, the structure of the post-war international system, the security concerns it produced, and the two countries' sharp domestic-level differences created the potential for antagonism between the Soviet Union and United States. Any leader would have found this context hard to navigate. Stalin's paranoia and Truman's foreign policy inexperience complicated the task further. Each tended to suspect the other's motives and respond to his counterpart's policy moves in ways that ultimately bred more mistrust and hostility.

When the Truman administration established the Marshall Plan to help rebuild war-torn Europe and revitalize its capitalist economies, Stalin viewed this project as a deliberate attempt to weaken the Soviet Union's own sphere of influence in Eastern Europe. When Czechoslovakia tried to participate, he clamped down in Eastern Europe and the Czech Communist Party seized control of the state. In turn, Soviet expansion into Eastern Europe alarmed U.S. leaders. Yet, consolidating control over the region was a logical defensive step, since Russia, then the Soviet Union, had been invaded three times through Eastern Europe since the nineteenth century. It also was not entirely dissimilar to earlier U.S. security concerns in the Caribbean and Central America, and the actions the United States had taken to address them. From a realist perspective, Stalin's early foreign policy appears more moderate and defensive, than merely expansionist. But Americans found it hard to view Soviet actions and security concerns in that light; to Truman and other U.S. officials, Stalin's moves reflected only Soviet imperialist ambitions. Fear of communist expansion is one reason the United States developed the anti-Soviet military alliance, NATO, in 1949—a prudent defensive precaution that in classic security dilemma fashion

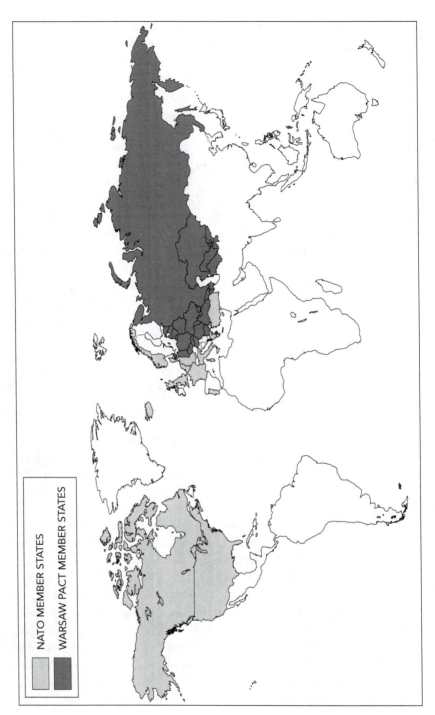

NATO MEMBER STATES

WARSAW PACT MEMBER STATES

Figure 6.2 Cold War Alliances, c.1955

prompted the Soviets to respond with their own Warsaw Pact alliance six years later. In a relatively brief time span, the U.S.-Soviet alliance had collapsed, mutual hostility emerged, mutual insecurity deepened, and rigid bipolarity had set in.

The Truman Doctrine and Containment

Throughout the Cold War, the United States sought to prevent the spread of Communism and Soviet power. Toward this end, it developed an overarching moral and ideological rationale to justify counter-measures against Soviet expansion. This rationale grew directly out of post-World War II problems in Greece and Turkey, where Britain had exercised a degree of influence before the war that it could not maintain afterward. When the Greek civil war resurfaced in 1946—and the communist side appeared to gain the upper hand— the United States faced a dilemma. A communist victory in Greece could threaten Turkey too. With Britain unable to play its traditional role, should Washington permit a Middle East power vacuum that could entice the Soviets to move in? Or should it provide aid to non-communist forces to ensure that both Greece and Turkey remained non-communist?

Ultimately, Truman decided to move into the Middle East, and based on advice from a key Republican senator, Arthur Vandenberg, he sold the decision to Congress and the public as a critical turning point in world politics. In a major 1947 foreign policy speech, Truman proclaimed that America faced a crisis of historic proportions, one in which the United States must shoulder the responsibility of protecting free people anywhere in the world against communist aggression. The concept of a global campaign against Communism in defense of freedom became the *Truman Doctrine*. Although its ideology was expressly anti-communist, in one sense the Truman Doctrine echoed elements of the 1823 Monroe Doctrine, but on a global, not regional level. The latter had aimed to prevent powerful European states from imposing their monarchical political system on the weak, newly independent American republics; the former sought to prevent the Soviet Union from imposing its communist political system on weaker, non-communist states around the world.

Closely related to the Truman Doctrine was the strategic policy of *containment*. In broad terms, containment sought to limit the spread of Communism and Soviet influence, and to promote more liberal economic and political systems around the globe. Initially formulated by State Department officer George Kennan in 1947, the containment policy was revised in April 1950, through a secret National Security Council document, NSC-68. Its

Box 6.1 The Truman Doctrine (1947)

Mr. President, Mr. Speaker, Members of the Congress of the United States. The gravity of the situation which confronts the world today necessitates my appearance before a joint session of the Congress. The foreign policy and the national security of this country are involved. One aspect of the present situation, which I wish to present to you at this time for your consideration and decision concerns Greece . . .

The United States has received from the Greek Government an urgent appeal for financial and economic assistance. Preliminary reports from the American Economic Mission now in Greece and reports from the American Ambassador in Greece corroborate the statement of the Greek Government that assistance is imperative if Greece is to survive as a free nation . . .

The very existence of the Greek state is today threatened by the terrorist activities of several thousand armed men, led by communists, who defy the Government's authority at a number of points . . . the Greek Government is unable to cope with the situation . . . Greece must have assistance if it is to become a self-supporting and self-respecting democracy. The United States must supply that assistance . . . There is no other country to which democratic Greece can turn.

One of the primary objectives of the foreign policy of the United States is the creation of conditions in which we and other nations will be able to work out a way of life free from coercion. This was a fundamental issue in the war with Germany and Japan . . .

To insure the peaceful development of nations, free from coercion, the United States has taken a leading part in establishing the United Nations . . . We shall not realize our objectives, however, unless we are willing to help free peoples to maintain their free institutions and their national integrity against aggressive movements that seek to impose upon them totalitarian regimes. This is no more than a frank recognition that totalitarian regimes imposed on free peoples, by direct or indirect aggression, undermine the foundations of international peace and hence the security of the United States . . .

At the present moment in the world history nearly every nation must choose between alternative ways of life. The choice is too often not a free one. One way of life is based upon the will of the majority and is distinguished by free institutions, representing government, free elections, guarantees of individual liberty, freedom of speech and religion, and freedom from political repression. The second way of life is based upon the will of the minority forcibly imposed upon the majority. It relies on terror and oppression, a controlled press and radio, fixed elections, and the suppression of personal freedoms.

I believe that it must be the policy of the United States to support free peoples who are resisting attempted subjugation by armed minorities or by outside pressures. I believe that we must assist peoples to work out their own destinies in their own way . . . The seeds of totalitarian regimes are nurtured by misery and want. They spread and grow in the evil soil of poverty and strife. They reach their full growth when the hope of a people for a better life has died. We must keep that hope alive.

The free peoples of the world look to us for support in maintaining their freedoms. If we falter in our leadership, we may endanger the peace of the world—and we shall surely endanger the welfare of our own Nation. Great responsibilities have been placed upon us by the swift movement of events. I am confident that the Congress will face these responsibilities squarely.

Harry S. Truman, Special Message to Congress, March 12, 1947

analysis began by discussing recent changes in the global balance of power that had placed the West at a strategic disadvantage, such as the fall of China to communist forces in 1949, and the Soviets' development of an atomic bomb the same year. It painted a terrifying view of the global, monolithic communist threat: Moscow's goal was nothing less than to "impose its absolute authority over the rest of the world"; it would pursue this goal through means violent or otherwise; its quest for world domination threatened not just the United States, but "civilization itself"; and it was likely to launch a direct military attack against the United States within four to five years. In this stark, zero-sum scenario the fundamental antagonisms between Communism and liberal, capitalist democracy excluded the possibility of compromise. To meet this challenge, NSC-68 called for an enormous increase in U.S. defense spending and the adoption of a "perimeter defense" approach: anywhere that Communism surfaced was evidence of Soviet expansion and a strategic concern to the United States. In Asia, the perimeter defense concept would lead to U.S. military engagement in Vietnam, and in Latin America, to a series of direct and indirect interventions from the 1950s through the 1980s.

As Communism spread beyond Soviet borders, the *domino theory* gained currency in U.S. policymaking circles. This theory held that if one country became communist, its surrounding neighbors were likely to follow, like falling dominoes. The 1949 communist triumph in China, followed in 1950 by North Korea's communist invasion of South Korea, encouraged this line of thinking. Once American leaders accepted the domino theory's underlying premises, stopping the spread of Communism assumed unparalleled priority. Some observers have argued that the United States misread aspects of the Cold War and consequently exaggerated the extent of the communist threat; in hindsight, there is evidence to support this position. But as the Cold War developed and deepened, the dangers seemed real: the Soviets did display open hostility toward the West; their ideology not only considered Western economic and political systems as antithetical to Soviet interests, but saw their destruction as the natural progression of history. Consequently, those charged with protecting U.S. security often accepted the premises of a Soviet-controlled, monolithic communist conspiracy without much question, perceived extraordinary security threats without much supporting evidence, and fashioned U.S. policy toward Latin America and elsewhere accordingly.

In 1950, for example, George Kennan filed a State Department report detailing his first field trip to Latin America and assessing its political situation. He found no "serious likelihood that the communists might . . . come to power by majority opinion" in any country there except perhaps Guatemala, and that even if they did, "they would hardly be a serious military threat to the hemisphere"; still, he maintained, "this gives us no justification for complacency about communist activities in this hemisphere." Because Latin America's democratic institutions were weak (or sometimes nonexistent), Kennan observed, to counter the communist threat the United States would need to support "harsh governmental measures of repression . . . from regimes whose origins and methods would not stand the test of American concepts of democratic procedures."[2] Although Kennan had no direct role in formulating U.S. policy toward Latin America, his 1950 policy prescription—to support anti-communist dictatorships rather than countenance Latin American governments that were, or could possibly become, communist—informed U.S. policy for decades to come, and intervening to preempt communist expansion became standard policy practice. Inevitably, how the Western Hemisphere's hegemon prosecuted the Cold War left its imprint on hemispheric relations.

Intervention and the Organization of American States

Strong states tend to benefit from the existing international order (and often have helped create it). Consequently, most great powers also are status quo powers. They have a vested interest in preserving existing arrangements, and can face powerful incentives to intervene in regions where they seem threatened. During the early nineteenth century, Austria and Prussia intervened in Italy and Spain's internal affairs to crush liberal insurrections that threatened to de-legitimize Europe's status quo practice of monarchical rule. Another example occurred during the ancient Greeks' Peloponnesian War. The island city-state of Melos requested that Athens respect its neutrality, but the Athenians refused. A Melos subordinate to Athenian authority, they explained, would demonstrate Athens' continued status as the dominant regional power, but a neutral Melos would challenge it and embolden others to do the same. "The strong do what they will," the Athenians forewarned the Melians, "while the weak do what they must." Thus, if Melos would not willingly become a vassal state, Athens vowed to conquer Melos, and enslave and decimate its people. In the end, Athens made good on its threat to intervene, and destroyed Melos in its drive to preserve the status quo.

During the Cold War, the United Sates believed that Soviet and communist expansion threatened the Western Hemisphere's status quo—a hegemonic America whose economic and political systems faced no viable ideological competitors. Like other great powers, the United States grew sensitive to any developments that might change the existing arrangement, and at times, it addressed cases of real and perceived regional communist expansion through unilateral interventions.

Guatemala, 1954

In 1954, the United States overthrew the democratically elected government of Guatemala in the first of a series of containment interventions. To effect regime change, Washington used a proxy force of Guatemalan exiles trained and equipped by the CIA. This indirect intervention occurred against the backdrop of threats to U.S. economic interests, growing concern over communist advancements, and the implementation of NSC-68's perimeter defense model.

Politically, Guatemala had long suffered dictatorial rule. Economically, it was uniquely dependent upon the U.S.-owned, Boston-based, United Fruit Company (UFCO), which produced bananas and began its Guatemala

Figure 6.3 U.S. Interventions in Latin America During the Cold War

operations in the late nineteenth century. In time, UFCO became the country's largest employer and landowner (over one-half million acres, 85 percent of which was uncultivated); it controlled Guatemala's railway system, principal port, and postal service (from 1930 onward); it also developed a close relationship with the dictatorship of General Jorge Ubico. In exchange for its political support, the regime provided UFCO enormous tax breaks, allowed it to import production goods and material duty-free, and guaranteed the company low-waged labor (capped by Ubico at 50 cents per day). UFCO's political ties also stretched into the U.S. government. During the Eisenhower administration, both the Secretary of State and the Director of Central Intelligence (John Foster Dulles and Allen Dulles) had worked for the Boston law firm that drafted UFCO's contracts with the Guatemalan government; moreover, Allen Dulles held stock in the company, as did other U.S. officials like UN Ambassador Henry Cabot Lodge, Jr., and Commerce Secretary Sinclair Weeks.

In 1944, a coalition of university students, middle-class businessmen, and junior military officers revolted against Ubico, toppled the dictatorship, and ushered in a democratic period of economic and political reforms, led by presidents Juan José Arévalo (elected in 1945) and Jacobo Árbenz (elected in 1950). The Arévalo government banned the insignificant Communist Party, eradicated forced labor, introduced collective bargaining, constructed new clinics, hospitals, and schools, instituted social security and housing programs, and pushed a moderate land reform project. The Árbenz government lifted the ban on the tiny Communist Party and expanded the land reform program dramatically. Under the Agrarian Reform Law of 1952, the state expropriated large tracts of unused land—including 1,700 acres that belonged to the president's family—and redistributed it to poor farmers. More than 100,000 families received property. As Guatemala's largest landowner, United Fruit became a prime target of the agrarian reform law (under which it saw 71 percent of its land holdings expropriated), and logically, a strong opponent. Negotiations on adequate compensation quickly reached an impasse: for tax purposes, UFCO had valued its land at $3 per acre; a government offer to compensate the firm on this basis led the U.S. State Department (acting on United Fruit's behalf) to revise the assessment substantially upward to $75 per acre, and stalemate ensued.

Although UFCO's banana crops had no strategic value (unlike, say, copper or oil), the company's appeals to Washington for help melded with Washington's own concerns over Communism. Guatemala received no aid from the Soviet Union, and its Communist Party was small and ineffective. Árbenz's cabinet did not contain any communists nor was the president himself a communist; however, some presidential advisors on labor and land reform issues were. Communists also occupied posts in organized labor and parts of the state bureaucracy, and held four seats in the legislature. As for the Soviet Union, its involvement was scant, notes political scientist Wayne Smith: it "provided neither economic nor military aid, did not send advisers, nor did it even bother to set up a Soviet mission" in Guatemala.[3]

The evidence of a communist take-over in Guatemala, then, was meager, but in the Cold War context, it was sufficient to trigger a U.S. containment response. Under Operation Success, the CIA trained and equipped a small group of Guatemalan exiles in Honduras and Nicaragua, and used clandestine radio broadcasts and air-dropped leaflets to insinuate distrust within the military, inflame popular opinion against the government, and raise calls for Árbenz to resign. In June 1954, the exiles—led by Colonel Carlos Castillo Armas—entered Guatemala from Honduras, engaged Guatemalan forces loyal to the president, and toppled the government. Árbenz's demise brought Castillo Armas to power, ended Guatemala's economic, political, and land reforms, and led to decades of staunch anti-communist, but harsh military rule. By the mid-1990s, more than 200,000 Guatemalans had been killed in the government's anti-communist campaigns against subversives.

Cuba, 1961

In 1961, the United States again intervened indirectly—this time unsuccessfully—in an effort to overthrow the new communist government in Cuba led by Fidel Castro. As we shall see in Chapter 7, Cuba's 1959 revolution had ousted dictator Fulgencio Batista, a U.S. ally, and its 1960 alliance with the Soviet Union greatly alarmed U.S. leaders. As bilateral relations deteriorated, the United States began imposing trade restrictions and Cuba began nationalizing U.S. commercial operations. More trade restrictions brought more nationalizations, including U.S. banks, oil companies, and telecommunications firms. In 1960, President Dwight Eisenhower authorized the Central Intelligence Agency to develop a plan to combat the communist advance in Cuba. In a page straight from the Guatemalan playbook, the CIA trained and equipped a force of Cuban exiles to invade the island at the Bay of Pigs, depose Castro, and reestablish a non-communist government. In 1961, newly elected President John Kennedy authorized the agency to put its plan into action.

Unlike Guatemala, however, the CIA's Cuba operation failed catastrophically. Castro's military defeated the exile forces decisively (capturing over 1,000), and won an enormous propaganda victory against the United Sates. Although Washington developed other projects to eliminate Castro and limit Cuba's international influence, the Bay of Pigs was the only intervention whose explicit, immediate goal was the overthrow of Cuba's government. As explained more fully in Chapter 7, its failure helped precipitate the 1962 Cuban Missile Crisis (whose resolution ultimately helped the island's communist government consolidate power), and led the United States to adopt an even more aggressive stance toward regional developments that conceivably might produce "another Cuba."

The Dominican Republic, 1965

Four years after the Bay of Pigs, the United States deployed 22,000 troops to the Dominican Republic, where it feared the collapse of political order had opened the door to a communist take-over. Following the 1961 assassination of rightwing dictator, Rafael Trujillo, Juan Bosch, a left-of-center opposition leader, was elected president in December 1962 (the first democratically elected in over three decades). Deep political polarization followed. Bosch took office in February 1963, and his public policies (including some land reform) quickly energized critics and center-right opponents. Just seven months into his term, Bosch was deposed by a military coup and fled to Puerto Rico; meanwhile, the military installed a civilian Triumvirate that in turn, abolished the Dominican Constitution. In April 1965, a faction within the military rebelled against the Triumvirate, demanding both a return to constitutional rule and Bosch's reinstatement. Within the Dominican military, a brief civil war erupted between those elements that had deposed the elected president and those that demanded his return. U.S. officials, meanwhile, feared that the Dominican situation would ultimately yield a Cuba-style regime.

Although there was little reliable evidence to support this scenario, U.S. leaders believed that communists had infiltrated the pro-Bosch movement, and that Bosch himself was either sympathetic or indifferent to their influence.[4] For his part, President Lyndon Johnson resolved to act decisively. "I am not willing to let this island go to Castro," he told an aide. "How can we send troops 10,000 miles [to fight communists in Vietnam] and let Castro take over right under our nose?"[5] Such thinking led Johnson to approve direct military intervention, which restored a measure of political order, brought Joaquin Balaguer to power (a protégé of former dictator Rafael Trujillo), and assuaged U.S. concerns that the Dominican Republic might enter the communist orbit. This overt intervention badly damaged America's image in the region. In special meetings of the Organization of American States, Latin American delegates sharply criticized their neighbor's actions. Despite opposition from Chile, Mexico, Peru, and Uruguay, the OAS ultimately approved a U.S. proposal to replace North American troops with an Inter-American peacekeeping force to maintain order in the run-up to Balaguer's election. To some Latin American states, Washington seemed to have secured a retroactive endorsement of the invasion, which, notes Chilean diplomat Heraldo Muñoz, "legitimized its unilateral policies but at the cost of delegitimizing the OAS."[6]

Subsequent Interventions

As the Cold War stretched on, periodic U.S. interventions into Latin America continued. In Brazil, Washington signaled its support for a 1964 military coup against the leftist, constitutional government of President Joào Goulart; 21 years of military dictatorship followed. In Bolivia, the United States dispatched CIA operatives and Special Forces personnel to advise, equip, and train Bolivian troops seeking to capture Ernesto "Che" Guevara—the famed Argentine revolutionary and Castro collaborator who had traveled to Bolivia specifically to raise a guerrilla militia and ignite a Marxist revolution similar to Cuba's. The intervention succeeded, and in October 1967, Guevara was captured and executed. In Chile, the United States intervened through the CIA—first in a failed attempt to prevent the 1970 election of socialist Salvador Allende as president (whose platform called for nationalizing key economic sectors and foreign firms, plus extensive land reform)— then in another failed effort to keep Allende from assuming power, and finally (and successfully) to facilitate his removal from office. The 1973 coup that deposed Allende (examined more closely in Chapter 8) led to a brutal 18-year dictatorship headed by General Augusto Pinochet. In the Caribbean state of Grenada, a 1983 U.S. military invasion removed a radical, leftist leadership that itself had overthrown a pro-Marxist, revolutionary regime, and in Nicaragua, the United States intervened throughout most of the 1980s through a proxy military force (the CIA-created *contra* guerrillas), in a failed bid to topple the revolutionary Sandinista government.

These interventions ran counter to the fundamental principles of the Organization of American States and Inter-American System: nonintervention and respect for states' sovereignty. In prosecuting the Cold War, the United States did not deliberately set out to undermine the regional arrangements it helped create, but its policies in Latin America played an important role in this outcome.

The Organization of American States

Although the Cold War became a key lens through which Washington viewed world politics and developments in Latin America, the two Americas did not always share the same level of concern regarding the communist threat. This divergence unfolded at both the global and regional levels, and in time, bred increasing difficulties for the Organization of American States.

After North Korean communists invaded South Korea in 1950, for example, the United States secured a UN Security Council resolution that authorized member states to protect South Korea's sovereignty through a multilateral force that would fight under the UN flag. The Organization of American States resolved to support the UN decision, yet OAS members felt little threat from events in Korea, and Bolivia, Brazil, Chile, Mexico, Peru, and Uruguay all rebuffed U.S. requests to join the Korean campaign. Only Colombia provided any boots on the ground (in hopes of obtaining U.S. economic aid), and its contribution was merely a token force. At the global level, then, divergent perceptions of the communist threat worked to separate Latin American states from their neighbor; at the regional level, they often divided the two Americas more forcefully.

The problems of threat perception emerged early on. In 1954, the United States had looked at Jacobo Árbenz's Guatemala and saw a government that was abandoning democratic principles and pursuing leftist, anti-capitalist economic policies—a government that if not communist itself, was at least tolerant of communism. Viewed through the lens of NSC-68, Washington traced this communist threat directly back to the Soviet Union, and defined Guatemala's situation as a case of external threat. Latin American states perceived something different. They saw a government that sought to be more democratic by allowing even the tiny Communist Party to have its say, and a sovereign state whose reformist policies aimed to address historic problems of inequality, poverty, and underdevelopment—problems whose roots had little to do with Moscow. These differences played out dramatically at the tenth Inter-American Conference held in Caracas in March 1954.

U.S. Secretary of State Allen Dulles had traveled to Caracas seeking an OAS resolution that would declare Communism an external threat to hemispheric security, and permit multilateral action against Guatemala under the terms of the Rio Treaty. But Latin American states displayed little interest in Dulles' proposal, and initially, only six states—all dictatorships—supported it. After considerable cajoling and veiled threats of economic and political reprisals, Dulles finally obtained a watered-down resolution that made no mention of Guatemala, did not commit OAS members to act collectively against it, and called only for future consultations "to consider the adoption of appropriate action in accordance with existing treaties." This vague statement passed on a 17–1 vote (Guatemala voted nay, Argentina and Mexico both abstained). Unsatisfied with these results, the United States turned to unilateral action and deposed the Árbenz government.

Similarly, in 1965 the United States looked at the Dominican Republic and saw a country about to go communist. Most Latin Americans, however, saw a country in the throes of its own domestic political problems; neither the Dominicans' problems nor their politics seemed to have much to do with Communism or Moscow. After the U.S. invasion, they had reluctantly agreed to establish a multilateral peacekeeping force, but many felt Washington had betrayed the principle of nonintervention, and manipulated the OAS into endorsing its intervention retroactively. By the 1970s, U.S.–Latin American estrangement had deepened. When Chileans elected socialist Salvador Allende as their president, the United States did not even try to address its concerns over communist encroachment through the OAS, and in the 1980s, it bypassed the organization completely to confront perceived communist threats in Grenada and Nicaragua.

In short, as the Cold War progressed, the Organization of American States grew increasingly irrelevant to the region's major security issues. In the 1970s and 1980s, it proved ineffective in resolving Central America's political problems (revolution in Nicaragua, civil war in El Salvador, and U.S. intervention in the region), and played no role in the 1983 U.S.-led invasion of Grenada. Moreover, during this period, Latin Americans themselves began to work outside the OAS through arrangements that deliberately excluded the United States. In the 1980s, Colombia, Mexico, Panama, and Venezuela tried to broker peace in Central America diplomatically (the Contadora Group); when this effort failed, the presidents of the Central American republics (the Esquipulas Group) picked up and completed the task in 1989, largely through the efforts of Costa Rican president Óscar Árias. By 1990, the OAS seemed to be in tatters and effective multilateral cooperation on regional security matters had virtually ceased.

Were U.S. actions primarily responsible for this development, or were Latin Americans' actions more to blame? Actually, the root causes went deeper than the actions of either side. They lay in the different visions and expectations the Organization of American States' founding members held at its creation.

The United States had supported Latin American desires to create the Inter-American System for reasons that included but transcended hemispheric relations. What Washington wanted most in the late 1940s, was a regional framework that would promote hemispheric unity in the face of a frightening Soviet Cold War challenge, and provide strong diplomatic support for U.S. initiatives in the new United Nations. What Latin American states wanted most was an arrangement that would bind the United States to the principles of nonintervention and respect for states' sovereignty. For Latin America, the system's security focus was intra-hemispheric, and designed primarily to curtail U.S. intervention; for the United States, it was extra-hemispheric, and designed principally to prevent intervention from abroad. These divergent visions and expectations ensured that the OAS and broader Inter-American System would not always function as their creators had envisioned.

Why did Intervention Return?

Cold War interventions badly damaged U.S.–Latin American relations. But aside from a U.S. determination to preserve the hemispheric status quo, how else might we analyze and explain the revival of interventionist practices?

A realist approach would identify pressing U.S. security concerns under anarchic conditions as the overriding factor. Just as earlier U.S. interventions aimed to counter the threat of European encroachment into the Western Hemisphere, so did U.S. Cold War interventions seek to preempt the threat of Soviet expansion into the region. In both instances, Washington acted in self-defense to prevent strong states from exercising power in the Americas. A liberal approach might suggest that the institutional framework developed to prohibit intervention—whose efficacy rested on a presumed harmony of interests between the American republics—had failed to work precisely because these states did not share the same interests in curbing communist expansion. Just as a house built on crumbling foundations inevitably slides into disrepair, so Latin Americans' reluctance to embrace what Washington defined as an external communist threat, incentivized the United States to act unilaterally. A dependency approach would assert that the United States intervened presumably at the behest of domestic economic commercial interests and primarily to defend its regional economic interests and maintain its economic dominance of Latin American states.

Beyond these theoretical approaches, historian Michael Grow offers a different explanation based on the importance of international credibility and domestic political calculations. In a study of eight U.S. Cold War interventions in the Western Hemisphere, Grow suggests that at the international level, the United States feared that its own credibility as a superpower—and that of its anti-communist alliances in Asia, Europe, and Latin America—would be damaged without aggressive, effective action against perceived communist expansion in the Western Hemisphere. A passive response or acceptance of communist advances in Chile, Cuba, the Dominican Republic, Grenada, or Guatemala, would "create a perception of U.S. weakness in the eyes of the international community, with potentially serious long-range consequences for the nation's security."[7] At the domestic level, U.S. presidents felt compelled to intervene for partisan gains or other political reasons. Thus, President Eisenhower—who had criticized Truman for "losing" China to the communists and faced mid-term elections in November 1954—chose to intervene in Guatemala in June. Kennedy, who during the campaign had criticized Eisenhower for "losing" Cuba, felt compelled to authorize intervention at the Bay of Pigs. Johnson, meanwhile, approved the Dominican Republic invasion against a potential Castro-style regime to protect his left-of-center Great Society agenda from sabotage by conservative lawmakers in Congress, and so on.

None of these explanations, however, is entirely convincing, and some exhibit serious shortcomings. A realist argument captures the case of Cuba, where the United States' intervention targeted a government that had become a genuine adversary and a military and political ally of its mortal enemy. But it does not provide an adequate explanation for U.S. interventions in Guatemala, the Dominican Republic, or Chile—countries that had no formal alliance with the Soviet Union and where Soviet involvement in their domestic politics was minimal or nonexistent. Nor can it explain why no U.S. containment interventions occurred in countries that *did* have more substantial relations with the Soviet Union during the Cold War, such as Peru (where in the 1970s the reformist but anti-communist government of General Juan Velasco Alvarado developed extensive military relations with Moscow, purchased Soviet tanks, fighter planes, and helicopters, and hosted hundreds of Soviet military trainers).[8] In short, a realist account is not sufficiently robust, because it leaves too many issues unexplained. A liberal argument fares better, but ultimately displays the same deficiencies: it explains why the United States intervened in some cases of perceived and real communist expansion (Guatemala, the Dominican Republic, Cuba, etc.), but not why it failed to do so in other cases where a strong Soviet presence was evident (Peru).

A dependency argument would seem to have bearing on the Guatemalan, Cuban, and Chilean cases, where U.S. assets faced the threat of nationalization. But the central thrust of a dependency account—that intervention was adopted primarily to protect America's regional economic interests—is problematic. In Guatemala, for example, just weeks after the coup that deposed President Árbenz, the U.S. government took anti-trust action against the very firm (United Fruit Company) that dependency suggests its foreign policy was designed to protect; ultimately, this action broke up UFCO's Central American holdings. And in Chile, Washington continued to support the post-coup, Pinochet dictatorship even after it refused to rescind the nationalization of U.S. copper firms. Moreover, a dependency argument cannot account for the interventions in the Dominican Republic or Grenada—where U.S. investments were relatively small and at any rate, not threatened with nationalization—nor can it explain the lack of intervention in countries like Bolivia and Peru, where important U.S. headquartered or U.S.-owned companies in the tin, copper, and telecommunications sectors were nationalized in 1952 and the 1970s, respectively. Grow's credibility and domestic politics account, meanwhile, shares some of the same problems that realist, liberal, and dependency approaches exhibit.

If such arguments cannot fully explain the return of intervention, what does? Some scholars suggest that ideology provides a better explanation; specifically, the anti-communist ideology articulated first in the 1947 Truman Doctrine, then formalized as U.S. containment policy in the 1950 NSC-68. In a detailed, multi-case study of U.S. interventions during the Cold War years (including interventions in Latin America), political scientist Stephen Krasner found no correlation between U.S. investments, and countries where the United States intervened overtly or covertly. Indeed, the common threads connecting these cases were political and ideological, not economic. Put simply, "The United States intervened when central decision-makers perceived the imminent danger of a communist takeover"—a perception triggered more by the presence of communist ideology in these countries than by actual Soviet agents or strong communist parties.[9] Harvard political scientist Jorge Domínguez agrees:

> [T]he United States deployed military force or otherwise sought to overthrow a Latin American government whenever it felt ideologically threatened by the prospects of communism in a Latin American country, and only then . . . [but] did not engage in such actions, even when other Latin American governments acted in ways seriously adverse to U.S. interests, if there was no ideological threat of communism.[10]

No doubt, elements of all these explanations above had some bearing on political outcomes. But whatever its ultimate cause, the return of U.S. intervention rekindled anti-Americanism and sharply degraded the pattern of cooperative relations American states had worked hard to create. Both the justifications for, and consequences of, these interventions raise important moral issues concerning this type of international politics.

Judging the Ethics of Intervention

Nonintervention and respect for state sovereignty are important norms in international politics. They provide a modicum of global order that helps offset the disorder anarchy generates, and their violation increases the likelihood of disorder and conflict between states. The prohibitions on intervention enshrined in international law and organizations have not stopped this practice, and though states typically intervene for reasons of self-interest, they often justify their actions in moral and ethical terms. The nineteenth-century European imperialists justified their interventions on the basis of bringing civilization to backward peoples (the "white man's burden"). The U.S. ideology of manifest destiny shared these high-sounding but self-serving themes. From the time of the Mexican-American War through the Wilson administration, the United States partly explained its incursions into the Caribbean, Central America, Mexico, and the Philippines in a similar vein to the Europeans. During the Cold War, Cuba justified its interventions in the Dominican Republic, Nicaragua, Panama, and Venezuela on the grounds that it sought to liberate the people of those countries from repressive, bourgeois rule and exploitation; the United States, meanwhile, justified its interventions on the basis that it was protecting the free people of the Americas from the horrors of totalitarian, communist domination.

Despite such claims to the moral high ground, all interventions violate the norm of nonintervention; but not all interventions are the same. Some can be more ethically just than others. How might we distinguish between such cases?

On this point, the traditional international relations theories do not provide much guidance. Realism sees little role for ethics in international politics. For realists, anarchy impedes the development of a strong international consensus on ethics or a robust international society in which shared norms define its members' rights and duties. Anarchy also requires states to prioritize their security and can impel them to act in ways deemed unjust in domestic settings. Liberalism sees more space for ethics in international politics. For liberals, anarchy is real, but less intense and isolating than realists suggest. Because cultural, diplomatic, economic, and political ties help bind states together, many liberals believe that states comprise a rudimentary global society in which at least some shared ethical norms influence its members' behavior. Like realism, however, liberalism provides little purchase on how to distinguish the ethical integrity of one intervention from another. The problem of differentiation, therefore, remains.

Political philosophy offers one way to approach this issue. In his 1977 book, *Just and Unjust Wars*, theorist Michael Walzer outlined several scenarios in which states that had not suffered direct aggression might violate the nonintervention norm in ways that still remain ethically just. One possibility is a "preemptive intervention," wherein one state intervenes in another because it faces a clear, imminent threat to its own security, sovereignty, or territorial integrity. If the threatened state does not act first, it will not have a chance to act later. By this criterion, Israel's 1967 attack on Egypt (which had mobilized its own troops along the Israeli border in preparation for an attack) would be justified, but the 2003 U.S. attack on Saddam Hussein's Iraq (which posed no immediate threat to the United States) would not. In other words, the clearer and more imminent the threat, the stronger the ethical justification for the intervention; since the converse is also true, many interventions undoubtedly lack the ethical integrity required for a truly just preemptive intervention.

A second scenario that might bend the rule is a "balancing intervention." If a prior intervention by one state has denied the citizens of another their right of self-determination, a second intervention by another state could be justified to enable those people to reclaim their self-determination rights. During the Cold War, the United States often explained its incursions into other states' domestic affairs along these lines (some prior Soviet meddling required a U.S. balancing intervention to ensure Latin Americans retained their right to reject Communism). This exception to the nonintervention rule also carries two important caveats. Balancing interventions are ethically just only in the face of a clear, prior intervention, and only so far as they counterbalance that prior intervention. If the state that intervenes to balance a prior incursion becomes too involved, it ultimately could deny the local population the right to decide its own fate.

"Salvation interventions" constitute a third exception to the nonintervention norm. Under this scenario, state intervention can be ethically justified when such action is needed to prevent a people from being slaughtered. During the 1990s in the former Yugoslavia, NATO initially dithered, but eventually intervened forcefully against Serb militias that were systematically targeting non-Serbs. The scope of persecution sets limits on this exception to the nonintervention rule. Broad, systematic attacks on a large, identifiable group of people might justify the involvement of external actors, but more localized episodes of persecution cannot. Unfortunately, not all situations that demand interventions on humanitarian grounds, stimulate such a response: throughout the 1990s, the genocide in Rwanda, and slaughter in Liberia and Sierra Leone failed to motivate other states to step in and stop the carnage.

Each of these exceptions can be analytically useful, and when assessing the moral aspects of an intervention, these rules of thumb are a good place to start. However, because the exceptions apply only to very specific situations, we need additional tools to evaluate the ethical merits of interventions that fall outside their parameters.

Toward this end, political scientist Joseph Nye offers a useful, three-dimensional framework to assess the morality of an intervention, consisting of motives, means, and consequences. By examining the motives states have for what they do, the means they use to accomplish their ends, and the consequences or net effects of their actions, this framework can yield a more comprehensive, satisfying assessment. The reason is straightforward. All states—whether imperialist, communist, democratic, or dictatorial—typically claim that their motives to intervene are just. But even if the intentions *are* honorable, we cannot be satisfied with such one-dimensional analysis.

Good intentions alone, or even good consequences, do not necessarily make an intervention morally sound. Even if an intervention leads to some objective good—say, the preservation of a democratic or a socialist regime, depending upon your perspective—but the means used to obtain that end have laid waste a country or produced excessive casualty rates within its population, we might still conclude that the intervention lacked moral integrity. When studying the morality of interventions, then, we should remember that a one-dimensional analysis can yield inappropriate conclusions, while a three-dimensional approach can help us avoid this pitfall.

Should the United States (or Cuba) have intervened in its neighbors' affairs during the Cold War? Because the question is normative, we cannot answer it fully from a security, strategic, or even ideological perspective. Ethical and moral judgment must be brought to bear. The anarchic nature of international politics may indeed limit the role that ethics can play in states' foreign policy, but it does not eliminate the possibility of understanding the moral implications and consequences of states' actions. America's Cold War interventions readily lend themselves to such analysis, and many of these actions aimed to prevent the kind of radical political change unleashed by the Cuban Revolution.

Study Questions

1. What caused the Cold War? How important were first-, second-, or third-level factors in its development?
2. What effects, if any, did the Cold War and "containment" have on U.S.–Latin American relations?
3. How did the United States' perception of the Cold War in the Western Hemisphere differ from the perception of Latin American states? Why did the two Americas not always see eye to eye?
4. Both Mecham and Smith address the issue of Communism in Guatemala during the Árbenz government, but reach decidedly different conclusions. For Mecham, communist influence and control over the Árbenz government was incontrovertible; for Smith, the communists "were really a side show" and the idea of Guatemala as a Soviet satellite was a "little short of absurd". Which author makes the more compelling case?

5. In what ways was the Organization of American States affected by the Cold War, U.S. foreign policies, and Latin American states' reaction to those policies?
6. Why is the principle of nonintervention a useful norm in international politics and why do states sometimes violate this norm? What ethical issues arise when states do intervene, and how might we assess the ethics of any particular intervention?

Selected Readings

Domínguez, Jorge I. "US-Latin American Relations During the Cold War and its Aftermath." In *The United States and Latin America: The New Agenda*, edited by Victor Bulmer-Thomas and James Dunkerley, 33–50. London and Cambridge, MA: Institute of Latin American Studies, University of London and David Rockefeller Center for Latin American Studies, Harvard University, 1999.

Gaddis, John Lewis. *Strategies of Containment*, 89–126. New York: Oxford University Press, 1982.

Grow, Michael. *Pursuing Regime Change in the Cold War*, ix–xiv, 185–194. Lawrence: University of Kansas Press, 2008.

Kennan, George. "Latin America as a Problem in United States Foreign Policy." In *Neighborly Adversaries: Readings in U.S.–Latin American Relations*, edited by Michael LaRosa and Frank O. Mora, 177–188. Latham, MD: Rowman & Littlefield, 1999.

Mecham, J. Lloyd. *A Survey of United States-Latin American Relations*, 208–220. New York: Houghton Mifflin, 1965.

Muñoz, Heraldo. "The Rise and Decline of the Inter-American System: A Latin American View." In *Alternative to Intervention: A New U.S.–Latin American Security Relationship*, edited by Richard J. Bloomfield and Gregory F. Treverton, 27–37. Boulder: Lynne Rienner, 1990.

Rabe, Stephen G. *Eisenhower and Latin America: The Foreign Policy of Anticommunism*, 1–5; 42–63, 84–116. Chapel Hill: University of North Carolina Press, 1988.

Smith, Wayne S. "Introduction: An Overview of Soviet Policy in Latin America." In *The Russians Aren't Coming: New Soviet Policy in Latin America*, edited by Wayne S. Smith, 1–24. Boulder: Lynne Rienner, 1992.

Further Readings

Blasier, Cole. *The Giant's Rival: The USSR and Latin America*, 129–151. Pittsburgh: University of Pittsburgh Press, 1983.

Gleijeses, Piero. *Shattered Hope: The Guatemalan Revolution and the United States, 1944–1954*. Princeton: Princeton University Press, 1991.

Larson, Deborah W. *Origins of Containment: A Psychological Explanation*. Princeton: Princeton University Press, 1985.

Lowenthal, Abraham F. *The Dominican Intervention*. Baltimore: Johns Hopkins University Press, 1995.

Rabe, Stephen G. *Eisenhower and Latin America: The Foreign Policy of Anticommunism*. Chapel Hill: University of North Carolina Press, 1988.

Schlesinger, Stephan and Stephen Kinzer. *Bitter Fruit: The Story of the American Coup in Guatemala*. Cambridge, MA: Harvard University Press, David Rockefeller Center for Latin American Studies, 1999.

Smith, Gaddis. *The Last Years of the Monroe Doctrine: 1945–1993*. New York: Hill & Wang, 1994.

Chronology: The Cold War Years, Part I

1939–1945	World War II
1945	FDR dies; Truman becomes U.S. president
1945	United Nations created
1945	U.S. tests first atomic bomb, destroys Hiroshima and Nagasaki with atomic bombs
1946	Greek civil war resumes
1947	Truman Doctrine announced; Rio Treaty of Reciprocal Assistance signed; Treaty of Peaceful Settlements signed
1948	Organization of American States created
1948	Czech Communist Party seizes power in Czechoslovakia
1949	North Atlantic Treaty Organization (NATO) created
1949	Communists seize power in China; Soviets explode their own atomic bomb
1950	Soviet Union and Communist China sign pact; NSC-68 drafted and U.S. adopts perimeter defense model
1950–1953	Korean War
1952	Eisenhower elected U.S. president; Greece and Turkey join NATO
1953	Stalin dies; Khrushchev becomes First Secretary of Soviet Communist Party
1954	CIA overthrows Árbenz government in Guatemala
1955	Soviets create Warsaw Pact alliance to oppose NATO
1961	CIA-sponsored Bay of Pigs invasion of Cuba fails
1964	U.S. supports military coup in Brazil
1965	U.S. invades Dominican Republic
1967	Bolivian forces trained and assisted by U.S. capture and kill Che Guevara
1979	Revolution in Nicaragua

1979	Revolution in Grenada
1979–1992	Civil War in El Salvador
1980s	U.S. seeks to overthrow Nicaragua's revolutionary Sandinista government via CIA-trained *contra* guerrillas
1980s	U.S. aid to Salvadoran military government
1983	U.S. invades Grenada
1989	Soviet hegemony in Eastern Europe collapses; Berlin Wall torn down; Cold War ends
1991	Soviet Union disintegrates

The Cold War, Part II   7

Figure 7.1
Fidel Castro arrives
at MATS Terminal,
Washington, DC,
April 15, 1959

The Cuban Revolution

In a little over six decades, Cuba transitioned from a Spanish colony, to a
nominally independent U.S. Protectorate, to a sovereign state and close U.S.
ally, to a revolutionary state and Cold War, U.S. adversary. The United States
was intimately involved in this progression. U.S. intervention in Cuba's war of

independence helped end Spanish rule; the Platt Amendment turned Cuba into a U.S. Protectorate; the abrogation of Platt gave Cuba its sovereignty; U.S. support helped sustain Cuba's governments in times of democracy and dictatorship; the 1959 revolution was a reaction against the U.S.-supported dictatorship of Fulgencio Batista; and revolutionary Cuba sought to sustain its independence from U.S. influence by forging an alliance with the Soviet Union. Cuba's revolution changed its relationship with the United States dramatically and, in important ways, it affected hemispheric relations throughout the Cold War and beyond.

The story of Cuba's revolution is complex, but among its many causes were the government's sharp loss of public support in the face of a twin challenge: nationalist aspirations for a government free of external influence and an armed insurrection. Both the American intervention in Cuba's war with Spain and the Platt Amendment had frustrated Cubans' nationalist desires, but not extinguished them. By the mid-1950s, these sentiments surged again and melded with strong political opposition to Fulgencio Batista, who seized power in a 1952 coup and governed Cuba unconstitutionally thereafter. Between 1952 and 1958, a large swath of Cuban society—politicians, the intelligentsia, students, workers, and rebels—had turned against the dictator. Radical students nearly assassinated Batista; parts of his navy had mutinied; one of Cuba's ex-presidents even financed a mini uprising in a failed attempt to topple him. The insurrection by Fidel Castro's 26th of July Movement succeeded. On New Year's Eve, 1958, Batista fled Cuba and Castro rapidly assumed power.

Castro's victory worried the United States. During the insurgency, he had revealed little about his own political philosophy or plans, beyond a desire to end dictatorial rule. American policymakers, therefore, were unsure where Castro intended to take Cuba, or how it would affect U.S. interests.

In April 1959, Castro visited the United States on the invitation of the Association of Newspaper Editors. He addressed the press, met with U.S. officials, and held a three-hour discussion with Vice President Richard Nixon (President Eisenhower had refused to meet him). Anxious to retain influence in Cuba, the Americans were prepared to offer Castro a generous package of economic aid (with strings attached). When Castro never requested aid, the Americans' uncertainty and suspicions heightened. After meeting with Cuba's new leader, Vice President Nixon penned a memo for President Eisenhower in which he advised that Castro was either naïve about Communism, or was a communist himself; Nixon was unsure. But "The one fact that we can be sure of," he noted, "is that he has those definable qualities which make him a leader of men. Whatever we may think of him he is going to be a great factor in the development of Cuba and very possibly Latin American affairs generally." Nixon's assessment would prove prophetic.

After returning to Cuba, Castro enacted a number of highly popular reforms. Among other things, the government cut urban rents by 50 percent, cut electricity and telephone rates, slashed the price of basic medicines, implemented wage hikes, ordered that Cuba's finest beaches and resorts be open to all Cubans (not just tourists, the wealthy, or military officers), and implemented agrarian reform. These measures increased the government's support among lower-income and rural Cubans, while their leftward tilt helped encourage middle and upper class Cubans to resettle in Miami.

Throughout 1959, Castro also worked to consolidate his power and reorient Cuba's economy. In June, he began dismissing moderate members of his cabinet (their replacements included members of the Communist Party). In August, his government began nationalizing not only U.S. firms, but all privately owned banks, commercial ventures, and sugar mills—the raw material on which Cuba's capitalist economy had been based. Migration to Miami accelerated. By September, Castro had begun denouncing the United States, and by early 1960, was courting the Soviet Union as a balance against Washington. In February 1960, the two countries penned important trade agreements: Cuban sugar went to the Soviet Union while Soviet oil flowed into Cuba. By June, they had formalized a military alliance—under which, according to a joint Soviet-Cuban communiqué—the Soviet Union pledged to "use all means at its disposal to prevent an armed intervention by the United States against Cuba."[1] The Organization of American States took note. In its August 1960 Declaration of San José, the OAS spoke directly to the Soviet Union when it condemned "energetically the intervention or the threat of intervention . . . by an extra-continental power in the affairs of the American republics," and to Cuba, when it advised that "the acceptance of a threat of extra-continental intervention by any American state" posed a danger to hemispheric security that the OAS was obligated to reject.

In this context, Cuban-U.S. relations deteriorated quickly. Each side adopted harsher rhetoric and ever-stronger economic and political reprisals. When the dust settled, Cuba had nationalized $1 billion of U.S. assets (without compensation), while the United States had tightened trade restrictions on the island and laid plans for the disastrous Bay of Pigs invasion. Despite initial sympathy from many of its neighbors, Cuba's relations with Latin American states deteriorated too, largely due to self-inflicted wounds. Its 1959 efforts to undermine the Dominican and Nicaraguan governments began the trend; its 1960 call for regional revolution (the first Declaration of Havana) accelerated it. Cuba's self-identification as a Marxist-Leninist state—proclaimed by Fidel

Castro in December 1961—led to its suspension from the Organization of American States for having embraced a governing philosophy "incompatible with the principles of the inter-American system." Cuba's acceptance of Soviet nuclear missiles in 1962 united the hemisphere against it, and in 1963, its decision to supply weapons to guerrillas seeking to overthrow Venezuela's government led the OAS to impose economic sanctions. Thereafter, every OAS member except Mexico severed its diplomatic relations with Havana.

These early Cuban foreign policies were conditioned, in part, by the Cuban government's ideology and security concerns, and in part, by its leader's inexperience and risk-taking personality. The result was a series of policy moves, often immoderate, that left Cuba diplomatically isolated within the hemisphere and subject to intense scrutiny by the regional hegemon. The reasons for the scrutiny are not hard to fathom.

Revolutionary Cuba challenged the United States politically on multiple fronts, beginning with U.S. hegemony. From its inception, the new government's highest foreign policy goal—and one it achieved decisively—was to free Cuba from U.S. influence and break its dependent relationship with the United States. Of course, the Cuban-Soviet alliance transferred this dependency from Washington to Moscow, but the alliance itself challenged the Monroe Doctrine by offering a nuclear-armed, extra-continental U.S. adversary entrée into the Western Hemisphere. Meanwhile, the Cuban regime's surprising resilience challenged the efficacy of standard practices Washington had used to influence Latin American states: diplomacy failed, political pressure failed, covert action failed, and economic carrots and sticks failed too. Finally, Cuba's efforts to export socialist revolutions challenged U.S. containment policy.

In short, Cuba was no bit player in the East-West conflict, but rather, an active, enthusiastic cold warrior. Its leaders were not "pushed" by the United States into the Soviet orbit, but went of their own volition. Cuba willingly expanded its relations with Soviet satellite states of Eastern Europe. It accepted Chinese economic and military aid, and in 1960, it recognized the People's Republic of China—i.e., "Red China"—19 years before the United States abandoned its own fiction that Taiwan alone constituted the "real" China. It engaged Washington head-on in the Cold War's ideological and geopolitical struggles. As historian Louis Pérez notes, in the 1960s Cuba "sought to replace hostile governments with friendly ones" to reduce its isolation in the Western Hemisphere. "It extended moral and material support to guerrilla movements across Latin America—in Guatemala, Colombia, Venezuela, Peru, and Bolivia."[2] In the 1970s and 1980s, it supported wars of national liberation in Angola and Ethiopia against pro-West or capitalist forces. Thanks to Soviet largesse and transport facilities, it became the only Latin American state with the capacity to project hard power beyond the Western Hemisphere. Yet, years before these events, Cuba's geopolitical profile had already shifted from a regional to global level, when it accepted Soviet nuclear missiles in 1962 and helped precipitate a crisis of global proportions.

The Cuban Missile Crisis

The failure of the 1961 Bay of Pigs invasion thwarted U.S. containment plans, humiliated the Kennedy administration, and increased both the Cuban government's domestic popularity and its sense of urgency and insecurity. By the summer of 1962, Cuba's leadership had concluded that Washington's inability to roll back the revolution covertly, increased the likelihood it would try again overtly through a full-scale military invasion. As a safeguard, Cuba "hard balanced" externally, and accepted the Soviet Union's offer of nuclear missiles to defend against a U.S. attack. In September, Cuba began receiving the weapons shipments; in October, the United States discovered their delivery, and the Cuban Missile Crisis began. This crisis constituted the single-most frightening chapter of the Cold War. It brought the world to the brink of thermonuclear war, and its resolution—a liberal approach to realist security concerns in an anarchic environment—increased security for Cuba, the Soviet Union, and the United States.

The introduction of nuclear missiles in Cuba did nothing to alter the absolute global balance of power between the Soviet Union, United States, and their respective allies (in fact, the Americans retained a 17:1 numerical superiority in nuclear weapons). However, it did much to alter the psychological perception of that balance in Havana, Washington, and Moscow. The weapons offered Cuba a greater sense of security and the Soviet Union a measure of satisfaction given its own exposure to U.S. missiles stationed at NATO bases in Europe and Turkey. By contrast, the missiles' proximity to the United States enhanced the U.S. perception of threat acutely (a dynamic the Americans had failed to understand when it came to placing their own missiles next to Soviet borders in Turkey). For the United States, the missiles' discovery also made time a critical factor: once they became operational, most major American cities including Washington would be vulnerable to a nuclear strike in less than 10 minutes. Chapter 1 briefly described the nature of the crisis and its causes, stemming from balance of power considerations, self-help incentives, and the security dilemma. Here, we shall explore more of its historical detail.

U.S. officials quickly determined there seemed but three options to remove the missiles: an air strike against Cuba followed by a full invasion; a naval blockade of Cuba; or a missile exchange that would remove arsenals from both Cuba and Turkey. Each option posed extraordinary risks. An air attack and invasion of Cuba would likely kill a number of Soviet military personnel (which the United States believed stood at around 22,000), and compel the Soviets to respond by attacking a U.S. ally that might produce similarly high American casualties. This option would cast America as a naked aggressor against tiny Cuba, which had not attacked the United States. Nor would it guarantee the destruction of all the missiles, and a strike by even one would kill tens of thousands of U.S. citizens. Finally, it held the potential to escalate to armed conflict between Washington and Moscow—a very troubling possibility. A naval blockade might stop further arms shipments to Cuba, but not remove the weapons already in place; it also could trigger naval clashes between U.S. and Soviet vessels patrolling the Caribbean that could easily escalate into a broader conflict. A public missile exchange would degrade the credibility of U.S. alliance commitments, whether in Latin America (the Rio Treaty), Europe (NATO), or Asia (the U.S.-Japan alliance), by suggesting that in a crunch, the United States would sacrifice its allies' security—in this case, Turkey—for the sake of its own. After considerable internal debate, President Kennedy settled on the naval blockade as a first response, and ordered the Pentagon to draw up backup plans for an invasion in case the crisis could not be resolved diplomatically.

On October 22, Kennedy addressed the nation. He called for the Soviet Union to withdraw the weapons and announced that any missile launched from Cuba against any state in the Western Hemisphere would be considered an attack by the Soviet Union on America, requiring a full retaliatory nuclear response. He also announced the naval blockade and U.S. intentions to stop all incoming ships to Cuba and seize any material related to the missiles.

To gain international support for the blockade—and equally important, legal sanction for an act that in most circumstances would violate international law—the United States turned to the Organization of American States. Because the Soviet Union held veto rights in the UN Security Council, there was little prospect of obtaining a Security Council resolution that condemned Moscow's actions or authorized military measures to remove the missiles. But this was not the case with the OAS; in an emergency meeting, its members voted unanimously to support the blockade. The vote effectively isolated Cuba and the Soviet Union diplomatically within the Western Hemisphere, and to some degree, justified U.S. policy legally through a body recognized by the UN Charter (Article 51). Having been suspended from the OAS, Cuba could not use this forum to argue its case that the missiles were needed to defend against an American invasion. Meanwhile, the momentum of events kept pulling the world ever closer to catastrophe.

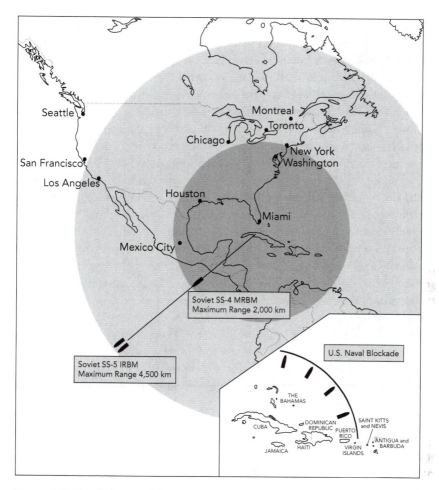

Figure 7.2 The Cuban Missile Crisis, October 1962

On October 23, Kennedy received a letter from Soviet Premier Nikita Khrushchev, accusing him of threatening the Soviet Union and its ally, labeling the blockade an act of "outright banditry," and informing Kennedy that Soviet ships would ignore the blockade. The same day U.S. reconnaissance photos revealed that some missiles were now ready for launch. On October 24, the blockade went into effect, and U.S. and Soviet naval forces began a dangerous game of cat-and-mouse. To defend Soviet ships streaming toward Cuba, Soviet submarines shadowed them, while U.S. war vessels monitored their progress. After having second thoughts about running the blockade, Moscow ordered those ships that had reached its perimeter to hold their positions. On October

26, Kennedy received a letter from Khrushchev in which he proposed to remove the missiles if the United States publicly guaranteed that it would not invade Cuba. Khrushchev himself received a cable from Fidel Castro urging him to launch a nuclear first-strike if a U.S. invasion of Cuba proceeded; and the CIA determined that construction on the remaining missile sites was accelerating.

On October 27, the crisis appeared to reach a breaking point. An American U-2 spy plane inadvertently strayed into Russian air space, prompting Soviet MiG fighters to scramble, and leading Washington to fear the Soviets would interpret the mistake as a preparation for attack. A second U.S. spy plane was shot down over Cuba, and Castro received a letter from Khrushchev urging Havana to refrain from any similar actions. Most chillingly, the naval cat-and-mouse game nearly produced calamity. A Soviet B-59 sub—pounded by depth charges from a U.S. destroyer intent on bringing it to the surface—came within a whisper of sinking the American vessel with a nuclear-tipped torpedo. Soviet military doctrine required three officers' approval to authorize a nuclear launch: two voted yea, but fortunately, the third, nay; had the nuclear launch gone forward, the pressure on Washington to respond in kind could easily have escalated into a broader nuclear exchange.[3] Both in the air and on the sea, events seemed to be slipping beyond Khrushchev and Kennedy's ability to control them.

The same day, Kennedy received a second letter from Khrushchev regarding a possible resolution. The Soviet Union would withdraw its missiles if the United States promised not to invade Cuba *and* removed its own missiles from Turkey. Anxious to find some escape from the crisis that avoided conflict without threatening U.S. alliance commitments, Kennedy chose to respond to Khrushchev's initial offer (which made no mention of Turkey), but in a way that still addressed the Soviets' broader security concerns. If the Soviet Union would immediately withdraw its missiles from Cuba, the United States would end its blockade and pledge not to invade Cuba. "The effect of such a settlement on easing world tensions," Kennedy wrote, "would enable us to work toward a more general arrangement regarding 'other armaments' [i.e., missiles in Turkey], as proposed in your second letter." This arrangement could not be linked publicly to the resolution of problems in Cuba, but through diplomatic back channels, Kennedy assured Khrushchev that the United States would remove its missiles from Turkey once the Cuban crisis had ended. Khrushchev accepted this formulation. In a final letter written on October 28 and broadcast on Radio Moscow, he announced his government's intention to dismantle and withdraw the missiles and reiterated Cuba's need for security from an attack.

For the Soviet Union and United States, the crisis was over. For Cuba, it was not. Khrushchev had not consulted Fidel Castro on the disposition of the missiles, and the Cuban government felt burned at being shut out. Although the deal brokered between Khrushchev and Kennedy protected Cuba from an invasion, Havana still deemed it inadequate. Cuba also demanded that the United States end its economic embargo, discontinue clandestine CIA operations against Cuba, and give up its naval base on Cuban territory at Guantánamo Bay. These demands, however, went nowhere. Neither Moscow nor Washington had any interest in prolonging the crisis. Their prior agreement left Cuba little negotiating leverage and the United States rejected the demands in total.

The Cuban Missile Crisis placed U.S. and Soviet leadership under tremendous emotional and psychological strain. One fortuitous by-product of this experience was that it literally scared the superpowers into more cooperative behavior. Both sides had walked right up to the precipice and taken a virtual "peep" into hell; after seeing the fires burning below, they wisely decided not to go to hell in October 1962 or anytime thereafter. Once the crisis ended, therefore, the two states worked to ensure that nothing like it ever happened again.

The Limited Security Regime

To prevent a repeat, the superpowers needed some mechanism that would block the way to Hades. Clearly, deploying more weapons in the region and pursuing balance of power policies were not the answer (this very approach had precipitated the crisis). Instead, they devised a mechanism along more liberal lines. Political scientists call this mechanism a *security regime*. Like other international regimes, a security regime consists of a set of mutual understandings and principles that guide the behavior of sovereign states, and delineate their mutual rights and obligations. By providing mutually acceptable standards of action, it helps reduce uncertainty between states, and can promote more orderly relations even under anarchic conditions. As with any international regime, a security regime does not guarantee that relations will be cordial, and does not eliminate international anarchy and its attendant problems. But when states agree to let a given set of norms govern their behavior, a security regime can make those problems easier to manage and instances of armed conflict easier to avoid.

In the wake of the Cuban Missile Crisis, the United States and Soviet Union set up such a regime in the Caribbean to avoid a future nuclear war. Like the Good Neighbor regime of an earlier era, it did not consist of a formal, written agreement, but rather, a set of tacit, informal understandings contained in the official letters exchanged by Khrushchev and Kennedy in October 1962. In essence, the regime boiled down to an implicit agreement between Moscow and Washington not to do anything in the Caribbean—or with respect to Cuba—that would go beyond the other's threshold of toleration and escalate into war.

What had worried the United States most was the presence of strategic nuclear weapons in Cuba. The Soviets agreed to dismantle and remove these weapons, and promised not to reintroduce them. This allowed the United States to breathe easy about the prospects of a nuclear attack launched from Cuba. What had bothered Moscow most was the possibility that the Americans might invade its only ally in the Western Hemisphere. In exchange for dismantling the missiles, therefore, the United States pledged to withdraw its missiles from Turkey, not to invade Cuba, and in effect, leave Castro in power. This "no invasion principle" was never formalized in any treaty, but has been honored by every U.S. administration from Kennedy to Obama—conservative or liberal, Democratic or Republican.

Cuba was a clear beneficiary of this arrangement. Castro's government not only gained greater security, but the opportunity to consolidate its power. However, the benefits were not limited to Cuba. By restraining the superpowers' actions in the Caribbean, the security regime enhanced their security too. The Soviet Union finally understood that to install nuclear weapons in Cuba was to push the United States beyond its limits, and the result would be a military strike against a key ally. The United States finally understood that an invasion of Cuba would trigger a Soviet response—probably against a U.S. ally in Europe. Since either scenario could lead to nuclear war, the security regime worked as a voluntary restraint on both states that provided each important gains. By contrast, the regime did not put any real restraints on Cuba, which continued to pursue its revolutionary ambitions in Latin America, and in the 1970s and 1980s deployed hundreds of thousands of troops to conflicts in Angola and Ethiopia.

Some people criticized the solution to the missile crisis, especially the U.S. pledge not to invade Cuba or impose stronger constraints on its foreign policy. The conservative columnist, George Will, for example, argued that the United States should have been much firmer with Moscow, and that Kennedy should have demanded that Castro cease further efforts to export "subversion and expeditionary forces in this hemisphere and Africa."[4] Not everyone agrees with such views. "The problem with these criticisms," suggests political scientist Jorge Domínguez, "is that they ignore two central facts. First, in 1962 the world was close to nuclear war; insistence on secondary issues would have carried the risk of crossing the nuclear threshold, thus sacrificing fundamental goals for the sake of worthy but less vital interests. Second, . . . Had the United States attempted to impose greater restraints on Cuba, the likelihood of war would have increased."[5]

Disagreements on what should or shouldn't have happened in 1962 are understandable. What is clear from the historical record, though, is that other than safeguard it from invasion, the agreement between the Americans and Soviets was never designed to do anything about communist Cuba, because in the grand scheme of things, it simply was not that important. The point of the security regime was to avert nuclear war—a scenario which could leave many tens of millions dead, destroy many of the world's great urban centers, contaminate the world's soil, water, and air—and in Walter Lippmann's words, "be followed by a savage struggle for existence as people crawled out of their cellars, and all the democracies [had been] converted into military dictatorships in order to keep some semblance of order among the desperate survivors."[6] Weighed against this sobering scenario, other issues paled in significance.

Given the intense hostility between Cuba, the Soviet Union, and the United States, their conflicting ideological and strategic interests—and most important, the added danger of nuclear weapons—the security regime helped generate greater regional stability in what otherwise was an explosive situation. The Soviet Union and United States continued to compete, but in the Caribbean and with respect to Cuba, each made sure it never crossed the boundary between acceptable and unacceptable actions. They did so mindful that in the nuclear age, events can easily slip out of control with catastrophic consequences. "There is a line of intolerable provocation and humiliation," Walter Lippmann wrote, "beyond which popular and governmental reactions are likely to become uncontrollable. It is the business of the governments to find out where that line is, and to stay well back of it."[7] Cuba and the Caribbean are one place where the Cold War antagonists found that line and appear to have heeded this good advice.

The Cold War and Economics: Nationalism and Development

Apart from its problematic security dimensions, the Cold War also strained U.S.–Latin American relations over economic issues, yet paradoxically, facilitated multilateral cooperation on regional development. On the one hand, it led Washington to interpret some expressions of Latin American economic nationalism as evidence of communist expansion; on the other, it provided the

Americas incentives and opportunities to cooperate on the most ambitious hemispheric development project ever attempted, the Alliance for Progress.

Economic Nationalism

Economic nationalism can be a confusing concept, in part because of its dual economic and political connotations, and in part because it lacks definitional clarity. As defined by economist William E. Rappard, for example, economic nationalism is a doctrine that seeks "to serve the nation by making it not richer, but freer, by promoting not its material welfare, but its independence of foreign influences";[8] by contrast, according to political scientist Robert Gilpin, "its central idea is that economic activities are and should be subordinate to the goal of state-building and the interests of the state."[9] Each definition is useful, but incomplete: they both capture the concept's political dimension, but understate the value economic nationalism typically puts on growth and development. States embrace economic nationalism for different reasons. Some seek to protect domestic industry and insulate themselves from the vagaries of the global economy, while others seek to place as much of the domestic economy as possible in the hands of nationals. Regardless of the motives, most economic nationalist projects share the goals of increasing national independence and promoting greater prosperity and national power.

Classic examples of economic nationalism in practice are post-World War II Japan—where the Ministry of International Trade and Industry protected Japanese industry from competition, promoted its access to foreign technology and foreign exchange, and strengthened Japan's economic base considerably—and the nineteenth-century U.S. "American School" of economic development described by historian Michael Lind. Drawing on ideas first developed by Alexander Hamilton (in his 1791 *Report on Manufactures*) and further elaborated by Henry Clay, the "American School" called for high tariffs to protect domestic industry, promote import-substitution, and provide resources to fund infrastructure upgrades—all in pursuit of national development and power.[10] Other examples include aspects of post-World War II import-substitution industrialization programs adopted by states like Argentina, Brazil, and Mexico. Under these programs, governments promoted national development by encouraging, protecting, and subsidizing domestic industry (to produce goods that were formerly imported), regulating foreign trade and investment flows, and nationalizing various foreign-owned operations.

As these examples indicate, states that implement economic nationalist projects can employ a variety of strategies to promote development and increase their independence. The strategy mix includes tariffs, quotas, licensing arrangements and other restrictions on foreign investment or trade. It can also include the establishment of a public sector that operates parallel to the economy's private sector, composed of businesses either created by the state or foreign operations that it has nationalized. Classic, liberal economists correctly point out that such policies do not always make "economic sense"; but they also are not necessarily "irrational." Studies indicate that economic nationalist programs can generate a type of psychological income—manifest in a greater sense of national pride or purpose—that offsets the deferral of more immediate material gain.[11]

History suggests that extensive foreign economic penetration can stimulate an upsurge in economic nationalism. In the nineteenth century, for example, Latin American states often welcomed foreign investors, whose capital was needed to fuel their own development. In many countries, British, German, and American investments poured into sectors like agriculture, banking, communications, industry, mining, oil, and transportation. But as the foreigners' share of the national economy grew, so did economic nationalism. In some cases, nationalist critics labeled governments, politicians, and economic elites who had cozied up with foreign investors *vendepatristas* (national sell-outs); in other cases, nationalist sentiments helped fuel revolution (Cuba, Guatemala, Mexico). Although less intense than in Latin America, the United States has also experienced spikes in economic nationalist sentiments when foreign investment seemed too pervasive or threatening. In the 1980s, Japanese acquisitions of U.S. banks, companies, and real estate led to much "Japan bashing" in the U.S. press and Congress. More recently, in 2006 the George W. Bush administration tried to sell the operating rights for U.S. port security to the United Arab Emirates firm, Dubai Ports World, but a popular backlash—produced both by nationalist sentiments and security concerns—quashed the deal.

Once the national economy of weak states has been deeply penetrated by foreign investors, it can be difficult to change course even if states want to. In Latin America, this was especially true in the nineteenth century when strong European and North American states tended to protect their nationals' investments with military force. From the mid-1930s onward, though, Latin Americans developed tools to implement their nationalist projects: just as they had sought protection from external intervention through international law (the Calvo Clause and Drago Doctrine), they used legal means to wrest control of their economies from foreign investors, and limit their exposure to external pressures. In Argentina, Bolivia, Chile, Mexico, Peru, Venezuela, and elsewhere, the state extended its control over key foreign investments—sometimes dramatically through outright nationalizations, and sometimes more gradually through laws that required foreigners to sell 51 percent of their equity to nationals. Typically, these states also sought greater independence from external forces through protectionist policies and trade and investment restrictions.

The Cold War did not create economic nationalism in Latin America. It arose independently of the conflict and was expressed vividly before it began. Argentina's nationalization of several British-owned railways in the 1930s, and Bolivia and Mexico's nationalization of foreign-owned oil firms during the same period, all reflected this dynamic. The strategies Latin American states pursued to realize nationalist aspirations—import-substitution programs that limited foreign investment, promoted state intervention in the economy, and nationalized foreign assets—often affected U.S. domestic economic interests, and consequently bred tension. But the Cold War compounded this tension because, in some instances, it led Washington to interpret these same strategies as evidence of communist expansion. Reclaiming parts of the national economy from foreign investors was a critical goal for Jacobo Árbenz's Guatemala and Salvador Allende's Chile. In each case, the American response to perceived Cold War threats ultimately strained U.S.–Latin American relations.

Development and the Alliance for Progress

Although the Cold War helped create tension over economic policy, it also facilitated a (brief) period of genuine hemispheric cooperation around economic development under the Alliance for Progress. In March 1961, President Kennedy announced the Alliance, employing rhetoric that still inspires and captures the imagination. The Alliance, he said, was a "vast new Ten Year Plan for the Americas" designed to make every American republic "the master of its own revolution." This "cooperative effort, unparalleled in magnitude and nobility of purpose," would "transform the American continent into a vast crucible of revolutionary ideas and effort," and ultimately, "demonstrate to the entire world that man's unsatisfied aspiration for economic progress and social justice can best be achieved within a framework of democratic institutions."

In August 1961, delegates to the Organization of American States met at Uruguay's beach resort, Punta del Este, and signed the Declaration of the Peoples of America in which they formally committed to a hemispheric development program based on the themes in Kennedy's speech. They also signed the Charter of Punta del Este, which served as the Alliance's basic operational plan.

Box 7.1 Declaration of the Peoples of America, August 1961

Assembled in Punta del Este, inspired by the principles consecrated in the Charter of the Organization of American States, in Operation Pan America, and in the Act of Bogotá, the representatives of the American republics hereby agree to establish an Alliance for Progress: a vast effort to bring a better life to all the peoples of the continent.

This Alliance is established on the basic principles that free men working through the institution of representative democracy can best satisfy man's aspirations, including those for work, home and land, health and schools. No system can guarantee true progress unless it affirms the dignity of the individual which is the foundation of our civilization.

Therefore the countries signing this declaration in the exercise of their sovereignty have agreed to work toward the following goals during the coming years:

- To improve and strengthen democratic institutions through application of the principle of self-determination by the people.
- To accelerate economic and social development, thus rapidly bringing about a substantial and steady increase in the average income in order to narrow the gap between the standard of living in Latin American countries and that enjoyed in the industrialized countries.
- To carry out urban and rural housing programs to provide decent homes for all our people.
- To encourage, in accordance with the characteristics of each country, programs of comprehensive agrarian reform, leading to the effective transformation, where required, of unjust structures and systems of land tenure and use; with a view to replacing latifundia and dwarf holdings by an equitable system of property so that, supplemented by timely and adequate credit, technical assistance and improved marketing arrangements, the land will become for the man who works it the basis of his economic stability, the foundation of his increasing welfare, and the guarantee of his freedom and dignity.
- To assure fair wages and satisfactory working conditions to all our workers; to establish effective systems of labor-management relations and procedures for consultation and cooperation among government authorities, employers' associations, and trade unions in the interests of social and economic development.

- To wipe out illiteracy; to extend, as quickly as possible, the benefits of primary education to all Latin Americans; and to provide broader facilities, on a vast scale, for secondary and technical training and for higher education.
- To press forward with programs of health and sanitation in order to prevent sickness, combat contagious disease, and strengthen our human potential.
- To reform tax laws, demanding more from those who have most, to punish tax evasion severely, and to redistribute the national income in order to benefit those who are most in need, while, at the same time, promoting savings and investment and reinvestment in capital . . .
- To stimulate private enterprise in order to encourage the development of Latin American countries at a rate which will help them to provide jobs for their growing populations, to eliminate unemployment, and to take their place among the modern industrialized nations of the world . . .

This declaration expresses the conviction of the nations of Latin America that these profound economic, social, and cultural changes can come about only through the self-help efforts of each country. Nonetheless, in order to achieve the goals which have been established with the necessary speed, domestic efforts must be reinforced by essential contributions of external assistance.

The United States, for its part, pledges its efforts to supply financial and technical cooperation in order to achieve the aims of the Alliance for Progress. To this end, the United States will provide a major part of the minimum of $20 billion, principally in public funds, which Latin America will require over the next ten years from all external sources in order to supplement its own efforts . . .

The United States intends to furnish development loans on a long-term basis, where appropriate funding up to fifty years and in general at very low or zero rates of interest.

For their part, the countries of Latin America agree to devote a steadily increasing share of their own resources to economic and social development, and to make the reforms necessary to assure that all share fully in the fruits of the Alliance for Progress.

Further, as a contribution to the Alliance for Progress, each of the countries of Latin America will formulate a comprehensive and well-conceived national program for the development of its own economy.

Independent and highly qualified experts will be made available to Latin American countries in order to assist in formulating and examining national development plans.

Conscious of the overriding importance of this declaration, the signatory countries declare that the inter-American community is now beginning a new era when it will supplement its institutional, legal, cultural, and social accomplishments with immediate and concrete actions to secure a better life, under freedom and democracy, for the present and future generations.

The Alliance for Progress sought to achieve three broad goals in Latin America: political democracy, structural change, and economic development. Its basic intent was to foster greater social wellbeing, higher living standards, more effective political participation and representation, and broader educational and employment opportunities. It laid out specific means to realize these ends, including anti-illiteracy programs and higher educational standards, expanded health care, tax reform, incentives for private enterprise, land reform, and a U.S. commitment to provide billions of dollars in economic and technical aid and billions more in private investments. It also set a specific target of 2.5 percent annual growth in Latin America's Gross Domestic Product. For its advocates, the Alliance's principal goals seemed to be mutually reinforcing. Economic growth would expand the private sector and middle class, stimulate job creation, and promote political democracy and stability. Structural change through land reform would eliminate gross inequalities, bring the large majority of Latin Americans back from society's margins, redistribute some of the income and fruits of progress, and transform the newly empowered into stakeholders in their country's political system and prosperity. The interaction between these objectives was critical, since without structural change and democratization, Latin American states stood little chance of providing their citizens greater social wellbeing or a more equitable distribution of rewards.

Alliance operations drew upon the machinery of the Inter-American System and the U.S. government. The Inter-American Committee on Agricultural Development helped Latin American states devise effective agricultural promotion programs, while the Inter-American Committee on the Alliance for Progress (the so-called Committee of Nine Experts) reviewed the countries' national development programs and served as the Alliance liaison with the global financial community. For its part, the Kennedy administration created a new entity within the State Department to channel U.S. foreign aid including Alliance funds—the Agency for International Development (AID)—and selected Puerto Rican politician Teodoro Moscoso as the first Coordinator of the Alliance for Progress, and Assistant Administrator of AID.

Carried out within a democratic framework, the Alliance for Progress envisioned a peaceful revolution across the Americas that would transform the continent, diminish the enormous economic gap between the two Americas, and unite them more strongly on an ideological, democratic basis. Underwritten in large part by the United States, this revolution would require Latin American states to commit some of their own resources to development, and also serve Cold War containment purposes by adhering more to the principles of John Locke than Karl Marx.

Over its 10-year life span, however, the Alliance amassed a less than stellar record. On the up side, it surpassed the target of 2.5 percent growth in GDP. From 1961 to 1965, the region's economies actually grew by 4.9 percent, and from 1966 to 1969, by 5.7 percent (Table 7.1). In terms of individual countries, Chile and Venezuela stood out as Alliance success stories. Both carried out major reform projects that redistributed land to thousands of small family farmers; both launched projects to improve social welfare for the poor (schools and education, health care and medicine, housing); and both made even stronger commitments to democracy. In Venezuela, the governing party *Acción Democrática* expanded mass political participation, bringing hundreds of thousands of people into the political party system. In Chile, the Christian Democrats and other political parties actively recruited members among the peasants, students, and workers.

But in the end, despite the expenditure of $20 billion, the Alliance for Progress did not achieve its more fundamental goals. Although national economies grew, populations grew faster; hence, there was little headway made on reducing poverty. There also was little progress on effective structural change: few governments adopted significant land reform, unemployment remained high, per capita income and illiteracy rates did not improve appreciably, and the inequalities that separated the highly affluent from the impoverished remained. Perhaps most distressing is that the scope of democratic governance did not expand: between 1962 and 1968, nine military coups toppled constitutional governments and authoritarian rulers took power in some of the region's largest, most economically important states—Argentina, Brazil, and Peru. By the 1970s, the Alliance for Progress had died a quiet death, its demise a sharp contrast to its bold unveiling.

Both the Alliance's creation and its record raise two important questions. Why was such an ambitious, collaborative development enterprise undertaken to begin with? And why did the Alliance for Progress ultimately fail?

Table 7.1   Latin America's Annual GDP Growth Rates, Selected Countries, 1961–1969

Country	1961–1965	1966–1969	1966	1967	1968	1969
Argentina	2.9	4.5	0.02	2.3	4.7	6.6
Barbados	3.5	5.5	4.0	7.8	6.5	2.3
Bolivia	5.9	6.1	7.0	6.3	7.2	4.8
Brazil	3.1	7.4	5.1	4.8	8.4	9.0
Chile	4.7	2.9	7.0	2.3	2.7	3.5
Colombia	4.6	5.2	5.4	4.2	5.5	5.8
Costa Rica	5.7	6.8	7.3	7.1	5.8	7.6
Dominican Rep.	2.3	4.5	12.4	3.3	3.1	7.0
Ecuador	4.8	5.5	4.6	6.5	5.2	4.9
El Salvador	7.7	2.8	7.2	5.4	−1.2	0.2
Guatemala	5.5	5.2	5.5	4.1	5.7	5.6
Haiti	1.3	1.9	1.9	1.4	2.0	2.5
Honduras	4.9	5.5	7.6	6.5	7.0	3.1
Jamaica	5.3	4.4	3.8	2.9	6.1	4.1
Mexico	7.7	7.2	6.9	6.3	8.1	7.3
Nicaragua	9.6	4.8	3.1	5.3	4.7	4.4
Panama	7.6	7.3	7.6	8.6	7.0	6.5
Paraguay	4.7	5.2	1.3	6.7	4.8	4.2
Peru	6.1	2.5	5.7	4.6	1.4	1.7
Trinidad & Tobago	3.3	3.2	3.7	5.7	3.3	1.0
Uruguay	0.3	−0.1	3.3	−6.6	1.2	5.5
Venezuela	7.9	0.3	2.3	4.0	5.3	3.5
Latin America	4.9	5.7	4.5	4.4	6.3	6.5

Source: Inter-American Development Bank, *Socio-Economic Progress in Latin America; Social Progress Trust Fund Annual Report* (Washington, DC: Inter-American Development Bank, 1970)

Why an Alliance for Progress?

Answering the first question can be challenging, in part because there is a great deal of confusion regarding the origin and nature of the Alliance for Progress. As early as 1962, Argentine economist Raúl Prebisch was troubled by "a rather peculiar tendency" in both Americas to cast the Alliance's basic ideas as "having been conceived in the United States, or as constituting a ready-made American blueprint to be applied in Latin America."[12] Even today, many still view it primarily as a *United States* policy toward Latin America—a Cold War program of U.S. economic aid launched mainly in response to the Cuban Revolution, spurred by the fear of more Cuban-style revolutions, and geared toward containing the spread of Communism in the Western Hemisphere. To be sure, the Alliance *was* a U.S. policy that Washington hoped would serve these ends. However, analyzing its creation solely through a U.S. lens can mislead us, because the Alliance for Progress also was a multilateral inter-American development initiative, much of whose conceptualization originated in Latin America. Its multilateral adoption had as much to do with Latin American states pursuing their self-interest, as with the United States pursuing its own.

Despite the general confusion, astute writers in both Americas agree that the Alliance concept originated in Latin America. According to political scientist Howard Wiarda: "One of the unique aspects of the Alliance was the degree to which it initially grew out of, and particularly incorporated, ideas emanating from Latin America." Similarly, historian Arthur Schlesinger, Jr., writes: "In its ideas the Alliance was essentially a Latin American product."[13] These North American views echo those from Argentinean economist Raúl Prebisch, and Chile's former president Eduardo Frei. According to Prebisch, "the basic ideas" underlying the Alliance—the importance of industrialization, "the inevitability of land reform and other changes in the social structure," and the need for greater "foreign funds" to supplement internal resources states could devote toward their own development—were all conceived in Latin America.[14] Frei states the matter even more succinctly: "The Alliance was essentially a Latin American conception which became reality because it was accepted by the United States and specifically by President Kennedy, who understood it and injected new life into it."[15]

HISTORICAL SETTING

The back-story to John Kennedy's 1961 announcement of the Alliance for Progress underscores the points above, and provides an historical explanation of its origin. It is an intriguing account of how Alliance precursors—post-World War II economic concerns in Latin American states, third-level security concerns in the United States, and domestic factors in both Americas—helped generate this ambitious, collaborative development enterprise.

During World War II, Latin American exports to the United States grew substantially. Because the war curtailed trade in manufactured products, Latin American states built up sizeable foreign currency reserves (Table 7.2), and as the war wound down, they hoped to safeguard their economic gains by persuading Washington to incorporate a strong economic development component into a new Inter-American System. When these efforts failed, many Latin

Table 7.2   Selected Latin American Countries' Economic and Trade Figures, 1940–1945

	Yearly Export Growth Rates	Percentage Change in Reserves	Growth Rates	
			Real per capita GDP	Exports
Argentina	4.0	+156	1.2	5.0
Brazil	12.1	+635	0.3	8.1
Chile	1.5	+214	2.4	2.2
Colombia	0.6	+540	0.4	17.5
Ecuador	18.9	—	1.5	17.0
Guatemala	12.0	—	0.8	—
Honduras	4.6	—	—	22.4
Mexico	4.6	+480	4.6	11.7
Paraguay	20.9	—	−0.1	3.1
Peru	4.5	+55	—	—
Uruguay	5.4	—	1.3	10.7
Venezuela	9.1	—	2.3	23.1

Source: Derived from Rosemary Thorp, "The Latin American Economies in the 1940s," in *Latin America in the 1940s*, ed. David Rock (Berkeley: University of California Press, 1994), Tables 3, 4, and 5

American states experienced economic hard times. With peace restored in Asia, primary product exports from Latin America to the U.S. market fell, while those from Asian suppliers grew;[16] and with peace in Europe, U.S. aid and technical assistance flowed into that continent's reconstruction, not Latin America's development.

For a time, foreign reserves and the U.S. need for commodities during the Korean War helped keep Latin American economies afloat, but regional governments still found Washington's unwillingness to extend them aid hard to swallow. Between 1945 and 1951, the tiny European states of Belgium and Luxembourg received more U.S. aid than all Latin American states combined, and in 1951, Latin America was the only regional bloc not covered by a U.S. aid program outside of the communist countries and Africa. By the mid-1950s, global prices for important commodities began to fall, and economic distress expanded. At special hemispheric meetings in 1954 (Rio de Janeiro) and 1956 (Buenos Aires), Latin American states continued to seek some type of U.S. development aid program, but without success; almost to its end, the Eisenhower administration insisted that private sector investment alone was sufficient to address the region's development needs. The deep resentment Latin American states held toward the U.S. position on aid, dovetailed with rising popular frustrations over aspects of U.S. foreign policy.

In the 1940s, the need for wartime solidarity had led the United States to recognize and work with stable governments in Latin America, regardless of their regime type, and undemocratic governments received consistent American support. The Cold War's onset intensified this tendency: U.S. economic, military, and political support went to dictatorships in Cuba, Nicaragua, Paraguay, Peru, and Venezuela. As George Kennan had foreseen, these dictatorships were able to keep a close eye on communists (real or imagined) and repress political movements that appeared too leftist. What Kennan had not foreseen, was the rising popular discontent against such repression and the "blowback" the United States could suffer as a result of supporting it. Just as some contemporary Muslim societies seethe with anti-Americanism owing in part to U.S. support for autocratic Middle East governments, so in the 1950s, anti-Americanism surged in some Latin American societies, especially in countries where U.S.-supported dictators had recently been overthrown.

These sentiments were revealed in dramatic fashion during Vice President Richard Nixon's goodwill tour of Latin America in May 1958. Except for Nicaragua, protestors confronted Nixon in every country he visited, but most strikingly in Peru and Venezuela. One night in Lima, the Vice President tried to catch some sleep while crowds outside his hotel shouted "¡Fuera Nixon! ¡Fuera Nixon!" (Get out, Nixon! Get out, Nixon!); the next day, students at San Marcos University pelted him with rocks. In Caracas—where four months before, Venezuelan society had risen up *en masse* and overthrown U.S.-backed dictator Marcos Pérez Jiménez—Nixon's reception was not just hostile, but life-threatening. Greeted on the airport tarmac by banners in English that proclaimed, GO HOME NIXON! TRICKY DICK, GO HOME! GO AWAY, NIXON! OUT, DOG!, the Vice President and Mrs. Nixon proceeded through a phalanx of soldiers restraining a crowd that seemed to hold the Americans (but more likely, the government they symbolized) in utter contempt—spitting over the soldiers' heads onto the foreign dignitaries. "I thought it was a new trick," Nixon said afterward, "someone busting water bags on us." A few minutes later, his motorcade was encircled by enraged Venezuelans. "Out of the alleys and the side streets," Nixon recalled in his book *Six Crises*, "poured a screaming mob of two to three hundred, throwing rocks, brandishing sticks and pieces of steel pipe . . . Those who had no weapons used their feet and bare fists to beat upon the car."[17]

Ultimately, Nixon escaped unharmed, but the event—captured by television cameras and broadcast around the world—led President Eisenhower to send his brother, Milton, on a fact-finding trip to evaluate the region's problems and recommend ways to counter them. The debriefing report that followed contained unwanted news and recommendations: Latin America's economic situation was so desperate, its need for external economic assistance so critical, that private sector investment (the administration's mantra) was simply insufficient; some type of state-to-state economic aid was required. Unwanted or not, these conclusions and Latin America's overall political climate finally moved Washington to reassess its proscription against using public funds to assist the region's development, and in August 1958, the United States embraced an OAS proposal to create a multilateral Inter-American Development Bank (IADB). This modest policy adjustment was real. But the loans the IADB might provide Latin America were nothing compared to the scale of aid some states believed was required, and to make this case, first Brazil then Colombia stepped onto the stage.

A month after Nixon's disastrous trip, Brazilian president Juscelino Kubitschek drew a sharp contrast between U.S. efforts to promote economic recovery in Europe and Latin America. In a major speech broadcast on television and radio, he praised Washington for aiding Europeans through the Marshall Plan, but lamented its disinterest in assisting its own neighbors' development. Without U.S. aid, he noted, Latin American states were "in a more precarious and afflicted position than the nations devastated by [World War II]." Well attuned to American concerns over Communism, Kubitschek painted his aid request in Cold War terms designed to capture U.S. attention: Latin America was now "the most vulnerable point within the Western coalition"; standard defense measures against external aggression like the Rio Treaty simply could not address the problems of poverty and underdevelopment that communists would most likely exploit. "The Western cause will unavoidably suffer," he warned, "if in its own hemisphere no help comes. It is difficult to defend the democratic ideal with misery weighing on so many lives."[18]

To meet this challenge, Kubitschek proposed Operation Pan America, a large-scale, 20-year assistance program that would attack the region's poverty, promote its development, and be funded largely through U.S. economic aid. Colombia's president Alberto Lleras Camargo echoed Kubitschek's call, and in September 1960, the United States reluctantly joined other OAS members in adopting the Act of Bogotá—under which Washington would contribute $500 million toward an IADB-administered fund to improve Latin Americans' social wellbeing, develop their economies, and strengthen their democratic institutions "within the framework of Operation Pan America."[19]

Neither the Act of Bogotá nor Operation Pan America would have come to pass within the OAS framework without U.S. approval; but their content, as well as the impetus and effort to establish them, did not originate in the United States. It was Latin American states and statesmen that offered a vision of hemispheric development, encouraged their northern neighbor to buy into it, and adeptly took advantage of the OAS machinery and Cold War climate to press their case. In the process, they established important precursors to the Alliance for Progress. The 1961 Declaration of the Peoples of America drew inspiration directly from these precursors (as noted in its opening paragraph), and the new Kennedy administration embraced them too: Kennedy pitched his own announcement of the Alliance as analogous to the "majestic concept of Operation Pan America." In short, just as Latin American states played a critical role in creating the Inter-American System, they played a similar role in developing the Alliance for Progress.

The historical narrative above provides one way to explain why the Americas adopted the Alliance for Progress. We also can employ more standard analytical concepts.

LEVELS OF ANALYSIS

What role, for example, did individuals play? Both Juscelino Kubitschek and John Kennedy clearly mattered. Not only did Kubitschek's Operation Pan America form a template for the Alliance, but his famous 1958 speech was not his first attempt to persuade the United States on the virtues of providing Latin America a comprehensive aid program. With a persistence the Eisenhower administration may well have found annoying, he broached the topic on prior occasions and in letters to the American president. Finally, his political savvy helped him frame the 1958 request in Cold War terms Washington could understand, and take advantage of the fallout from Vice President Nixon's ill-fated goodwill tour. As president of the country that would assume much of the Alliance's financial burden, Kennedy's active support and full throttle embrace of the program's underlying ideas were also critical. Eduardo Frei's comment that the Alliance became a reality "because it was accepted by the United States and specifically by President Kennedy" was a veiled jab at Dwight Eisenhower's unwillingness to do the same. But his observation that JFK "understood . . . and injected new life into" the Alliance ideas was very much on point,[20] since the Alliance for Progress depended a great deal on Kennedy's decision to sponsor and support it with his own political capital. Of course, the Alliance was not simply the product of the Brazilian and U.S. presidents. There were other causal factors too.

At the systemic level, both the structure of the international system and the global distribution of power within it helped expand U.S.-Soviet competition into Latin America in ways conducive to a multilateral hemispheric development program. In terms of structure, Cold War competition played out within a rigid, bipolar system that encouraged zero-sum thinking (any perceived gain by one side translated into a loss for the other). Consequently, the superpowers not only tried to balance each other in hard power terms through conventional forces and nuclear arsenals, but also in terms of their regional influence. The Soviet Union's 1956 announcement that it would extend diplomatic, economic, and technical aid to Latin American states, was in part, a reflection of this dynamic; and America's belated decision to support a hemispheric development project was the response (some Eisenhower officials advocated a new aid approach much earlier but lost the internal policy debates). The global distribution of power also tended to push superpower competition into the developing world and Latin America. The United States had already locked down parts of Asia through defense agreements with Japan and South Korea; and in Europe, where Soviet influence extended across much of the East, an uneasy Cold War stability had settled onto the continent, where the NATO and Warsaw Pact alliances produced a relative balance of forces. This distribution of power led the superpowers to seek further gains outside these regions.

Domestic-level factors in both Americas also influenced the course of events. In Latin American states, three types of factors—economic, political, and social—were important. First, economic distress led many states beyond Brazil and Colombia to view development as an imperative, not a luxury. In private conversations Vice President Nixon held with state leaders during his 1958 visit, Ecuador's president Camilo Enríquez confided that his country's "principal problem was that of raising the living standards of the people"; Colombia's president-elect Alberto Lleras explained that "if a better way of life could not be available to the people, an 'explosion' was inevitable"; and Bolivia's president Hernán Zuazo had worried he would be assassinated if Bolivia's growing economic and social problems remained unsolved.[21]

Second, a wave of political transitions away from authoritarianism had swept over Latin America, reflecting a mounting popular desire for greater democracy with social justice. In 1955, Costa Rican president José Figueres had proclaimed that "The Latin American people are ripe for democracy,"[22] and by the late 1950s, unconstitutional governments had fallen not just in Costa Rica, but in Cuba, Peru, and Venezuela too. Moreover, except for Cuba, in all these countries plus Colombia, reformist leaders and parties of the Democratic Left had emerged. Consequently, explained Kennedy aide and Cuban historian

Arturo Morales Carrión, "The Alliance responded to Latin America's yearning for democracy with social justice."[23] Equally important, however, in many Latin American countries political discontent over the status quo was clearly evident. The Cuban Revolution cast shadows over the region's future and suggested the possibility of similar socialist revolutions elsewhere. For many Latin American governments, the Alliance for Progress seemed to offer a way to avoid replicating Cuba's experience.

Finally, across the region and in some countries more than others, Latin America's social structures were changing. A new middle class—or what Stanford historian John Johnson labeled the "middle sectors"—was emerging. This new social group, Johnson explained, exhibited a moderate, more democratic stance toward politics, demanded political change including "government by law and by the people,"[24] and seemed poised to grow stronger and larger as development progressed. The Alliance's democratic and development thrust aimed to capitalize on these changes.

In the United States, three domestic factors were also critical. First, in 1960, U.S. domestic politics brought to power a new administration with a fresh perspective on Latin American policy and a determination to distance itself from what John Kennedy considered the failed policies of his predecessor. Especially critical of America's "failure to understand the rapidly changing hopes and ambitions of the people to the south . . . [and to] identify ourselves with the rising tide of freedom," Kennedy alleged that Eisenhower's policies had convinced U.S. neighbors "that we are more interested in stable regimes than in free governments; more interested in fighting against Communism than in fighting for freedom." What was needed, he claimed in the campaign, was an approach "not merely directed against Communism, but aimed at helping our sister republics for their own sake."[25] As president, Kennedy stacked his inner Latin American policy circle with like-minded individuals, who quickly helped put these policy critiques into practice.

Second, notwithstanding Kennedy's public arguments on the need to help the American republics for their own sake, the administration saw the Alliance as a response to the Cuban Revolution—a means to bolster the region against further communist inroads and undercut the potential for violent, socialist revolution á la Cuba. Strong anti-communist sentiments in Congress ensured initial funding for the Alliance, and similar public sentiments provided political support for a new-style containment effort. Consequently, in the wake of Cuba's revolution, Kennedy did not find it too difficult to convince lawmakers and the public that promoting and financing Latin America's economic and political development were in the United States' national interest.

A third domestic factor was the rise of new social science theories that posited a strong correlation, if not a causal relationship, between economic development and political democratization. These *modernization* theories—advanced by scholars like Gabriel Almond, Seymour Martin Lipset, Max Millikan, Lucian Pye, and Walt Rostow—gained strong currency within the Kennedy transition team and White House. Although modernization arguments varied, most shared several core assumptions. They viewed modernization as an evolutionary process in which societies moved from a traditional status to one of modernity, a revolutionary process that transformed major patterns of human life, a complex process that encompassed industrialization, urbanization, social differentiation, and expanded political participation, and a progressive process that was desirable on its own merits. Most important, countries that passed through the stages of modernization exhibited a strong correlation between economic growth and political democracy. Scholars like Rostow (who served in the Kennedy and Johnson administrations) also posited that exposure to advanced, modern societies could assist, even accelerate this transition. In the early 1960s, these ideas exerted a powerful influence not only on how U.S. policymakers thought about the political and strategic value of a large-scale aid program, but also about its overall viability.

Box 7.2 Modernization and Democracy in Latin America

[I]ndustrialization, urbanization, wealth, and education, are so closely interrelated as to form one common factor [i.e., economic development]. And the factors subsumed under economic development carry with it the political correlate of democracy . . . Perhaps the most widespread generalization linking political systems to other aspects of society has been that democracy is related to the state of economic development. Concretely, this means that the more well-to-do a nation, the greater the chances that it will sustain democracy . . . If Latin America is allowed to develop . . . and is able to increase its productivity and middle classes, there is a good chance that many Latin American countries will follow in the European (democratic) direction. Recent developments, including the overthrowal of a number of dictatorships, in large measure reflect the effects of an increased middle class, growing wealth, and increased education.

Seymour Martin Lipset, "Some Social Requisites of Democracy: Economic Development and Political Legitimacy," *The American Political Science Review* 53 (March 1959): 80, 75, 102

Three Perspectives on the Alliance's Failure

Of course, the Alliance did not prove to be viable, and by the end of the 1960s, it had fallen well short of its objectives. Across Latin America, the number of dictatorships, not democratic governments, had grown; more people were living in poverty, not less; a good share of new capital that came into the region had flowed back out to repay debt and repatriate foreign investors' profits; perhaps a million peasant families received land under agrarian reform programs, but 10–14 million families eligible for land received none; and U.S. Alliance efforts focused more on fighting Communism and promoting American business, than advancing regional social, economic, and political change. What explains these outcomes? On this point, there are three competing views.

The traditional *liberal* perspective held by many who helped formulate or advocate the Alliance, takes its stated goals at face value. Despite important differences between the Western Hemispheric states, liberals believe that the Americas were united by a community of interests and a shared desire to provide their citizens greater economic prosperity, political liberty, and security. They also believe the U.S. national interest was distinct from the more parochial interests of American private business, and that it was in the U.S. interest to help Latin America progress economically, democratically, and socially.

Liberals, therefore, see the Alliance as a genuine commitment to cooperate multilaterally toward achieving the ambitious goals laid out in the Declaration of the Peoples of America. For Alberto Lleras, former president of Colombia, the Alliance was an "enormous rehabilitation enterprise . . . [an] audacious plan to transform the lives of millions of human beings";[26] for Lincoln Gordon, a Harvard economist and member of JFK's transition team task force on Latin America, it represented "the hopes for a major advance in social and economic development" in Latin America.[27] Liberals concede that the United States saw the Alliance as a means to enhance U.S. security in the Cold War, and even promote private American economic interests. But for liberals, these factors affirm rather than vitiate the essential truth that the Alliance was a vehicle for all Western Hemispheric states to pursue their shared interests in greater progress, prosperity, and security.

Liberals explain the disparity between the Alliance's stated goals and its results largely on the basis of first- and second-level factors. At the first level, John Kennedy's murder was critical because many who advised JFK on Latin America left government service after his death, which diminished U.S. commitment to the Alliance's original goals. Under Kennedy's successor Lyndon Johnson, U.S. policy toward Latin America moved away from its initial focus on promoting democracy, structural change, and poverty reduction.

Moreover, as president, Johnson replaced Teodoro Moscoso as Alliance Coordinator with Thomas Mann, then made Mann the Assistant Secretary of State for Inter-American Affairs. An Alliance skeptic, Mann did not believe land reform was economically viable or that democracy promotion was politically feasible. Intensely anti-communist and pro-U.S. business, he deemphasized those aspects of the Alliance unrelated to security, anti-communism, and corporate America. For liberals, these personnel changes help explain why the Alliance for Progress increasingly displayed less resemblance to its initial incarnation over time.

Box 7.3 The Mann Doctrine

In March 1964, Thomas Mann—President Johnson's new Assistant Secretary of State for Inter-American Affairs and coordinator of the Alliance for Progress—delivered a closed-door speech to high-level U.S. officials and ambassadors serving in Latin America. In the speech, Mann outlined dramatic changes to U.S. policy toward the region that downplayed key elements of the Alliance for Progress. The Johnson administration never published Mann's policy announcements in any official document, but did leak their substance to the press and key lawmakers. Quickly dubbed the "Mann Doctrine," Washington's new policy stressed regional stability over dramatic democratic change and exhibited an ambivalence toward democracy promotion in sharp contrast with the original Alliance for Progress goals. The substance of Mann's 1964 address and its policy implications were recorded by New York Times reporter, Tad Szulc:

> The United States was reported today to be considering modification of its policy of actively opposing rightist and military dictatorships that might emerge in the future in Latin America.
>
> The reported shift in policy, under which the United States would no longer seek to punish military juntas for overthrowing democratic regimes, was outlined last night by Thomas C. Mann, Assistant Secretary of State for Inter-American Affairs . . .
>
> Mr. Mann, who is President Johnson's chief Latin-American policy-maker, discussed his views on dictatorships and democracy in the Western Hemisphere in an address to a group of high-ranking United States officials serving in Latin America . . .

Mr. Mann is said to have emphasized four purposes United States policy in Latin America should serve.

They are the fostering of economic growth in the area, the protection of $9 billion in United States investments there, non-intervention in the internal political affairs of the hemisphere's republics, and opposition to Communism . . .

Mr. Mann's views were considered as representing a radical modification of the policies followed by the Kennedy Administration under the Alliance for Progress.

President Kennedy believed that economic and social development under the Alliance must move hand-in-hand with the development of democracy and that, therefore, the United States had the duty actively to encourage the practice of democracy and refuse its help to regimes that had overturned representative democracies.

This concept was recognized in the Alliance's charter, signed at Punta del Este Uruguay, by 20 American governments in August, 1961.

It proclaimed in its "declaration to the peoples of America" that "this alliance is established on the basic principle that free men working through the institution of representative democracy can best satisfy man's aspirations."

Diplomats who attended last night's session said that in his entire presentation Mr. Mann made no mention of the Alliance for Progress.

Tad Szulc, "U.S. May Abandon Effort to Deter Latin Dictators," *New York Times*, March 19, 1964

Liberals also believe the Alliance failed due to second-level domestic factors. In the United States, bureaucratic inertia and a lack of interagency coordination hampered the implementation of Alliance projects in the field. In Latin America, the region's middle class did not perform its expected function as a catalyst for change, champion of democracy, and wedge against the status quo; instead, it often aligned itself against the region's downtrodden groups and with those forces opposing dramatic change. Latin American oligarchies, meanwhile, fiercely resisted structural changes like land reform and political liberalization and, in league with military leaders, constrained and in some cases, helped overthrow reformist governments that aimed to promote them. More generally, the region's rapid birthrate increased the number of those living in poverty faster than the Alliance could lift them out. Liberals believe that despite the good intentions of all parties in 1961, those who championed the Alliance in both Americas overestimated the potential for peaceful revolutionary change in Latin America, and underestimated the intensity of resistance to it.

The *radical* perspective offers a very different interpretation, one linked closely to Marxist analysis and dependency theory. The radicals wrote primarily in the late 1960s and early 1970s, during the Vietnam War. Unlike liberals who view the two Americas' basic interests as essentially compatible, radicals see a clear distinction between U.S. goals to dominate America's neighbors on the one hand, and Latin Americans' quest for sovereignty and independence on the other. Owing to the nature of U.S. capitalism and its commanding influence over U.S. foreign policy, they maintain that the United States' national interest *as a state* is virtually indistinguishable from the interests of U.S. capitalists. Following dependency theory, U.S. development produced—and required— underdevelopment in Latin America; hence, the United States had a vested interest in preserving Latin America's dependence.

Radicals, therefore, view the Alliance as a tool to re-open the markets in Latin America that import-substitution industrialization and economic nationalism had closed. Less crude than gunboat or Dollar Diplomacy, they deem it a sophisticated policy instrument to advance American corporate interests at the economic and political expense of U.S. neighbors, and in the words of Susanne Bodenheimer, "one more means of integrating Latin America into the international system that creates dependency and hinders development in the region."[28] For radicals, there is no mystery to explain respecting the gap between the Alliance's stated goals and its divergent outcomes, since the program's "real" goals were never the expansion of liberty, democracy, or economic prosperity for Latin Americans. In the end, its net results—maintenance of the region's status quo, greater U.S.–Latin American economic linkages, greater hemispheric unity behind the U.S. drive to staunch communist expansion (which would curtail U.S. capitalist expansion), and less political freedom if that is what it took—were produced not by individuals or domestic factors, but by design.

The *bureaucratic* perspective, as exemplified by political scientist Abraham F. Lowenthal, takes issue with both liberals and radicals. As a U.S. policy, it views the Alliance not as the product of a unitary actor called "the U.S. government," which worked either to advance its own singular interest or those of corporate America. Instead, it was the product of jostling and competition between different segments of the U.S. government and business—each of which had their own interests and whose capacity to influence the content and direction of policy varied over time. Thus, "The Alliance," writes Lowenthal, "was not dictated by big-business interests nor was it a mere rhetorical pose, adopted simply to camouflage traditional North American imperial designs. Rather, [it] resulted from a political and bureaucratic process tacked temporarily to weight the influence of persons and groups genuinely interested in the Alliance's stated goals."[29]

According to this perspective, at the beginning of the Kennedy administration in 1961, relative outsiders ("Kennedy men") enjoyed an unusual ability to influence Washington's signature policy toward Latin America. Those close to President Kennedy who helped formulate U.S. policy—Adolf Berle, Lincoln Gordon, Richard Goodwin, and Arthur Schlesinger, Jr.—had a personal interest or ideological stake in promoting democracy and development in Latin America, and some like Berle had extensive personal contacts with key Latin American reformist leaders, in Colombia, Costa Rica, Puerto Rico, and Venezuela. By contrast, in 1961 traditional bureaucratic heavyweights like the CIA, Pentagon, and State Department, as well as corporate America, all experienced a temporary reduction in their capacity to influence the content and direction of U.S. policy.

Since the Alliance's goal to induce peaceful revolutions fell well outside these actors' core areas of competence and preferences, they had little input on its design or objectives. Not only were career diplomats at the State Department "little more than bystanders," Lowenthal suggests, but, adds Schlesinger, Richard Goodwin wrote the president's speech announcing the Alliance from within the White House precisely because "it could never have come out of the State Department that Kennedy inherited from Eisenhower." Corporate America's influence over the initial program was negligible too: "Big-business did not participate in any meaningful way in the formulation of the Alliance," notes political scientist Federico Gil.[30]

But the diminution of these actors' influence was only temporary. Even before Kennedy's death, the outsiders' influence on policy began to wane. As the president's attention shifted away from Latin America (after the Cuban Missile Crisis) to Southeast Asia, his advisors' influence declined too. Meanwhile, actors like the State Department—that had not devised the Alliance, contained staff that actively opposed it, but were charged with implementing it nonetheless—gained ground. So did U.S. security agencies concerned with averting the spread of Communism. Both the CIA and Pentagon worked to ensure that U.S. Alliance funds bypassed reform projects developed in Latin America that seemed too progressive or infiltrated by communists, and instead, flowed to development projects controlled by status quo elites. Thus, the perversion of the Alliance for Progress steadily progressed over time.

Whereas Kennedy had turned to scholars for innovative policy ideas (and in the process, elevated their influence above that of usual bureaucratic actors or business), Johnson relied more on traditional organs of state that had never truly embraced the Alliance's original goals of land reform and political democratization. The advice Johnson received from agencies like the CIA did little to advance a dramatic, positive regional transformation.

As early as 1964, the CIA warned the president that through its call for revolutionary change, the Alliance was fomenting security dangers by stimulating destabilizing, popular demands "for positive and radical changes" in social and economic structures, and for "accomplishments in short periods of time" that simply were "impossible of attainment, even granted unlimited resources and extensive periods of time."[31] Ironically, at the 1961 Punta del Este meeting, Che Guevara had warned Kennedy aide Richard Goodwin on this same point: "By encouraging the forces of change and the desires of the masses," Che said, "you might set loose forces beyond your control, ending in a revolution which would be your enemy."[32] Accordingly, Alliance aid began flowing to governments that were politically stable and strongly anti-communist, but which displayed little progress on democratization or land reform (including dictatorships in Brazil, El Salvador, Guatemala, and Honduras). Corporate America also regained influence over policy, and lobbied Congress to enact legislation that transformed parts of the Alliance into vehicles for private gain. For its part, Congress became disillusioned with the Alliance's lack of achievement by the mid-1960s and, faced with calls to increase spending on the Vietnam War, began decreasing America's financial contribution to the Alliance. In short, suggests the bureaucratic perspective, the Alliance failed to promote democracy and structural change, not due to U.S. imperialist designs or individual intent, but largely due to the standard, inner workings of the U.S. foreign policy process.

Cold War Legacies

At the height of the Cold War, John Kennedy and Fidel Castro each granted interviews to French journalist, Jean Daniel, in which they offered their assessments of each other and discussed the Alliance for Progress. Their personal assessments expressed a surprising level of understanding for each other's actions—perhaps even a measure of admiration. They found common ground on the Alliance's Cold War aim to inoculate Latin America from further Cuban-style revolutions, but their hopes and judgments regarding its prospects of success differed; of the two, Castro's assessment seems more vindicated by history.

On October 24, 1963, Daniel visited Kennedy at the White House, where he captured the president's thoughts on Cuba, U.S.-Cuban relations, and U.S. foreign policy toward Latin America as it pertained to the Alliance for Progress.

John F. Kennedy: "I believe that there is no country in the world, including the African regions, including any and all the countries under colonial domination, where economic colonization, humiliation and exploitation were worse than in Cuba, in part owing to my country's policies during the Batista regime. I believe that we created, built and manufactured the Castro movement out of whole cloth and without realizing it. I believe that the accumulation of these mistakes has jeopardized all of Latin America. The great aim of the Alliance for Progress is to reverse this unfortunate policy . . . I can assure you that I have understood the Cubans. I approved the proclamation which Fidel Castro made in the Sierra Maestra, when he justifiably called for justice and especially yearned to rid Cuba of corruption. I will go even further: to some extent it is as though Batista was the incarnation of a number of sins on the part of the United States. Now we shall have to pay for those sins . . . [But] Castro betrayed the promises made in the Sierra Maestra, and . . . has agreed to be a Soviet agent in Latin America . . . [Through the Alliance] The United States now has the possibility of doing as much good in Latin America as it has done wrong in the past."[33]

Leaving Washington, Daniel flew to Havana where in November 1963, he relayed Kennedy's comments to Castro and recorded his response.

Fidel Castro: "I believe Kennedy is sincere . . . But I feel that he inherited a difficult situation . . . I also think he is a realist: he is now registering that it is impossible to simply wave a wand and cause us [the Cuban revolutionary regime], and the explosive situation throughout Latin America, to disappear . . . In a way, [the Alliance] was a good idea, it marked progress of a sort . . . I am willing to agree that the idea in itself constituted an effort to adapt to the extraordinarily rapid course of events in Latin America . . . [But] Kennedy's good ideas aren't going to yield any results . . . For years and years American policy—not the government, but the trusts and the Pentagon—has supported the Latin American oligarchies. All the prestige, the dollars, and the power was held by a class which Kennedy himself has described in speaking of Batista. Suddenly a President arrives on the scene who tries to support the interests of another class (which has no access to any of the levers of power) to give the various Latin American countries the impression that the United States no longer stands behind the dictators, and so there is no more need to start Castro-type revolutions. What happens then? The trusts see that their interests are being a little compromised (just barely, but still compromised); the Pentagon thinks the strategic bases are in danger; the powerful oligarchies in all the Latin American countries alert their American friends; they sabotage the new policy; and in short, Kennedy has everyone against him."[34]

On November 22, 1963, Daniel was at Castro's summer home on Varadero Beach, wrapping up his interviews with the Cuban leader. At around 1:30 p.m. Havana time, Castro received a phone call relaying startling news about the President of the United States. Daniel recorded the one-sided conversation as follows: "¿Como? ¿Un atentado? ¿Herido? ¿Muy gravemente?" ("What's that? An attempted assassination? Wounded? Very seriously?"). Castro explained the events in Dallas to Daniel, and told him repeatedly: "This is bad news." Along with a translator, the two men then followed the breaking story through radio broadcasts from Miami. When the president's death was finally announced, a stunned Castro pondered its implications for the Cold War and Latin America's future. "Everything is going to change," he said. "The United States occupies such a position in world affairs that the death of a President of that country affects millions of people in every corner of the globe. The cold war, relations with Russia, Latin America, Cuba . . . all will have to be rethought . . . This is an extremely serious matter."[35]

Castro was right about the gravity of Kennedy's death, but perhaps less so about the future. The Cold War outlived the Alliance for Progress by almost two decades, during which it continued to frame the relations between the United States and Cuba, the Soviet Union, and much of Latin America. The Alliance's failure to transform the region's economic, political, and social landscape allowed pressing problems to fester. Efforts to address those problems—whether by reformist politicians and civil society working within the political system, guerrilla militias working outside it, or militaries that had overthrown it—played out within the Cold War context. Often, these efforts bred instability, civil wars, revolutions, coups, and dictatorships that in the 1970s and 1980s, ensured the Cold War would become very hot for both Latin America and the United States.

Study Questions

1. How might realist theory explain revolutionary Cuba's foreign policies and its relations with the United States? How might a dependency perspective?
2. Why might realist theorists *not* be surprised by the development of the Cuban Missile Crisis? How did the resolution of the crisis provide greater security to Cuba, the Soviet Union, and the United States?
3. Does the Cuban Missile Crisis demonstrate the importance that individuals play in international affairs, or does it show individual leaders virtually overwhelmed by impersonal factors and the rush of events?
4. What is economic nationalism and why do states sometimes embrace it? In what ways can it influence states' domestic and foreign policies? Why did the United States sometimes equate Latin American economic nationalism with communist encroachment?
5. How did Juscelino Kubitschek's actions and vision of hemispheric development contribute to the birth of the Alliance for Progress? What were the Alliance's main goals and to what extent were they achieved?
6. Like Latin American states, the Kennedy administration had high hopes for the Alliance for Progress. On what grounds did this optimism rest? At the time, were the judgments of U.S. officials reasonable?

Selected Readings

Castro, Fidel. "History Will Absolve Me." In *The Cuba Reader: History, Culture, Politics*, edited by Aviva Chomsky, Barry Carr, and Pamela Maria Smorkaloff, 306–314. Durham, NC: Duke University Press, 2003.

Domínguez, Jorge I. *To Make a World Safe for Revolution: Cuba's Foreign Policy*, 44–56. Cambridge, MA: Harvard University Press, 1989.

Frei Montalva, Eduardo. "The Alliance that Lost its Way." *Foreign Affairs* 45 (1967): 437–448.

Garthoff, Raymond L. "The Cuban Missile Crisis: An Overview." In *The Cuban Missile Crisis Revisited*, edited by James A. Nathan, 41–53. New York: St. Martin's, 1992.

Kagan, Donald. *On the Origins of War and the Preservation of Peace*, 437–548. New York: Anchor Books, Doubleday, 1995.

LaFeber, Walter. "Thomas C. Mann and the Devolution of Latin American Policy: From the Good Neighbor to Military Intervention." In *Behind the Throne: Servants of Power to Imperial Presidents, 1898–1968*, edited by Thomas J. McCormick and Walter LaFeber, 166–198. Madison: University of Wisconsin Press, 1993.

Levinson, Jerome and Juan de Onis. "The Alliance that Lost its Way: A Critical Report on the Alliance for Progress." In *Neighborly Adversaries: Readings in U.S.–Latin American Relations*, edited by Michael LaRosa and Frank O. Mora, 189–202. Latham, MD: Rowman & Littlefield, 1999.

Lippmann, Walter. "Cuba and the Nuclear Risk." *The Atlantic Monthly*. February 1963.

Pérez, Jr., Louis A. *Cuba: Between Reform and Revolution*, third edition, 285–290. New York: Oxford University Press, 2005.

Schlesinger, Jr., Arthur. "The Alliance for Progress: A Retrospective." In *Latin America: The Search for a New International Role*, edited by Ronald Hellman and H. Jon Rosenbaum, 57–88. New York: Sage, 1975.

Will, George F. "Lessons of the Cuban Missile Crisis." *Newsweek*. October 11, 1982.

Wright, Thomas C. *Latin America in the Era of the Cuban Revolution*, revised edition, 1–38. Westport, CT: Praeger, 2001.

Further Readings

Blight, James G. and David A. Welch. *On the Brink: Americans and Soviets Reexamine the Cuban Missile Crisis*. New York: Hill & Wang, 1989.

Bonilla, Heraclio. "Commentary on Lowenthal." In *Latin America and the United States*, edited by Julio Cotler and Richard R. Fagen, 236–237. Stanford, CA: Stanford University Press, 1974.

Cobbs, Elizabeth A. "U.S. Business: Self-Interest and Neutrality." In *Exporting Democracy: The United States and Latin America, Themes and Issues*, edited by Abraham F. Lowenthal, 123–154. Baltimore: Johns Hopkins University Press, 1991.

Domínguez, Jorge I. "The @#$%& Missile Crisis: (Or, What was 'Cuban' about U.S. Decisions during the Cuban Missile Crisis?)." *Diplomatic History* 24 (Spring 2000): 305–315.

Domínguez, Jorge I. *To Make a World Safe for Revolution: Cuba's Foreign Policy*. Cambridge, MA: Harvard University Press, 1989.

Fursenko, Aleksandr and Timothy Naftali. *"One Hell of a Gamble": Khrushchev, Castro and Kennedy, 1958–1964*. New York: W. W. Norton, 1997.

Gordon, Lincoln. "The Alliance at Birth: Hopes and Fears." In *The Alliance for Progress: A Retrospective*, edited by L. Ronald Scheman, 73–79. Westport, CT: Praeger, 1988.

Guevara, Che. *Guerrilla Warfare*. Lincoln: University of Nebraska Press, 1985.

Latham, Michael E. "Ideology, Social Science, and Destiny: Modernization and the Kennedy-Era Alliance for Progress." *Diplomatic History* 22 (Spring 1998): 199–229.

Lowenthal, Abraham F. "'Liberal,' 'Radical,' and 'Bureaucratic' Perspectives on US Latin American Policy: The Alliance for Progress in Retrospect." In *Latin America and the United States*, edited by Julio Cotler and Richard R. Fagen, 212–235. Stanford, CA: Stanford University Press, 1974.

May, Ernest R. and Philip D. Zelikow (eds), *The Kennedy Tapes: Inside the White House During the Cuban Missile Crisis*. Cambridge, MA: Belknap and Harvard University Press, 1997.

Moscoso, Teodoro. "The Will to Economic Development." In *The Alliance for Progress: A Retrospective*, edited by L. Ronald Scheman, 81–87. Westport, CT: Praeger, 1988.

Packenham, Robert A. *Liberal America and the Third World: Political Development Ideas in Foreign Aid and Social Science*, 3–22, 59–84; 111–160. Princeton: Princeton University Press, 1973.

Rabe, Stephen G. *The Most Dangerous Area in the World: John F. Kennedy Confronts Communist Revolution in Latin America*. Chapel Hill: University of North Carolina Press, 1999.

Chronology: The Cold War Years, Part II

1956	Soviets extend diplomatic relations and economic/technical aid to Latin America
1958	Vice President Nixon attacked in Caracas, Venezuela
1958	Brazil's president Juscelino Kubitschek urges continental developmental aid program, Operation Pan America
1959	Inter-American Development Bank created
1959	Cuban Revolution; Castro prevails, Batista flees; Castro visits U.S.
1960	Cuba aligns with Soviet Union; Kennedy elected U.S. president
1961	Castro proclaims Cuba a Socialist state; CIA-sponsored Bay of Pigs invasion of Cuba fails; Alliance for Progress announced; Declaration of the Peoples of America signed
1962	Cuban Missile Crisis; Limited security regime established by U.S. and USSR in Caribbean
1963	JFK assassinated; Johnson becomes president
1964	Thomas Mann replaces Teodoro Moscoso as Alliance for Progress Coordinator, announces Mann Doctrine
1964–1969	Alliance for Progress fails

Cold War Challenges to U.S. Hegemony

8

Figure 8.1 Chile's President Salvador Allende speaking at the UN, 1972

The Cold War brought unprecedented challenges to American hegemony in the Western Hemisphere, but not from the Soviet Union directly. Instead, they emanated from regional powers themselves, and from the political dynamics that engulfed them. The nature of these challenges varied. But whether unilateral, multilateral, or the product of domestic instability and revolutionary fervor, they formed part of the broad Cold War context. This chapter examines both the challenges to American hegemony and the U.S. response to them. Because the idea that weaker states could challenge a hegemon effectively seems counterintuitive, it's useful to dispel a common misperception about hegemony and U.S.–Latin American relations—namely, that America's power advantage so restricted its neighbors' agency that it left the United States virtually unlimited influence over their external and internal affairs. The United States did wield great influence, and in some instances, did restrict other states' agency. But hegemons do not always get their way in international politics; the belief that they do can be as misleading as the notion that hegemons routinely dominate weaker states through belligerent actions. The simplest way to avoid confusion on these matters is to revisit a point discussed briefly in Chapter 4, and clarify the difference between hegemony and other types of great power influence.

Primacy, Dominance, and Hegemony

The degree of influence that strong states enjoy over weaker ones and the type of relationship that develops between them can assume diverse forms: primacy, dominance, and hegemony. Each form provides the strong state significant leverage over lesser powers, but typically, that influence is acquired and exercised in different ways.

Primacy occurs when weaker states voluntarily concede a leadership status to a stronger power without that state having to resort to coercion, force, or threats. States that acquire primacy typically exercise influence through multilateral arrangements or institutions, and avoid displaying excessive disregard for the rights of lesser powers or other established international norms. Ancient Greece provides one example. When the Greek city-states were battling the Persians 2600 years ago, Athens—encouraged and supported by other city-states—assumed leadership of the Greek cause when the Spartans abdicated this role. Athens' leadership and naval power were important factors in the Persians' defeat, and Athens retained its leadership status among many Greek states (the Delian League) long after the Persian threat had been stamped out. Another example was Britain's position among its "Old Dominions" during the inter-war period. After World War I, London established the British Commonwealth whose other members (Australia, Canada, Ceylon (Sri Lanka), India, Ireland, Newfoundland, New Zealand, and South Africa) willingly accorded Britain leadership in Commonwealth affairs. As these examples suggest, primacy reflects a type of *primus inter pares* (first among equals) relationship, and the leadership it connotes often reflects the contributions weak states believe a stronger power makes toward achieving some common purpose.

By contrast, *dominance* refers to one state's acquisition of military, political, and economic superiority, its routine use of force against weaker powers, and a habitual disregard of the weaker states' rights of equality, independence, and sovereignty. Dominant states are not classical empires, and do not impose strict, imperial rule over weak states. They do, however, treat them much like second-class members of international society—members whose rights can be ignored with impunity. In the late nineteenth century, Britain's behavior toward and relations with Egypt, Iraq, and Jordan reflected this concept of dominance. In the Western Hemisphere, from the Spanish-American War through the adoption of the Good Neighbor Policy, the United States displayed similar attitudes toward and patterns of relations with its immediate neighbors in the Caribbean and Central America. Australian political scientist Hedley Bull notes:

> In both these cases the preponderance of the great power was expressed in habitual and uninhibited military intervention in the internal affairs and external relations of the local states, including prolonged military occupation, and in failure to pay more than lip service to notions of the sovereignty, equality and independence of these states.[1]

Hegemony is similar to dominance, yet different. A hegemonic state possesses a preponderance of military, political, and economic power over others. Such states do resort to force (or the threat of force) in relating to lesser powers, but not in a habitual or uninhibited fashion. More often, hegemons use force reluctantly and, instead, prefer to exercise influence through other instruments. Hegemonic states concede that weaker states possess rights of equality, independence, and sovereignty; but they remain fully prepared to violate these rights in situations where they perceive (accurately or not) their vital interests are at stake.

During the Cold War, the Soviet Union exercised hegemony over Eastern Europe. It recognized these states had rights, but still used force against them in 1953, 1956, and 1968 (to quell an internal challenge to the communist East German government, and to overthrow the governments of Hungary and Czechoslovakia). Despite these military incursions, Moscow preferred to exercise hegemonic influence through its positions as the hub of international Communism, the Eastern bloc's principal defense against Western, capitalist states, and through its Warsaw Pact multilateral security alliance (through which it crushed the political reforms of the 1968 "Prague Spring" that threatened the socialist order of Czechoslovakia and other East European states). After transitioning from dominance to hegemony after the advent of the Good Neighbor Policy, Washington's behavior toward its neighbors displayed similar dynamics. Despite its interventions, the United States still officially recognized the rights of lesser powers, and when it violated those rights, it often did so covertly (as in Cuba, Chile, Guatemala, and Nicaragua), or under the auspices of international institutions (as in the Dominican Republic and Grenada). Generally, however, Washington preferred to exert influence through economic and diplomatic pressure, not force. And because diplomacy involved compromise by default—while economic pressures weren't always effective—U.S. hegemonic influence was extensive but never as smothering as often perceived.

As discussed in Chapter 3, when an international system acquires a unipolar structure, the state that functions as the central "pole" of power can set that system's rules and then "milk" them to its advantage. In the Western Hemisphere, the United States guarded its unipolar position jealously, especially during the Cold War. Among the implicit rules that emerged under unipolarity were that Latin American governments must defer to the United States on matters of strategic significance and show fidelity to U.S. regional leadership, while the United States would serve as interlocutor between extra-hemispheric powers and the Americas. At times during the Cold War, hegemonic influence was exercised through American military power, but more often through multilateral arrangements like the Organization of American States, the broader Inter-American System (including the Inter-American Development Bank), and unilateral economic and diplomatic initiatives.

Hegemony itself can be a confusing concept, partly because it's mistaken for dominance, and partly due to its normative connotations: the very act of exercising hegemony casts value judgments on the stronger state's behavior toward weaker powers. Discussions of U.S. hegemony, therefore, sometimes carry a negative overtone that can yield imprecise conclusions regarding

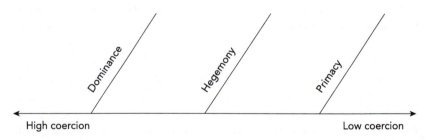

Figure 8.2 Types of Great Power Influence

its actual consequences. For example, one common belief is that American hegemony imposed high costs on Latin American states, but provided them no real benefits.

In reality, U.S. hegemony did accord weaker powers some important benefits, although not enough to offset the resentment it kindled among Latin American states. One benefit was simply the relative order the United States provided in an otherwise anarchic environment. This order sprang from the very rules that Washington set to govern inter-state relations, and is the type of benefit weak states could never have secured on their own. Another benefit was the enhanced, less costly security against stronger states (save America) that derived from Washington's efforts to safeguard its own expansive zone of influence. "Lower defense expenditures," explains political scientist David Lake, "are one of the benefits that subordinate states receive" whenever they come into a hierarchical security relationship with a strong or hegemonic one.[2] Since the United States first acquired the power to enforce the Monroe Doctrine in the late nineteenth century, the security blanket it extended southward into Latin America to protect its own flanks impinged on weaker states' sovereignty, but relieved them of the need to fully fund their own defense. Thus, throughout much of the Cold War, many U.S. neighbors enjoyed a type of "security on the cheap." Between 1950 and 2000, South American states spent less than half (47 percent) of the global average on defense, while Caribbean and Central American states even closer to U.S. borders spent just over a quarter (26 percent).

Hegemony constitutes one of the realities of international politics, and hegemonic states can hold sway over lesser powers for long periods. But in an anarchic world, hegemony can also be fleeting. Throughout history, strong states have sometimes lost their preeminent position. Understanding exactly why a hegemon declines can offer useful insights into the challenges against U.S. hegemony that developed during the Cold War.

According to Yale historian Paul Kennedy, from the sixteenth through the twentieth centuries, the world's great powers rose and fell based on changes in their economic productivity and wealth, military and defense expenditures, military successes, and overseas commitments. Strong states that diverted too many resources from wealth creation to defense, security, or expansion, saw their power diminish over time.[3] In a similar vein, Princeton political scientist Robert Gilpin suggests that a hegemonic state typically can hold sway until the costs of maintaining the status quo exceed its capacity to do so. Beyond this threshold, a disequilibrium results that yields "the eventual economic and political decline of the dominant power."[4] These disequilibria present subordinate states opportunities to expand their independence from a hegemon and improve their standing in the international system.

Nonviolent Challenges to American Hegemony

For reasons detailed later, in the late 1960s and early 1970s regional powers believed that geopolitical and economic trends had produced a systemic disequilibrium, and seized their opportunities to challenge U.S. hegemony and economic influence in the Western Hemisphere. Two such challenges warrant close examination: Chile's unilateral attempt to chart an independent course toward Socialism under President Salvador Allende, and a more multilateral effort by various regional powers to slip out of America's zone of influence. In each case, the challenge to American hegemony was nonviolent, and in each case, it would ultimately end in failure.

Chile's Unilateral Challenge

Chile's challenge to U.S. hegemony was similar to Guatemala's in the late 1940s and early 1950s, in that the challenge was nonviolent, displayed economic and ideological dimensions, and emanated from the election of a leftist government determined to chart its own course. To appreciate the Chilean case, we need to know a bit about the country's economic and political development. Historically, Chile's economic profile resembled those of other Latin American countries, in that foreign investors had penetrated the economy deeply and gained control of key sectors like copper and communications (American), nitrate and transportation (British), and electricity (German). Initially, European—especially British—investment was predominant. But when the Panama Canal opened in 1914, U.S. capital poured into Chile at a rate well beyond its British counterpart. Whereas in 1913, U.S. and British investment in Chile stood at $29 million and $391 million respectively, by 1929, U.S. investment had grown to $395 million while British investment had fallen to $389 million. This transposition was a boon to American business, but did little to distinguish Chile's economic profile from its neighbors'.

Politically, however, Chile was something of a regional outlier. While instability and authoritarianism plagued much of Latin America, Chile had been one of the region's most stable constitutional democracies since the late nineteenth century. Its vibrant, multi-party system afforded representation to those across the political spectrum. Although Chilean presidents typically came from the parties in the Center or the Right, parties of the Left, Right, and Center all won seats to Congress. Socially, Chile developed a fairly large middle class relative to its regional counterparts; by 1960, 30–35 percent of Chileans were either middle or upper class, and many more people whose incomes denied them middle-class status, held middle-class aspirations and values. Many Chileans also lived in urban areas where there was greater access to education and employment.

Still, for those who remained in the countryside there were clear winners and losers—the products of highly skewed patterns of land tenure and elite political domination. As late as 1955, less than 3 percent of all estates in Chile made up 41 percent of all the arable land; 64 percent of all properties accounted for only 12 percent of the arable land; and through vote manipulation, literacy tests, and obscure voter-registration procedures, large landowners held enormous political leverage over the rural poor.

In the early 1960s, the Kennedy administration sought to make Chile an Alliance for Progress showpiece, pumping ample Alliance funds into one of the region's few genuine democracies. Between 1964 and 1970, Chile experienced six years of progressive, but moderate reform under the government of Eduardo Frei and the Christian Democratic party. The Frei administration embraced the Alliance and promised a bevy of economic and social measures that mirrored its objectives. Agrarian reform, greater investments in education and housing, profit sharing in industry, programs to increase the organizational capacity and thus, political inclusion of Chile's marginalized social groups, and the "Chileanization" of the copper sector (i.e., at least 51 percent state ownership)—as opposed to its outright nationalization—were all part of Frei's agenda. By 1970, his government had achieved Chileanization (and even nationalized the U.S. firm, Anaconda Copper). It also had passed unionization and wage legislation that improved workers' status and diminished landowners' capacity to dominate the rural population, established a host of local organizations to facilitate self-help projects among the poor, and made moderate progress in education, housing, and agrarian reform. But this solid record of achievements only whetted many Chileans' appetite for even greater reforms, and set the stage for a pivotal election when Frei's term expired.

In 1970, Salvador Allende ran for president of Chile as the candidate of Popular Unity, a coalition of various communist and socialist parties. Popular Unity's agenda was similar to Frei's, but given the philosophy of its constituent parties, it was even more reformist, less wedded to following America's Cold War lead, and saw a stronger economic role for the state (for example, the complete nationalization of the copper, communications, and transportation sectors, as well as large-scale agrarian reform). In a three-way race, Allende won the September election with 36.6 percent of the vote; conservative candidate Jorge Alessandri of the National Party won 34.9 percent, and the centrist, Christian Democratic candidate Radomiro Tomic captured 27.8 percent. Since no candidate had won a majority, Chile's constitution mandated a run-off election in the Congress, where lawmakers traditionally followed the principle of majority rule and chose the candidate who had received the most popular votes. On the campaign trail, Allende had vowed to broaden Chile's international relations beyond the bipolar, Cold War framework, and take Chile on a "peaceful road to Socialism"; with the election's ultimate outcome hinging on a congressional vote, he also promised to govern within constitutional parameters.

In the midst of the Cold War, though, the possibility of an Allende presidency unnerved U.S. officials. In fact, U.S. President Richard Nixon became obsessed with Allende, and along with his National Security Advisor, Henry Kissinger, immediately began plotting ways to keep him from becoming president. So ingrained had anti-communist, Cold War ideology become in American policy circles, that rather than see Allende's victory as symbolic of Chilean democracy in action, U.S. leaders viewed it exclusively through a Cold War lens. Two months shy of Chile's presidential inauguration, Kissinger spoke ominously about what an Allende presidency would mean, described it as a "takeover" rather than an election victory, and ascribed to it dangerous hemispheric significance:

> In a major Latin American country you would have a Communist govern-
> ment, joining, for example, Argentina, which is already deeply divided,
> along a long frontier, joining Peru, which has already been heading in
> directions that have been difficult to deal with, and joining Bolivia, which
> has also gone in a more leftist, anti-U.S. direction . . . So I do not think we
> should delude ourselves that an Allende *takeover* in Chile would not pre-
> sent massive problems for us, and for democratic forces in Latin America,
> and indeed to the whole Western Hemisphere [emphasis added].[5]

In fact, both Nixon and Kissinger disdained the outcome of Chile's demo-
cratic vote, and were of one mind regarding their desire to reverse it. Just nine days after the Chilean elections (September 15), the president gave CIA director Richard Helms clear marching orders, telling him bluntly that an Allende government was simply "not acceptable to the United States." For his part, Kissinger opined: "I don't see why we need to stand by and watch a country go communist due to the irresponsibility of its own people. The issues are much too important for the Chilean voters to be left to decide for themselves."[6]

Accordingly, under direct orders from Nixon, U.S. agencies devised a two-
pronged strategy (Track I and Track II) to prevent Allende from assuming power. Under Track I, Washington looked for ways to stop Allende from taking power legally. As with prior attempts to eliminate Fidel Castro, some elements of the Track I scheme bordered on the absurd—they entailed a wild plan to

bribe enough lawmakers to select Allesandri in the congressional run-off election, who after his inauguration would resign, and thereby clear the path for outgoing President Frei to return to power in a new election (the Constitution barred Frei from consecutive re-election). But when Frei made clear his disinterest in the scheme, Track I collapsed and Washington shifted its focus to Track II.

Under Track II, the United States sought to provoke a military coup that would disrupt constitutional government in Chile and prevent Allende's accession. To work, this strategy required cooperative Chilean military officials who opposed the presumed new president, and the removal of the Chilean Army's strict constitutionalist commander-in-chief, General René Schneider. The CIA set to work executing the plan—which Washington ultimately called off, but its Chilean collaborators resumed. In the end, the result was a bungled attempt to kidnap Schneider that left him mortally wounded. Rather than hinder Allende's election, Schneider's death had the opposite effect. Besides traumatizing the country, it prompted leaders of major parties to urge lawmakers to cast their ballots for Popular Unity. A majority did, and on November 3, 1970, Allende was inaugurated.

Once in power, the Allende government promptly pushed policies to raise average Chileans' living standards and help solidify its support base among the working class. It launched a free milk program for school children and new mothers, cut rent payments and expanded public works to create jobs, hiked social security and pension payments, lowered taxes on the working poor and middle class, and raised taxes on the wealthy. It also raised the minimum wage and imposed a moderate price freeze on basic goods and food. These initial measures stimulated the economy, boosted the government's popularity in some quarters, and helped Popular Unity do well at the polls in 1971 municipal elections.

The Allende government also followed through on important aspects of its socialist election platform: it maintained relations with the United States, but reestablished relations with Cuba (in 1971 Allende welcomed Castro to a month-long visit to Chile), recognized communist China, and sought warmer relations with the Eastern bloc. It nationalized the banking, communications, transportation, and copper sectors (including, without compensation, the U.S. firm Kennecott Copper), and by June 1972, had completed one of the most sweeping land-reform programs in the world, expropriating nearly every estate larger than 80 hectares and turning them over to rural workers. Allende's domestic policies especially, made sense to many Chileans; but since the Popular Unity government held power by virtue of only a plurality of voters, its program also polarized society. Meanwhile, Allende's redistributive policies made for good populist politics, but bad economics. Raising the minimum wage while freezing prices, for example, helped workers buy more food, but eliminated the market dynamic that would stimulate more food production. As economic problems mounted, foreign reserves dwindled, and steep inflation set in.

Having failed to prevent an Allende presidency, the United States endeavored to stop the socialist government from completing its term of office through covert interventions that would culminate in a military coup. Toward this end, it left virtually no stone unturned. To help create economic hardship that would turn Chileans against their government, Washington discouraged private U.S. investment in Chile, cut bilateral aid to Santiago drastically, declined to extend Chile loans or credit guarantees through the U.S. Export-Import Bank, and used its influence to deny Chile credits from the Inter-American Development Bank and the World Bank. As Nixon explained to CIA director Richard Helms, the goal was to make the Chilean economy "scream." To create a political climate conducive to a coup, the CIA pumped money into political parties that opposed Popular Unity and funded anti-government propaganda campaigns in the media; Washington also increased aid to Chile's military, while simultaneously conveying its displeasure with the military's civilian leadership. Indirectly, some U.S. funds also went to support a long truckers' strike that paralyzed the economy and produced food shortages and rationing. The coup came on September 11, 1973: military units took control of key port cities and other locations; air force planes bombed the presidential palace; and before taking his own life, President Allende took to the airwaves in a final address which asked Chileans to remember him as a man of honor whose loyalty to the peaceful path to Socialism remained undiminished.

Although many Chileans who had opposed Allende's agenda welcomed the president's downfall, eventually many of these had second thoughts about the government that replaced his administration: for the next 17 years, Chilean democracy was dead. In its place, an iron dictatorship emerged, led by General Augusto Pinochet. Under the dictatorship, over 3,000 Chileans perished, parties were banned, politicians exiled, union labor repressed, "subversives" tortured, and Congress was dissolved. The Nixon administration denied any involvement in the coup, but across Latin America and beyond, U.S. complicity was taken as a given. Colombian Nobel Laureate Gabriel García Márquez captured the sentiments of many when he accused U.S. agencies and officials of orchestrating the coup, telling readers of *Harper's* magazine it was "impossible to suppose that Kissinger and President Nixon himself was not aware" of U.S. anti-Allende machinations.[7]

As for official state responses, not all regional powers grieved over the Chilean government's downfall. Brazil's president, Emílio Médici, for example, sup-

ported U.S. efforts to destabilize Chile's socialist government and his administration collaborated with Nixon's toward this end. But several states expressed
sharp disapproval of U.S. involvement. Cuba, of course, condemned the coup,
and when reporters asked Castro for his thoughts on the rise of dictatorship in
Chile, his response was unambiguous: "The United States," he said, "is father
of the creature" (i.e., the coup and resulting military crackdown).[8] Mexico
condemned the coup too, and extended asylum to any Chileans who might seek
it; in 1974, President Luis Echeverría also severed diplomatic relations with
Chile, and in 1975, he publicly accused the United States of "intolerable"
intervention in its internal affairs.[9] Other regional powers soon downgraded
their relations with Santiago (Colombia and Venezuela), and some states that
initially endorsed the coup (Argentina) wound up breaking ties with the
Pinochet regime. Many other extra-hemispheric powers either condemned the
coup (India, the Soviet Union, Yugoslavia), expressed dismay at the death of
Chilean democracy (West Germany), or felt compelled to break or downgrade
their bilateral relations (Belgium, France, Italy, Sweden, and Zambia).

While Latin Americans took Washington's involvement in Allende's downfall
as a given, in America, the degree of U.S. culpability for the coup is still hotly
debated. Kissinger's memoirs, for example, paint the United States as having
little involvement in the coup itself. More recently, former Nixon secretary of
state William Rogers observed there simply was no "smoking gun" linking the
United States directly to the coup. In a 2004 letter to the journal *Foreign Affairs*,
he largely dismissed assertions that Washington destabilized Chile's government
or worked to foment a coup climate. The coup, Rogers suggested, was essentially the product of Chile's armed forces and Allende's polarizing domestic
politics and economic blunders.[10] But documents declassified during the Bill
Clinton administration paint a different picture, detailing the extent to which
American policy was bent on creating optimal coup conditions, and the efforts
and resources devoted toward this end. Analyst Peter Kornbluh makes such a
case for American involvement in his book *The Pinochet File*,[11] and based on a
review of the declassified documents, historian Kenneth Maxwell contends that
to "claim that the United States was not actively involved in promoting Allende's
downfall in the face of overwhelming evidence to the contrary verges on
incredulity."[12] Kissinger himself actually confirms some level of U.S. complicity.
In a phone conversation between him and Nixon (which was taped and the
National Security Archives acquired through a Freedom of Information
petition), Kissinger tells the President: "We didn't do it [the coup] . . . I mean we
helped them."

Given its heated nature, the debate over the degree of U.S. complicity seems
unlikely to end anytime soon. But there are two things we can conclude with

high confidence. First, U.S. policy did actively seek to overthrow the elected government of Chile; and second, it is misleading to hold the United States, alone, completely responsible for the coup.

In terms of Chile's economy, the economic problems Allende's populist policies created were real, painful, and politically damaging; the 500 percent inflation of 1973 wiped out any gains average Chileans had made in Allende's first year. Important aspects of Chile's enormous domestic political problems also were not manufactured in the U.S. As a minority president, Allende presided over both a highly polarized society, and a divided government. Almost two-thirds of Chileans had voted against him; Popular Unity controlled only the presidency, not the legislature; and congressional resistance to some of the president's policies led Allende to advance them by virtue of his own authority as chief executive—or through questionable legal tactics—which polarized the political climate even more. Finally, the Popular Unity coalition itself was internally divided. Because its more radical elements were farther to the Left than Allende himself, the president sometimes had to take positions or accept measures that were more extreme than he preferred—for example, unauthorized peasant land seizures, unsanctioned worker takeovers of private firms, and the left wing's insistence that the U.S. firm Kennecott Copper be nationalized without compensation. Despite Popular Unity's rapid reforms, the core of Allende's supporters wanted still more, and the president sometimes labored simply to keep up with events on the ground. In short, Chile's three-year experiment with Socialism was a time of dramatically heightened economic stress, political uncertainty, and political excess. American economic pressure and covert intervention did not create all these conditions. But there is no doubt they certainly helped aggravate them.

In February 2003, U.S. Secretary of State Colin Powell conceded that U.S. policy toward Chile and President Allende, "is not a part of American history that we're proud of."[13] America's actions injured hemispheric relations and badly damaged its image in Latin America, perhaps more among its population than even among its governments. Since working to overthrow a democratically elected government violated Washington's long-standing claims (and efforts) to support and promote democracy, a critical question is what drove the United States to adopt such a policy?

EXPLAINING U.S. POLICY TOWARD CHILE

On this point, realist balance of power explanations are unsatisfying. U.S. military power dwarfed Chile's, and the Allende government never forged a close security or economic alliance with the Soviet Union. While Moscow was pleased by Allende's election, gave the president a warm welcome when he visited the USSR in 1972, and extended credits to Chile, the Kremlin maintained its distance from the Popular Unity government and never assumed the role of economic and military patron it had with Cuba.

Moreover, the global balance of power was not at stake in Chile, nor were any critical U.S. national interests. A September 1973 CIA intelligence assessment, for example, found that "the world military balance of power would not be significantly altered by an Allende government" [and] "the United States has no vital national interests within Chile."[14] Similarly, a State Department memorandum produced three weeks before Allende's election victory (August 18, 1970) advised the White House that while problematic, an Allende victory would not pose unique challenges: "In examining the potential threat posed by Allende, it is important to bear in mind that some of the problems foreseen for the United States in the event of his election are likely to arise no matter who becomes Chile's next president."[15] After Allende won the election, the State Department recommended the adoption of a "wait and see" policy approach to determine what kind of productive bilateral relationship might be developed (an idea Nixon vetoed). Given the government's own assessments of developments in Chile, it is hard to explain U.S. policy in strict realist terms.

A dependency explanation fares poorly too. From this Marxist perspective, keeping Chile safe for American investments would be paramount. Toward this end, U.S. capitalists would either dictate the government's policy or seek its help in staving off Allende's expected nationalizations. To be sure, the prospects of nationalization concerned Nixon and Kissinger (and greatly alarmed Treasury Secretary John Connolly). They also concerned American multinational corporations that would be likely nationalization targets— commercial U.S. banks operating in Chile, Cerro Copper, Kennecott Copper, Bethlehem Steel, and Ralston Purina. But none of these firms sought U.S. government assistance to protect their interests before Allende came to power, and most worked out compensation measures with the Allende government when their holdings were eventually nationalized. The one multinational that did seek government help—International Telephone and Telegraph (ITT)— offered the CIA, then the State Department and national security advisor Henry Kissinger, $1 million to fund efforts that might prevent an Allende presidency. But the government refused the offer and needed no corporate lobbying to take action: the CIA had already been given an explicit charge to undermine Allende before ITT president Harold Geneen pitched his plan. As political scientist Stephen Krasner notes, in the end, "American policy cannot be explained by corporate pressure."[16]

If strategic, balance of power, or economic factors don't fully explain U.S. policy, what does? In hindsight, the most important factors were ideology and the distortion of America's containment policy produced by NSC-68. As we saw in Chapter 6, NSC-68 shifted the emphasis of containment from restricting the growth of Soviet power, to stopping the spread of communist ideology. The stronger containment's ideological dimension became, the less containment itself was linked to realist, hard power considerations, and the more that Cold War competition centered (at least in Washington's eyes) on intangible factors like American versus Soviet prestige or the perceived credibility of capitalist versus socialist economic systems.

Concerns over these ideological intangibles grew directly out of NSC-68's perimeter defense concept. These concerns were captured by the CIA assessment cited earlier. The Agency warned Nixon that while an Allende Chile did not threaten the global balance of power, it did pose risks to "U.S. prestige . . . at a time when the U.S. can ill afford problems *in an area that has been traditionally accepted as the U.S. 'backyard'*" (emphasis added); it also "would represent a definite psychological set-back to the U.S. and a definite psychological advantage for the Marxist idea"; and finally, "the reactions it would create in other countries" would undermine hemispheric cohesion. Based on these intangible criteria, an Allende presidency did threaten the concept of perimeter defense because it represented a second pathway for the Left to assume power: whereas Castro had brought Socialism to Cuba through violent revolution, Allende would bring Socialism to the hemisphere's mainland through legitimate elections. And just as Castro's victory inspired a host of copycat insurgency ventures, CIA analysts worried an Allende presidency would inspire leftist parties and candidates, producing a series of socialist states across the region.

Moral Issues and Other Lessons

How might we assess the morality of U.S. covert intervention in Chile? Drawing upon the three-dimensional framework introduced in Chapter 6, motives, means, and consequences are all essential to derive a sound ethical judgment. One-dimensional analysis is more likely to yield inaccurate conclusions. For example, American officials who authorized and designed U.S. policy toward Chile did so believing it would protect Chile, the United States, and other countries from the dangers of Communism. In their eyes, the policy motivations were honorable. But good intentions alone are insufficient grounds on which to base a moral judgment. The means of the intervention as well as its consequences must also be considered. If we assume Allende's removal was just, and would secure a greater good (an assumption a plurality of Chileans would no doubt contest), we must then examine whether the means of intervention were proportional to the goal policymakers sought. At first blush, Washington's covert initiatives—as opposed to, say, a full military invasion—may seem prudent and proportional. But did they include any serious efforts to minimize risks and injury to Chilean citizens, or did the Nixon administration's "make the economy scream" approach have the opposite effect? And what about the consequences of the coup—the destruction of Chile's democracy and the systematic deaths and torture that followed? Sound moral judgment requires us to examine all three dimensions before we can render a balanced conclusion.

What does the Chilean case teach us about international politics more generally? One important lesson it illustrates is the concept of *blowback*, which refers to the adverse, unintentional consequences of covert policies. A good example of blowback is the 1979 Iranian Revolution that toppled the Shah of Iran's iron dictatorship, and imposed an Islamic fundamentalist regime that demonized the United States, held American diplomats hostage, and became an avowed U.S. enemy. The Shah held power only by virtue of a secret 1953 CIA-sponsored coup against an earlier Iranian government, and stayed in power thanks to his secret police and American political support and weapons. Many Iranians suffered brutally under the Shah's rule, and when large segments of society finally overthrew the dictator, the vehemently anti-U.S. regime that emerged was the harvest of seeds laid a quarter-century before.

Blowback is more than simply a matter of a country reaping what it sows. As political scientist Chalmers Johnson noted in his book *Blowback: The Costs and Consequences of American Empire*, in some instances, the unintended consequences of a policy are felt more strongly among third parties, than by the state whose action initially started the ball rolling. In the case of Chile, for example, neither the United States nor its citizens experienced much concrete blowback from Washington's efforts to provoke a coup. But thousands of Chileans—leaders, students, teachers, workers, journalists, intellectuals, politicians, and families—did. There is no evidence at all to suggest that when American officials first adopted a pro-coup policy in 1970, they intended to establish a literal police state under General Pinochet or unleash the extraordinary repression many Chileans suffered thereafter. Nor did they anticipate the international reach the dictatorship would attain in its quest to silence opponents and crush "leftist subversion." Under Pinochet, Chile developed Operation Condor—a transnational terrorist network composed of Chile and five other South American military states—designed to hunt down, kidnap, and assassinate their nonviolent critics, committed guerrillas, and other subversives (real and imagined) beyond their borders. By 1975, U.S. officials had learned, and apparently approved of, Operation Condor; at times, they also facilitated its operations and impeded some of its kills in Western Europe. But they did not dream up the enterprise; Operation Condor was the brainchild of Colonel Juan Manuel Contreras, the director of Pinochet's National Directorate of Intelligence. As with the Pinochet dictatorship itself, in 1970, establishing a transnational, state-sponsored terrorist network was not a goal of anti-Allende U.S. policy; it was, however, an inherent and monstrous facet of that policy's blowback.

States employ covert measures when they deem it necessary. However, because the blowback from such operations sometimes assumes frightening proportions and can take directions policymakers could scarcely conceive, prudence suggests that covert interventions—especially those designed to restructure an entire country's government—should be a last resort.

Box 8.1 Operation Condor: A Cold War, State-sponsored Terrorist Network

Operation Condor [was] a shadowy Latin American military network whose key members were Chile, Argentina, Uruguay, Bolivia, Paraguay, and Brazil . . . Condor enabled the Latin American military states to share intelligence and to hunt down, seize, and execute political opponents in combined operations across borders. Refugees fleeing military coups and repression in their own countries who sought safe havens in neighboring countries were "disappeared" in combined transnational operations. The militaries defied international law and traditions of political sanctuary . . . [T]op U.S. officials and agencies, including the State Department, the Central Intelligence Agency, and the Defense Department, were fully aware of Condor's formation and its operations from the time it was organized in 1975 . . . U.S. executive agencies at least condoned, and sometimes actively assisted, Condor "countersubversive" operations . . . Condor's victims included guerrillas and militants as well as political leaders, activists, and dissidents who denounced social injustice, organized political opposition, or challenged the military states . . . The most secret aspect of Condor ("Phase III") was its capability to assassinate political leaders especially feared for their potential to mobilize world opinion or organize broad opposition to the military states. Victims included former Chilean

[Defense and Foreign Affairs] minister Orlando Letelier—a fierce foe of the Pinochet regime—and his American colleague Ronni Moffitt, in Washington, D.C.; Chilean Christian Democratic leader Bernardo Leighton and his wife, in Rome; nationalist ex-president of Bolivia Juan José Torres, in Buenos Aires; and two Uruguayan legislators known for their opposition to the Uruguayan military regime, Zelmir Michelini and Héctor Gutiérrez Ruíz, also in Buenos Aires . . . Condor allowed the militaries in the Southern Cone to put into practice a key strategic concept of Cold War national security doctrine: *hemispheric defense* defined by *ideological frontiers.* The more limited concept of territorial defense was superseded . . . Security forces in Latin America classified and targeted persons on the basis of their political ideas rather than illegal acts.

J. Patrice McSherry, "Operation Condor: Clandestine Inter-American System," *Social Justice,* 26, 4 (1999)

The Regional Multilateral Challenge

Efforts by Allende's Chile to break from American Cold War orthodoxy and distance itself from U.S. economic and political influence were part of a broader, multilateral endeavor toward the same objectives. In the late 1960s and early 1970s, a number of states charted foreign policies more independent of Washington and flouted the implicit "rule" regarding non-U.S.-mediated relations with extra-hemispheric powers. They aspired to reject the East-West Cold War construct as *the* organizing framework for hemispheric relations. They also proposed fundamental revisions in global commercial and financial relations. This regional challenge was not monolithic; some states pressed harder for dramatic change than others, and Central American states were generally uninvolved. But its central thrust aimed to undermine the Western Hemisphere's unipolar structure, alter its systemic "rules," and expand Latin America's independence from its northern neighbor.

Within a five-year span (1969–1974), this broad challenge targeted U.S. institutional, political, and economic influence. To limit the leverage Washington could exert through institutional means, for example, Latin American states proposed reforming the Organization of American States in ways that curtailed U.S. influence. When Washington resisted this measure, its neighbors devoted more energy toward coordinating regional policies through the Economic Commission for Latin America—a UN agency they viewed as more genuinely *Latin American* than the Washington-headquartered OAS. Some states even proposed creating an new entity without a U.S. presence to replace the OAS.

To liberate themselves from America's political influence more generally, major Latin American states also began to adopt foreign policies more independent of U.S. preferences. Eduardo Frei's Chile established diplomatic or consular relations with the Soviet Union and Eastern bloc states; Salvador Allende's Chile recognized communist China, nurtured warmer ties with General Juan Velasco's leftist military government in Peru, and drew closer to Castro's Cuba. Rafael Caldera's Venezuela established relations with the USSR and Eastern bloc states too. Emílio Médici's Brazil, meanwhile, spurned U.S. aims to curtail nuclear proliferation: it refused to sign the Nuclear Non-Proliferation Treaty (which it argued established an unjust balance of power between nuclear and non-nuclear states), then imported nuclear technology and a reactor from West Germany. For its part, Velasco's Peru established military ties with the USSR, purchased Soviet military equipment, and hosted Soviet military advisors to provide instruction in its use. Both Mexico and Peru increased their participation in the Non-Aligned Movement—a group of developing countries that strove to retain their political independence by eschewing both the American and Soviet Cold War blocs. Finally, Argentina, Colombia, Mexico, and Peru all rejected the bipolar, Cold War construct and openly voiced a desire to replace bipolarity (and essentially, unipolarity within the hemisphere) with a multipolar structure that afforded greater autonomy from the United States.

On the economic front, regional powers pursued a mix of strategies to expand their economic independence and limit Washington's economic influence in the hemisphere. Some states, for example, worked to strengthen and diversify their commercial relations with extra-hemispheric powers. Argentina concluded an agricultural agreement with the European Economic Community; Brazil purchased French fighter jets rather than the American models; Mexico pursued stronger commercial ties with China, Japan, Western Europe, and the Soviet Union; and Venezuela brokered a petrochemical deal with the Kremlin. Several states also linked the quest for greater economic independence with their long-held desire to end Western Hemispheric unipolarity: when Argentina called on its neighbors to establish "an autonomous center of economic gravitation" to balance U.S. influence, both Colombia and Peru echoed this aspiration.[17]

Other economic strategies included imposing new restrictions on foreign direct investment (FDI), devising trade schemes that excluded U.S. participation, and nationalizing foreign—often American-owned—assets. Mexico increasingly pushed a policy of "Mexicanization" that compelled foreign investors to sell up to 51 percent of their holdings in key sectors to Mexican nationals. Chile pushed the "Chileanization" of copper. The Andean states of Bolivia, Chile, Colombia, Ecuador, and Peru established a regional trade bloc in 1969 (the Andean Pact), which imposed tough restrictions on FDI in 1971. The same year, OAS Secretary-General Galo Plaza captured the sentiments of many Latin American delegates when he called for a general prohibition on foreign investment in any economic sectors that member states deemed to be of strategic, national importance.

Latin American states also embraced calls by other developing countries for a New International Economic Order (NIEO)—a set of proposals formulated largely by Argentine economist Raúl Prebisch, and officially set forth through the United Nations Conference on Trade and Development. Designed to improve the terms of trade between the industrialized North and developing South, the NIEO called on the United States and other wealthy countries to increase their levels of development assistance and technology transfers, reduce the tariffs imposed on developing country exports, establish arrangements to stabilize the global price of commodities and raw materials, and recognize the poor states' twin rights to regulate multinational corporations operating in their territory, and nationalize foreign companies on favorable terms.

All these actions raised tensions between Latin America and the United States, but from the U.S. perspective, the region's most serious economic challenge came from the growing wave of nationalizations. Between 1968 and 1976, nearly a dozen regional powers expropriated or nationalized U.S.-owned firms, often without compensating their prior owners.[18] In 1968, Peru nationalized the U.S.-owned International Petroleum Company (and other companies later); in 1971, Chile seized Kennecott Copper (and later, International Telephone and Telegraph); Venezuela accelerated its timetable to nationalize American (and other foreign) oil interests; Bolivia, Guyana, and even Jamaica all nationalized U.S. holdings too.

These nationalizations bedeviled the Nixon administration. To deter even more expropriations, Washington adopted a "get tough" policy: it vowed to suspend bilateral economic assistance and veto multilateral loans (for example, through the Inter-American Development Bank) to any expropriator unwilling or unable to make adequate, timely compensation. But this approach backfired: it not only failed to deter further nationalizations, but sparked a broad, nationalist backlash. From Mexico to Argentina, major newspapers harshly criticized the U.S. position; Chile denounced the policy as an attack on its independence and sovereignty; Peru and Venezuela labeled it contrary to traditional norms of hemispheric cooperation; and the OAS resolved that its members retained a sovereign right to chart their own national development and should be granted multilateral loans based on the merits of their request, not issues unrelated to them (i.e., nationalization).

Yet, despite the concerted efforts, Latin America's multi-pronged challenge ultimately bore little fruit. By the mid-1970s, solidarity among the challengers had dissipated; the prospects of offsetting U.S. regional influence went largely unrealized; and the bipolar, Cold War construct remained intact. These outcomes raise intriguing questions. Why did such a broad challenge emerge when it did, and why did this collective effort ultimately fail?

EXPLAINING THE REGIONAL CHALLENGE

The timing of Latin America's challenge has much to do with the notion of a hegemonic "disequilibrium" discussed earlier. Regional powers believed such a disequilibrium had arrived and modified their foreign policies accordingly, based on four systemic factors: the collapse of the Bretton Woods international monetary system, balance of power struggles between East and West, power readjustments between the North and South, and rising global prices for the region's principal commodities exports. In different ways, each suggested that the United States had reached the limits of its power, that Cold War bipolarity was receding, and that the prospects of changing their position vis-à-vis the United States had improved accordingly.

To many regional powers, for example, the breakdown of Bretton Woods seemed to indicate an America in decline. Created to stabilize and integrate the world economy after World War II, the Bretton Woods System had required member states to maintain the convertibility of their currencies into either gold or a currency that was itself convertible into gold. In practice, most member states maintained large reserves of U.S. dollars, which they bought and sold to stabilize their own currency's value at preordained, "pegged" exchange rates. The system worked well as long as the dollar's market value hovered near the official peg of $35 per ounce of gold. But by the late 1960s, U.S. trade deficits along with persistent budget deficits (due to spending on the Vietnam War and domestic social programs) created a "glut" of dollars with dwindling value. Unable to defend the official exchange rate, President Nixon suspended gold convertibility of the dollar in August 1971, essentially ending the Bretton Woods System. While the dollar remained the principal global currency, Nixon's action seemed symbolic of America's economic distress and hegemonic decline.

Even stronger indicators of America's waning influence were U.S. setbacks in the ongoing East-West balance of power struggle in Southeast Asia, and its subsequent rapprochement with communist China and the Soviet Union. By the mid-1960s, America had become bogged down in a losing effort to contain Communism in Vietnam, and by the late 1960s, it showed no signs of winning the Vietnam War. By 1972, the United States had conceded that Taiwan was not the only "real" China, and had agreed with Beijing to move toward normalizing bilateral relations. It also had adopted the policy of *détente* (relaxing of tensions) toward the Soviet Union. Government leaders in Chile, Cuba, Peru, and elsewhere saw the Vietnam imbroglio as evidence that U.S. power was stretched thin, and that Washington's ability to act decisively in Latin America had been compromised. Other regional leaders interpreted the U.S.-communist rapprochements as evidence of U.S. retreat, the dawn of a post-bipolar era, and enhanced opportunities for greater political independence. Nearly coterminous power readjustments between the rich states of the industrialized North and some poorer states of the developing South strengthened these assessments.

In 1973, the Organization of Petroleum Exporting Countries (OPEC) demonstrated a degree of power that stunned the strong, industrial states and inspired governments in many developing countries. In retaliation for U.S. support of Israel in the Yom Kippur war, OPEC quadrupled the price of a barrel of oil and imposed an oil embargo on the United States and other Western powers it deemed unfriendly to Arab interests. States that supported Israel unreservedly would receive no oil at all from OPEC; states that were neutral on Arab/Israeli matters could purchase some oil; and states that supported the Arab cause could purchase as much oil as they wanted. In rapid fashion, the embargo's shock waves rippled through many national economies; the price hikes spawned massive inflation and transferred hundreds of billions of dollars from the industrialized (and other consumer) countries to the relatively poor oil-producing states. Moreover, when London, Paris, and Tokyo shifted their positions to support the Arabs, OPEC's embargo achieved what Moscow's Warsaw Pact never could—it split the alliances between the United States, some NATO countries, and Japan.

At the same time OPEC's price hikes brought record profits to Latin America's oil exporters (Venezuela, Ecuador, and Bolivia; Mexico did not become a major exporter until 1976), the region's non-oil states saw prices surge for their commodities exports too, including cocoa, copper, sugar, and zinc. By 1973, Latin America had a $3 billion trade surplus; by 1974, its exports had jumped 70 percent and its trade surplus registered $4.8 billion.[19] In short, the external shocks and price fluctuations of the early 1970s dramatically changed economic power relations: they damaged Northern and Western economies badly, and brought unprecedented profits to many poorer countries. In this context, many Latin American states believed the opportunity had finally come when new policies might rectify long-standing grievances and perceived inequalities.

WHY DID THE CHALLENGE FAIL?

But if there were plausible reasons to believe the time was ripe to challenge U.S. hegemony and reorder hemispheric relations, why did these efforts prove unsuccessful? Realists might tell us the answer is simple: the challenge was doomed from the start, because regional states never amassed sufficient hard power to give their diplomatic efforts real political muscle, and never forged a durable, anti-hegemonic coalition that could mount and sustain a credible challenge. By contrast, liberals might suggest that failure was a function of the regional powers' inability to develop strong, autonomous institutions through which they could realize their economic and political objectives. There is something to be said for each of these positions. More broadly, however, at least three factors mattered: Latin American states simply misread the indicators of U.S. decline and underestimated the constraints on America's ability to act in the region; they overestimated the willingness of extra-hemispheric powers to balance the United States in its zone of influence; and they misjudged the degree of their own shared interests, and Washington's ability to preempt the formation of a solid, regional anti-U.S. bloc.

Détente and rapprochement with China did constitute a recalibration of U.S. Cold War policies, but not a U.S. retreat in the contest with Communism. These moves were actually a shrewd balance of power tactic designed to play upon the Sino-Soviet security dilemma, and pit the two communist giants against each other in competition for the benefits a new relationship with Washington could provide. The mistrust each harbored against the other allowed Washington to strike useful deals—for example, if the Soviets hoped to expand trade with the United States or preferred Washington not give aid to China, they had to agree to nuclear arms reduction talks or limit their actions that might threaten U.S. interests; similar criteria held for China. The more Beijing and Moscow valued these potential benefits, the less inclined they were to offend Washington through aggressive competition for influence in the Western Hemisphere.

Extra-hemispheric powers did establish closer commercial and political links to Latin American states, but never to a degree that enabled regional powers to exit the U.S. zone of influence as decisively as Cuba had. Again, with U.S.-Soviet *détente* and Sino-American normalization in play, Moscow and Beijing steered clear of any actions that could be read as excessive foreign "meddling." Enhanced commercial exchanges between Latin America and Europe, meanwhile, were real, but simply insufficient to achieve an effective political counter-weight against U.S. influence. Nor did European states have much interest in trying to balance America in the Western Hemisphere: their own security depended on the U.S.-led NATO, and they stood to lose a lot more economically than they gained if their regional commercial ventures sparked a Europe-U.S. trade war.

In short, the only strong power willing to act decisively in the region was the United States, whose setbacks in Vietnam, it turned out, only enhanced its proclivity to act against perceived threats. Washington's covert interventions in Chile laid to rest any questions on this point.

But the United States did more than intervene to protect its interests. It also picked apart Latin American solidarity by appeasing its neighbors on a major issue of concern, and by courting governments that might share some of its interests or be persuaded to help advance them. In February 1974, America and Panama signed a Joint Framework of Principles that established the parameters for negotiating a new treaty to govern the Panama Canal. Like the Platt Amendment in Cuba decades before, the original 1903 Hay–Bunau-Varilla Treaty had long been a sore point in Panamanian-U.S. relations. The con-cessions it gave America—a five-mile wide swath of land on each side of the canal, and control of the canal itself in perpetuity—were a constant reminder of Panama's stunted sovereignty. Pressured strongly by Panamanian leader Omar Torrijos (whose government spoke against the existing canal treaty in the UN Security Council and lined up support for renegotiations within the hemisphere and beyond), the Nixon administration acceded. By 1977, two new treaties had been negotiated and signed by President Jimmy Carter and President Omar Torrijos: the Panama Canal Treaty returned the canal to Panamanian sovereignty as of January 1, 2000, while the Neutrality Treaty gave the United States the right to defend the canal's neutrality even after it relin-quished sovereign control. Although highly unpopular in conservative, domes-tic U.S. political circles, Washington's appeasement of Panama kept the canal issue from blossoming into a unifying cause that might solidify regional anti-U.S. sentiments even more.

The United States further undermined regional solidarity by courting other governments to act as surrogates on behalf of its interests. U.S. attempts to woo Mexico failed to pan out, but similar efforts toward Brazil and post-Allende Chile struck gold. Due to their economic and strategic positions, the latter two proved especially useful. Take Brazil, for example. Despite some sharp critiques by American politicians over Brazil's sorry human rights record (the anti-communist, military government's routine torture of domestic opponents), the United States refused to deny Brazil U.S. aid, treated President Médici to a

State Dinner in December 1971, sent high-level delegates to visit Brasilia (including the secretaries of State and Treasury, and the Chairman of the Federal Reserve), sold Brazil supersonic fighter planes, and made other minor concessions to Brazil's interests. Brazil, in turn, opposed proposals to develop a "Latin American" replacement for the OAS that would exclude the United States. It also accommodated U.S. interests in stopping the advance of Latin America's Left: privately, the Médici government supported and collaborated with covert U.S. actions against Salvador Allende; it cooperated with U.S. efforts to prevent the leftist, multi-party *Frente Amplio* from coming to power in Uruguay (more precisely, as Nixon explained to British Prime Minister Edward Heath, "Brazil helped rig the Uruguayan elections");[20] and it encouraged a coup against Bolivia's left-of-center regime.

Like Brazil, Chile served as a bulwark against regional anti-American designs after General Augusto Pinochet seized power. Staunchly anti-communist, Pinochet's Chile was even more pro-American than Brazil, and adopted policies that warmed the hearts of Washington's cold warriors. Domestically, it rolled back most of Allende's economic and social policies, reprivatized many businesses that had been nationalized (although not the copper companies), and compensated the firms that Allende's government had seized. In terms of foreign policy, it withdrew from the Andean Pact (whose preferential trade arrangements and restrictions on foreign investment riled U.S. business interests). From Washington's perspective, even more useful was Chile's capacity to "balance" the anti-U.S., left-wing military regime in Peru. In less than two years, the Chilean-Peruvian relationship shifted from one of comradeship to one of confrontation and war plans (Peru hoped to recover territory it lost to Chile during the late nineteenth-century War of the Pacific). Under Pinochet, there would be no anti-American Chilean-Peruvian entente, and when Secretary of State Henry Kissinger met the dictator at the OAS general assembly in 1976, Pinochet left no doubt about where his allegiance lay in the battle against communists and leftist subversion: "We are behind you," he told Kissinger. "You are the leader."[21]

By 1976, the potential for an anti-American bloc in South America had dissipated, and the East-West, Cold War construct had been reaffirmed. Brazil and Chile were firm, anti-communist pro-U.S. friends. U.S.-Uruguayan relations were good too: in 1973, the military ousted civilian leaders and declared the leftist *Frente Amplio* illegal. In Argentina, the military had seized power and with U.S. approval, was prosecuting a "dirty war" against communist subversives, both real and imaginary; and in Peru, General Velasco had been ousted and replaced by a new nationalistic junta that displayed less open hostility to the United States. For most Southern Cone governments, anti-Communism trumped anti-Americanism, and the prospects of multipolarity replacing either the hemisphere's traditional unipolarity—or the Cold War's broader bipolar framework—were dead.

By the late 1970s, even the economic dynamics that once encouraged a diplomatic challenge to U.S. hegemony had begun working against states hoping to change the status quo. Yes, OPEC's price hikes had damaged economies of the North and enriched petroleum-producing states, but they did not produce a permanent shift in the economic balance of power. Instead, they spurred industrialized states to devise energy-conservation measures and new institutions to facilitate energy policy cooperation (for example, the International Energy Agency in which the United States would play an important role). In the end, the northern economies weathered the storm much better than most Latin American states. Besides raising the price of oil, OPEC's policies also raised the cost of imports. For a brief time, the spike in commodities export prices helped mask the ramifications of these cost increases. But as import costs exceeded their export earnings, many regional powers borrowed extensively to finance their trade deficits, development projects, and oil purchases. When the price of coffee, copper, and other commodities declined in the late 1970s, they borrowed even more. By 1978, the region's total outstanding debt stood at $159 billion (compared to just $29 billion in 1970)—80 percent of which was sovereign, that is, state-owed, debt.

By the 1980s, some regional powers were so indebted that they lost the capacity to govern their own economies and turned to the International Monetary Fund and World Bank for relief—ironically, institutions in which the United States wielded considerable leverage. For many states, renegotiating external debt became a higher foreign policy goal than challenging U.S. hegemony. In the end, Latin America's nonviolent diplomatic challenges died a quiet death that left hemispheric relations largely unchanged. But as the Cold War dragged on, new dynamics challenged U.S. hegemony even more force-fully, and to some extent, more successfully too.

Violent Challenges to American Hegemony

Had the Alliance for Progress realized the visions of Juscelino Kubitschek and John Kennedy, much of Latin America's Cold War experience could have been different. A successful Alliance would not have completely resolved the vexing problems of grinding poverty, inadequate education, political marginalization, and oppression. But it might have addressed them sufficiently to vent pressures that ultimately found more violent expression in revolution and revolutionary movements. Both developments challenged America's regional hegemony, but often less directly than their nonviolent counterparts. Their primary aim was to change the status quo in the countries where they developed.

Revolutions and Revolutionary Movements

Revolutions are complex phenomena that entail the overthrow of a government, followed by the rapid transformation of a country's political, economic, and social institutions. Their most important roots are domestic, and they culminate after long gestation periods. While not all revolutions follow the same trajectory, most tend to occur when countries experience some combination of the following: the state faces an economic, military, political, or social crisis it can't resolve; divisions erupt between the state and domestic elites; a revolutionary movement emerges to challenge the state's authority; and armed struggle ensues between the state and the forces demanding change. If the state falls, a new government comes to power and begins pushing its revolutionary agenda. Revolutions in Cuba (1959), Grenada (1979), Nicaragua (1979), and Venezuela (1958) all shared most of these features.

Revolution can be a fuzzy concept, however, because the terms "revolution" and "revolutionary" are commonly used in different ways. In the commercial realm, businesses pitch their products as revolutionary to distinguish them from the competition; in the political realm, political parties and leaders do likewise to distinguish their policies from their opponent's (the "Reagan Revolution"). Given these terms' broad and imprecise usage, the best way to understand what revolutions are, is to understand what they aren't.

As we see in Box 8.2, revolutions are distinct from other types of dramatic political phenomena such as revolts, insurrections, coups, or reform movements. Revolts occur when people rise up against constituted authority. Typically, these unorganized and unarmed uprisings break out in a certain region or city, but remain localized. One example of a revolt would be the 1992 *Caracazco* in Venezuela, when riots erupted in six cities (including the capital) after the Carlos Ándres Pérez government imposed a painful and surprising set of economic austerity measures. Ultimately, Venezuela's military quelled the unrest. Another example is the 1992 Los Angeles riots after the "Rodney King trial," when masses of unorganized people—enraged over the acquittal of police caught on tape beating Mr. King relentlessly—refused to obey the law.

By contrast, insurrections are armed, organized uprisings against constituted authority. Guerrilla armies that have opposed governments in Colombia (Revolutionary Armed Forces of Colombia), El Salvador (Farabundo Martí

Box 8.2 Revolutions vs. Coups, Insurrections, Reform Movements, and Revolts

	An organized challenge to authority?	An armed challenge to authority?	Does incumbent government fall and power change hands?	Typical political outcomes
Coup d'état	Yes	Yes	Yes	State policies and the country's basic institutions usually remain unchanged.
Insurrection	Yes	Yes	No	Prolonged, unresolved conflict or stalemate.
Reform Movement	Yes	No	No	Gradual modification of some aspects of the country's basic institutions.
Revolt	No	No	No	The challenge to authority is put down.
Revolution	Yes	Yes	Yes	Rapid transformation of the country's basic economic, political, and social institutions.

National Liberation Front), Peru (Shining Path), and Mexico (Zapatista National Liberation Army) are all examples of organized insurrections. An important distinction between revolts, insurrections, and revolutions is that the former two don't topple the existing government. Usually, revolts are put down while insurrections can yield prolonged, unresolved conflicts or stalemate. Either way, the absence of any change of power precludes the possibility of a genuine revolution.

In a *coup d'état*, a country's military or some faction of it seizes power from government leaders. In this case, power does change hands, and perhaps some government policies change too. Most coups don't constitute revolutions because they fail to change a country's basic institutions. An important exception is the 1973 coup in Chile, which deposed President Salvador Allende and brought General Augusto Pinochet to power. The coup not only changed Chile's form of government (from a multi-party democracy to dictatorship), but the Pinochet regime also changed Chile's basic economic model and social arrangements (the imposition of a market-based model and systematic efforts to demobilize civil society, political parties, organized labor, intellectuals, students, and the working class).

Finally, like revolutions, reform movements can also yield significant political change. But unlike revolutions, they only aim to change some aspects of a country's economy, politics, or society—not replace its major institutions. They also produce political change far more gradually. The U.S. Civil Rights Movement of the 1950s and 1960s seemed revolutionary to some people, yet in reality, it was merely a reform movement. It never tried to overthrow the federal government, or destroy America's capitalist economic system or representative democracy; instead, it merely sought to open up the existing institutions so everyone could participate equally, and it took decades to realize meaningful progress on this front.

Revolutions, then, are unique, and they generate dramatic change that threatens the interests of powerful actors. Those with power don't want to lose it, and those who benefit from the status quo don't want it changed. Consequently, most revolutions are violent, and can have sweeping effects on other states and inter-state relations more generally. The French Revolution, for example, produced prolonged conflict between France and much of Europe. Russia's 1917 Bolshevik Revolution incited external powers to attempt its suppression, led the Bolsheviks to attempt communist revolution in Eastern Europe and China, and generated nearly five decades of Cold War struggle between the Soviet bloc and Western states. The Cuban Revolution not only helped inspire the Alliance for Progress, but generated tension with various members of the Organization of American States.

Why do revolutions exert such influence on international politics? One reason is that revolutionary states often seek to export their revolution and ideology beyond their borders. Cuba, France, Iran, Nicaragua, Russia, and eventually, the United States all sought to export their revolution or political ideology to more distant lands, and since Hugo Chávez instituted the Bolivarian Revolution in Venezuela, Caracas has too. Another reason is that modern revolutionary leaders often take sharp issue with their state's prior foreign policies, view them as illegitimate, and adopt a radically different policy course. Iran's 1979 revolution led Tehran to break its close relationship with, and begin demonizing, the United States. Cuba's 1959 revolution led to a similar policy change. Such transitions upset prior relations and induce inter-state friction. A third reason is that revolutions can threaten the strategic and material interests of external powers. Some revolutionary states not only shift from allies to adversaries (thus, affecting alliances and the balance of power), but adopt domestic policies that endanger an external power's economic interests too (investments, trade relations).

Even a potential revolution or revolutionary movement can destabilize inter-state relations, since the violence it spawns often spills over national borders or generates refugee flows that damage neighboring powers. And when governments targeted by revolutionary movements seek external assistance to fend off an insurgency, or outside powers intervene unilaterally to prevent the fall of a friendly government, these anti-revolutionary measures merely expand the scope of instability. Summing up, revolutions influence international relations because they produce a level of instability or "messiness" that transcends national borders, affects the security and interests of other states, and gives rise to all kinds of uncertainties that influence states' foreign policy calculations.

In the Western Hemisphere, the Cuban Revolution was an important catalyst for further revolutionary dynamics because it affected regional governments and societies alike, and did so partly due to its timing. It erupted at a period when civilian, not military rule, was an increasing norm—an era New York Times correspondent Tad Szulc once labeled the "twilight of the tyrants." Between 1955 and 1959, dictators fell in Argentina (Juan Domíngo Perón), Peru (Manuel Arturo Odría), Colombia (Gustavo Rojas Pinilla), and Venezuela (Marcos Pérez Jiménez). Although dictatorships still remained in some countries, elected (if not entirely democratic) governments held power in much of Latin America, and many were susceptible to the fallout Cuba's revolution unleashed.

This fallout was enormous. By realizing a clean break from U.S. hegemony, the Cuban Revolution inspired a host of political actors, would-be revolutionaries, and copycat guerrilla forces. In the years immediately following the revolution, guerrillas and other pro-Castro groups popped up in Argentina,

Colombia, Guatemala, Panama, Peru, and Venezuela. Castro's early policy initiatives in literacy, healthcare, and land reform also energized Marxist elements, leftist parties, organized labor, and student organizations, and as the Left mobilized, strikes, protests, and calls for dramatic reform spiked across Latin America. These developments exerted significant pressure on governments either to adopt somewhat similar reforms, or resist these demands. They also alarmed more conservative, traditional actors and in some cases, led to preemptive coups against governments the military deemed too sympathetic to the Left, or too incompetent to quell revolutionary ferment.

In short, the Cuban Revolution radicalized, polarized, and ultimately helped destabilize regional politics. Throughout the 1960s, its impact on political stability hinged on the degree of political institutionalization a government enjoyed. Generally, governments that were the least institutionalized were also the most prone to severe instability: by 1964, Argentina, Brazil, the Dominican Republic, Ecuador, Guatemala, Honduras, and Peru had all suffered military coups. At the other extreme, governments that were more highly institutionalized democracies or authoritarian regimes—Costa Rica, Chile, Uruguay, and Mexico—experienced less intense instability. They not only avoided coups, but had a greater capacity to address (through crackdowns or reform) at least some demands for social change. Meanwhile, moderately institutionalized governments like Venezuela's experienced unrest, but survived (albeit with a good dose of martial law).

The Cuban Revolution also demonstrated that Cold War hemispheric security required more than a traditional readiness to repel external aggression (the basic goal of the Rio Treaty of Reciprocal Assistance). While Latin American governments rarely shared the inordinate fear the United States harbored of a Soviet attack, their militaries did draw the same lesson from Cuba that Washington did: states could be overthrown and communized from within. Consequently, after 1961 the United States reoriented its military assistance programs toward the region, shifting the focus from the delivery of hardware for external defense, to instructing and equipping local forces in counterinsurgency and civic action. The former entailed teaching Latin American militaries how to develop and deploy smaller, more agile units akin to their potential guerrilla counterparts, and to live and mount operations in the jungle; it also involved the provision of lightweight weapons, communications technology, and helicopters to enhance troops' mobility. The latter entailed training troops to perform what traditionally were nonmilitary tasks— building roads, schools, clinics, or water systems—that would increase the military's approval among local populations and win the hearts and minds of rural populations where guerrillas typically found sanctuary.

The Pentagon deployed Military Assistance Advisory Groups throughout much of the region to disseminate its new doctrine, and trained Latin American officers in counterinsurgency in many locations on the U.S. mainland and at the School of the Americas in the Panama Canal Zone (which moved to Fort Benning, Georgia, in 1984). Military schools in Latin American countries also provided such training.

By stressing internal security, this new warfare doctrine helped shift the local militaries' focus inward, by depicting the domestic political landscape as a potential Cold War battleground. Aside from U.S. contributions to this development, Latin American militaries had their own reasons for heightened vigilance against internal threats: having seen how Cuba's successful revolution led to the complete dismantling of the old Batista army, they did not want to share its fate. In Southern Cone states especially, the military added an element to the counterinsurgency doctrine that U.S. training manuals omitted—a sharp focus on the economic, political, and social dynamics that might help generate instability and revolutionary potential. As political scientist Alfred Stepan notes, these military institutions "began to study such questions as the social and political conditions facilitating the growth of revolutionary protest and to develop doctrines and training techniques to prevent or crush insurgent movements."[22]

Counterinsurgency, internal security, and virulent anti-communism proved a potent mixture. In the wake of Cuba's revolution it led military institutions to seize power from civilian governments that seemed overwhelmed by economic, political, or social problems (Argentina, Brazil, Ecuador, Peru), engendered harsh crackdowns on groups calling for social justice, and unleashed bloody attempts to crush all forms of perceived subversion. Because its broad conception of internal threat allowed governments to brand much unwanted activism or dissent as "communist inspired," it facilitated violent, security-oriented measures that were both systematic and indiscriminate. Those who authorized and perpetrated these actions generally believed they were preventing their country from going the way of Cuba. The human rights abuses that flowed from these campaigns constitute some of the region's darkest Cold War experiences, and—rightly or wrongly—were officially justified on the premise that Latin America's economic, political, and social conditions pulled powerfully in the direction of revolution. States and state militaries took this matter seriously, and acted accordingly.

In the 1960s, local militaries trained in counterinsurgency (and often assisted by U.S. advisors) either defeated or held at bay rural revolutionary movements in Argentina, Bolivia, Brazil, Colombia, Guatemala, Peru, and Venezuela. Of this set, by the 1970s, only the guerrillas in Colombia and Guatemala remained, and neither were well positioned to challenge their respective states. But in other Central American states—Nicaragua and El Salvador—Marxist revolutionary movements developed that, by the decade's end, had turned the Cold War very "hot."

The Cold War and Revolution in Central America

The roots of Central America's revolutionary potential lay in its long history of military rule, political repression, oligarchic economic domination, and elite collaboration with foreign (usually American) economic and political interests. With the exception of Costa Rica, during the Cold War, wealth and privilege derived principally from land and agricultural production, land holdings were highly concentrated, and landed elites maintained close ties with national militaries, which in turn, dominated politics. This situation afforded average Central Americans little chance for upward mobility or meaningful political participation; among some social segments, it also encouraged a brand of revolutionary nationalism that defined itself in opposition to the United States. The Cold War's rigid bipolarity, meanwhile, heightened U.S. concerns over any regional dynamics that might alter the balance between East and West.

Following the advice of the UN Economic Commission for Latin America, in 1969 the five Central American states created the Central American Common Market in an effort to expand regional trade, capture economies of scale, and spur growth and employment. The Common Market led to an increase in foreign investment, moderate industrialization, and a significant upturn in intra-regional trade (from only $33 million in 1960 to over $1 billion by 1980). But these gains were never distributed equitably (the rich got much richer, and the poor the reverse); they were not accompanied by meaningful political or social reforms; and they were offset by external economic dislocations (oil shocks) and by the region's expanding population (from 8 million to 30 million between 1950 and 1980). By the end of the 1970s, 60 percent of Guatemalans, Hondurans, Nicaraguans, and Salvadorans were still illiterate, poverty and malnutrition remained deep and widespread, and only Costa Ricans enjoyed robust, democratic liberties. These conditions transformed Central America into a political tinderbox.

In 1979, the Nicaraguan government led by Anastasio Somoza Debayle fell to revolution. Its downfall cost the United States a close ally, ended the longest family dynasty in Latin American history (both Somoza's brother Luis and father Anastasio Somoza García had ruled as dictator), and marked the first successful leftist revolution in Latin America since Castro's triumph 20 years earlier. Somoza had run Nicaragua as his personal *finca*: he used his political position to enrich himself and friends, and used the National Guard as his personal army. Peasants, the urban middle class, the poor, students, and much of the bourgeoisie comprised this revolutionary movement, but a Marxist-oriented guerrilla force—the Sandinista Front of National Liberation— spearheaded its military campaigns. When the dictatorship finally fell, the movement's broad, multi-class cohesion ebbed too, and the Sandinistas ultimately assumed control of the new revolutionary state.

As events unfolded in Nicaragua, El Salvador's military government faced growing opposition from three principal guerrilla forces: the Popular Forces of Liberation—Farabundo Martí, the Revolutionary Army of the People, and the Armed Forces of National Resistance. Each shared a desire to overthrow the state, but were separated by ideological and tactical differences. Political repression, exploitation, economic pressures, landlessness, and fraudulent elections all spurred their armed resistance, which in turn, triggered reprisals by the military and private, rightwing death squads. With Fidel Castro's assistance, in October 1980, the guerrillas put aside their differences sufficiently to form an umbrella group, the Farabundo Martí National Liberation Front (FMLN). The FMLN engaged the Salvadoran military in battle, was capable of major offensives, and by 1981, had nearly pushed the government to the point of collapse.

Faced with the Salvadoran insurgency, the Sandinista government, and a 1979 Marxist revolution in the Caribbean mini-state of Grenada, the new U.S. administration led by Ronald Reagan determined to "draw the line" against further communist expansion. Reagan had been a harsh critic of his predecessor's foreign policy. As the Somoza dictatorship was crumbling, President Jimmy Carter had looked for ways to stabilize the situation. He withdrew aid from Somoza, engineered his resignation, and proposed an OAS peacekeeping operation to facilitate the transition to a new—hopefully moderate and pro-American—government. But OAS members quickly torpedoed this proposal, largely due to their sympathy with the Sandinistas' cause, and their smoldering resentment over past U.S. interventions in the Dominican Republic and Chile. Mexico, Panama, Venezuela, and other Andean states spearheaded the opposition. After the Sandinistas prevailed, Carter still hoped to retain U.S. influence with the new government by responding favorably to its request for aid, and refusing to block World Bank and Inter-American Development Bank loans to Nicaragua. Carter also cautioned Managua that continued good relations hinged on Nicaragua staying out of El Salvador's turmoil. The Sandinistas' decision to aid the FMLN insurgency anyway (including material and weapons assistance) produced a broad, anti-revolutionary campaign from the United States when Ronald Reagan took office.

Beginning in 1981, Washington cut aid to Nicaragua and increased military aid to El Salvador dramatically (by the mid-1980s, only Israel and Egypt received more U.S. aid, and only this aid stood between the Salvadoran government and military defeat). The same year, President Reagan charged that the Sandinistas had betrayed the Nicaraguan revolution by importing a Cuban-style Socialism that denied Nicaraguans freedom. In 1982, he authorized the CIA to create the *contras*—a proxy army commanded by ex-Somoza National Guardsmen—to interdict arms still flowing from Nicaragua into El Salvador, and enlisted the Argentine military government to help train them. In 1983, the United States built four military bases in Honduras to support *contra* and American military operations. Meanwhile, the *contras'* initial arms interdiction mission quickly morphed into a new objective: the overthrow of the Sandinista government itself.

Toward this end, the CIA schooled the *contras* in tactics of *low-intensity warfare*—one of three types of armed struggle for which the Pentagon makes contingencies (Figure 8.3). Under the Defense Department's typology, high-intensity conflicts involve nuclear confrontation, generate heavy casualties, and pose an immediate threat to U.S. security; mid-intensity conflicts require a major commitment of forces (like the Korean War), risk high casualties, but pose no risk to America's survival; low-intensity conflicts entail a minimal commitment of forces, a low probability of U.S. casualties, and the pursuit of limited, political objectives.

Low-intensity warfare became a key military doctrine in the Reagan era. Its object was not to defeat an opposing army on the battlefield by applying maximum military power, but to weaken the opponent through attrition, neutralize its popular base of support, degrade its economy, demoralize its population, and create conditions in which the enemy appeared to collapse under its own weight. Applying this concept to the Sandinista government, the *contras* engaged in military ambushes, black operations, asset and infrastructure

Counterinsurgency	Vietnam and Korean wars	Nuclear war
Minimal U.S. troop commitment No security threat Limited political objectives Low U.S. casualties	Minimal U.S. troop commitment No security threat Limited political objectives Low U.S. casualties	All-out commitment Immediate security threat National survival at stake Heavy U.S. casualties

◄───►

Low intensity	Mid intensity	High intensity

Figure 8.3 Typology of Warfare

sabotage, assassinations, and various terrorist acts against peasant villagers designed to drive a wedge between the government and rural populations, and delegitimize the government's credibility as an effective provider of common defense. As *contra* activities expanded, the Soviet Union began supplying Nicaragua military aid to balance U.S. operations; in turn, Nicaragua, Honduras, and most of Central America became a "hot" Cold War theater.

Washington's counter-revolutionary policies were highly controversial and raised difficult questions. What kind of threat, if any, did Nicaragua present? Was it a communist threat, simply a threat to American hegemony, or merely a nationalist, revolutionary state? Were the factors behind its revolution and the broader instability across Central America products of local repression, poverty, and injustice, or exogenous agitation by Moscow and Havana? Different people answered these questions in different ways.

Assistant Secretary of State for Latin America Thomas Enders viewed the situation as fairly straightforward: Central America had become the locus of external communist subversion. "Cuba is now trying to unite the radical left," he warned, and "commit it to the use of violence, train it in warfare and terrorism, and attempt to use it to destroy existing governments and replace them with Marxist-Leninist regimes on the Cuban model."[23] For President Reagan too, external subversion was the root cause of Central America's turmoil. "A new kind of colonialism stalks the world today and threatens our independence," he told the Organization of American States in February 1982. "It is brutal and totalitarian. It is not of our hemisphere but it threatens our hemisphere and has established footholds on American soil for the expansion of its colonial ambitions."[24] In a 1983 television address, the president elaborated:

> Many of our citizens don't fully understand the seriousness of the situation, so let me put it bluntly: There is a war in Central America that is being fueled by the Soviets and the Cubans. They are arming, training, supplying, and encouraging a war to subjugate another nation to communism, and that nation is El Salvador. The Soviets and the Cubans are operating from a base called Nicaragua. And this is the first real Communist aggression on the American mainland.[25]

Reviving the old *domino theory*, Reagan's scenario envisioned Communism threatening the United States as it expanded state-by-state through Central America toward the U.S. border.

Not everyone, of course, agreed. Mexico's president José López Portillo, for example, saw things quite differently. On a 1982 state visit to Nicaragua, López Portillo suggested that Central American instability had little to do with

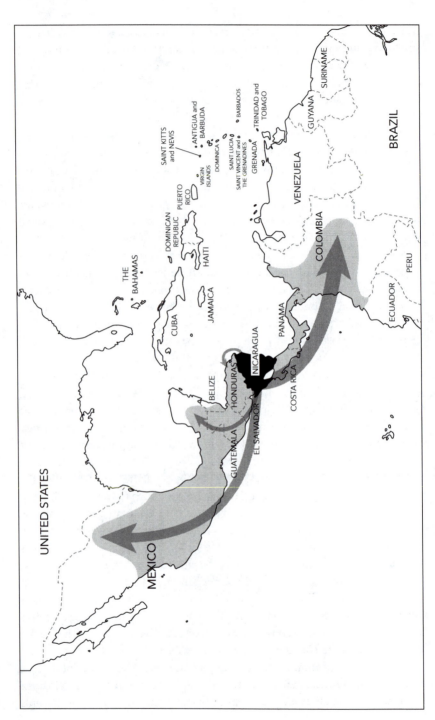

Figure 8.4 The "Red Menace": The Potential Expansion of Communism from Nicaragua

external subversion and was more the product of poor, oppressed people wanting a better life and more freedom. "I can assure my good friends in the United States," he said, "that what is taking place here in Nicaragua, and what is taking place in El Salvador, and what is blowing throughout the whole region does not constitute an intolerable danger to the basic interests or national security of the United States."[26] His successor Miguel de la Madrid argued that Central America's "internal dynamics" had been placed "in the context of East-West rivalry"—a context bolstered by "simplistic analyses" that overlooked "the reality of complex social and political processes . . . "[27] A Bipartisan Commission on Central America (headed by former Secretary of State Henry Kissinger) tried to split the difference. It determined that while longstanding economic, political, and social problems plagued Central America, external actors were deliberately exacerbating these issues for ideological and strategic reasons:

> Just as Nicaragua was ripe for revolution, so the conditions that invite revolution are present elsewhere in the region as well. But these conditions have been exploited by hostile outside forces—specifically, by Cuba, backed by the Soviet Union and now operating through Nicaragua—which will turn any revolution they capture into a totalitarian state, threatening the region and robbing the people of their hopes for liberty.[28]

Neither side ever "won" this debate. At times, the American position devolved into a crude, 1950s-era black–white, Cold War framework that obscured the situation's nuances. Like Cuba, the new Sandinista government had quickly launched a series of popular reforms, including a national literacy campaign, significant land reform, and campaigns in health care and education. But unlike Cuba, the Sandinista government created a mixed rather than command economy, and preserved greater press and political freedoms. It nationalized a number of assets (many of which were owned by Somoza, or his family and cronies) and retained the private sector; it censored the opposition press periodically, but never closed it outright; and in 1984, it held national elections in which Sandinista leader Daniel Ortega won the presidency. In foreign policy, it maintained relations with regional powers, enjoyed warm relations with Canada, Eastern Europe, Western Europe, and the Soviet Union (and especially warm ties with Cuba). But from the beginning, in realist fashion it sought to safeguard its sovereignty and establish political independence from Washington, thus challenging America's hegemony over Nicaragua.

In this context, U.S. fears and policy actions helped create a self-fulfilling prophecy. For example, the Soviet Union had little interest, and played virtually no part, in the Sandinistas' successful revolution; but the more Washington pressed Managua through its *contra* proxies, the more it stimulated Soviet efforts to balance the United States by aiding the Sandinista military. Similarly, U.S. actions induced a security dilemma vis-à-vis Nicaragua that only heightened America's own concerns over regional security. In response to *contra* attacks, the Sandinistas increased the size of their military and bolstered their defensive posture (through arms secured from France, as well as Cuba and the Soviet Union). Washington saw these measures as proof that Nicaragua threatened its interests and posed a regional military threat. But to Daniel Ortega, these moves were simply prudent defense: "We are a very small country," he explained, "confronting a truly colossal force—U.S. power—and, honestly, the only way to resist those attacks is to close ranks, strengthening the country's defense at all levels."[29] The Sandinista government had been suspicious of Washington's intentions even under Jimmy Carter; under Ronald Reagan, these suspicions hardened into an animus toward the United States that Washington fully shared of Managua, and bound the two in conflict through negative, mutually reinforcing dynamics. As former National Security Council member Robert Pastor notes: "Each action by the Reagan Administration prompted the Sandinistas toward a higher level of vituperation against U.S. imperialism, thus justifying and reinforcing the Reagan Administration's strategy."[30]

Washington's Central American policy also became entangled in a fierce domestic tug of war between the White House and Congress. Lawmakers were willing to finance the *contras*' arms interdiction mission, but refused to finance efforts to overthrow the Sandinista government (the United States was not at war with Nicaragua). Thus, between 1982 and 1984, Congress passed a series of "Boland Amendments" (named after Representative Ed Boland of Massachusetts) to defense appropriation bills that aimed to restrict U.S. support for *contra* operations.

The first Boland Amendment (1982) prohibited CIA funds from being used for covert operations against the Nicaraguan government. To keep the *contras* going, the administration funded some of their operations through the National Security Council rather than the CIA, and engaged in creative bookkeeping (for example, charging some *contras* expenses to non-*contra* accounts, and building airfields in Honduras for Pentagon maneuvers, then turning them over to the *contras* as transport bases). When Congress discovered the CIA had mined Nicaragua's shipping harbors in support of *contra* activities, lawmakers passed a second Boland Amendment (1984) whose proscriptions appeared absolute: no monies could be used by the CIA, Defense, or any "agency or entity of the United States," to support directly or indirectly any military or paramilitary operations in Nicaragua.

But the administration circumvented this law too. The National Security Council established a network of private, nongovernmental aid to sustain the *contras* (soliciting donations from wealthy, conservative Americans, and governments like Saudi Arabia and Brunei). It also created a stand-alone commercial "Enterprise" that sold U.S. military equipment to America's avowed enemy, Iran—then at war with Iraq, and considered by the State Department to be a supporter of international terrorism. In exchange for Iranian efforts to free American hostages held in Lebanon, the Enterprise sold Tehran a thousand TOW anti-tank missiles, and other war materiel, then diverted proceeds from these sales to *contra* operations. The Enterprise kept the *contras* going despite the congressional prohibition. It also violated U.S. law (the Boland Amendment and Arms Export Control Act), the U.S. weapons embargo imposed on Tehran, and the president's public pledge not to negotiate with terrorists. In 1986, it exploded in a high-profile scandal dubbed "Iran-Contra."

The Invasion of Grenada

In the 1980s, Cold War conflict was not confined solely to Central America. It extended into the Caribbean too, and flared dramatically when the United States invaded Grenada. A former British colony of 100,000 citizens, Grenada gained independence in 1974. In March 1979, its first Prime Minister—Eric Gairy—was deposed in a bloodless coup, spearheaded by Maurice Bishop, leader of the Marxist, New Jewel Movement opposition party. After Bishop became Prime Minister, his government suspended elections, banned political parties except New Jewel, established much closer relations with Cuba, and proclaimed anti-imperialism and nonalignment with either Cold War bloc as its basic foreign policy principles (this, despite the New Jewel Movement's obvious ideological leanings). But unlike Cuba, the Bishop government eschewed a command economy in favor of a mixed economy with an enhanced state role; to bolster the tourist trade, it also began construction on a new international airport (the Point Salines International Airport), with expanded runways to accommodate large jumbo jets. Financial assistance for the project came from Cuba, the European Community, and Venezuela; Cuba also provided personnel for the actual construction.

Grenada's new leftist orientation, close Cuban ties, and expanded airport facilities captured the attention of U.S. Cold War strategists. Those who believed the airport's real purpose was to accommodate long-range Soviet Backfire Bombers, not commercial tourist jets, deemed revolutionary Grenada a threat to stability in the Caribbean. Others believed that Marxist Grenada—

Figure 8.5 Daniel Ortega, Maurice Bishop, and Fidel Castro at May Day Celebration, Havana, Cuba, 1980

acting on the Soviets' behest and in league with Cuba and Nicaragua—posed an even broader threat to NATO's defense of Western Europe. In the event of a Soviet invasion, the Europeans' defense hinged on a "swing strategy," in which American reinforcements and materiel would be airlifted or ferried through Caribbean sea routes to the European theater. But if Moscow secured access to Grenada's new airport, Soviet bombers—along with Soviet naval vessels operating from Cuba and perhaps Nicaragua—could cripple this swing strategy and leave Western Europe undefended (Figure 8.6). The fact that neither Grenada nor Nicaragua had established formal military alliances with the USSR did not dim the fears some American strategists harbored, and the Reagan administration continued to eye Grenada with concern. When the Grenadian government plunged into political chaos in 1983, the United States seized the opportunity to remove communist influence from the tiny island state.

In October 1983, a power struggle within the New Jewel Movement led to Bishop's own overthrow by supporters of Deputy Prime Minister Bernard Coard. On October 13, the Coard faction placed Bishop under house arrest, then subsequently released—and later, murdered—the Prime Minister along with members of his cabinet. The violence and political vacuum the coup generated provided the backdrop for U.S. intervention. On October 25,

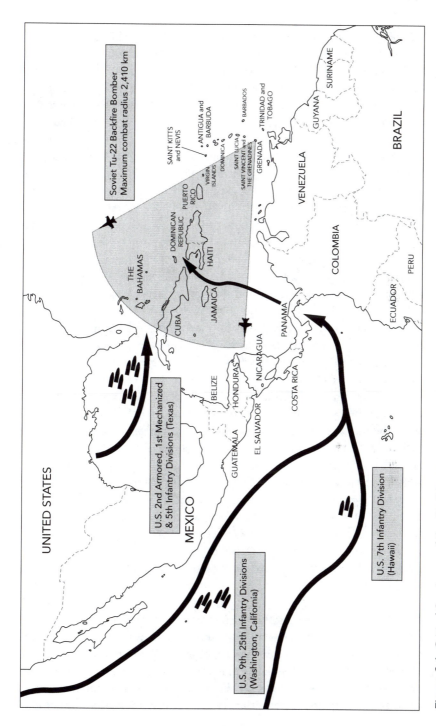

Figure 8.6 Critical Sea Lanes of the Caribbean

President Reagan authorized a military invasion code-named Operation Urgent Fury—ostensibly to restore order and democracy, and safeguard several hundred American citizens on the island (who were never in danger). Since Grenada had not aggressed against any state and posed no direct threat to the United States, there was little chance of obtaining OAS or UN authorization for this action, and Washington did not try to secure it. Instead, the administration used a request for assistance from the Organization of Eastern Caribbean States (a small regional organization composed of Grenada and six other tiny Caribbean nations) to justify its actions.

In the end, U.S. forces secured the island in a matter of days. Casualties were moderately light (45 Grenadians, 24 Cubans, and 19 U.S. military personnel were killed). Eventually, moderate political forces assumed power and Grenada transitioned away from Cuba. But since many Latin American governments did not share Washington's more extreme view of the Grenadian threat, the spectacle of a superpower beating up on a small state reaffirmed regional sentiments against U.S. intervention, and strengthened misgivings regarding U.S. Cold War policy in Central America.

The Cold War in Central America, meanwhile, exacted heavy human, economic, and social costs. In Nicaragua, the *contra* war dragged on for eight years. According to the Correlates of War Project housed at Pennsylvania State University, it killed 43,000 Nicaraguans (mostly civilians), and destroyed clinics, schools, agricultural cooperatives, bridges, electric power grids, and other infrastructure. By the mid-1980s, economic production had declined to 1960 levels; by 1987 defense spending swallowed up 62 percent of Nicaragua's state budget; and by 1988 inflation reached 33,000 percent. During this period, El Salvador's FMLN insurgents and U.S.-backed military government battled each other to a stalemate. By 1986, the government was spending half its budget on defense, gross national product per capita had shrunk to nearly half its 1977 level, capital flight was extensive, and average living standards had plummeted. Both conflicts also generated significant refugee flows. Roughly one million Salvadorans and 150,000 Nicaraguans tried to escape the violence by leaving their country—primarily for Honduras and Mexico, but also the United States.

Despite determined U.S. backing, the *contras* failed to make meaningful progress either in outfighting the Nicaraguan military, holding a sizeable chunk of Nicaraguan territory that might house a "government in exile" (which Washington might then recognize as Nicaragua's "true" government), or in toppling the Sandinistas. On the other hand, their low-intensity warfare tactics damaged Nicaragua's revolution economically, programmatically, and politically. These operations diverted scarce state resources from planned social welfare programs to defense, and induced war fatigue among Nicaraguans that helped cost the Sandinistas the 1990 election. After more than a decade of war— first against Somoza then between the *contras* and Sandinistas—voters who wanted peace believed the prospects were higher under a new, non-Sandinista government. In 1990, they chose opposition candidate Violeta Chamorro over incumbent President Daniel Ortega, and essentially voted the revolution out of power.

Ultimately, Central America's wars and revolutionary turmoil ended not by bullets or military might, but through diplomacy and politics. While Guatemala and Honduras had gone along with U.S. policy under Reagan, other regional powers took a much dimmer view. Under Mexico's leadership, officials from Colombia, Panama, and Venezuela established the Contadora Group in 1982 (named for the Panamanian island on which delegates first met) to develop a framework for regional peace settlements. Argentina, Brazil, Peru, and Uruguay all supported Contadora efforts, as did the Soviet Union, Western Europe, and the UN. But the United States had no use for a negotiated settlement that would leave the Sandinista government in power, and in any event, Nicaragua would not sign a Contadora peace accord until the United States first disbanded the *contras*, which the Reagan administration refused to do. But Costa Rica—close to the epicenter of the conflicts—pressed on. Drawing upon the Contadora framework, Costa Rican president Óscar Arias developed a new proposal—*Esquipulas II*—that won the backing of the five Central American governments in 1987, and for Arias, the Nobel Peace Prize. The *Esquipulas Accords* outlined a number of steps to end hostilities and promote national reconciliation, including demilitarization, free elections and democratization, a cut-off in aid to paramilitary units, refugee assistance, and arms-control talks.

By the mid-1990s, *Esquipulas* had forged a durable, regional peace. In El Salvador, the FMLN signed a peace treaty with President Alfredo Cristiani's government in January 1992, and the United Nations monitored national elections in 1994. In Guatemala, the insurgent Guatemalan National Revolutionary Unity signed a peace accord with President Álvaro Arzú Irigoyen's government in 1996. And in Nicaragua, the *contras* eventually demobilized after the 1990 election, while the Sandinistas transitioned into a political party and vied for office under democratic procedures.

As peace was coming to Central America, the Cold War was ending too. Beginning in 1989, democratic revolutions swept across Eastern Europe, Soviet hegemony over the region collapsed, and East German citizens tore down the Berlin Wall separating East and West Germany. In 1991, the Soviet Union itself disappeared. In the process, Cuba lost its principal patron, along with an annual multibillion-dollar aid package.

For over 40 years, the great ideological struggle had dominated international politics, and helped shape the interactions between the two Americas. It led to a resumption of U.S. intervention, weakened the Inter-American System, and reinvigorated anti-American sentiments throughout the region. It affected domestic politics in many Latin American countries—often for the worse. At times, it brought the United States and some regional powers closer together; at other times, it drove these neighbors apart. It encouraged nonviolent challenges to America's influence, and formed the context in which more violent challenges emerged, were confronted, and contained. The end of the Cold War did not alter the Western Hemisphere's systemic unipolarity or quench Latin America's desire for greater independence from its northern neighbor. As we shall see in Chapter 10, in the post-Cold War era, these aspirations would find renewed expression, gain greater traction, and mark the early twenty-first century as a time of declining U.S. regional influence.

Study Questions

1. What is the difference between primacy, dominance, and hegemony, and under what conditions can hegemonic states lose their preeminent position? Of the three concepts, why does hegemony best capture the United States' relationship with Latin America during the Cold War?

2. How did world events in the 1960s and 1970s persuade Latin American states that the time was ripe to challenge America's regional hegemony nonviolently? Why did this challenge ultimately fail?

3. What did Salvador Allende hope to achieve as Chile's president? How did the United States interpret his agenda and why?

4. Did Allende's Chile pose a national security threat to the United States? If not, what might explain American policy toward Chile during this time, and how would you assess the ethics of U.S. intervention in Chile's domestic affairs?

5. Why are revolutions and revolutionary movements often of special concern to other states? In what ways do these political phenomena tend to unsettle inter-state relations?

6. How did Cuba's 1959 revolution exacerbate Cold War concerns through the 1960s, 1970s, and 1980s?

7. Why did Nicaraguan-U.S. relations deteriorate after the Sandinista Revolution? In explaining the breakdown of relations, how would a realist account differ from a dependency argument?

8. Compare McColm's analysis of Central America's political situation and the United States' regional interests with those of Fagen and Maidanik. Which author provides the most persuasive interpretation? Given your assessment, was the U.S. policy response appropriate, or did American policy become a self-fulfilling prophecy?
9. Was Central America's political turmoil during the 1980s the product of external communist subversion or long-standing internal problems? On what basis might different analysts reach different conclusions?
10. Was U.S. intervention in Central America during the 1980s ethically just?
11. According to Scott, what was the "Reagan Doctrine" and how did it affect U.S. policy toward Nicaragua in the 1980s? What factors explain why the President—and Congress—exerted different levels of influence over the policy agenda at different times?
12. Why did Latin American governments and the United States alike try to resolve Central America's political problems outside the framework of the Organization of American States?

Selected Readings

Fagen, Richard. *Forging Peace: The Challenge of Central America.* New York: Basil Blackwell, 1987.

Fagen, Richard R. "The United States and Chile: Roots and Branches." *Foreign Affairs* 53 (January 1975): 297–313.

Kornbluh, Peter. "Opening up the Files: Chile Declassified." *NACLAS Report on the Americas* 37 (July/August 2003): 25–31.

LaFeber, Walter. "The Reagan Administration and Revolutions in Central America." *Political Science Quarterly* 99 (Spring 1984): 1–25.

Maidanik, Kiva. "On the *Real* Soviet Policy Toward Central America, Past and Present." In *The Russians Aren't Coming: New Soviet Policy in Latin America*, edited by Wayne S. Smith, 89–95. Boulder, CO: Lynne Rienner, 1992.

Maxwell, Kenneth. "Maxwell Replies." *Foreign Affairs* 83 (January/February 2004): 163–165.

Maxwell, Kenneth. "The Other 9/11." *Foreign Affairs* 82 (November/December 2003): 147–151.

McColm, R. Bruce. "Central America: The Larger Regional Scenario." In *Central America and the Reagan Doctrine*, edited by Walter F. Hahn, 1–23. Lanham, MD: United States Strategic Institute, 1987.

Rogers, William D. "Mythmaking and Foreign Policy," *Foreign Affairs* 83 (January/February 2004): 160–163.

Scott, James M. "Interbranch Rivalry and the Reagan Doctrine in Nicaragua." *Political Science Quarterly* 112 (1997): 237–260.

United States Senate. *Senate Select Committee to Study Governmental Operations, Covert Action in Chile: 1963–1973, Staff Report.* Washington, DC: US Government Printing Office, 1975.

Winn, Peter. "Salvador Allende: His Political Life . . . and Afterlife." *Socialism and Democracy* 19 (November 2005): 129–159.

Further Readings

Aronson, Cynthia J. *Cross-Road: Congress, the Reagan Administration, and Central America*. New York: Pantheon Books, 1989.

Hove, Mark T. "The Árbenz Factor: Salvador Allende, U.S.-Chilean Relations, and the 1954 U.S. Intervention in Guatemala." *Diplomatic History* 31 (Summer 2007): 623–663.

Johnson, Chalmers. *Blowback: The Costs and Consequences of American Empire*. New York: Henry Holt & Company, 2000.

Kornbluh, Peter. *The Pinochet File: A Declassified Dossier of Atrocity and Accountability*. New York: Free Press, 2004.

Krasner, Steven D. *Defending the National Interest*, 298–312. Princeton: Princeton University Press, 1978.

Márquez, Gabriel García. "The Death of Salvador Allende." *Harper's* March 1974, 46–53.

McSherry, J. Patrice. *Predatory States: Operation Condor and Covert War in Latin America*. Lanham, MD: Rowman & Littlefield, 2005.

Moreno, Dario. *U.S. Policy in Central America: The Endless Debate*. Miami: Florida International University Press, 1983.

Muñoz, Heraldo. *The Dictator's Shadow: Life under Augusto Pinochet*. New York: Basic Books, 2008.

Nogee, Joseph L. and John W. Sloan. "Allende's Chile and the Soviet Union: A Policy Lesson for Latin American Nations Seeking Autonomy." *Journal of Interamerican Studies and World Affairs* 21 (August 1979): 339–368.

The Report of the President's National Bipartisan Commission on Central America. New York: Macmillan, 1984.

United States Congress. "Executive Summary." *Report of the Congressional Committees Investigating the Iran-Contra Affair*, 3–21. Washington, DC: Government Printing Office, 1987.

Walt, Stephen M. "A Theory of Revolution and War." In *Revolution: International Dimensions*, edited by Mark N. Katz, 32–62. Washington, DC: CQ Press, 2001.

Chronology: Cold War Challenges to U.S. Hegemony

1960s	Cuban Revolution's demonstration effect radicalizes Latin America's political Left and Right; U.S. military assistance programs help train Latin American forces in counterinsurgency
1969–1974	Latin American states challenge (unsuccessfully) U.S. regional hegemony nonviolently, seeking to limit America's economic and political influence and escape bipolar, Cold War framework
1970	Salvador Allende wins Chilean Presidency; United States seeks to prevent his assumption of power, and failing this, lays plans to create conditions conducive to a military coup
1973	Allende overthrown in bloody coup; General Augusto Pinochet seizes power
1973–1989	Chilean democracy replaced by Pinochet dictatorship
1979	Nicaraguan Revolution; dictatorship of Anastasio Somoza Debayle falls, Sandinistas take power
1979–1992	El Salvador civil war between U.S.-backed military government and Farabundo Martí National Liberation Front leftist guerrillas
1979	Grenadian Revolution; New Jewel Movement takes power, allies with Cuba
1982	Reagan Administration creates the *contras* guerrilla force to fight Sandinista government
1982–1989	*Contras* engage in low-intensity conflict against Sandinista government
1982, 1984	Boland Amendments (I and II) prohibit U.S. funds from supporting *contra* efforts to overthrow Nicaraguan government
1982	Contadora peace process begins but proves unsuccessful
1983	United States invades Grenada
1984	Sandinista leader Daniel Ortega wins national election for President of Nicaragua
1987	*Esquipulas II* peace accords brokered by Costa Rican President Oscar Árias, win backing of Central American states

1989	Cold War ends; democratic revolutions in Eastern Europe; Soviet hegemony over region collapses; Berlin Wall torn down
1990s	*Esquipulas* accords implemented; Central America's wars end
1991	Soviet Union disintegrates

Interdependence and Globalization

9

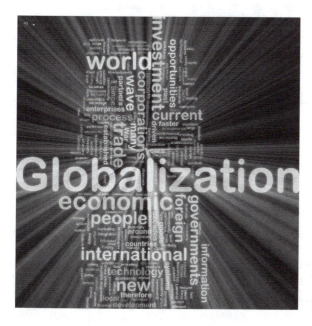

Figure 9.1
Globalization's
Increasing
Complexity

Economic interdependence accelerated after World War II. Thanks to the cessation of hostilities, the creation of the International Monetary Fund and World Bank in 1945, and of the liberal General Agreement on Tariffs and Trade in 1947, trade outside the Soviet bloc expanded along with transnational investments. International politics became more complicated too. States enjoyed new opportunities, but also faced new challenges. Important issue areas multiplied, and the concept of security itself expanded. No longer could "high politics" be reserved solely for matters of military security. With greater interdependence, economic security issues began moving into this realm, and sometimes intruded in dramatic, urgent fashion.

How have these changes affected international politics in the Western Hemisphere? The short answer is that interdependence generally decreased the utility of hard power as a state's tool of choice, induced new sources of conflict and motives for cooperation, and increased the importance of non-state actors in international affairs. In the 1980s, Latin America's debt crisis brought these points home forcefully.

As we saw in Chapter 8, Latin American states began borrowing heavily in the 1970s. By 1982, some of the region's major powers had incurred so much debt that even the interest payments exceeded their export earnings, and thus, their ability to service these obligations. This put their creditors—mostly commercial banks—in a real bind. Had a major debtor like Brazil or Mexico defaulted, some of America's largest (and over-exposed) banks would have faced the prospect of writing off billions in loans, and a potential collapse triggering a cascade of other failures among business and international financial circles. To complicate matters further, the highly indebted states remained sovereign, so the banks could not compel repayment, or seize a state's assets as they might a private borrower's.

The economist John Maynard Keynes said: "If you owe the bank a thousand dollars, you have a problem; if you owe the bank a million dollars, the bank has a problem." In the 1980s, Latin American states owed billions of dollars. The banks indeed had a problem; but so did the indebted states, the international financial system, and governments that were not even a party to the crisis. Each was bound to and dependent on the other in complex ways, and this interdependence led to a kind of international politics that veered sharply from realist depictions.

The 1980s debt crisis presents important questions. What caused the crisis? Why did the rich states where over-exposed commercial banks were headquartered, not use force to compel repayment and stave off potential economic catastrophe? Why did indebted states not simply repudiate their debts or form a debtors' cartel to leverage their numbers and negotiate the most favorable terms of settlement? What role did non-state actors play in resolving the crisis, and what influence did this resolution have on the course of U.S.–Latin American relations? To address these questions we need to understand the concept of interdependence, and how the international politics of interdependence differs from a more traditional realist view.

Interdependence

Interdependence refers to situations where at least two states are mutually dependent, and more broadly, to situations where changes in one part of a system affect another part. It is not limited to the economic sphere, and can develop around other issue areas too. The effects of interdependence can be beneficial or adverse and the extent of interdependence can vary according to time and circumstance.

An example of economic interdependence is Canada, Mexico, and the United States. Tri-national economic interdependence was a fact before the governments negotiated the North American Free Trade Agreement (NAFTA). North America's auto industry—a leading industrial sector—had already dispersed its operations across the three countries, producing cars and car parts in each, and shipping parts made in Mexico to plants in Canada, Mexico, and the United States. Given the auto industry's large workforce, the effects of interdependence were felt throughout each national economy. With NAFTA's advent in 1994, interdependence deepened: trade barriers fell, jobs in one country grew even more dependent on exports to others, and for many years Canada and Mexico became the United States' top trade partners. The Venezuelan-U.S. relationship offers another example of economic interdependence. The United States relies on Venezuela for roughly 11 percent of its oil imports; oil shipments, in turn, constitute 60 percent of Venezuela's total exports, and 95 percent of its exports to America. Although sharp political differences soured bilateral relations in the twenty-first century and spurred mutual acrimony (especially between 2001 and 2005), interdependence helped restrain both states from severing their ties completely or engaging in overt aggression.

As the Venezuelan-U.S. relationship suggests, interdependence has an obvious economic dimension, but also a political one. Consider Argentina and Brazil. Both before and after the South American Common Market (MERCOSUR) was established, Argentine-Brazilian trade yielded levels of mutual dependence whose economic gains required the political cooperation of each state. The same is true for the three North American states. With or without NAFTA or MERCOSUR, realizing the joint gains from trade entailed statecraft, and by mixing the economic and political, interdependence created a more challenging policy environment for states to navigate.

Interdependent relationships are not necessarily symmetrical. One state might be much more dependent on another than vice versa. In terms of their national security, for example, Mexico and the United States are mutually dependent on each maintaining a politically stable and friendly government. But Mexico's security is much more dependent on the United States than is

America's on Mexico. After its defeat in the Mexican-American War, Mexico largely retreated inward. Through the twentieth century, it never disarmed unilaterally vis-à-vis the United States, but it also never devoted its resources toward significant weapons development or procurement, and never again tried to vie with the United States militarily. In the 1980s, its army was smaller than Nicaragua's. Even today, if Mexico were ever attacked by a strong, external power, its soldiers would fight valiantly, but its ultimate defense would rest with the United States.

One common misperception about interdependence is that it always breeds cooperation; but in fact, cooperation is not a default setting. This misperception stems from the idea that interdependence invariably generates positive-sum, joint gains whereby each party involved stands to benefit. NAFTA, for example, lets Canada, Mexico, and the United States trade a variety of commodities and manufactured goods, making each nation better off. But interdependence can also generate zero-sum outcomes (your gain is my loss) and even negative-sum outcomes (we both lose). In 1992, U.S. presidential candidate Ross Perot argued that the interdependence NAFTA promised would be a net "bad" for America, because as U.S. capital flowed into Mexico under the accord, U.S. jobs would too. Ultimately, Perot's prediction (which he described as a "giant sucking sound") failed to materialize; but his warning exemplified the potential zero-sum effects that interdependence could bring. In the October 1962 Cuban Missile Crisis, the future of Cuba, the United States, and the Soviet Union were all bound together and dependent on each other's actions. If cool heads and good fortune had not enabled a successful resolution to the crisis, a nuclear war could have produced a negative-sum outcome for all involved. When analyzing international politics under conditions of interdependence, we should bear in mind that its benefits are not always positive-sum, and that how they are apportioned can vary from case to case.

Besides producing benefits, interdependence can also levy two types of costs, often described as short-term *sensitivity*, and long-term *vulnerability*. When change occurs in one part of the system—say, another state alters its foreign policy, experiences economic collapse, or suffers a revolution—other states and actors can incur high costs in a very short time frame. A revolution, for example, can change one state's ally into its enemy overnight; similarly, the collapse of a state's chief trading partner can have immediate ramifications for the other state. These short-term costs reflect a state's sensitivity to the effects of interdependence; the higher the costs and the faster a state incurs them, the greater is its sensitivity.

The 1994–1995 Mexican peso crisis exemplifies the short-term, sensitivity costs of interdependence. By 1994, the peso had become overvalued. At the same time, Mexico was running enormous current account deficits (more than 7 percent of its GDP) that it financed primarily through surging, foreign capital portfolio investments. The peso's overvaluation made it subject to speculative attacks, which did, in fact, occur through the spring and summer. Although many analysts expected—and some even called for—a currency devaluation, the outgoing government of Carlos Salinas ruled this out. A few weeks after Salinas left office, the new government of Ernesto Zedillo did devalue the currency on December 20, hoping for a modest 15 percent "soft landing." But after months of refusing to devalue, the government's sudden action caught investors by surprise. In response, they began selling off their debt instruments, pulling billions of dollars out of Mexico, and in the process depressing the peso's value even more. By December 31, the government's planned 15 percent devaluation had become a 50 percent free-fall. In this case, Mexico had depended on foreign capital, while foreign investors depended on Mexico to earn profits. This interdependence, however, left Mexico highly sensitive to changes in transnational capital flows, and this sensitivity wreaked economic havoc in a very short time.

Box 9.1 The Mexican Peso Crisis

The recent plunge in the value of Mexico's peso and the collapse of its stock market are a stark reminder of the risks of investing in emerging markets . . . [T]he main cause of Mexico's present troubles was the country's current-account deficit. This rose to around 8% of GDP in 1994, higher even than it had been on the eve of the 1980s' debt crisis. Many other emerging economies, in Latin America and Asia, are also running large external deficits. In recent years these have been financed easily by the foreign capital that has flooded eagerly into these economies. Mexico shows that what flows in can also flow out . . . A large current-account deficit financed by speculative capital leaves an economy exquisitely vulnerable to swings in investor confidence.

"Under the Volcano," *The Economist*, January 7, 1995, 14

Where sensitivity refers to the short-term costs of interdependence, vulnerability reflects the long-term costs a state would incur to break out of or change the situation of interdependence it is in. For example, when the U.S. economy goes into recession, the Canadian and Mexican economies suffer too. This is hardly a surprise, given their degree of interdependence: in 2009, the

United States absorbed 73 and 80 percent of all Canadian and Mexican exports, respectively. Of course, Canada and Mexico could reduce their vulnerability to U.S. economic downturns, but the policies and steps needed to accomplish this—forgoing guaranteed access to the world's largest market next door via NAFTA, and establishing new markets for the vast bulk of their exports in more distant countries—would prove extremely costly.

Several additional points are worth noting. First, interdependence can alter a state's perception of its national interest. In the 1830s and 1840s, Mexican leaders could worry about U.S. economic expansion, since America's economic growth might stimulate territorial expansion at Mexico's expense. Back then, an economically weaker United States was not necessarily bad for Mexico. By contrast, because of today's economic interdependence, Mexico prospers when the U.S. economy is booming, and the new worry is that when America's economy "catches a cold," Mexico's will likely "catch the flu."

Second, interdependence tends to blur the distinction between domestic and foreign policy matters. Consider the issue of undocumented immigration to the United States. Although America attracts undocumented immigrants from many countries, the vast majority comes from Mexico, and is pulled northward by job opportunities, prospects for a better life, and familial ties. In some regions of America, the agricultural, construction, services, and tourism sectors are highly dependent on undocumented workers. The United States has adopted several different policies in response to this phenomenon: it has legalized those in the country without proper documents, deported them, punished employers who hire them, and beefed up border security to prevent their entry. But whatever its official action, was the United States addressing a domestic policy issue, a foreign policy issue, or both? Sometimes the line between domestic and foreign politics is hard to draw when interdependence prevails.

Similarly, when Mexico's peso lost 50 percent of its value in 1994, the price Mexicans paid for U.S. exports jumped by 50 percent too. Because fewer Mexicans could buy the products American business had been shipping, the United States stood to lose hundreds of thousands of export sector jobs. President Bill Clinton and the International Monetary Fund quickly put together a $50 billion loan to keep the Mexican economy going. But was Clinton's action strictly a U.S. domestic policy to protect American jobs? Was it a foreign policy? Was it both? Again, in situations of interdependence, it's hard to tell.

Finally, because interdependence engenders complex linkages among economic, political, and social phenomena, change in one part of the system can produce unexpected consequences in others. A good example is the events in the early 1970s that affected American, Brazilian, Japanese, and Russian interests. In 1971–1972, a harsh winter destroyed Russia's winter wheat crop, and in response, the United States sold the Soviets enormous quantities of wheat in July 1972. Both ethics and strategic concerns motivated the sale: it was immoral to permit broad hunger among Soviet citizens, and it seemed unwise not to alleviate conditions that might produce political instability in a nuclear-armed adversary. The scale of the wheat sale, however, decreased domestic wheat supplies and produced much higher food costs at home, plus an angry American citizenry; it also caused domestic grain prices to soar, along with the price of soybeans. To address these issues, the next year the United States suspended soybean exports to Japan, which led Tokyo to invest heavily in Brazilian soybean production. In the end, domestic food and grain prices eventually stabilized, but U.S. soybean farmers lost much of their Japanese market while Japan acquired a cheap, reliable soybean source, and Brazil overtook Argentina, Canada, and China to become the world's second largest soy exporter after the United States. None of these outcomes were envisioned as by-products of the Soviet wheat purchase.

Complex Interdependence vs. Realism

How does interdependence relate to the traditional realist view of international relations? Realists have long contended that several assumptions form the basis of international politics: states constitute the only significant actors; military security is the states' highest priority; and force or hard power is their tool of choice. As we have seen, international politics is filled with examples of political behavior that fall squarely under a realist rubric; yet, there also are many examples that don't conform to realist assumptions. In the 1970s, Robert Keohane and Joseph Nye addressed this gap in international relations theory. Drawing upon a more liberal approach to international politics, they posed an intriguing question. What would the world look like if the key assumptions of realist theory were relaxed? The answer was obvious, and its insights compelling. Relaxing the assumptions would yield a world quite different from the one realists posit: (1) states are not the only major actors; non-state actors operating across borders play important roles too; (2) military security is not always the chief objective; economic welfare can be valued just as highly; and (3) actors pursue their objectives not through military force, but through diplomacy, manipulating economic interdependence, or international institutions. Keohane and Nye dubbed this alternate world one of *complex interdependence*.

Like Realism, complex interdependence is a heuristic device that helps us examine and explain certain relationships and episodes of real-world international politics. Because they are nearly mirror opposites, both concepts can facilitate profitable analysis, depending on the actors involved and issues at stake. The kind of politics observed, as well as the objectives and tools actors use, will differ if a relationship is closer to the realist or complex interdependent model. For example, in much of the nineteenth and twentieth centuries, Argentina and Brazil's relationship was much closer to the realist "ideal type" where military security and hard power politics prevailed. These states fought two wars and vied for regional prominence. They eyed each other warily into the 1970s, and even competed for nuclear weapons technology. But since the mid-1980s, their relationship has shifted away from the realist model and closer to complex interdependence. Not only are their economies linked closely through MERCOSUR, but they have put away the most potent symbol of their mutual security concerns and military competition by renouncing the testing of nuclear explosive devices, and establishing a bilateral security regime to monitor and account for their nuclear materials. Both states also signed (finally) the Nuclear Nonproliferation Treaty: Argentina did so in 1995, followed by Brazil in 1998. National security, of course, remains important for each state, but their actions—on trade via MERCOSUR and on nuclear defense—suggest it now shares the stage with a desire to ensure economic prosperity.

In short, over time Argentina and Brazil managed to change the "theoretical world" of international politics that characterized their relationship. Other states have too, such as America and Russia, and France and Germany. Today, most relations between different states fall somewhere between the realist and complex interdependence models. For example, during the 2000s, periodic saber rattling by Caracas and Bogotá pushed Venezuelan-Colombia relations closer to the former; by contrast, U.S.-Canadian-Mexican relations fall consistently closer to the latter.

Transnational Politics and the Sovereign Debt Crisis

The 1980s debt crisis illustrates a number of elements found in a complex interdependent world. The fact that Latin America was in the thick of the crisis is ironic since many regional powers had deliberately avoided the post-war era's increasing interdependence. By 1953, for example, only Brazil, Chile, Peru, and Uruguay had signed the General Agreement on Tariffs and Trade (GATT); Argentina did so in 1967, and Bolivia, Colombia, Mexico, and Venezuela did not accede to the GATT until the 1980s and 1990s. In general, regional powers saw greater advantages and fewer potential risks in pursuing state-led, inward-oriented development policies. Import-substitution industrialization (ISI), protectionist trade policies, and restrictions on foreign investment all offered a way for regional powers to grow their domestic manufacturing base, safeguard it from foreign competition, and capture the benefits of external investment while limiting foreigners' influence in their economies. Yet, despite their best efforts, by the 1980s many of these same states had become ensnared in a web of interdependent economic relationships that affected their own welfare, posed risks to other states, and threatened the global financial system. They also became central actors in an international debt crisis of epic proportions. Why did it develop?

CAUSAL FACTORS

One important cause was the "match made in heaven" between cash-stuffed commercial banks and capital-thirsty regional powers. Under ISI, states actively promoted economic growth: many created public enterprises in key sectors (transportation, steel, mining, manufacturing), invested heavily in infrastructure upgrades, and provided domestic industries various subsidies to nurture their growth (tax breaks, cheap credit, electricity, and energy). States usually financed ISI through a mix of internal savings, inflationary monetary policies, more orthodox fiscal and monetary policies, and external credit. As the industrial sector grew, however, sustaining ISI required more sophisticated equipment and intermediate inputs that were unavailable domestically, and expensive to import. Eventually, balance of payments problems developed and foreign borrowing became a more attractive financing mechanism. In the 1970s, borrowing grew even more attractive, thanks to cheap credit. Oil price hikes transferred hundreds of billions of dollars into OPEC's coffers, whose Middle East members deposited enormous quantities of "petrodollars" into Western (often American) commercial banks. The banks, in turn, recycled these funds to credit hungry regional powers—often at extremely low but variable interest rates. This happy union of supply and demand was the match made in heaven.

Since new credit was readily available at low, even negative real interest rates, for a time debt servicing was not a problem. Borrower countries increasingly relied on cheap, new credit, while banks increasingly made imprudent loans. When the 1979 Iranian Revolution cut global oil production and stimulated another round of oil price hikes, regional powers borrowed still more: OPEC required U.S. dollars for all oil purchases and a drop in global commodities prices left Latin American states unable to earn enough dollars through exports to finance their energy needs. By 1982, Latin America's aggregate debt totaled hundreds of billions of dollars (Table 9.1).

Table 9.1 Total External Debt of Selected Latin American Countries During the "Lost Decade" ($ billions)

	1980	1981	1982	1983	1984	1985	1986	1987	1988	1989	1990
Argentina	27.2	35.7	43.6	45.1	47.0	49.3	51.4	54.7	58.5	63.3	62.2
Bolivia	2.3	2.7	2.8	3.2	3.2	3.3	3.5	4.2	4.0	3.5	3.8
Brazil	70.6	80.4	91.9	97.5	104.9	105.1	111.0	21.2	113.5	15.1	123.4
Chile	11.2	15.6	17.2	18.0	19.7	20.4	20.7	20.6	19.0	17.5	18.6
Colombia	6.8	8.5	10.3	11.5	12.4	14.1	15.0	15.7	18.0	17.6	17.8
Ecuador	4.2	5.3	5.4	7.4	7.6	8.1	9.1	10.3	10.7	11.5	12.2
Mexico	50.7	74.9	87.6	93.8	96.7	97.8	100.5	102.4	100.9	95.1	101.9
Peru	9.6	9.6	11.5	12.4	12.1	13.9	15.6	15.3	16.5	18.5	20.0
Uruguay	2.1	3.1	4.2	4.6	4.7	4.9	5.2	5.9	4.2	4.3	4.5
Venezuela	29.6	33.1	32.1	34.7	33.9	33.4	32.9	34.4	31.6	31.6	36.6

Source: Economic Commission for Latin America and the Caribbean, *Statistical Yearbook for Latin America and the Caribbean: 1989 Edition* (Chile: United Nations, 1990)

Excessive borrowing laid the seeds for the debt crisis. But interdependence provided the catalyst—specifically, a change in U.S. domestic economic policy that reverberated across the hemisphere. In the late 1970s and early 1980s, persistent inflation plagued the United States. To break inflation, in 1981 Federal Reserve Chairman Paul Volcker raised domestic interest rates sharply (nearly 9 percent). The Fed's policy change worked: between 1981 and 1983, U.S. inflation fell from 13.5 to 3.2 percent. In Latin America, however, the effects of this policy change were not so beneficial. The Fed's interest rate hike rippled through commercial banks' loan portfolios, raising interest payments across the board. Latin American states that had variable interest rate loans quickly discovered their debts had grown exponentially. In August 1982, Mexico became the first regional power to announce it could not make its scheduled interest payments. Commercial banks quickly pulled back from extending new loans—not just to Mexico, but also to other states that had planned to roll over existing debts with fresh credit. As a result, Mexico's payment problem expanded rapidly to other states, and Latin America's debt crisis was on.

The crisis posed extraordinary problems for indebted states, commercial banks, the economies of "creditor states" where the banks were headquartered, and the international financial system. Regional powers still required external credit for a variety of reasons, and failure to meet their debt obligations could transform them into pariahs—permanently shunned by international credit sources. Although commercial banks' exposure varied, some of America's largest banks were heavily over-exposed: on average, they had lent over 100 percent of their capital assets; some like Manufacturers Hanover Trust had lent over 200 percent. The nine largest U.S. banks had loaned 44.4 percent of their capital to Mexico alone. The banks' potential collapse, in turn, threatened the U.S. economy, as did Latin America's declining ability to purchase U.S. exports. In just 1981 and 1982, a sharp drop in Mexico's imports cost American workers 250,000 jobs. Finally, both the banks' wobbly position and the possibility that the region's largest debtors might default, threatened the international financial system. The welfare of all depended on the debtor states' capacity to service their loans, and without additional credit, they were in no position to do so.

The transnational politics that helped resolve the debt crisis bore little resemblance to traditional realist dynamics. For all states involved, military security was never the overarching goal, but rather, economic welfare. Nor did states necessarily play the most important roles. Yes, the Latin American states were intimately involved, and the United States (through the Treasury and Federal Reserve) also helped manage the crisis, as to some extent did Britain, Germany, and Japan. But non-state actors—specifically, the commercial banks, International Monetary Fund, and World Bank—did much of the heavy lifting.

Box 9.2 Interdependence as Seen by the U.S. Federal Reserve

In all of this [debt crisis], the mutual dependency of the U.S. economy and the stability of the international financial system should be apparent. Failure to deal successfully with the immediate international pressures could only jeopardize prospects for *our* recovery—for *our* jobs, for *our* export markets, and for *our* financial markets [emphasis in original] . . . This is not an abstract, esoteric problem of marginal interest to our economy . . . Unless it is dealt with effectively, it could undermine our own recovery and the economies of our trading partners and friends abroad.

Paul Volcker, Federal Reserve Chairman, Testimony before the U.S. Senate Subcommittee on International Finance and Monetary Policy, 98th Congress, February 2 and 17, 1983

As for the instruments actors used to work toward a settlement, intensive negotiations, manipulating economic interdependence, and international institutions were the dominant means employed.

The actual resolution was a muddied process of fairly long duration. As a group, commercial banks wanted Latin American states to receive new credit so they could service their existing obligations, but individually, each bank preferred to see one of its counterparts bite this bullet. Especially in the early years of the crisis, large banks that had the most exposure (and thus, the most to lose) contributed more than they wanted to new loan packages; but they also combated the free-rider problem by pressuring and persuading less exposed banks to contribute too. Central Banks in America, Britain, and some European countries put additional pressure on private banks. So did the International Monetary Fund. To cite one example, the IMF drew up a list of 1,400 banks that had made loans to Brazil, determined what each bank's proper contribution to a Brazilian rescue package should be, based on its individual exposure, then made these data available to all the banks. By making bank operations more transparent, the IMF also made it harder for individual banks to free ride and shirk their responsibility.

Through cooperation, non-state actors managed to form a fairly unified front toward debtor states—a sort of "creditors cartel"—that developed jumbo rescue packages for Latin America's largest debtors (Brazil and Mexico), and dealt with other regional powers on a case-by-case basis. In the end, the cartel adopted a multi-pronged strategy to weather the crisis. It entailed rescheduling states' interest payments (often with a grace period), new credit lines from commercial banks, and additional funds from international financial institutions whose provision would hinge on regional powers adopting painful austerity budgets and other "structural adjustment" policies—deregulation, privatization, and trade liberalization—that dismantled the ISI model and opened up the economy to greater trade and foreign investment.

Latin American states resented this type of "conditionality," but generally could not avoid it. Faced with creditor unity, and for some, potential insolvency, regional powers had few viable political options. The creditors' cartel kept them from playing one lender off the other, and for most states, unilateral debt repudiation was impractical since it ultimately would lead to a pariah status, and thus, a sharp reduction in economic choices over the long term. A more appealing option was forming a multilateral "debtors cartel" that could threaten mass debt repudiation (something creditors would take much more seriously), and thus, negotiate better terms of settlement. But the key to such a cartel was participation by the region's largest debtors—Brazil and Mexico—and neither had much interest in joining. For one thing, their regional economic significance worked in their favor. Each secured better debt restructuring terms negotiating on its own, than say, Bolivia, Ecuador, or Peru. The shared U.S.-Mexican border also gave Washington a special interest in Mexico's political stability and economic recovery; consequently, the Treasury, Federal Reserve, and other U.S. agencies helped Mexico through its initial distress in 1982, and remained supportive thereafter. Both Brazil and Mexico feared that a confrontational approach or any actions that suggested bad faith on the part of the debtors would only make matters worse. As a result, in 1984 Mexico took the lead in formulating and contributing to a stopgap financial package for Argentina that kept Buenos Aires from defaulting on its payments (Brazil, Colombia, and Venezuela also pitched in).

Although a debtors cartel was out of the picture, Latin American states found unity on other matters. One was their opposition to IMF conditionality—which again, required states receiving IMF loans to adopt austerity budgets and other reforms before the loans were disbursed. The Fund insisted its prescriptions made economic sense, but they had extraordinarily adverse social and political domestic consequences, including exceptionally high unemployment, sharply reduced public service provision, and widespread public dissatisfaction with incumbent governments. Debtor states also found unity in their opposition to the exorbitant interest rates their loans had acquired through Federal Reserve policies, and the northern governments' protectionist measures that reduced their export earnings at a time when every dollar mattered. These concerns preoccupied the region's largest, mid-range, and more modest debtors, as reflected in a letter the presidents of Argentina (Raúl Alfonsín), Brazil (João Figueiredo), Colombia (Belisario Betancur) and Mexico (Miguel de la Madrid) issued to their regional counterparts: "[T]he successive increases of interest rates . . . and the proliferation and intensity of protectionist measures have created a somber scenario for our nations and for the region as a whole . . . we do not accept being pushed into a situation of forced insolvency and continuous economic stagnation."[1]

In tackling these issues, regional powers largely bypassed the Organization of American States (due to the United States' presence), and instead, asked the UN Economic Commission for Latin America to prepare a statistical analysis of the region's economic situation and the IMF policies' deleterious effects, along with proposals for how Latin American states might respond. Armed with this analysis, they convened several international conferences in Quito, Cartagena, and Mar del Plata, and ultimately hashed out a "linkage" strategy to address their concerns.

In broad terms, their goals were to (1) link debt discussions with interest rates, northern protectionism, and the political and social consequences of IMF policy requirements, (2) replace the dyadic creditors vs. debtors negotiation model with a tripartite model that brought creditor states directly into the discussions, and thereby (3) establish a state-approved, debt reduction framework *for Latin America as a region* that would eclipse the creditors' case-by-case approach. If creditor states became involved at the highest decision-making levels, regional powers believed they stood a better chance of extracting political concessions on issues that technically were unrelated to debt repayment. The Declaration of Quito (issued after the January 1984 Quito conference) typified this linkage approach:

> The magnitude of the regional economic recession and the persistence of *adverse external factors* make it imperative that any external debt arrangements and negotiations . . . should harmonize the requirements of debt servicing with the development needs of each country, by minimizing the social cost of the adjustment processes underway [emphasis added].[2]

On multiple occasions in 1984 and 1985, regional powers tried to operationalize their linkage strategy by calling on America and other industrialized states to engage them in formal dialogue.

Ultimately, however, linkage proved largely ineffective. Western states had clear interests in resolving the debt crisis, but refused to be dragged directly into the fray. For its part, Washington did accept the debtor states' position that policy reforms required to secure new IMF loans must prioritize economic growth along with austerity measures. Beginning in 1985, the Treasury began pushing the Baker Plan (named after Treasury Secretary James Baker), which stipulated policies designed to promote growth—and not simply restrict spending—should be part of the conditions for receiving new IMF loans. The World Bank also assumed a more active role following the Baker Plan, and began providing "structural adjustment" loans to countries that sought to expand their economies by privatizing state-owned enterprises, liberalizing trade, and deregulating domestic markets. But creditor states remained unwilling to link other issues like interest rates and protectionism to debt negotiations, or raise debt discussions to a level involving talks between states' chief executives. The locus of negotiations, therefore, stayed between borrowers, lenders, and international financial institutions, and the creditors cartel maintained its case-by-case approach.

Most regional powers had little recourse but to accept these terms, and for many, meeting them proved a bumpy ride. In 1984, Argentina nearly defaulted, and Bolivia and Ecuador were forced to suspend debt payments; in 1985, Mexico fell out of compliance with the terms of its IMF loan, while Peru refused to allocate more than 10 percent of its export revenues to debt service; and in 1987, Brazil was so cash-strapped it imposed a moratorium on its debt payments. Regional debt restructuring continued into the 1990s under the Brady Plan (named after then-Secretary of the Treasury Nicholas Brady). Debtor states received more relief through new debt-reduction instruments and additional credit, and economic growth gradually returned across Latin America. From 1995 onward (Table 9.2), many states' debt levels rose, fell, and rose again; but the return of modest growth—and the reacquisition of credit worthiness— meant that governments could also borrow again and roll over existing debts. The crisis was over.

One important analytic lesson the debt crisis teaches us is not to approach the study of world politics indiscriminately. Instead, we must take care to select our analytic tools and frameworks carefully, and use them appropriately. The debt crisis, for example, posed enormous threats to many states, non-state actors, and the international financial system—clearly, the stuff of high politics. Yet, the international politics of the crisis period bore little resemblance to a traditional realist world. Since both the interdependent and non-military nature of the threats of the crisis rendered hard power instruments ineffective, neither creditor nor debtor states ever hinted that a settlement would be imposed or resisted through force. Instead, they sought remedies and worked to protect their interests through negotiations, diplomacy, and international institutions.

Table 9.2 Total External Debt of Selected Latin American Countries ($ billions), 1995–2009

	1995	2000	2005	2009
Argentina	110.6	140.3	113.8	128.1
Bolivia	4.4	4.4	7.6	5.9
Brazil	186.5	226.1	169.4	198.3
Chile	26.3	8.5	44.9	64.8
Colombia	31.1	39.0	38.5	46.4
Ecuador	14.6	14.4	17.2	16.5
Mexico	157.2	144.5	130.7	150.1
Peru	33.8	27.2	28.7	34.6
Uruguay	5.4	5.9	11.4	12.0
Venezuela	34.1	32.4	46.4	46.4

Source: Economic Commission for Latin America and the Caribbean, *Statistical Yearbook for Latin America and the Caribbean: 2002, 2004, and 2009 Editions* (Santiago: United Nations, 2002, 2004, 2010)

States still mattered, of course (a resolution could not have been achieved without them). But by and large, non-state actors played a more direct and dominant role than creditor states (who worked indirectly through institutions but stayed somewhat on the sidelines).

For students of international politics, do these outcomes mean that realist theory is "wrong"? The prudent answer is "not necessarily." As a heuristic, in most cases of international politics realist theory still offers a useful "first cut" at analysis (even in situations of interdependence, states are still important actors). However, given the complexity that interdependence generates, a realist approach does have obvious limits. Especially when assessing contemporary international politics, therefore, our analytic task is to recognize these limitations, determine which real-life situations best approximate the realist vs. complex interdependence world, and proceed accordingly.

The 1980s debt crisis had far-reaching effects. To begin, it imposed heavy costs on Latin American states and their citizens. Widespread unemployment, sharply reduced social welfare spending, stagnant wages, deepening poverty, corporate bankruptcies, and minimal (even negative) growth were all hallmarks of what became a "lost decade." Beyond the domestic misery it unleashed, the crisis—along with other factors—delegitimized many authoritarian and military governments, thereby paving the way for a wave of democratic transitions. By 1990, elected governments held power in nearly every Latin American state. In terms of hemispheric relations, meanwhile, the crisis drove the final nails into the coffin of regional anti-hegemonic efforts from the 1970s. Latin American states became so absorbed with domestic problems that debt negotiations—rather than challenging U.S. influence—comprised the bulk of their foreign policy agendas.

Neoliberal Economics Triumphant

The Latin American debt crisis also produced dramatic shifts in regional powers' development policies, primarily by undermining states' capacity to sustain ISI programs, and compelling them to accept more market-oriented prescriptions touted by international financial institutions and the U.S. government. Many eventually embraced elements of the so-called *Washington Consensus*—a term coined by economist John Williamson to denote the neoliberal economic policies advocated by powerful actors in Washington, DC (the IMF, World Bank, and U.S. Treasury). In broad terms, this consensus proposed that countries could achieve sustainable growth by pursuing macroeconomic stability, liberalizing trade and investment policies, and shrinking the state's economic role through privatizing state-owned enterprises and economic deregulation. In essence, it argued that international market forces, rather than the kind of state economic intervention typical of import-substitution industrialization, offered countries the surest means to growth and prosperity.

To varying degrees, by the early 1990s governments in Argentina, Brazil, Colombia, Mexico, Peru, and other states had all embraced aspects of neoliberalism and adopted elements of Consensus prescriptions—often to the surprise of their citizens. In Argentina, it was the populist Peronist government of Carlos Menem which took up the torch of neoliberalism in 1989; in Brazil, it was the government of erstwhile *dependency* advocate Fernando Henrique Cardoso; in Mexico, it was the government of Carlos Salinas (head of the long-time, ruling Institutional Revolutionary Party, whose leaders had engineered Mexico's ISI development model); and in Peru, it was President Alberto Fujimori, who like Carlos Menem, had campaigned for the presidency on a populist platform. Chile, too, was among those that marketized its development model, although the Augusto Pinochet dictatorship did so long before the Washington Consensus had become vogue.

As states adjusted their economic policies in line with Consensus prescriptions, some acquired greater interest in pursuing liberal trade agreements with other states. The South American Common Market, North American Free Trade Agreement, and proposed Free Trade Agreement of the Americas all gained momentum in the wake of these regional domestic adjustments. With the Cold War's demise, expanding free trade became a U.S. foreign policy mantra during the George H. W. Bush and Bill Clinton administrations. To a significant, but lesser extent, the same was true in Latin America, and for several years, much of the continent appeared to be marching to the same tune. Under the banners of economic liberalism (free market capitalism) and political liberalism (democracy), the United States led the procession, and hemispheric relations seemed more cordial, albeit still hierarchical.

Box 9.3 The Origin of the Washington Consensus

The story of the Washington Consensus dates back to 1989, when the press in the United States was still talking about how Latin American countries were unwilling to undertake the reforms that might give them a chance to escape the debt crisis. It seemed to me that this was a misconception and that, in fact, a sea change in attitudes toward economic policy was occurring. To determine whether this was correct, the Institute for International Economics decided to convene a conference at which authors from 10 Latin American nations would present papers detailing what had been happening in their respective countries. To try to make sure that they all addressed a common set of questions, I wrote a background paper in which I listed 10 policy reforms that I argued almost everyone in Washington thought were needed in Latin America as of that date. I labeled this reform agenda the "Washington Consensus," never dreaming that I was coining a term that would become a war cry in ideological debates for more than a decade. Indeed, I thought the ideas I was laying out were consensual, which is why I gave them the label I did. The 10 reforms that constituted my list were as follows:

Fiscal discipline. This was in the context of a region where almost all the countries had run large deficits that led to balance of payments crises and were experiencing high inflation that hit mainly the poor because the rich could park their money abroad.

Reordering public expenditure priorities. This suggested switching expenditure, in a pro-growth and pro-poor way, from things like non-merit subsidies to basic health care, education, and infrastructure.

Tax reform. The aim was a tax system that would combine a broad tax base with moderate marginal tax rates.

Liberalization of interest rates. In retrospect, I wish I had formulated this more broadly as financial liberalization, stressed that views differed on how fast it should be achieved, and recognized the importance of accompanying financial liberalization with prudential supervision.

A competitive exchange rate. I fear I indulged in wishful thinking in asserting that there was a consensus in favor of ensuring that the exchange rate would be competitive, which implies an intermediate regime; in fact, Washington was already beginning to edge toward the two-corner doctrine, which holds that a country must either fix firmly or float "cleanly."

Trade liberalization. I acknowledged that there was a difference of view about how fast trade should be liberalized, but everyone agreed that this was the appropriate direction in which to move.

Liberalization of inward foreign direct investment. I specifically did not include comprehensive capital account liberalization because I did not believe that it commanded a consensus in Washington.

Privatization. This was the one area in which what originated as a neoliberal idea won broad acceptance. We have since been made very conscious that it matters a lot how privatization is done: it can be a highly corrupt process that transfers assets to a privileged elite for a fraction of their true value, but the evidence is that privatization brings benefits (especially in terms of improved service) when done properly, and the privatized enterprise either sells into a competitive market or is properly regulated.

Deregulation. This focused specifically on easing barriers to entry and exit, not on abolishing safety or environmental regulations (or regulations governing prices in a noncompetitive industry).

Property rights. This was primarily about providing the informal sector with the ability to gain property rights at an acceptable cost (inspired by Hernando de Soto's analysis).

John Williamson, "From Reform Agenda to Damaged Band Name: A Short History of the Washington Consensus and Suggestions for What to Do Next." *Finance & Development* (September 2003): 10–11, http://www.imf.org/external/pubs/ft/fandd/2003/09/pdf/williams.pdf, accessed January 23, 2011

Neoliberal economic policies helped bring economic stability to the region and a modest return to growth, but they did not generate widespread prosperity. Instead, the benefits of growth were highly skewed. Large domestic firms that were competitive internationally or produced for export markets did well; smaller firms that lacked capital, technology, or produced for domestic markets did less well; organized labor generally saw its fortunes decline; and across the region, the privatization of state-owned enterprises and rollback of state bureaucracies cut hundreds of thousands of jobs. As a result, Latin America's inequality—already notorious—grew even more.

From the late 1990s on, "reform fatigue" set in across much of the region as the public and politicians alike soured on the reform results. A Latinbarométro survey of 17 Latin American countries found that between 1998 and 2003, the percentage of Latin Americans who believed privatization policies were beneficial for their country fell from over 50 to 25 percent, while those who believed a market economy was good for their country dropped from 77 to 18 percent. In many countries these trends, coupled with periodic economic crises, helped propel left-of-center candidates and parties into office. Since Hugo Chávez was elected President of Venezuela in 1998, leftist politicians have claimed the presidency in Argentina, Bolivia, Brazil, Ecuador, El Salvador, Honduras, Nicaragua, Paraguay, and Uruguay (and almost in Mexico and Peru). Not all these governments are as stridently anti-neoliberal as those in Bolivia, Nicaragua, or Venezuela; but their economic policies all stress a greater focus on fighting poverty and inequality than is typical of conventional free market advocates. Regardless of where governments ultimately come down on neoliberalism, however, today's leaders manage their economic policies in an increasingly complex and interdependent world that offers new opportunities, and poses new challenges

Globalization

Interdependence is related to the larger phenomenon of *globalization*, and sometimes is mistaken for its equivalent. They do share certain properties: both can be facilitated by technological changes (in communications and transportation) that link different states and actors together and speed the flow of capital, information, products, and people across borders. But where interdependence implies reciprocal effects between two states or different parts in a system, globalization entails broader networks of interdependence that span larger geographic distances. And whereas interdependence constitutes a settled situation or state of affairs, globalization is a process through which communication, transportation, and trade tend to integrate regional economies, societies, and cultures.

By minimizing the effects of distance between geographic regions and sharply reducing communication and transportation costs, advocates claim globalization provides a range of widely distributed benefits to consumers (product variety and lower prices), business (markets), farmers (agricultural technology), the sick (wider dispersal of health care knowledge), and societies (cultural enhancement). At the same time, it's clear that globalization can generate "losers" too. States that fail to adjust their economic policies adequately to globalization can fall behind; industrial workers may see their jobs "migrate" to lower wage regions; capital- and technology-deficient firms can lose market share to foreign competitors; and farmers in developing countries can lose ground to agricultural imports from rich countries where production costs are lower and harvests often dramatically larger.

Interpretations of globalization differ. Some equate it with the "Americanization" of regions beyond U.S. borders—especially the extension of American culture, values, politics (democracy), and most important, capitalist economics. As journalist Thomas Freidman argued in his book *The Lexus and the Olive Tree*, "Globalization means the spread of free-market capitalism to virtually every country in the world . . . Culturally speaking, globalization has tended to involve the spread (for better or for worse) of Americanization—from Big Macs to iMacs to Mickey Mouse." Friedman sees globalization as an international system unto itself, composed not of sovereign states, but of dynamic free market forces that compel "the inexorable integration of markets, nation-states and technologies to a degree never witnessed before."[3]

Not everyone shares this view. Some observers believe Freidman's universalist conception exaggerates globalization's impact and leaves out most of the world. After all, most people in the world don't have telephones, much less personal computers with Internet access. Hundreds of millions subsist as peasants, living in remote areas with little access to their national economy, the global economy, or global flows of information and ideas. The equation "globalization = Americanization" also rubs some the wrong way. Political scientist Kenneth Waltz, for example, finds it hard to credit perceived Americanization to the effects of globalization alone, and not more traditional motives behind imitative behavior: "In any competitive system," he suggests, "the winners are imitated by the losers, or they continue to lose . . . Competition among states has always led some of them to imitate others politically, militarily, and economically."[4] Waltz's point is well taken. In just the Western Hemisphere, regional powers historically looked to Europe and the United States for inspiration and consciously sought to emulate aspects of their economic, military, or political models.

Nor is it just North Americans who view globalization differently. Latin Americans hold varying opinions too. In September 2000, Chilean president Ricardo Lagos declared that Chileans embraced globalization "with enthusiasm and optimism . . . We know that this is a revolution that impacts on the economy, technology, politics and culture and which affects the daily life of people everywhere on the planet. We in the south of the world are not afraid of this great transformation."[5] By contrast, others are more skeptical and view globalization as little more than disguised Americanization. Mexican sociologist Néstor García Canclini, for example, notes how difficult it is to see a "Latin American film outside its country of production . . . unless [it is] distributed by American firms and [fits] their standards of length, entertainment, and profit. In Mexico, although Televisa [a Mexican media conglomerate] controls the video market, almost the entirety of material offered comes from Hollywood Pictures, Paramount, Columbia, Touchstone, Turner, Universal, and Walt Disney." The "unilateral North Americanization"[6] García Canclini sees globalization generating, differs sharply from Lagos' perspective.

Economists often equate globalization and the world market. But globalization is not confined solely to economics; it has important environmental, cultural, and social dimensions too. There are many examples. The spread of deadly viruses, pathogens, and foreign vegetation has affected human populations and ecosystems from Asia to the Americas. Scientists attribute increased incidence of floods, droughts, and storm intensity to global climate change produced by carbon emissions from developed and developing countries that compete in the world economy. The global flow of information, ideas, people, and products helps reshape cultures and societies: business practices that originate in one part of the world are imitated in others, while political ideas that span great distances lead to "waves" of democratization, anti-Western Jihadist movements, and rising awareness in Northern countries of struggles to secure indigenous people's rights in the South. Religious ideas and believers migrate trans-regionally too, bringing Islam to "Christian" North America, and expanding Protestant beliefs deep into Catholic and historically non-Christian regions.

Understanding that globalization has economic, environmental, or social dimensions can help us appreciate the significance in their periodic interaction. Consider how transnational trade (a facet of globalization's economic dimension) has influenced its environmental dimension. Dutch Elm Disease is believed to have originated in Asia; it spreads locally via the elm bark beetle, and globally via lumber exports. It first arrived in Europe in 1910, Britain in 1927, and reached North America in 1928. By the 1970s, it had decimated millions of majestic elm trees across Europe and North America. Today, scientists, environmentalists, and Mexican farmers worry about the export of U.S. genetically modified corn to Mexico under NAFTA, and its impact on Mexico's *maize*—the original source of the world's many corn varieties. Mexican corn evolved over millennia and is adaptable to a broad range of climates and growing conditions; most U.S. corn lacks its counterpart's broad adaptability, and has been genetically modified to enhance its flavor and increase its resistance to pests and herbicides. The fear is that genetically modified corn will contaminate Mexico's seed reserves and eventually displace the country's natural corn stock, yielding a net loss to global food biodiversity, to farmers who cultivate the natural varieties, and to societies whose diets depend on them. This scenario sees clear disadvantages in the interaction between globalization's economic dimension (NAFTA) and its social dimension (societies).

Such dimensional interaction suggests that even as states seek to capture gains from globalization, they also must contend with its complexity and unexpected consequences. To complicate matters further, globalization multiplies both the number of issues states confront, and the number of actors who can participate meaningfully in transnational politics. Consider how global communications via the Internet helped empower activists who "wanted in" on particular political issues. Better regulation of garment manufacturing in low-wage countries (that produce, for example, college logo apparel or Nike shoes), better financial returns to farmers who produce shade-grown or "fair exchange" coffee, and the international landmines treaty are all examples where individuals exploited global communications technology to advocate change and pressure sovereign states and multinational corporations to adopt or enforce policies they might otherwise have not.

As globalization deepens interdependence, it can create new, unanticipated vulnerabilities for states. Global economics provides useful illustrations. In the 1990s and early 2000s, American financial, insurance, and mortgage firms developed and traded "mortgage bundles" with foreign financial institutions. When the U.S. sub-prime mortgage market collapsed in 2008, its effects ricocheted around the globe, threatened many countries' financial systems and societies, and caused governments in Asia, Europe, and beyond to scramble in response. Similarly, 10 years earlier the 1998 Asian financial crisis unnerved world markets to the point that it compelled states as far apart as Brazil and Russia to devalue their currencies and alter their economic policies.

Globalization has become a buzzword of the new millennium, but it is not a new phenomenon. Before World War I, mass immigration had transformed countries like Argentina and the United States, while trade and finance linked economies on both sides of the Atlantic and beyond. Much earlier, of course, globalization left a defining mark on the Western Hemisphere. Especially in Spanish and Portuguese America, the dramatic encounter between Europeans and indigenous populations fused their cultures and linked the two regions economically; meanwhile, the transcontinental flow of ideas and agricultural products influenced their economic development, populations, societies, and even cuisines. Every potato and tomato in British, Irish, and Italian cuisine has its origins in this early phase of globalization; Mexico's superb beers are the offspring of German immigrants; and Latin America's historic hacienda economic model, religious and political organization, and social arrangements owe much to their European heritage.

Whether contemporary globalization has been good for the Americas depends on whom you ask. A 2010 survey conducted by the Chicago Council of Global Affairs found that 56 percent of U.S. citizens believed globalization has been "mostly good" for the United States. By contrast, a 2009 survey conducted by Barómetro Iberoamericano found Latin Americans held a broad range of opinions: 78 percent of Chileans, for example, said globalization had "a positive impact" on their country, as did 77 percent of Brazilians and 70 percent of Peruvians. Still positive, but less so were Guatemalans (66%), Costa Ricans (64%), Colombians (60%), Hondurans (58%), Venezuelans and Dominicans (55% each). States in which only a minority of citizens believed globalization had been good for their country included Mexico (49%), Panama and Uruguay (48% each), Ecuador (47%), Nicaragua (39%), and Bolivia and El Salvador (37% each). While the 2010 report did not include globalization data for Argentina, a 2007 Iberoamericano survey found that only 40 percent of Argentines believed globalization had a positive impact on their country.[7]

Globalization and Hemispheric Relations

How has globalization affected hemispheric relations? In general, it has deepened regional economic integration, fostered greater inter-state political dialogue and policy coordination, and provided some states a new framework to express traditional anti-American nationalist sentiments. By some measures, it also has reinforced America's preeminent position vis-à-vis its neighbors, and by other measures has weakened America's regional political influence. Finally, it has created vulnerabilities for some states by facilitating certain unwanted trans-border flows that adversely affect their societies, economies, and politics. These dynamics, in turn, have stimulated new sources of inter-state conflict.

Increasing Economic Integration, Political Dialogue, and Policy Coordination

Since the 1990s, regional economic integration has acquired both greater density and scope, as new integration schemes were established and existing ones reinvigorated. NAFTA (1994), for example, established a free trade zone among the North American states, while the Dominican Republic–Central America Free Trade Agreement (2005) established a similar arrangement between the United States, Central American countries, and the Dominican Republic. MERCOSUR (1991) created a common market among Southern Cone economies in which members of the Andean Community (established as the Andean Pact in 1969) now hold associate status and vice versa. Meanwhile, the Caribbean Community (established in 1973) has grown from a small organization of mostly English-speaking states, into a 15-member, multilingual single-market economy that permits the free movement of labor and capital. In short, economic integration now crisscrosses the Western Hemisphere in a variety of ways.

Globalization also has stimulated economic integration in ways beyond state-authorized trade accords. Today, informal integration—reflected in money transfers or remittances sent by immigrants in the United States back to their Latin American homelands—increasingly links the two Americas. Even after a global economic crisis decreased the level of remittances in 2009 by 15 percent, nearly $59 billion still flowed into many Latin American states,[8] a sum much greater than levels of either foreign investment capital or official aid. Mexico, Brazil, Central America, Colombia, the Dominican Republic, and Ecuador are all major beneficiaries of this economic interchange: in 2009, for example, Mexico received over $21 billion in remittances, Brazil $4.7 billion, and Guatemala and El Salvador $3.9 and $3.4 billion respectively. Beyond simply transferring funds back home to help sustain their families, Latino immigrants have deepened economic integration through their travel and consumption habits. For example, 30 percent of tourists that travel to the Dominican Republic are Dominicans living abroad (mostly in America); 40 percent of tourists to El Salvador are Salvadorans, and similar patterns hold for Nicaragua and Honduras. Studies indicate that these "diaspora tourists" typically spend $1,000 per stay (excluding air fare) on local goods and services, which has a multiplier effect in local economies. Conversely, while in the United States, their demand for certain familiar "home products" creates niche markets in the U.S. economy that benefit Latin American exporters and U.S. importers alike.[9]

Greater political dialogue and policy coordination have developed between states too, and in ways that compete with similar functions performed through the Organization of American States. While all OAS heads of state still meet periodically in the Summits of the Americas, Latin American chief executives increasingly hold their own summits in venues that exclude the United States, like the Rio Group and Ibero-American Summits. Such regionally exclusive frameworks are not new. Organizations created in the 1960s and 1970s—like the Latin American Free Trade Association, Latin American Economic System, and Latin American Integration Association—worked to stimulate trade, economic cooperation, and a common market, and they engaged the energy of the various states' economic bureaucracies. What is different today is that issues beyond trade and commercial regulations are discussed—matters ranging from social policies, gender equality, and multilateral cooperation—and they are discussed at the highest levels of government in a consistent fashion.

Retooling Anti-Americanism

Especially in countries where left-of-center governments have come to power, globalization provides a new framework to express traditional anti-American nationalist sentiments. The governments of Argentina, Bolivia, Ecuador, Nicaragua, and Venezuela, for example, tend to equate globalization with "Americanization," the Washington Consensus, or U.S. imperialism. Consequently, they give their policy pronouncements a stronger anti-American spin than their counterparts, and exhibit greater resistance to some U.S. multilateral proposals, such as those concerning trade or narcotics trafficking.

For these states, "Americanized" globalization has become something to rally against. One antidote pushed heavily by Venezuela is the Bolivarian Alternative for the Americas (ALBA). This regional integration framework deliberately omits the United States, and is based on principles of complementarity, cooperation, and solidarity, rather than on liberal trade and free market dynamics. To date, ALBA's official membership includes Antigua and Barbuda, Bolivia, Cuba, Dominica, Ecuador (Honduras withdrew in January 2010), Nicaragua, St. Vincent and the Grenadines, and Venezuela, but none of Latin America's more economically advanced countries. Some of its core members view ALBA as an alternative to Washington's preferred integration project—a market-based, Free Trade Agreement of the Americas (FTAA). The latter would promote *hemispheric* integration in ways that likely would preserve U.S. influence, while the former would promote a *regional* integration in ways that dilute it. At the 2005 Summit of the Americas, Venezuela (along with Argentina and Brazil) took the lead in blocking the creation of a FTAA, and there has been little progress on this front since.

Differential Effects on U.S. Regional Influence

Globalization dynamics seem to have both enhanced and diminished America's regional standing. Certain aspects of globalization, for example, have penetrated the United States more deeply than Latin America, and in the process, bolstered its position vis-à-vis its neighbors. One way to assess the depth of penetration is by examining the region's communication and trade links with the "world beyond." How extensive, for example, is use of the Internet? How many free trade agreements has a state signed with other states? Most data show the United States has experienced more globalization than its southern neighbors (which is not surprising), yet globalization is making significant inroads into Latin America too.

According to figures compiled by the firm Internet World Stats, in 2010 the United States had about 240 million Internet users, or about 77 percent of the U.S. population, and between 2000 and 2010, the number of Americans using the Net grew 152 percent. Collectively, Latin American states boasted only 200 million Internet users, or about 35 percent of the region's population; but between 2000 and 2010, the number of Latin Americans who used the Internet jumped over 1,000 percent. And it's not just that more people are using the Net; they are using it to send and receive ever-larger quantities of data. According to TeleGeography, a firm that measures the geography and scope of telecommunications, between 2002 and 2005 Latin America's Internet bandwidth usage grew faster than any other region outside of Asia (Figure 9.2). Within Latin

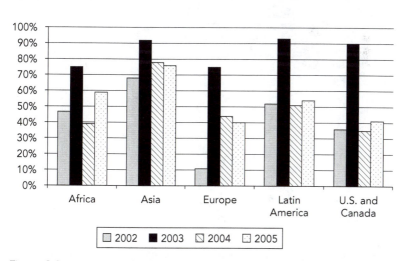

Figure 9.2 International Internet Bandwidth Growth, 2002–2005

Source: © TeleGeography

America itself, Brazil leads the pack. In 2010, it had the largest number of Internet users (76 million), followed by Mexico (30.6 million), Argentina (26.6 million), and Colombia (21.5 million). The states "least connected" to the Net in terms of users were Nicaragua (10%), Bolivia (11%), Honduras (12%), Cuba (14%), and Paraguay (15%).

Internet usage data reflect a clear digital divide between the two Americas, one that remains wide despite recent trends that suggest it may be starting to close. Even if the number of Internet users continues to grow faster in Latin America than the United States, America will probably retain a significant edge. As a leader in technological breakthroughs in computers, communications, and software, it is better positioned to adapt these innovations to its commercial, financial, industrial, and military operations. It also will likely continue to capture more gains than Latin American states from its digital connections to regions of high financial activity and economic output. As shown in Figure 9.3, in 2010 the United States (and Canada) exchanged much more digital data with Asia and Europe than did Latin America, and this pattern will likely continue

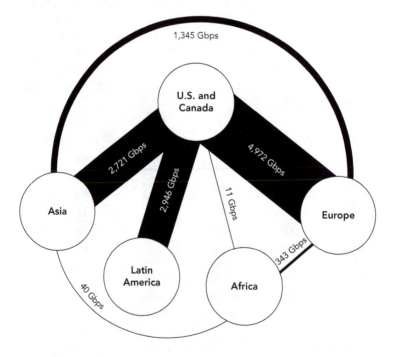

Figure 9.3 Inter-regional Internet Bandwidth (in gigabytes per second), 2010 (interregional bandwidth below 10 Gbps not depicted)

Source: © TeleGeography

for some time. If "knowledge is power," as the English philosopher Francis Bacon suggested—and modern communications speed the acquisition and use of knowledge-based power—the digital divide will continue to accord the United States greater informational power (and by extension, other advantages) than its regional peers.

In terms of their free trade links, there is asymmetry in this realm too, although it is less pronounced. Free trade agreements are useful globalization proxies not because they guarantee booming economies or robust levels of inter-state trade (many don't have these effects at all), but rather, because states enter into these accords voluntarily; hence, they reflect a country's willing embrace of economic globalization. In 2010, the United States had free trade agreements in force with 17 states—nine with Latin American states, and others with states in Asia, the Middle East, and Oceania (free trade agreements with Colombia and Panama were pending congressional approval). In Latin America, Chile and Mexico are the region's leading free traders. In 2010, Chile had 15 full-fledged free trade agreements in force—eight with Latin American states, and others with states in Asia, Europe, and Oceania. Mexico followed closely with a dozen free trade agreements: six with Latin American states, and others spread across Asia, Europe, and the Middle East. By contrast, Peru had five, while Argentina, Brazil, Colombia, and Venezuela had fewer. Put differently, these economically significant states exhibit less inclination to embrace economic globalization as fully as Chile, Mexico, or the United States. Currently, the winds of global free trade blow more toward America's favor than Latin America's.

Despite U.S. advantages in communications and trade, in some respects the outworking of globalization has weakened America's regional influence. We have already noted the growth of forums that facilitate regional cooperation without a U.S. presence, and the creation of ALBA through which some states seek the same ends. These developments permit Latin American states to identify and pursue common interests on their own terms without U.S. involvement. Even more ambitious is the economic and political regional integration project envisioned under the Union of South American Nations (UNASUR)—an intergovernmental framework established in 2008 and modeled after the European Union. UNASUR seeks to integrate states comprising both the Andean Community and MERCOSUR, and eventually provide them a common currency, parliament, and passport. Like ALBA, UNASUR remains embryonic and faces a long gestation period (it took the European Union nearly four decades to be realized). It is far too early to say whether any of these developments will completely displace older frameworks under the Inter-American System. They do, however, reflect Latin America's efforts to distance itself from the United States and address regional issues independently; thus, any successes achieved will likely come at the expense of America's traditional regional influence.

Globalization's "Darker" Side

In the Western Hemisphere, states face the problems of unwanted trans-border flows in people and drugs. Complex, transnational criminal organizations—sometimes in league with legitimate private and public sector actors—support these operations. Unregulated immigration, along with narcotics trafficking, reflect aspects of globalization's darker side. While neither trend is new, thanks to globalization they have grown enormously, and created complicated domestic political problems. Because they operate outside the law, these transnational activities challenge states' sovereignty and stimulate new points of inter-state conflict.

Undocumented Immigration

The trans-border flow of people—just like other flows in finance, commerce, ideas, or information—reflects the intensity of globalization. Today, every state in the world is either receiving, sending, or transshipping immigrants, especially immigrant laborers. Although states seek to regulate these flows through their immigration policies, they have not been able to stem the tide of illegal immigrants.

Undocumented immigration is not a direct by-product of contemporary globalization. But in important ways, the globalization of trade, investment, and communications—supported by technological innovations—has helped shape and facilitate it. Transportation costs, for example, are lower, while communication and money transfers are easier. Meanwhile, rich countries' investments in poorer countries' export manufacturing operations have forged economic, cultural, and ideological ties between the two that stimulate immigrant flows. Japan, for instance, historically had very limited immigration, and shares no common border with a potential immigrant-sending country. But after the Japanese invested heavily in other countries' export manufacturing sectors, Japan began to experience illegal immigration from those countries it had invested in: Thailand, Bangladesh, Pakistan, the Philippines, and South Korea. Studies suggest that since the late 1970s, American investments in manufacturing and component assembly operations in Mexico and the Caribbean have contributed to similar outcomes.[10]

For centuries, people have moved across the Western Hemisphere's political borders with and without the consent of established governments. In recent years, unregulated immigration has grown more intense, and is not confined to the movement of people from Latin American countries into the United States. Bolivians and Paraguayans, for example, move to Argentina; Salvadorans move to Honduras; Guatemalans and Salvadorans move to Mexico; and Hondurans, Guatemalans, Salvadorans, and Mexicans move to the United States (along with Colombians, Brazilians, Dominicans, Ecuadorians, Haitians, and people from other Latin American states). Unregulated immigration can have enormous consequences for states' economic development, labor markets, demographics, and social cohesion, as well as their education, healthcare, and housing policies.

Since 1980, the number of undocumented immigrants living in the United States has grown from less than 1 million to over 11 million (Table 9.3). The vast majority comes from Latin America (especially Mexico and Central America), the Caribbean, and Asia. Many Latin American immigrants have settled in the southern, southwestern, and western regions of the United States, where they contribute to the domestic economy (primarily through low or unskilled positions), utilize education and at times, healthcare services, and become the targets of periodic, anti-immigrant backlashes.

Unauthorized immigration into the United States has long been a sore point in Mexico-U.S. relations. In America, it has produced spates of "Mexico bashing" against the Mexican government and its citizens who cross the border illegally seeking work, and occasional policy spurts aimed at sealing the border. In

Table 9.3   Growth of Undocumented U.S. Immigrant Population, 1980–2009

Years	Undocumented Immigrants
1980–1984	900,000
1985–1989	1,310,000
1990–1994	1,800,000
1995–1999	3,260,000
2000–2004	3,250,000
2005–2009	700,000
All Years	11,122,000

Source: Derived from Rytina Hoefer and Baker, "Estimates of the Unauthorized Immigrant Population Residing in the United States: January 2008," Department of Homeland Security, February 2009; and Jeffrey S. Pasel D'Vera Cohn, "U.S. Unauthorized Immigration Flows Are Down Sharply Since Mid-Decade," *Pew Hispanic Center Report*, September 1, 2010, accessed January 6, 2011

Mexico, it has engendered a deep sense of grievance against the United States, who Mexicans believe undervalues the contributions their countrymen make to the U.S. economy, and some of whose policies (border fences, limits on work visas) they deem insulting. For good or ill, how the United States responds to the immigration issue is viewed by regional powers as a bell-wether of U.S.–Latin American relations writ large. Even measures adopted by individual U.S. states that are less immigrant-friendly provoke consternation south of the border. When Arizona adopted a tough immigration enforcement law in 2009, for example, Mexico, Bolivia, Colombia, El Salvador, Guatemala, Nicaragua, Paraguay, and Peru all challenged the state law in U.S. federal court.

Box 9.4 U.S. Immigration Policies as Viewed from Latin America

Although many Americans believe that immigration is a domestic issue that should be excluded from any international negotiations, such an approach is neither a U.S. tradition nor the view held by other nations in the hemisphere . . . [Mexico] is by no means the only country of the hemisphere for which immigration is a crucial issue. In the Caribbean, Cuba (even now, to say nothing of later), the Dominican Republic, Haiti, and Jamaica all have a similarly high proportion of their citizens residing in the United States and depend as much on remittances. The same is true for much of Central America: El Salvador has the largest share of its citizenry living abroad of any country in Latin America (more than 20 percent, compared with 12 percent for Mexico), and remittances are by far its most important source of hard currency. Nor is South America exempt from this trend. Eighteen percent of Ecuadorians reside abroad, and large and growing numbers of Colombians, Paraguayans, Peruvians, and Venezuelans live in the United States. These countries are deeply affected by the current immigration climate in the United States . . . The [George W.] Bush administration's regrettable decision to build fences along the U.S.-Mexican border, raid workplaces and housing sites, detain and deport foreigners without papers, and, more recently and more tragically, launch criminal proceedings against workers with false or stolen papers and subsequently sentence them to several months in jail before deportation is seen in Latin America as a hypocritical and vicious offense . . . These actions are accurately perceived as futile, nasty, and unfair, and, worst of all, they are conducive to growing anti-American sentiment in many countries. They play straight into the hands of the "anti-imperialist" faction of the Latin American left.

Jorge G. Castañeda, "Morning in Latin America: The Chance for a New Beginning," *Foreign Affairs* 87 (September/October 2008): 126 ff. *Academic OneFile*, accessed January 23, 2011

U.S. IMMIGRATION CONTROL POLICIES

Throughout the twentieth century, U.S. policy sometimes tolerated, encouraged, or tried to restrict unauthorized immigration from Latin America. Before the 1930s, the United States adopted an informal "open border" policy toward Mexico that helped American employers hire unskilled Mexican workers on a seasonal or cyclical basis. After the Great Depression struck, Washington forcefully repatriated 300,000 Mexicans (and in the process, exacerbated Mexico's own depression-induced employment woes). In 1942, Mexico and the United States instituted the *bracero* program, under which Mexican migrants replaced U.S. agricultural workers who had been called to military service in World War II. *Bracero* made it easier for Mexicans to enter the United States legally, and over 4 million Mexicans passed through the program before it ended in 1964. During its lifespan, many Mexicans overstayed their visits and many others entered the United States outside of *bracero*. Consequently, in 1954, the Eisenhower administration launched "operation wetback," which forcefully deported hundreds of thousands of illegal Mexican workers.

Yet, this crackdown—like others that followed—failed to stem the flow of unauthorized immigrants. The 1986 Illegal Immigration Reform and Control Act (IRCA), for example, sought to restrict the flow of illegal immigrants by imposing fines on employers who knowingly hired them, increasing funds for the Border Patrol, and granting amnesty to undocumented workers who had been in the country since 1982. Despite the new legislation, unauthorized immigration continued. Still tougher measures followed in the 1990s. Between 1993 and 2004, spending on border control quintupled from $750 million to $3.8 billion, and the size of the Border Patrol was tripled to over 11,000. Some of these measures grew out of the 1996 Illegal Immigration Reform and Immigration Responsibility Act (IIRIRA), which toughened penalties against immigrants who overstayed their legal visas (making them ineligible to reapply for another three years), and triggered new rounds of deportations. Throughout the decade, key border crossing areas in Arizona, California, and Texas were "plugged" with border fortifications, surveillance equipment, and more patrols. These border enforcement initiatives targeted El Paso, Texas (Operation Hold-the-Line, 1993), San Diego, California (Operation Gatekeeper, 1994), portions of Arizona (Operation Safeguard, 1995), and McAllen, Texas (Operation Rio Grande, 1997).

The goal was to increase the probability of apprehending border crossers in these high-traffic areas, force migrants to face life-threatening risks at other geographically inhospitable crossing points (fierce deserts, high mountain ranges), and thus, deter Central Americans and Mexicans from leaving home in the first place. However, as seen in Table 9.3, between 1995 and 2004, undocumented immigration surged dramatically even as the United States spent significantly more on border enforcement. By 2005, the policy's results were not what Washington had envisioned. Research by political scientist Wayne Cornelius determined that despite 10 years of enhanced border vigilance, unauthorized immigration had not been deterred, immigrants had not been discouraged by repeated apprehensions, and their employment prospects in the United States had not been reduced. On the other hand, because of tighter border surveillance, those who managed to cross over were staying longer in the United States than before the new policies began, and more of them were choosing to resettle permanently, rather than pass back and

Figure 9.4 Sign Warning of Illegal Immigrants Crossing Road

forth in time with shifts in the U.S. labor demand.[11] Finally, more Mexicans had turned to professional people smugglers—*coyotes*—to increase their prospects of a successful passage. The flow of Latin American immigrants entering the United States declined between 2005 and 2009 (Table 9.3), most likely from a combination of the U.S. recession that began in 2007—and deepened dramatically in 2008–2009—as well as stepped-up border control efforts. But despite this decline, in 2009 the number of undocumented immigrants residing in the United States was still nearly a third larger than in 2000.

WHY U.S. IMMIGRATION CONTROL POLICIES FAIL

Why have U.S. efforts proved largely ineffective? One reason is because they focused more on the supply side of illegal immigrants than the U.S. labor demand for undocumented workers. As economists remind us, market forces are powerful, and a strong demand for certain items—whether legal or not—inevitably stimulates a supply. Immigration control efforts in the 1930s, 1950s, and 1990s focused almost wholly on cutting off the supply of unauthorized immigrants. The 1986 reforms, meanwhile, did authorize sanctions for U.S. firms that knowingly hired such workers, but the legislation was written in a way that allowed employers to hire undocumented workers and still obey the law. IRCA required employers to obtain official citizenship or residential documents from job candidates, but not to verify their legitimacy. This loophole proved a boon to document counterfeiters, employers, and unauthorized workers alike. High-quality, fraudulent identification documents can be obtained easily in Mexican cities along the U.S. border and in American cities with large immigrant populations. Government officials also displayed little interest in enforcing IRCA's employer sanctions once U.S. policy turned toward border enforcement in the 1990s: between 1992 and 2002, worksite inspections by the Immigration and Naturalization Service fell more than 70 percent (from 7,053 to 2,061), and in 2002, the agency fined only 53 employers for hiring violations.

Another reason U.S. efforts have fared poorly is that even a reinforced border can be circumvented by professional people smugglers and determined immigrants. Some of the 10-foot steel, border fencing the United States constructed in parts of California, Arizona, and Texas has fallen prey to tunnels. According to a secret briefing by the U.S. Northern Command (which was subsequently leaked and reported by the American Federation of Scientists), 93 separate transborder tunnels were discovered between 1990 and November 2008; 35 were discovered in California, 57 in Arizona, and one in Washington state;[12] in June 2010, another tunnel was discovered between Mexico and El Paso, Texas.

Perhaps a more fundamental reason America's unilateral efforts have not been successful is that illegal immigration has become globalized. Not only do transnational labor market forces and investment patterns fuel immigrant flows, but individual immigrants of different nationalities, multiple sending countries, and non-state actors (smuggling operations) are all involved. Over a hundred large-scale people smuggling networks operate in Mexico alone, along with thousands of other smaller operations. Similar groups operate from other sending countries.

Important imbalances within sending countries themselves and the United States also interact in a globalized fashion that helps perpetuate the flows. One imbalance is between the supply and demand for labor in Mexico and other sending countries. For example, while over a million people enter Mexico's labor force each year, the economy creates only a fraction of the jobs needed to absorb them. In a speech to the Mexican Congress, President Vicente Fox lamented this dilemma: "One of the things that hurts most," he told lawmakers in 2000, "is to see how every year hundreds of thousands of Mexicans . . . have to emigrate to the United States and Canada . . . to find work and opportunities there which are denied to them in their own country."[13] High unemployment rates in other sending countries reflect a similar imbalance. According to the World Bank's World Development Indicators, between 1985 and 1989, and from 1990 through 1999, Colombia's unemployment rate averaged 11.4 and 11.5 percent respectively, El Salvador's was 11 and 6.3 percent, and Haiti's 24 and 13 percent; throughout the 1990s, unemployment in the Dominican Republic averaged 17 percent.

These imbalances inside sending countries interact with another imbalance in the United States, whose labor demand is out of sync with its immigration policy. From the 1970s onward, the U.S. economy transitioned from a primarily industrial and agricultural base, to an industrial, agricultural, and service sector base. Thanks in part to lower birth rates and higher educational levels, there is a greater demand for low and unskilled workers than there are Americans able or willing to fill these positions. Proposals to address this imbalance through immigration reforms, typically flounder in a tough domestic political terrain. The latest effort—a 2006 proposal by the George W. Bush administration— would have provided a mechanism to legalize the nearly 12 million undocumented immigrants already in the United States, and established a guest worker program to accommodate seasonal and cyclical labor demands. But the U.S. Senate rejected the proposal in 2007 (23 Democrats and 37 Republicans voted against it). Congress *did*, however, pass a bill that once again, sought to shut off supply by closing the border through high-tech surveillance and sensor equipment, and a 700-mile fence. Absent an immigration policy that syncs with

America's labor demand, illegal migration and employment will likely become more deeply embedded structural features of the U.S. economy. At the same time, America's imbalance will interact with those in sending countries, producing an equilibrium that perpetuates unauthorized immigrant flows.

IMMIGRATION PROBLEMS BEYOND THE UNITED STATES

America's "illegal immigration problem" also generates problems for other states. Efforts to cut off immigrant flows and deport undocumented workers can have severe economic consequences for sending countries that depend on remittances as a major source of hard currency. Recall that in 2009, Mexico received over $21 billion in migrant remittances, while tiny El Salvador and Guatemala received $3.9 and $3.4 billion respectively. For small states especially, the loss of these remittances can be devastating. In 1987, El Salvador's president José Napoleón Duarte was so concerned over the possibility of losing Salvadorans' remittances (which were greater than his country's annual U.S. economic aid package) that he personally asked President Reagan to allow Salvadorans in America illegally, permission to stay longer, rather than be deported under the 1986 IRCA law (Reagan was sympathetic but ultimately declined the request).

Violent, criminal youth gangs have also flourished in some sending countries, partly as a result of U.S. immigration policy. The *Mara Salvatrucha* gang (MS-13), for example, was formed in Los Angeles by Salvadorans whose families had fled their country's violent civil war. The *Calle Dieciocho* gang (18th Street, or M-18) was also formed in Los Angeles, but by Mexicans. Both have expanded their operations into Central America—an expansion triggered largely by the U.S. deportations that began under the 1996 IIRIRA.

Box 9.5 Central American Youth Gangs

Ultraviolent youth gangs, spawned in the ghettos of Los Angeles and other U.S. cities, have slowly migrated south to Central America, where they have transformed themselves into powerful, cross-border crime networks . . . [These gangs] now pose the most serious challenge to peace in the region since the end of Central America's civil wars . . . [T]he gangs are spreading, spilling into Mexico and beyond—even back into the United States itself . . . Central America's governments, meanwhile, seem utterly

> unable to meet the challenge, lacking the skills, know-how, and money necessary to fight these supergangs. The solutions attempted so far—largely confined to military and police operations—have only aggravated the problem; prisons act as gangland finishing schools, and military operations have only dispersed the gangs' leadership, making bosses harder than ever to track and capture.
> Ana Arana, "How the Street Gangs took Central America,"
> *Foreign Affairs* 84 (May/June 2005): 98 ff. *Academic OneFile*,
> accessed January 23, 2011

Between 2000 and 2004 alone, the United States deported nearly 20,000 immigrant criminals back to Central America. Many deportees had been held in U.S. prisons on gang-related felonies, where they became even more disciplined gang members. Their deportation helped "export" the Los Angeles gang culture back to countries whose police had little capacity or experience in effective gang control operations. In Central America, the gangs recruit new members, while battling each other and the police for control of neighborhoods and municipalities. Robbery, drug dealing, contract killings and simple murder have spread markedly (while official statistics remain relatively low, the journal *Foreign Affairs* reports that in 2005, Honduras' murder rate of 154 per 100,000 was twice as high as Colombia's).[14] Kidnappings and auto and weapons smuggling have spread too. The U.S. Southern Command estimates the region's total gang membership at about 70,000—an alarming figure in countries with relatively small populations. Although the problem is most severe in El Salvador, Guatemala, and Honduras, MS-13 now operates in Mexico, from Chiapas in the south, to Tamaulipas along the northern border. It also has moved back into the United States, where gang members supplement Latin American drug operations' efforts to distribute narcotics within the U.S. market.

Drug Trafficking

GLOBALIZATION AND THE DRUG TRADE

Like undocumented immigrants, illicit drugs are another unwanted transnational flow that globalization did not create, but whose expansion it facilitates. The United Nations Office on Drugs and Crime estimates that global drug trafficking generates $500 billion in annual sales—a figure greater than the gross domestic product of 90 percent of the world's states. Although marijuana, methamphetamines, heroin, and cocaine are all smuggled across borders, in the Western Hemisphere cocaine trafficking has been the leading cause of concern for several decades. Produced from coca leaves grown mainly in remote areas of Bolivia, Colombia, and Peru, cocaine is transshipped primarily through the Central America–Mexico corridor to the United States. It is easy to manufacture, sells retail in America for 500 percent above its cost in Colombia, and thus, is extraordinarily profitable. Most cocaine enters the United States disguised inside legally imported products and transport containers. Once inside the country, some of the powdered cocaine is reprocessed into its more highly addictive form, crack.

The hemisphere's cocaine trade links states from the Andes through North America, and affects their economies, politics, societies, and security. It provides employment to hundreds of thousands in producer states, funnels billions of dollars back into local economies, supports guerrilla insurgents and paramilitary groups in Colombia, spawns crime and violence on both sides of the U.S.-Mexico border, and sustains criminal organizations throughout the region.

Figure 9.5 Mayport, Florida: Drugs Seized by U.S. Navy and U.S. Coast Guard, December 12, 2008

Coca grows plentifully in all three Andean countries, but most cocaine manufacturing is concentrated in Colombia. Consequently, close to 90 percent of all cocaine sold in the United States originates in Colombia—90 percent of which passes through Mexico—and in 2008, 42 percent of these shipments had passed through Central America.

Even more than unauthorized immigration, globalization has been a boon to narcotics trafficking. Transnational drug operations display the central features found in other legitimate, highly successful multinational commercial

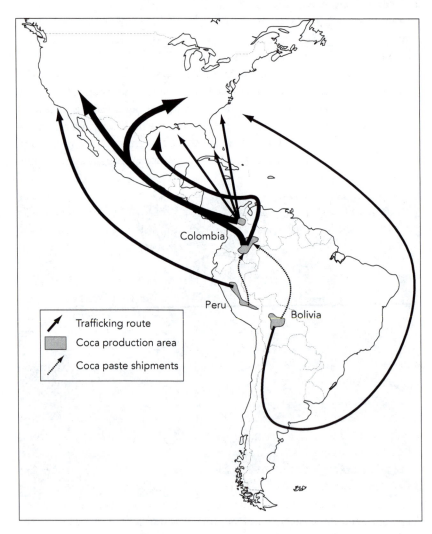

Figure 9.6 Cocaine Trafficking Routes in Latin America

enterprises: subcontracting, transnational division of labor, niche marketing, vertical integration, and complex distribution routes. These organizations take advantage of the latest innovations in communications to stay ahead of authorities, and in capital transfer technology, financial regulations, and offshore banking to hide, launder, and repatriate profits. Through their transnational investments in legitimate enterprises—from construction firms, real estate, and tourist centers, to manufacturing industries, commercial businesses, and financial entities—drug operations have woven themselves deeply into the fabric of the world economy.

THE U.S. AND HEMISPHERIC "WAR ON DRUGS"

Since the 1970s, the U.S. federal government has waged a "war on drugs." The Nixon administration targeted heroin, whose use among both American soldiers returning from Vietnam and inner-city residents, had raised crime rates and generated deep concern. Since the 1980s, however, the chief focus has been cocaine (although campaigns against marijuana, heroin, methamphetamines, and other illicit substances continue). In 1986, President Ronald Reagan signed National Security Decision Directive 221, which declared drug production and trafficking a U.S. security concern. The same year, Congress amended the 1961 Foreign Assistance Act to require the president to "certify" every year whether other states were cooperating with U.S. anti-narcotics efforts. Those the president deemed uncooperative, would face a cut-off in U.S. foreign aid, and be denied loans from the Inter-American Development Bank, World Bank, or International Monetary Fund. Latin American states routinely decried this annual ritual, and found it deeply humiliating and hypocritical: it cast Washington in the role of passing judgment on their internal anti-drug policies, while doing nothing to address the U.S. demand for drugs that stimulated the drug trade in the first place.

However, as a form of coercive diplomacy, America's unilateral certification process did help enlist its neighbors' support for a hemispheric war on drug trafficking. Since its inception, the war's primary goal has been to stop the influx of cocaine into the United States by eradicating coca fields in source countries and interdicting cocaine shipments bound for the U.S. market. This strategy was formalized at two regional anti-drug summits—the 1990 Cartagena summit, and the 1992 summit in San Antonio, Texas—and it has underpinned virtually every regional anti-drug initiative the United States has promoted. Under the "Andean Initiative" and "Plan Colombia" of the George H. W. Bush and Bill Clinton administrations, as well as the "Andean Regional Initiative" and "Mérida Initiative" of the George W. Bush administration,

Washington provided its neighbors billions of dollars in economic, technical, and material assistance to enhance their police and security forces, eradicate coca crops, combat, prosecute, or extradite drug actors, and seize and interdict drug shipments. In the 1980s, most funds went to Bolivia and Peru, which then were the region's leading coca producers. In the 1990s, Colombia began receiving a larger share of funds, as did Mexico in the 2000s. Some interdiction funds also went to Venezuela, and states in Central America and the Caribbean.

Participation in the hemispheric drug war has cost some Latin American governments and their people dearly. Examples abound. The use of Bolivian, Colombian, Peruvian, and Mexican militaries in the anti-drug campaigns has exposed these nations' armed forces to the same financial lure that has corrupted elements of their political, judicial, and police institutions. In rural Bolivia and Peru, police and soldiers tasked with manually eradicating coca crops have been implicated in human rights violations; meanwhile, aerial fumigation of Colombian coca fields has destroyed farmers' legitimate crops too, leaving rural families without means of support. During the 1980s, when Colombia began to extradite alleged drug leaders indicted for narco-trafficking in the United States, the Medellín drug cartel first tried to buy the state off (cartel leader Pablo Escobar offered to pay off Colombia's foreign debt). When this failed, the cartel retaliated ferociously with a wave of terrorist assassinations, bombings, and other attacks against public servants, presidential candidates, the state internal security service, journalists and the media—even shopping malls and other public venues. In 1985, Colombia's entire Supreme Court was held hostage by members of the "19th of April" guerrilla movement (M-19), who—presumably at the cartel's behest—burned all court records on pending extradition cases. Many judges died in the shootout that ended the hostage crisis.

Confrontation between Mexico's government and drug organizations unleashed a similar wave of violence, but a greater river of blood. When Mexican President Felipe Calderón launched a crackdown against drug organizations in 2006, the organizations responded by assassinating public officials, police, military personnel, journalists, and civilians. By 2010, the organizations' battle with authorities (and each other) for control of smuggling routes into America had left over 28,000 Mexicans dead.

Besides generating various costs, the drug war affects regional powers' domestic politics in other ways too. It's not just that public approval of political leaders may rise or fall depending on the outcome of a government's campaign against drug organizations; sometimes a country's political landscape can be wholly transformed. For example, in Bolivia where the coca plant has deep historical roots and cultural significance, eradication projects engendered a backlash among indigenous coca farmers that helped propel former *cocalero* leader Evo Morales into high office. Morales' 2005 election to the presidency gave Bolivia its first indigenous, national political leader in centuries. Since coming to power, the Morales government has approved coca production for legitimate cultural and commercial uses, maintained a ban on cocaine, but cooled its support for U.S. eradication programs.

Besides seeking its neighbors' support, the United States also pressed the drug war unilaterally on the domestic and international fronts. At home, it established specific anti-drug units such as the Drug Enforcement Agency and Office of National Drug Control Policy, and expanded other agencies' drug war responsibilities. In the 1980s, it stiffened penalties for cocaine use and trafficking dramatically—including mandatory minimum sentences, the death penalty for drug "kingpins," and highly asymmetrical punishments for those involved with powdered versus "crack" cocaine. Under the 1986 anti-Drug Abuse Act, possessing 500 grams of the former (a quantity large enough to infer cocaine trafficking) could yield a 5-year prison sentence, while possessing just 5 grams of the latter *required* a 5-year prison stint. Since powdered cocaine is preferred by white and more affluent customers, while minorities and the less affluent tend to consume the lower-priced crack, these penalties distributed jail time disproportionately along racial and socioeconomic lines and contributed to a soaring incarceration rate. Between 1979 and 2006, the number of U.S. citizens imprisoned climbed from less than 500,000 to over 2 million—leaving America with both the world's largest prison population (44 percent of which is non-white), and highest rate of incarceration (topping even Cuba, China, and Russia's). In 2010, Congress passed legislation to reduce the sentencing disparities between crack and powdered cocaine.

THE INVASION OF PANAMA

On the international front, the United States took the drug war directly to an important transshipment country. In December 1989, U.S. forces invaded Panama to apprehend its leader, General Manuel Noriega, whose links to the Medellín drug cartel (and other infractions) placed him in the U.S. crosshairs. Noriega actually worked for the United States *and* the Medellín cartel simultaneously. As early as 1967, he was a paid CIA informant. In the 1980s, he assumed control of Panama's National Guard and used this position to control Panamanian politics; he also began cooperating with U.S. efforts to overthrow Nicaragua's Sandinista government, and established a working relationship with Colombian drug dealers. Drawing salaries from the Americans (reportedly between $200,000 and $340,000) and Colombians (allegedly $4 million in drug payoffs), Noriega worked both sides. On the one hand, he allowed Washington to establish listening posts in Panamanian territory, and at a time when the Boland Amendment prohibited American money, weapons, government agencies, or personnel from assisting *contra* efforts to overthrow the Sandinistas, he facilitated the transshipment of weapons from third countries through Panama to *contra* bases in Honduras. (Oddly, he collaborated with Washington's anti-Sandinista military project at the same time Panama publicly sought a diplomatic peace settlement through the Contadora peace process.) On the other hand, he placed Panama's bank secrecy laws at the service of the Medellín cartel's money laundering operations, and allowed the cartel to ferry cocaine through Panama into Florida and the U.S. market.

In February 1988, U.S. federal prosecutors obtained an indictment against Noriega for drug trafficking, which led to a fallout between the General and Panama's puppet president, Eric Arturo Delvalle, as well as Delvalle's ouster and replacement by an interim president, Manuel Solís Palma. In May 1989, Panamanians went to the polls to vote for a new president. But the election—a contest between Noriega's candidate Carlos Duque, and opposition candidate Guillermo Endara—was stolen by the Noriega faction, and the fraud denounced by international observers, including former U.S. president Jimmy Carter. When the Organization of American States singled Noriega out for condemnation and sent a delegation to Panama to broker a peaceful transfer of power, the General rejected the OAS mission as a symbol of U.S. meddling in Panama's internal affairs. As U.S.-Panamanian relations soured, President George H. W. Bush ordered stepped-up military exercises around Panama, and on December 15, Panama's pro-Noriega General Assembly declared a "state of war" with the United States, under which it also named Noriega as chief of state. The following day, a car containing four U.S. military officers ran a roadblock and was fired upon by Panamanian soldiers; one officer was killed, another wounded, and a third interrogated and beaten; the same day another U.S. officer and his wife were arrested; the officer was beaten repeatedly while his wife was physically abused and sexually threatened.

The American invasion—code-named Operation Just Cause by the Pentagon—came four days later on December 20, 1989. It deposed Noriega and installed Endara in the presidency. With Panama under U.S. military occupation, Noriega took refuge in the Papal Nunciature, but surrendered to American forces on January 4, 1990. Flown to Florida, he was tried, convicted on drug charges, and spent 15 years (of a 30-year sentence) in a U.S. federal prison.

Because the United States had not consulted any Latin American governments about its invasion plans, regional opposition—quick, sharp, and uniform—cut through ideological divisions, and united governments that were friendly and less friendly toward Washington. Virtually every state criticized the move as a breach of international law and Panamanian sovereignty. Argentina's foreign minister, Domingo Cavallo, said Buenos Aires "deplored" the U.S. intervention; Brazilian president José Sarney labeled it a "step backward in international relations," and declared that all Brazilians "profoundly lament this event"; Mexico's government censured Noriega for his political malfeasance and drug-running activities, but maintained that combating "international crimes cannot be a motive for intervening in a sovereign nation . . . The Panamanian crisis must be resolved only by the Panamanian people." Costa Rica, Guatemala, and Nicaragua also condemned the use of force. Nicaragua's interior minister, Tomás Borge, urged regional powers to unleash a "thermo-nuclear bomb of reactions against this infamous, intervening Government." Peru recalled its Ambassador to the United States in protest, and Venezuela vowed not to recognize the new Endara government until U.S. forces were withdrawn. Cuba also excoriated the United States for its "new imperialist aggression against our Latin American peoples," and cited the invasion as "incredible evidence of the disdain of the United States for international law." Even Chile's pro-U.S. Pinochet dictatorship rejected America's military action and called for "a rapid restoration of Panama's sovereignty."[15] On December 22, the Organization of American States passed a resolution that deplored the U.S. intervention and urged the quick withdrawal of U.S. troops, and on December 29, the UN General Assembly followed suit, condemning the invasion as a violation of international law.

Operation Just Cause took Noriega out of circulation, but ultimately made little difference in the war on drugs. Its most notable consequences for the cocaine trade were the adjustments that traffickers made in their product distribution routes. Along with other interdiction efforts in the Caribbean, the invasion reduced Panama's role as a drug transshipment point and closed Florida as the gateway into the U.S. cocaine market. In turn, Colombian traffickers linked up with Mexican marijuana smugglers, who began moving cocaine across the U.S. border. By 2005, most cocaine was entering the United States through Mexico; Mexican drug organizations had displaced their Colombian counterparts as the trade's most prominent actors; and Mexico was transformed into the latest epicenter of drug operations and associated violence.

Since its inception in the 1980s, the regional drug war has generated what its critics (and some advocates) might call pyrrhic victories. Vast swaths of coca fields in Andean countries have been eradicated, hundreds of tons of cocaine have been interdicted or seized, large drug operations like Colombia's Medellín and Cali cartels have been dismantled, and over $13 billion in U.S. assistance has been disbursed. Yet, the cocaine trade has not only continued, but flourished. The price for a gram of cocaine on U.S. streets is lower today than in the 1980s, and its purity—and thus, potency—is greater. Americans' casual and recreational use of cocaine and other drugs has declined, but not disappeared (hardcore use has remained steady); and in Latin America, cocaine consumption has recently increased in several countries, especially in regions along the main transit routes to the U.S. market.

WHY HAS THE DRUG WAR FAILED?

Why have states been unable to eliminate (or even largely reduce) the unwanted flows in illicit drugs? Among the many reasons, one is that their efforts have focused primarily on reducing the supply of illicit drugs rather than the demand for them. Interdiction, seizure, and crop eradication all target the supply of drugs. This supply-side approach was developed largely at U.S. insistence, and rests on the notion that if cocaine did not enter U.S. territory, there would be no U.S. cocaine problem (and even if the border cannot be sealed completely against its influx, reducing the cocaine supply will increase the street price to the point it drives users out of the market). But this premise rests on the fallacy that other states are largely responsible for America's drug woes.

Americans often conceptualize their country's cocaine problem as a function of Latin America's rampant corruption, drug lords, and coca farmers. To be sure, the lure of profits, threats of violence, and lucrative payoffs have induced considerable corruption south of the border among public officials, police, and even the military. Meanwhile, drug organizations operating in the Andes, Mexico, and elsewhere compete for a share of U.S. sales and market their product aggressively. And for many small farmers in remote areas of Bolivia, Colombia, and Peru, coca—which can yield harvests 3 to 4 times per year—offers the highest return of any crop they might plant. But the root cause of the coke trade does not lay in Latin America; rather, it resides in the persistent demand for drugs among U.S. consumers. Americans spend roughly $35 billion a year on cocaine alone—more than they spend on airline tickets or cigarettes. Were there no demand, there would be no supply.

A second and related reason states have been unable to eliminate the cocaine trade is because of its profitability, which itself is a function of the drug's illegality. Because cocaine is illegal, its costs increase as the product moves up the production, processing, transportation, and distribution chain. The net effects are highly inflated retail prices, and a profit margin that consistently entices new entrants into the market to replace those who have been incarcerated or killed. Indeed, profits from the trade are so enormous, they reinforce the drug organizations' capacity to bribe, combat, and compete with states on many fronts. Although precise data are unavailable, the U.S. National Drug Intelligence Center estimates that drug organizations working out of Colombia and Mexico repatriate between $18 billion and $39 billion every year (in 2003 and 2004 alone, over $17 billion in *bulk drug cash* was smuggled back into Mexico; billions more may have been laundered). The magnitude of these revenues buys drug organizations extraordinary levels of political protection, shrewd money managers, advanced intelligence technology and operations, and high-performance weaponry that rivals or exceeds the arms states employ. Put simply, in important ways the drug trade's sheer economic force defies state actions.

A third reason is because of the trade's complex, globalized nature. It has a clear transnational economic dimension, but also a cultural, social, and political one too. It is comprised of multiple transnational actors (seven major drug organizations in Mexico alone; others in Colombia and beyond) and hundreds of thousands of consumers from all socioeconomic backgrounds. It has dense linkages with international finance and banking centers, and it intermingles freely with legitimate transnational commerce. Coca production itself is transnational, and nearly impossible to restrict due to the so-called "balloon effect": just as squeezing one part of a latex balloon yields a bulge elsewhere, so a clampdown on coca production in one region triggers its expansion in another. When Bolivia and Peru launched coca eradication programs in the 1990s, more production simply shifted to Colombia, where output soared 103 percent between 1996 and 2000; similarly, once intense fumigation efforts began to force Colombia's output down in 2006, more coca production shifted back into Bolivia and Peru.

Most important, the trade has flourished under neoliberal market reforms that were designed to facilitate legitimate international commerce, and which form the cornerstone of modern, economic globalization. Liberal trade, financial, and investment policies, along with deregulation and other measures that speed transportation and reduce shipping costs, have all worked as drug trade "enablers" that reinforce its capacity to meld with the legitimate world economy.

Consider the effects that trade-enhancing policies have on narcotics trafficking. Robust liberal trade rests on subsidiary programs that reduce tariffs, upgrade transport infrastructure, and deregulate financial systems. In the wake of the international debt crisis, these measures obtained broad consensus among developed and developing countries alike (including Colombia, Mexico, and Peru), and they expanded trade volume by lowering trade barriers and transport/transaction costs. These same benefits, however, come at the expense of effective supply-side, anti-trafficking efforts: liberalized trade increases the volume of legally traded goods, *plus* the variety of nooks and crannies where traffickers can hide illicit ones; infrastructure upgrades (roads, ports, railways, airports) lower transport costs for legal *and* illegal products; and financial deregulation facilitates legitimate transactions *and* money laundering. Put simply, the rise of the neoliberal economic creed and coterminous intensification of the cocaine trade is no accident, and the relationship has grown stronger as globalization deepened. Since the early 1990s, trade arrangements like NAFTA and the Dominican Republic–Central America Free Trade Agreement have not only integrated regional economies, but integrated the drug trade further into these economies too.

In a globalized, largely neoliberal economic context, states face an uphill battle against cocaine trafficking because the underlying logic of liberal trade policies and the war on drugs are in sharp conflict. The former requires increasingly open borders to facilitate commercial transactions; the latter requires ever-tighter controls over those same borders. Journalist Douglas Payne observed:

> If a drug trafficker or money launderer were asked what are the optimum conditions for conducting their operations, the answer would be low trade barriers, deregulation, relaxed international banking standards, border-erasing technology, and weak rule of law. Those are the prevailing trends or conditions in the world today, and every means the worlds of business and finance have to offer, linked by wireless and fax transmissions, are today used by traffickers and the managers of their illicit proceeds.[16]

WILL THE AMERICAS PART WAYS OVER DRUG CONTROL?

In 2003, libertarian scholar Ted Galen Carpenter labeled America's war on drugs "The Bad Neighbor Policy," in light of its failures and negative effects on U.S. neighbors. Despite little prospects of winning the war, the United States' commitment to it appears undiminished. But in Latin America, a growing number of states and elite political figures have called for a fundamental rethinking of anti-drug policies. In February 2009, the Latin American Commission on Drugs and Democracy passed judgment on the Western Hemisphere's 30-year anti-drug effort. The Commission—led by former Brazilian president Fernando Henrique Cardoso, former Colombian president César Gaviria, and former Mexican president Ernesto Zedillo—concluded that the war on drugs and supply-side strategies had failed, and that the Americas were "farther than ever from the announced goal of eradicating drugs." Rather than eliminating narcotics trafficking and drug consumption, the drug war induced ever-higher levels of corruption, stronger organized crime syndicates, and greater waves of violence that threatened democratic governments and societies. The Commission called for a region-wide dialogue on drug policy— one that included domestic societies and non-state actors, not just politicians. And as a starting point for this dialogue, it offered a Latin American, "harm reduction" approach that would treat drug use as a public health issue, educate individuals away from drug consumption (as has occurred with cigarettes in the United States), and reserve state coercion for organized crime.

Box 9.6 Latin America's Verdict: The War on Drugs Has Failed

Confronted with a situation that is growing worse by the day, it is imperative to rectify the "war on drugs" strategy pursued in the region over the past 30 years. Prohibitionist policies based on the eradication of production and on the disruption of drug flows as well as on the criminalization of consumption have not yielded the expected results. We are farther than ever from the announced goal of eradicating drugs . . . Colombia is a clear example of the shortcomings of the repressive policies promoted at the global level by the United States. For decades, Colombia implemented all conceivable measures to fight the drug trade . . . [but] the areas of illegal cultivation are again expanding as well as the flow of drugs coming out of Colombia and the Andean region. Mexico has quickly become the other epicenter of the violent activities carried out by the criminal groups associated with the narcotics trade . . . Mexico is thus well positioned to ask the government and institutions of American society to engage in a dialogue about the policies currently pursued by the US . . . The traumatic Colombian experience is a useful reference for countries not to make the mistake of adopting the US prohibitionist policies and to move forward in the search for innovative alternatives . . . [T]he Latin American Commission on Drugs and Democracy addresses the present statement to our countries' governments and public opinion, to the United Nations and the international community, proposing a new paradigm based on three main directives:

- Treating drug users as a matter of public health.
- Reducing drug consumption through information, education and pre-ventions.
- Focusing repression on organized crime.

César Gaviria (co-president); Fernando Henrique Cardoso (co-president); Ernesto Zedillo (co-president), *Drugs and Democracy: Toward a Paradigm Shift: Statement by the Latin American Commission on Drugs and Democracy* (February 2009), http://www.drogasedemocracia.org/Arquivos/declaracao_ingles_site.pdf, accessed January 23, 2011

In short order, some regional governments began moving in the Commission's direction. In August 2009, Mexico decriminalized possession of small amounts of drugs—marijuana, cocaine, heroin, methamphetamines, and LSD—and established government-financed treatment measures for drug dependency. The same month, Argentina's Supreme Court essentially decriminalized marijuana possession when it ruled (unanimously) the state could not prosecute adults who possessed the drug for personal use, so long as there was no harm to another: "Each adult is free to make lifestyle decisions without the intervention of the state," the Court declared. The next month, Colombia's Supreme Court followed suit and ruled that prosecuting adults who possessed any illegal drug for personal use was unconstitutional.

While these developments veer from traditional anti-drug orthodoxy, there is an obvious tension between the legal consumption of certain drugs, and the continued illegality of their production, distribution, and sale. In August 2010, former Mexican president Vicente Fox spoke to this point when he called for Mexico to legalize the drug trade outright. Writing in his personal blog, Fox suggested that Mexico

should consider legalizing the production, sale and distribution of drugs. Legalization in this sense does not mean that drugs are good or don't harm those who use them; that's not the point. But we have to see it as a strategy to weaken and break the economic system that allows cartels to make huge profits, which in turn increases their power and capacity to corrupt.[17]

Fox elaborated in a subsequent interview with a *Miami Herald* columnist:

> Prohibition of alcohol in the United States [in the 1920s] never worked, and it only helped trigger violence and crime. What I'm proposing is that, instead of allowing this [drug] business to continue being run by criminals, by cartels, that it be run by law-abiding business people who are registered with the Finance Ministry, pay taxes and create jobs.[18]

Current Mexican president Felipe Calderón refused to back outright legalization, but did call for an open, public debate on the topic—a call echoed by Colombia's president Juan Manuel Santos. The prospects of legalization seem remote in the United States, but as governments in the Western Hemisphere grapple with the problem of globalized narcotics trafficking, the two Americas may find themselves moving in very different directions, with Latin America increasingly unwilling to follow the U.S. lead.

Globalization and interdependence have not created an entirely "new" international politics. However, they have added a new dimension of complex, transnational political issues, provided states new opportunities and benefits, and generated new challenges. Some of these challenges—like economic or debt crises, unauthorized immigration, or narcotics trafficking—cannot be addressed adequately through traditional instruments of hard power. The changes wrought through economic integration, technological innovation, and the offsetting of geographic distance, make international politics more complicated and unpredictable. They also have helped empower non-state actors (including private sector actors, international institutions, and criminal organizations), while eroding some of the traditional capacities states enjoyed to control their borders, manage their economies, and regulate commerce. In the Western Hemisphere, the effects of interdependence and globalization have both strengthened and weakened America's position and influence vis-à-vis its neighbors. These dynamics will continue to play out as the twenty-first century unfolds.

Study Questions

1. What do Keohane and Nye mean by "complex interdependence"? How does this view of world politics differ from that of realist theory? Where might we find complex interdependence most developed today?

2. What were the underlying and immediate causes of the 1980s international debt crisis? How did it influence regional powers' domestic economic and

development policies? In what ways, if any, did it reorient U.S.–Latin American relations?

3. Why in the 1980s, did creditor states not use force to compel repayment of Latin America's enormous debt? In terms of resolving the crisis, who played the more prominent role—states or non-state actors?

4. What is globalization? Is it synonymous with "Americanization" or interdependence? Does it transcend economics? How does globalization complicate the political issues states confront?

5. In what ways has globalization strengthened connections between the two Americas? In what ways does it tend to separate them?

6. Why have state efforts to eliminate drug trafficking and control undocumented immigration proved unsuccessful?

7. Why does Flynn believe the "thugs" are more likely to advance their interests in drug trafficking than nation states are likely to curtail this illicit trade? What advantages does one side have that the other lacks?

Selected Readings

Coatsworth, John H. "Cycles of Globalization, Economic Growth, and Human Welfare in Latin America." In *Globalization and the Rural Environment*, edited by Otto T. Solbrig, Robert Paarlberg and Francesco Di Castri, 23–44. Cambridge, MA: Harvard University Press, 2001.

Dermota, Ken. "Snow Business: Drugs and the Spirit of Capitalism." *World Policy Journal* 16 (Winter 1999/2000): 15–23.

Flynn, Stephen E. "The Global Drug Trade Versus the Nation-State: Why the Thugs Are Winning." In *Beyond Sovereignty: Issues for a Global Agenda*, edited by Maryann Cusimano, 44–66. Boston: Bedford/St. Martins, 1999.

Friman, H. Richard and Peter Andreas. "Introduction: International Relations and the Illicit Global Economy." In *The Illicit Global Economy and State Power*, edited by H. Richard Friman and Peter Andreas, 1–23. Lanham, MD: Rowman & Littlefield, 1999.

Jacoby, Tamar. "Immigration Nation." *Foreign Affairs* 85 (November/December 2006): 50–65.

Keohane, Robert O. and Joseph S. Nye, Jr. *Power and Interdependence*, Second Edition, chs 1–3. Glenview, IL: Scott Foresman, 1989.

Latin American Commission on Drugs and Democracy. *Drugs and Democracy: Toward a Paradigm Shift: Statement by the Latin American Commission on Drugs and Democracy* (February 2009), http://www.drogasedemocracia.org/Arquivos/declaracao_ingles_site.pdf.

Nadelmann, Ethan. "Drugs: Think Again," *Foreign Policy* 162 (September/October 2007): 24–30.

Payne, Douglas. "Why Drug Traffickers Love Free Trade." *Dissent* 44 (Summer 1997): 59–64.

Roett, Riordan. "The Debt Crisis: Economics and Politics." In *United States Policy in Latin*

America: A Century of Crisis and Challenge, 1961–1986, edited by John D. Martz, 237–259. Lincoln: University of Nebraska Press, 1988.

Smith, Peter. "Political Dimensions of the Peso Crisis." In *Mexico 1994: Anatomy of an Emerging-Market Crash,* edited by Sebastian Edwards and Moises Naim, 31–54. Washington, DC: Carnegie Endowment for International Peace, 1997.

Williams, Phil. "Transnational Organized Crime and the State." In *The Emergence of Private Authority in Global Governance,* edited by Rodney Bruce Hall and Thomas J. Biersteker, 161–181. New York: Cambridge University Press, 2002.

Further Readings

Aggerwal, Vinod K. "International Debt Threat: Bargaining Among Creditors and Debtors in the 1980s." *Policy Papers in International Affairs* 29. Berkeley, CA: Institute of International Studies, 1987.

Andreas, Peter. "When Policies Collide: Market Reform, Market Prohibition, and the Narcotization of the Mexican Economy." In *The Illicit Global Economy and State Power,* edited by H. Richard Friman and Peter Andreas, 125–141. Lanham, MD: Rowman & Littlefield, 1999.

Bagley, Bruce M. and Juan G. Tokatlian. "Dope and Dogma: Explaining the Failure of U.S.–Latin American Drug Policies." In *Neighborly Adversaries: U.S.–Latin American Relations,* edited by Michael LaRosa and Frank O. Mora, 219–235. Lanham, MD: Rowman & Littlefield, 1999.

Berger, Mark T. "Up From Neoliberalism: Free-Market Mythologies and the Coming Crisis of Global Capitalism." *Third World Quarterly* 20 (1999): 453–463.

Brands, Hal. "Mexico's Narco-Insurgency and U.S. Counterdrug Policy." Carlisle, PA: Strategic Studies Institute, U.S. Army War College, May 2009.

Chaudhuri, Adhip. "The Mexican Debt Crisis, 1982." *Pew Program in Case Teaching and Writing in International Affairs,* case 204. N.p.: 1988.

Domínguez, Jorge I. "Immigration as Foreign Policy in U.S.–Latin American Relations." In *Immigration and U.S. Foreign Policy,* edited by Robert W. Tucker, Charles B. Keely, and Linda Wrigley, 150–166. Boulder, CO: Westview Press, 1990.

Friedman, Thomas L. *The Lexus and the Olive Tree.* New York: Anchor Books, 2000.

Gómez, Ricardo. "The Hall of Mirrors: The Internet in Latin America." *Current History* 96 (February 2000): 72–77.

Huntington, Samuel P. "The Hispanic Challenge." *Foreign Policy* 141 (March/April 2004): 30–46.

Keohane, Robert and Joseph Nye, "Globalization: What's New? What's Not? (And So What?)." *Foreign Policy* 118 (Spring 2000): 104–120.

Nadelmann, Ethan A. "Global Prohibition Regimes: The Evolution of Norms in International Society." *International Organizations* 44 (1990): 479–526.

Naím, Moisés. "Mexico's Larger Story." *Foreign Policy* 99 (Summer 1995): 112–130.

National Drug Intelligence Center. *National Drug Threat Assessment 2010.* Washington, DC: U.S. Department of Justice, National Drug Intelligence Center, February 2010, http://www.justice.gov/ndic/pubs38/38661/index.htm.

Peceny, Mark and Michael Durnan. "The FARC's Best Friend: U.S. Antidrug Policies and the Deepening of Colombia's Civil War in the 1990s." *Latin American Politics and Society* 48 (Summer 2006): 95–116.

Sassen, Saskia. "U.S. Immigration Policy Toward Mexico in a Global Economy." *Journal of International Affairs* 43 (Winter 1990): 369–383

Stavig, Ward. "Latin American Globalization in Historical Perspective: Human Reality and the First and Second 'Global' Eras." *Journal of Developing Societies* 21 (2005): 233–251.

Yergin, Daniel and Joseph Stanislaw. *The Commanding Heights: The Battle Between Government and the Marketplace That Is Remaking the Modern World*, Introduction, chs 5, 9, and Conclusion. New York: Simon & Schuster, 1998.

Youngers, Coletta A. and Eileen Rosin (eds). *Drugs and Democracy in Latin America: The Impact of U.S. Policy*. Boulder, CO: Lynne Rienner, 2005.

Chronology: Economic Independence

1970s	Latin American states borrow heavily from foreign, private commercial banks to finance ISI and energy purchases
1981	U.S. Federal Reserve raises interest rates to fight domestic inflation, triggering interest-rate hikes on Latin American loans drawn on U.S. commercial banks
1982	Mexico unable to meet debt obligations; 1980s debt crisis begins, threatens large foreign private banks and international financial system
1982–1990	Debt negotiations between creditor banks and indebted states
1982–1990s	Latin American states get some debt assistance from IMF and World Bank, come under their tutelage, and lose economic autonomy
1985	Baker Plan adopted
1989	Brady Plan adopted
1988–1990s	Growing number of Latin American states adopt market-oriented, neoliberal economic policies and development models
1991	South American Common Market (MERCOSUR) goes into effect
1994	North American Free Trade Agreement (NAFTA) goes into effect
1994–1995	Mexican peso crisis threatens Mexican and U.S. economies; United States and IMF provide emergency $53 billion loan

Hemispheric Relations in the Twenty-First Century **10**

Figure 10.1 The Future

At the end of the Cold War, U.S.–Latin American relations retained several historic characteristics. Wide asymmetries in economic and military power, for example, still separated the two Americas, and regional resentment lingered over the United States' Cold War interventions, Central American policy, and relatively hands-off posture toward international debt negotiations. Moreover, while global bipolarity had ended, the Western Hemisphere's unipolarity had not. If anything, unipolarity had been enhanced by the Soviet Union's disappearance and America's new status as the world's only superpower.

Still, there were important changes. The end of the Cold War liberated American foreign policy from the relentless anti-communist logic of NSC-68, and gave many Latin American governments a reprieve from concerns over internal subversion. Globally, it produced high expectations for a new, more just and peaceful world order. Regionally, it raised two fundamental questions. Could U.S.–Latin American relations finally escape their historic cycles of optimism and cooperation, conflict and disillusion; and would relations in the twenty-first century be more cordial and mutually beneficial than in the past?

Visions of the Post-Cold War Era

As Cold War practices and insecurities were put away, other developments gave reasons for hope. Liberal democracy had prevailed over communist ideology, and free market capitalism had triumphed over the socialist command economy model. Along with progress toward resolving Latin America's debt crisis and Central America's wars, the region's increasing embrace of neoliberal market reforms and transitions to democratic rule offered the potential for a new beginning. But what kind of future could leaders create for their countries and people? How might relations between the two Americas be restructured to minimize tensions and provide states the most benefits? As the twenty-first century approached, many state leaders dreamed big, and gravitated toward a vision of the future in which economic and political liberalism might foster increasing regional harmony, liberty, and prosperity.

Hemispheric Economic Integration

One dimension of this future envisioned the integration of all national economies (save Cuba's) throughout the Western Hemisphere. Hemispheric integration could play to the strength of each country's comparative advantage, realize greater economies of scale, facilitate foreign investment flows, and expand the exchange of goods and services across national borders.

This scenario appealed to U.S. leaders. In 1990, for example, President George H. W. Bush outlined a future centered on a free trade system that linked "all of the Americas: North, Central and South . . . [as] regional partners in a free trade zone stretching from the port of Anchorage to Tierra del Fuego."[1] Part of integration's appeal was that it offered America a modest economic counterweight to the acceleration of West European integration, and an informal trade bloc that seemed to be developing in Asia, anchored by Japan. U.S. economic prosperity might suffer if relatively closed trade blocs arose in the world's more economically dynamic regions without a corresponding arrangement in the Western Hemisphere. Former Ecuadorian president Osvaldo Hurtado captured this point well when he suggested that "The United States will not be able to respond to the challenge presented by Europe and Japan if it does not form a larger economic unit."[2] More important for Washington, though, were the prospects that the benefits of integrating with America's liberal economy would impel Latin American governments to continue reforming their own economies and adopt the range of neoliberal policies required to mesh economically with their larger neighbor—especially measures that would unleash market forces, attract foreign investment, liberalize trade, and protect intellectual property.

Surprisingly, this scenario also appealed to many Latin American leaders. Although hemispheric integration did raise the obvious specter of potential U.S. economic domination, it also offered guaranteed access to the U.S. market, and a better chance of attracting foreign investment in a post-Cold War world. As Mexican analyst Jorge Castañeda observed, the Cold War's end produced real fear among Latin American policy elites "that private credit and investment flows would be diverted from their region to the new capitalism of Eastern Europe," where countries no longer dominated by Moscow were transitioning to market economies.[3] Formal integration with the U.S. economy would help regional powers attract capital, escape a zero-sum contest for investment with East European states, and avoid marginalization should the world move toward regional trade blocs.

Meaningful steps toward economic integration began as soon as the Cold War ended. In June 1990, Mexico formally proposed negotiating a North American Free Trade Agreement (NAFTA) with the United States and Canada. The same month, the United States unveiled the "Enterprise for the Americas Initiative," through which it offered to negotiate free trade accords with any state or group of states in the hemisphere, beginning with Mexico. To a degree that surprised the Bush administration, Latin America's reception of this U.S. initiative was overwhelmingly positive. As Peter Hakim observed, in the early 1990s "The Enterprise Initiative . . . helped to reshape the discourse of U.S.–Latin American relations . . . Traditional Latin American concerns about U.S. economic exploitation, hegemonic impulses, or threats of unilateral intervention have faded into the background. The region's main preoccupation now is how to go about building stronger economic ties to the United States."[4]

NAFTA—which went into effect on January 1, 1994—was crafted to permit its expansion through the accession of new states, and constituted one path toward hemispheric integration. Full multilateral negotiations offered an alternate route. In December 1994, U.S. President Bill Clinton invited Latin America's elected chief executives to the first Summit of the Americas in Miami. Thirty-three heads of state accepted the invitation, but many did so on the condition that free trade be a focal point of the discussions. The Latin Americans had their way, and in the end, the Summit produced a multilateral agreement in principle to negotiate and implement a Free Trade Agreement of the Americas (FTAA) by the end of 2005. At the 1998 Summit of the Americas in Santiago, the leaders formalized their commitment to proceed. If realized, the FTAA would supersede all other sub-regional arrangements, including NAFTA. The result would be a single market of 800 million consumers with an annual gross domestic product of over $7 trillion—an environment in which FTAA backers believed that prosperity might be deepened and shared more broadly.

Hemispheric Democratic Community

Complementing economic integration was the vision of a hemispheric community of democratic states. By 1990, nearly every Latin American country was governed by elected, civilian leaders. Many of these governments were new democracies with limited economic and political track records; most also exhibited various democratic deficits (pertaining to robust representation, free and fair elections, effective rule of law, or complete military subordination to civilian authorities). Still, there was no mistaking that democracy had come to Latin America in a big way, or that a genuine and fairly broad consensus for democratic governance prevailed.

The United States, of course, embraced the democratic community scenario enthusiastically, but so did its regional counterparts. Throughout Latin America, rightwing, non-democratic elements had been widely discredited. Moreover, years of state repression had convinced almost all left-of-center actors that whatever their faults, bourgeois, civilian "democratic" governments were indeed different from—and preferable to—the anti-communist dictatorships that had decimated their ranks and brutalized their countrymen. But given Latin America's historic political experience, neither the United States nor its neighbors harbored any illusions regarding democracy's permanence. Sustaining democracy would require more than statesmanship and political skill among the region's new democrats; it would also require a strong, multi-lateral commitment to defend democracy. Consequently, the Organization of American States created several new mechanisms to institutionalize the defense of democratic governance, nurture the hemisphere's embryonic democratic community, and safeguard against political backsliding.

The most important measures were the creation of a new Unit for the Promotion of Democracy (UPD) in 1990, the adoption of the "Santiago Commitment" and General Assembly Resolution 1080 in 1991, and a 1992 amendment to the OAS Charter called the "Washington Protocol." Each represented greater dedication on the organization's part to promote and protect democracy. Under the UPD, for example, OAS delegations began monitoring the integrity of regional elections. The Santiago Commitment, meanwhile, articulated a forceful, unambiguous declaration in support of democracy, and Resolution 1080 provided some political muscle to back it up. Through this resolution, the OAS *mandated* its Secretary-General to convene an emergency meeting of the Permanent Council to investigate and respond to any regional democratic crisis within 10 days of its occurrence. If the Permanent Council found that a situation warranted action, a special meeting of the General Assembly or Foreign Ministers would ensue to determine an appropriate OAS response, which could include mediation, sanctions against an offending state, or other forms of diplomatic pressure to restore demo-cratic governance. Finally, in the event of a coup, the "Washington Protocol" empowered the General Assembly to suspend (by a two-thirds vote) any member state "whose democratically constituted government has been over-thrown by force."[5]

This vision of a united hemisphere composed of integrated, market democracies would take many years to realize. But it offered a very positive future for inter-American relations based on shared norms and mutual self-interest. Democracy would provide the foundation for the regional community (which the OAS would help protect multilaterally), while increased trade and capital flows would fuel even greater political reform and further integration. The early post-Cold War period seemed especially propitious for such a venture. With Cuba's socialist model having little appeal, the Soviet Union gone, and the United States strong, the Americas appeared poised to follow Washington's lead and construct a new order that would exile ideological squabbles, allow community members to pursue common economic interests, and work collaboratively to address other common concerns such as drug trafficking, environmental problems, or immigration.

Setbacks to Achieving the Post-Cold War Vision

Despite high enthusiasm for hemispheric integration at the 1994 Miami Summit, in succeeding years, progress toward realizing this vision stalled as the consensus on liberal economic integration eroded, and ideological differences separated some regional powers from others and from the United States. There were speed bumps on the road to a community of democracies too. By the end of the twenty-first century's first decade, mass approval of democratic governance had declined from its early 1990s levels, the United States cast doubt on its commitment to protect democracy by supporting a failed coup against Venezuela's elected president Hugo Chávez in 2002, a 2009 coup removed Honduras' democratically elected leftist president, Manuel Zelaya, and the OAS democracy-protection mechanisms had worked well in some cases, but less well in others. Perhaps most surprising, America exercised less influence in the Western Hemisphere—and conversely, Latin American states enjoyed greater independence—than at any time in the preceding hundred years. By the mid-2000s, Washington had lost control of the Organization of American States, saw its credibility and soft power resources decline, could not garner support for various diplomatic initiatives, and watched as regional powers increasingly worked together through arrangements that excluded the United States. Much of the story behind these developments had to do with economic and political dynamics in Latin America, U.S. domestic politics, China's emergence as an economic heavyweight, and regional reactions to U.S. foreign policy after the terrorist attacks of September 11, 2001.

Latin American and U.S. Developments

In Latin America, a string of currency and economic crises struck states that had figured among the region's more celebrated economic reformers. These crises—in Mexico (1994–1995), Brazil (1999), and Argentina (2001)—helped blunt some of the early enthusiasm for integration. So did the negotiating stance of South America's largest economic power, Brazil. Although Brazil accepted the FTAA's 2005 timetable, it was in no hurry to proceed. Instead, Brasilia's first priority was to build up and consolidate MERCOSUR, then leverage its economic clout to ensure that any FTAA would address U.S. policies that hurt Brazilian exporters, but which Washington was loath to alter, such as farm subsidies. Finally, a popular backlash against many new democracies' market reforms and their failure to alleviate unemployment and growing inequality, helped sweep to power new leaders that displayed less enthusiasm for an FTAA than their predecessors—first in Venezuela and Argentina, and later in Bolivia, Ecuador, El Salvador, Honduras, Nicaragua, Paraguay, and Uruguay. Some of these new governments moved further away from the United States ideologically, and as noted in Chapter 9, viewed economic globalization (and thus, an FTAA) as a mask for undesirable "Americanization."

During the 2000s, political change in Latin American countries—and U.S. attempts to stop or reverse it—coincided with deteriorating relations between Washington and some of these neighbors. After a clumsy effort to influence Bolivia's 2006 presidential election backfired, Bolivian-U.S. relations cooled (the U.S. Ambassador's threats that bilateral relations would suffer if leftist Evo Morales prevailed, only increased his popularity and ensured his victory); so did relations between Washington and Buenos Aires, Quito, Managua, and Tegucigalpa. Venezuelan-U.S. relations deteriorated the most. The Hugo Chávez government terminated bilateral military programs with Washington, pursued friendly ties with Cuba, Iran, Libya, and Saddam Hussein's Iraq, and went out of its way to criticize U.S. officials (including the president) publicly. In February 2002, the United States endorsed a failed coup against Chávez, after which he continued to insist that Washington still planned to invade Venezuela or assassinate its president. The United States consistently denied these charges, but U.S. officials did exchange periodic verbal barbs with Chávez, helped finance some of his domestic political opponents, tried to "contain" Venezuela via military alliances with Peru and Paraguay, accused Caracas of failing to cooperate in the wars on drugs and terror, and forbade the sale of U.S. arms to Venezuela.

In the United States, Congress denied President Clinton "Fast Track" authority to negotiate expansive trade deals. Fast Track is special legislation that empowers the executive branch to negotiate trade agreements that Congress can either approve or reject—but cannot amend or filibuster—and was in effect when the United States, Canada, and Mexico negotiated NAFTA. The Senate had ratified NAFTA by only a slim majority, and its passage opened a rift between the Democratic administration and key constituencies (especially organized labor and environmentalists). After the president's Fast Track authority expired in 1994, Clinton was never able to secure its renewal. "Without Fast Track," observed political scientist David Scott Palmer, "any possibility that the Clinton administration could pursue the U.S. commitment to advance the FTAA by 2005 evaporated" too.[6]

The George W. Bush administration hoped to revive the project, but failed. As a candidate, Bush argued that "the North American Free Trade Agreement promised to be a blueprint for free trade throughout the hemisphere," but "the promise of that moment has been squandered"; as president, he exhorted his regional counterparts at the April 2001 Summit of the Americas in Quebec City, to forge ahead on hemispheric integration and build "an age of prosperity in a hemisphere of liberty."[7] But after the terrorist attacks that September, U.S. attention shifted decidedly from Latin America to Afghanistan, the Middle East, and the global war on terror. Brazil and the United States co-chaired the negotiations framework in 2003, but the process stalled due to their conflicting interests. When national leaders met again in Mar del Plata for the 2005 Summit of the Americas, Venezuela joined Argentina, Brazil, and other MERCOSUR states in opposing a consensus declaration to restart the negotiations. At least in terms of its original timetable, the FTAA was dead.

The Rise of China

There were other developments. China, for example, transformed itself into a major economic player in the Western Hemisphere, which indirectly helped boost regional governments' economic and political independence. China not only displaced Mexico as America's second largest trade partner by 2003, but between 2000 and 2007, its exports to Latin America mushroomed from $4.2 billion to $44.4 billion; during the same period its imports from Latin America jumped from $5.1 billion to $46.7 billion. China's rise, however, did not translate into an unqualified "good" for the region. China's low-wage labor, for example, increasingly siphoned foreign investors away from Mexico; its producers often out-competed regional manufacturers of shoes and apparel; and its ravenous appetite for Latin American commodities strengthened these sectors, which worked against some governments' desire to diversify their economies beyond commodity exports.

Still, many Latin American countries benefited handsomely as a result of their growing exports to China, especially Argentina, Brazil, Chile, Peru, and Venezuela. The enormous upsurge in Chinese imports raised both the global demand for, and global price of, many regional powers' commodity exports. This, in turn, enhanced their international financial position considerably. Between 2001 and 2008, the international reserves of many Latin American countries climbed dramatically (Table 10.1). To cite just a few examples, Mexico's reserves doubled, while Argentina and Venezuela's tripled; Brazil's reserves grew fivefold, while Bolivia's grew sevenfold. Thanks to these dynamics, Latin American governments acquired financial independence from the International Monetary Fund, and for the first time since the 1980s, many could chart their own economic and trade policies outside of IMF conditionality constraints. Not only had the IMF "been relegated to the sidelines," but "as a

Table 10.1 Latin America's International Reserves ($ billions), 2001–2008

	2001	2008
Argentina	15.3	46.2
Bolivia	1.1	7.7
Brazil	35.9	193.8
Chile	14.4	23.2
Colombia	9.9	23.7
Mexico	44.8	95.3
Paraguay	0.7	2.7
Peru	8.8	31.2
Uruguay	3.1	6.9
Venezuela	18.5	28.9

Source: Economic Commission for Latin America and the Caribbean, *Economic Survey of Latin America and the Caribbean, 2008–2009* (Santiago: United Nations, 2010), Table A-17

result" notes Harvard political scientist Jorge Domínguez, "the U.S. government could not influence Latin American economic policies through this indirect route either."[8] As their financial independence increased, so did their capacity to bargain harder over—or even resist—initiatives the United States promoted, like the FTAA.

Post-9/11 U.S. Foreign Policy

The United States foreign policy played a critical role both in reversing the momentum of the 1990s toward a hemisphere of integrated market democracies, and in the extraordinary diminution of its own regional influence. Just the opposite, however, appeared more likely when George W. Bush became president in 2001. On the campaign trail, Bush expressed a desire for warmer ties with U.S. neighbors, proclaimed that the United States' future "cannot be separated from" Latin America's, and vowed to "look South, not as an afterthought, but as a fundamental commitment of my presidency."[9] As president, he strongly endorsed the free trade-democratic community project at the Quebec City summit. He also broke with tradition by visiting Mexico—rather than Canada—on his first official State Visit, and by hosting Mexican President Vicente Fox at the White House for his administration's first official State Dinner. Finally, the Bush administration was receptive to Mexico's February 2001 proposal to craft a comprehensive immigration reform policy that might address its own concerns and those of other immigrant-sending countries.

These developments sparked cautious optimism among many regional governments, and laid the seeds for productive inter-American relations in the future. But *al Qaeda's* September 11, 2001 terrorist attacks—which came just four days after Vicente Fox's historic visit—altered the fundamental priorities of U.S. foreign policy. Overnight, securing U.S. borders became critical (which foreclosed any move toward comprehensive immigration reform), and going on the offensive against *al Qaeda* and international terrorism took precedence over all other matters. After moving hemispheric integration to the back burner, the administration unwittingly degraded its regional influence further by encouraging, then supporting the failed Venezuelan coup. Along the way, it also increased frustration with the United States by exempting America from collective, global initiatives like the International Criminal Court and efforts to address global climate change, and by withdrawing from the Anti-Ballistic Missile Treaty with Russia.

Box 10.1 The Venezuelan Coup and U.S. Response

Since at least the time of Woodrow Wilson, democracy promotion has periodically been one aim of U.S. policy toward Latin America. Sometimes, however, democracy brought to power governments the United States disliked intensely, as exemplified by the leftist, democratically elected governments of Guatemala's Jacobo Arbenz and Chile's Salvador Allende. Each tested the U.S. commitment to democracy, and ultimately, Washington failed these tests by orchestrating or encouraging their overthrow.

In Latin America, these actions severely damaged the United States' moral and political standing. But in America, officials often justified them on the basis of realist, Cold War calculations: the communist threat was such that it was safer to facilitate a democratically elected socialist regime's downfall than to permit its continuation. This line of reasoning led Latin American governments and intellectuals to criticize the credibility gap between Washington's pro-democracy policy pronouncements, and its anti-democratic policy actions. Some observers believed the Cold War's demise had finally afforded America the luxury of supporting democracy even when it spawned governments Washington disliked. But the U.S. response to Venezuela's 2002 coup suggested the credibility gap remained.

After winning the presidency in 1998, Hugo Chávez unleashed the "Bolivarian Revolution" which rewrote the federal constitution, reorganized the Congress and Supreme Court, concentrated power within the executive, and polarized Venezuelan society along sharp class and ideological lines. Bilateral Venezuelan-U.S. relations remained "appropriate" if not cordial through 2000, but then spiraled downward dramatically. In 2001, President Chávez criticized civilian casualties in the U.S. war against Afghanistan's Taliban regime. This, plus his admonishment that President Bush not respond to terror with more terror (implicitly equating America's self-defense actions in Afghanistan to the 9/11 terrorist attacks) damaged relations further: Chávez routinely ridiculed and insulted U.S. leaders, and some American officials responded in kind. As relations deteriorated, so did Venezuela's domestic political stability. On April 12, 2002, Venezuelan military officers placed Chávez under house arrest and announced his "resignation." Businessman Pedro Carmona assumed the presidency (inexplicably bypassing Vice President Diosdado Cabello), then proceeded to suspend the Constitution, dissolve the Congress, Supreme Court, and Attorney General's office, and lay the grounds for a government-by-decree until elections the following year.

In Latin America, the coup aroused a swift, collective defense of Venezuela's democratically elected government, even from countries like Mexico whose government was hardly a Chávez fan. Nineteen regional powers quickly condemned the putsch and threatened to invoke sanctions against Venezuela under the OAS Inter-American Democratic Charter; several Latin American states refused to recognize the Carmona government. By contrast, the United States appeared to endorse Chávez's downfall, refused to label his ouster a coup ("That is not a word we are using," one official told the *Washington Post*),[3] and promised to work with the government that had just steamrolled Venezuela's democratic institutions. The attempt to depose Chávez crumbled two days later, after a faction of Venezuela's military refused to back the coup, and the president's civilian supporters took to the streets demanding his reinstatement. Only after Chávez had returned to power did Washington temper its enthusiasm and bring its official statements more in line with its official pro-democracy policy stance.

The Bush administration's diplomatic clumsiness and failure to demand that Venezuela's crisis be resolved *constitutionally*, sparked intense speculation over U.S. complicity in the events. There were many reasons to speculate. Since 2001, the United States had funneled over three-quarters of a million dollars through the National Endowment for Democracy to various anti-Chávez media, business, and labor groups inside Venezuela. In November 2001, State Department, Pentagon, and CIA officials convened to strategize over the Venezuelan situation. Beginning in December, Venezuelans who planned and participated in the coup held periodic meetings—in Washington and at the U.S. Embassy in Caracas—with senior U.S. officials from the State Department, Pentagon, and National Security Council. Both Secretary of State Colin Powell and CIA Director George Tenet spoke critically of Chávez just two months before the military moved against him; their comments made the front page in Venezuelan newspapers, and might easily have been interpreted by coup plotters as a "green light." As one Defense Department official later explained, "We were not discouraging people. We were sending informal, subtle signals that we don't like this guy."[b]

The Bush administration strongly denied any involvement in the coup, but the damage had already been done. Editorials around the world scoffed at U.S. denials of complicity, and made much of the point that it was the Western Hemisphere's small players, not its moral leader, who stood up to defend democratic principles. By appearing to encourage the coup, then accepting an unconstitutional end to a distasteful democratically elected government, the administration revived America's credibility gap, re-sensitized Latin America to U.S. intervention, and made it easier for states to oppose Washington's regional diplomatic, economic, and political initiatives.

[a] Scott Wilson, "Leader of Venezuela Is Forced To Resign; Ex-Oil Executive Takes Office as Interim President," *Washington Post*, April 13, 2002, A1.
[b] Christopher Marquis, "Bush Officials Met With Venezuelans Who Ousted Leader," *New York Times*, April 16, 2002.

But it was Washington's response to the 9/11 terrorist attacks that proved most damaging both to U.S.–Latin American relations and the United States' world standing. Initially, the attacks unleashed a broad wave of sympathy for America. In Europe, NATO invoked Article 5 of its charter, while in the Western Hemisphere, Brazil invoked the Rio Treaty of Reciprocal Assistance; under the terms of these treaties, an external attack on one signatory was considered an attack on all. With few exceptions, most states supported the

2001 U.S. war against Afghanistan's Taliban regime (which was harboring *al Qaeda* leadership). But Washington's decision to attack Iraq in March 2003 depleted this sympathy dramatically, and fractured regional solidarity behind U.S. foreign policy.

The Bush administration had accused Saddam Hussein's Iraq of stockpiling weapons of mass destruction (including nuclear arms), and having operational links to the 9/11 terrorists. Just weeks after Saddam's downfall, the international community discovered that none of these claims were true. Based on these assertions, though, the administration made its case for war publicly, privately, and diplomatically, but for many governments, never compellingly. Consequently, the United States failed to obtain UN Security Council authorization for military action against Iraq, and went to war on a largely unilateral basis. The "coalition of the willing" Washington assembled to prosecute the war included several important states like Britain, Italy, Japan, and Spain; but it was composed mostly of lesser powers. By contrast, a number of key states opposed U.S. war plans, such as Russia, China, and America's NATO allies Canada, France, Germany, and Turkey. The vast majority of Latin American states did too, including Chile and Mexico who at the time sat on the UN Security Council. Those regional powers that did back U.S. policy were basically client states—governments in Central America where Washington still wielded influence, or in Colombia, which was a recipient of large-scale U.S. military aid.

Both Chile and Mexico's refusal to support America's Iraq policy dismayed U.S. leaders. The United States was unaccustomed to its neighbors expressing such open resistance to an American proposal in the Security Council, especially one deemed to be of vital, national interest. Bilateral relations between these states and America suffered as a result, especially those with Mexico. After a promising beginning at the dawn of the Fox and Bush administrations, Mexico-U.S. relations remained frozen through 2006 when Fox left office.

Neither Mexico nor Chile opposed Washington's war plans because they were unsympathetic to America's security needs. Both based their opposition on principled reasoning. First, the ethics of waging war on Iraq were important to Mexican president Vicente Fox, who believed that since Iraq had not aggressed against the United States (or any other state), a U.S. attack on Iraq was immoral. Second, morality aside, both Chile and Mexico simply did not believe the United Sates had presented any credible evidence to support its claims that Iraq had amassed weapons of mass destruction or had conspired with the 9/11 terrorists. Instead, they believed that a multilateral approach to any Iraqi infractions—sanctioned by the international community—was more appropriate and legitimate than a largely unilateral one. As Fox later explained, "Our conviction—our belief is in multilateralism. We don't believe in one nation . . . policing the world. We believe in the United Nations doing that job."[10] Finally, the official position both governments took inside the Security Council squared with public opinion back home: in 2003 pre-war public opinion polls, over 80 percent of Chileans opposed the war, 85 percent of Mexicans did too, and 61 percent of Mexicans did not believe the evidence the United States offered to support its allegations against Iraq was true.

The Iraq War was highly unpopular in much of Latin America. It drove a wedge between the United States and other regional powers, and typified the growing disillusionment U.S. neighbors felt toward U.S. foreign policy. But it was not the only point of contention. Many Latin American states also parted company with the Bush administration over matters of its foreign policy style and broader substance. Stylistically, they resented the arrogance top U.S. officials sometimes exhibited by ignoring their concerns, disparaging the United Nations, and dismissing the opinions of other states, even allies. In terms of policy substance, the main concerns were (1) their perception that the Bush administration sought to solidify a global, unipolar order, (2) American unilateralism—which the administration displayed on various occasions, and was exemplified by its official national security strategy, and (3) the United States' treatment of terrorist suspects held at its military base in Guantánamo, Cuba.

UNIPOLARITY AND UNILATERALISM

In an anarchic environment where states value their independence and security, those that do not harbor hegemonic aspirations or capacities generally display a natural antipathy toward unipolarity. A unipolar order can serve the interests of the hegemon (and even its friends); but it also can disadvantage other states and systematize inter-state injustices, since the hegemon is too strong to be balanced against, can establish and enforce rules of behavior on weaker states, and can intervene in others' affairs without serious repercussions. In the run-up to the Iraq War, statesmen were not the only ones concerned over potential unipolarity. Some Latin American intellectuals deemed avoiding this outcome a political imperative, and justified UN Security Council opposition to U.S. war plans on this basis.

Box 10.2 A Mexican's Response to Global Unipolarity

Mexico's political independence in the case of Iraq will contribute forcefully to what the world most needs: a counterpoint to U.S. power. The real

> danger in our time is not the miserable [Saddam] Hussein. It is a unipolar world dominated by Washington. Creating that counterbalance is a political necessity. Future governments, but especially the democratic government of the United States, will end up thanking France, Germany, Chile, Mexico, Russia and China for their efforts to create a counterpoint to the United States.
>
> Carlos Fuentes, "The Insulting Insinuations of the Bush Regime:
> Mexico Must Stand for Principles Not Interests,"
> *CounterPunch*, March 14, 2003

As we saw in Chapter 2, Latin American states were too weak to prevent the development of a unipolar order in the Western Hemisphere. But historically, states in a position to oppose unipolarity effectively have done so. In the early nineteenth century, Austria, Britain, Prussia, and Russia joined forces to prevent Napoleon's France from establishing a unipolar system in Europe. In the twentieth century, World War I, World War II, and the Cold War had many causes, but an important one was the perception that one state—whether imperial Germany, Nazi Germany, the Soviet Union, or the United States—had unipolar designs.

In the early twenty-first century, the Bush administration's new National Security Strategy (NSS) fueled perceptions that the United States was reaching for global unipolarity. Unveiled in September 2002, the NSS formed the doctrinal justification for the Iraq War. Its overarching goals were to protect U.S. security and use American power to expand the global zone of peace and order. Yet, it was viewed even by some U.S. friends as misguided, and was caricatured by those less charitable as a blueprint for world domination.

The NSS enshrined the doctrine of unilateral, preemptive strikes and regime change against states that Washington determined *might* be trying to acquire weapons of mass destruction or have links to terrorism; in essence, this doctrine repudiated the sanctity of state sovereignty, and cast America as the final arbiter in determining global threats, applying force, and administering justice. It called for the development of U.S. military capacity to the point it could never be challenged by any other state or combination of states; this raised the specter of a global, unipolar system in which Washington might use its military power as it deemed fit, unconstrained by international law, institutions, or norms. The NSS also asserted that free markets and democracy alone (the bedrock of America's economic and political systems) offered the world's "single sustainable model for national success"; this proposition ignored the possibility that some countries might develop arrangements that differed from America's, yet still served them well. Finally, portions of its security policy discussions seemed to equate America's extraordinary capacity to act unilaterally, with the self-evident legitimacy of any such actions. Ultimately, applying elements of the new NSS to Iraq—over substantial international opposition and where no weapons of mass destruction or credible ties to *al Qaeda* were ever discovered—would vindicate Iraq war skeptics and undermine U.S. credibility.

GUANTÁNAMO DETAINEES

As Washington's global war on terror picked up in 2002, the United States began using the Guantánamo military base it had leased from Cuba since 1903, as an interrogation and jail site for suspected terrorists captured in Afghanistan and Pakistan. The Castro government had never accepted the leasing arrangement as legitimate, but initially, no regional power (including Cuba) made much say over how Washington was using Guantánamo in its war on terror (in fact, in 2002, Cuba even promised to return any escaped detainee it caught seeking access to Cuban territory to U.S. custody there). But this changed in 2004, after a scandal exploded over the treatment of prisoners at U.S. detention facilities: photographs surfaced that depicted prisoners held at the Abu Ghraib prison in Iraq being tortured and sexually abused by U.S. military and civilian personnel, and similar accounts regarding detainee treatment at Guantánamo began circulating too. Globally, the United States' image suffered terribly as a result of these revelations. Regionally, the result was much the same. For states predisposed to be skeptical of U.S. intentions, Guantánamo conjured up the worst images of American malfeasance and became yet another source of Latin America's estrangement from U.S. foreign policy.

Box 10.3 Outcry over Guantánamo

[W]ith America's image in shambles, the [Guantánamo] base—retained over the objection of the host nation and used for the indefinite detention of suspects in the war on terror . . . again emerged as a symbol of malignant U.S. power not only in Latin America but well beyond America's historic sphere. In a chapter of history pregnant with irony and meaning that even the most anti-American of observers could not have hoped to

> invent, a strategically useless military base on a strategically insignificant island in a region of the world that only a handful of years ago was poised to embrace U.S. leadership and values had become . . . an archetype of what has gone wrong with America.
>
> Julia Sweig, *Friendly Fire: Losing Friends and Making Enemies in the Anti-American Century* (New York: PublicAffairs 2007), 221

Following the terrorist attacks of September 11, 2001, regional sympathy for America and support for U.S. foreign policy collapsed in a relatively short time span. The Bush administration's go-it-alone posture on the Iraq War, perceived drive toward unipolarity, treatment of detainees, and unilateral stance on various global issues (climate change, the International Criminal Court, and the Anti-Ballistic Missile Treaty) led other governments to resist U.S. initiatives, and sparked a mode of state behavior that forced political scientists to develop a new concept to explain it.

Balancing Against the United States

When the Soviet Union and global bipolarity first disappeared, realist theorists like Kenneth Waltz anticipated that international anarchy would inevitably induce balancing behavior against the United States, the world's one remaining superpower. Waltz suggested in 1993:

> [O]ver time, unbalanced power will be checked by the responses of the weaker who will, rightly or not, feel put upon . . . Even if the powerful state's intentions are wholly benign, less powerful states will, from their different historical experiences, geographic locations, and economic interests, interpret events differently and often prefer different policies.[11]

Waltz was not alone. Other scholars like Samuel Huntington suggested that aside from any systemic power imbalance, imperious behavior on Washington's part could also induce balancing by other states. In particular, Huntington warned of a possible anti-hegemonic coalition developing in light of America's tendency to behave as if the entire international system—not just the Western Hemisphere—were unipolar. "American officials," he wrote, "tend to act as if the world were unipolar. They boast of American power and American virtue, hailing the United States as a benevolent hegemon. They lecture other countries on the universal validity of American principles, practices, and institutions."[12] Beyond boasts and preaching, Huntington cited a number of specific U.S. practices that could provoke a balancing coalition, such as pressuring other states to adopt U.S. values and practices about human rights and democracy, grading them according to how closely they mirrored U.S. standards on the drug war, terrorism, and other issues, applying sanctions to states that failed to meet these U.S. standards, shaping World Bank and IMF policies to serve U.S. corporate interests, and pressing other states to adopt economic policies that would benefit those same interests.

But traditional hard balancing against America did not materialize. Instead, another pattern of behavior did: *soft balancing*. Soft balancing is a type of state behavior whose underlying logic mirrors that of traditional balancing, but whose manifestations differ. Historically, states in the anarchic system have sought to preserve their independence and security through "internal" or "external" hard balancing, manifest in domestic defense build-ups or formal military alliances with other states. Their main objective has been to protect the interests of the weak against the strong and potentially threatening. But these defensive moves are impractical in situations where one state's power exceeds that of a weaker state (or coalition of states) by orders of magnitude. This is one of the basic reasons that traditional balancing did not emerge against the United States—which since the Cold War ended, had enjoyed unrivaled military power and spent more on defense than the next dozen strongest states combined. Yet, despite America's power advantage and professed benign intentions, other states still valued their independence; moreover, given the uncertainties of anarchy, many did not relish a world where any single state could act unilaterally if it chose, without serious fear of international opposition.

Consequently, as American unilateralism increased during the Bush administration, other states began to balance the United States "softly," through shrewd diplomacy, more subtle policy coordination, and limited or tacit ententes. Their goal was to check U.S. hegemonic influence non-militarily, frustrate or delay disagreeable U.S. policy designs, and on certain issues, undermine Washington's ability to realize its preferred outcomes. Strategically, soft balancing offered an added virtue. Because it does not threaten the stronger power's security directly (unlike traditional balancing), soft balancing is unlikely to generate a security dilemma.

Some notable episodes of soft balancing appeared in the run-up to the Iraq War. Chile, France, Germany, Mexico, and Russia, for example, worked to entangle the United States within UN institutional procedures in order to forestall U.S. military action against Iraq; and when Washington made clear its determination to invade Iraq without UN authorization, Turkey refused to permit U.S. ground forces to use its territory as a staging area for the invasion, thereby limiting Washington's power-projection capabilities. In the end, these efforts did not prevent the United States from attacking Iraq; they did, however, raise the political and economic costs of doing so, and denied U.S. policy the international legitimacy it may otherwise have achieved.

Some soft balancing strategies have longer time horizons than others. To cite two examples, through economic statecraft, governments might seek to arrange regional economic cooperation in ways that exclude the hegemonic power, limit the economic benefits it derives, and diminish its influence over the long term. By contrast, states might realize more immediate results by using the procedures of international institutions to bottle up and derail the stronger state's policy initiatives. The Bolivarian Alternative for the Americas (ALBA)—a regional integration scheme that excludes the United States and has been pushed by Venezuela as a substitute for the Free Trade Agreement of the Americas—exemplifies the former; the Chilean, French, German, Mexican, and Russian efforts to avert a U.S. attack on Iraq illustrate the latter. Both long- and short-term tactics, however, share the same goal: rather than try to balance America's hard power, they seek to limit its influence and degrees of freedom.

In the first decade of the twenty-first century, soft balancing against the United States became a prominent foreign policy tool of several South American states, including Argentina, Brazil, other Southern Cones countries, and especially Venezuela. For example, as part of its long-term soft balancing agenda, in the mid-2000s Venezuela created three energy alliances under the ALBA banner, composed of state-owned oil firms: Petroandina (Venezuela and four other Andean Ridge countries), Petrocaribe (Venezuela and 14 Caribbean nations), and Petrosur (Venezuela and Argentina). Through these alliances, member states can purchase Venezuelan oil at preferential prices and on credit, develop jointly operated refineries and storage facilities, and where feasible, share costs and benefits in the exploration, exploitation, and processing of oil and natural gas. Caracas' ultimate goal is to unite these initiatives into a single entity—Petroamérica—that will integrate the region's energy sectors, develop and commercialize its energy resources, upgrade its energy infrastructure, and generate funds for social welfare programs. Geopolitically, however, the end game is soft balancing. Venezuela touts Petroamérica as a "new geoeconomic and geopolitical initiative . . . geared towards buttressing both Latin American integration and the conformation of a multipolar world."[13] This vision rests on a simple logic: over time, a strong union of regional state petroleum firms will diminish America's influence by excluding U.S. multinational oil firms from future energy development within member states.

Caracas also was instrumental in launching Telesur, a satellite television network funded largely by Venezuela, with contributions from Argentina, Bolivia, Cuba, Ecuador, Nicaragua, and Uruguay. Telesur employs correspondents from a half-dozen Latin American countries, and operates bureaus in nine Latin American states and Washington, DC. Its mission is to promote regional integration through transnational communications exchanges and to counterbalance the "northern bias" emanating from U.S.-dominated satellite broadcasters like CNN, and other Spanish-language broadcasts headquartered in Miami. More bluntly, in the words of Telesur director Aram Ahoronian (a Uruguayan journalist formerly of CNN), it seeks to provide an "alternative to the hegemonic message with which they bombard us from the North,"[14] and challenge the United States' perceived "informational hegemony" in the Western Hemisphere, much as Qatar's *Al Jazeera* satellite network has done across the Muslim world.

Control over the dissemination of information—and the ability to frame issues and the official interpretation of a state's foreign policy—can exert great influence in international politics. Political scientist Robert Keohane writes:

> Consider what the [1991] Iraq war would have been like if the worldwide broadcast of events had been based in Cairo or Oman instead of in Atlanta. The framing of the issue would have been fundamentally different. The world would have had a very different picture of what was going on than it had with CNN's American perspective . . . One can imagine a world in which there still exists this kind of global communication structure, but not with the Americans at the helm.[15]

That scenario is what Telesur backers hope to achieve in the Western Hemisphere.

Each of these initiatives seeks to diminish U.S. regional influence over the long term, by denying American oil firms access to Latin America's oil sector, and diluting the United States' soft power by limiting its control over the production and flow of information beamed to and consumed by Latin American viewers. Only time will tell the long-term effects of these soft balancing ventures, and their immediate significance should not be exaggerated. Two key states, for example—Chile and Brazil—have not joined Venezuela's Petrosur energy alliance; Trinidad and Tobago have opted out of Petrocaribe; and a substantial decline in global petroleum prices could threaten Venezuela's capacity to continue selling its partners oil at preferential rates.

Telesur, meanwhile, has not acquired a wide viewership since its launch in 2005. Most Latin Americans don't have satellite TV, and the network's availability through private cable TV companies has been restricted due to its coverage of sensitive political events in some countries. Also, unlike *Al Jazeera*, Telesur's broadcasts have yet to acquire a strong public perception of credibility and independence, due to its close association with President Chávez. A proper reading of Telesur's influence, then, cautions against the more dire warning expressed by U.S. Congressman Connie Mack (R-FL), who in 2005, worried the network posed "a threat to the United States [because it] tries to undermine the balance of power in the western hemisphere."[16]

While the jury is still out regarding the success of these long-term soft balancing projects, the verdict is in on other short-term initiatives. Most effective have been regional powers' efforts to undercut America's capacity to realize its policy preferences—especially respecting Venezuela and hemispheric free trade—by entangling them within the constraining procedures of the Organization of American States and Summit of the Americas framework.

In May 2005, for example, U.S. neighbors used entangling diplomacy to deny the OAS secretary generalship to Washington's preferred candidate, former Salvadoran president Francisco Flores. This was the first time member states had ever rejected the "U.S. candidate." Venezuela was especially determined to defeat Flores' bid. Along with the Bush administration, under Flores, El Salvador was the only other state in the hemisphere to recognize the regime that briefly took power in the failed 2002 coup. Given the strained Venezuelan-U.S. relationship, Caracas placed high value on electing a Secretary General who was not a close U.S. ally and could act independently of U.S. preferences. Toward this end, it joined Argentina, Brazil, and Uruguay and threw its support to Chilean foreign minister José Miguel Insulza, cast the election as a referendum on U.S. hegemonic influence, and predicted Flores' ultimate defeat: "The times in which the OAS was an instrument of the government in Washington," President Chávez asserted, "are gone."[17] In the end, Insulza prevailed and in May 2005, became the first Secretary General since 1948 who was not Washington's preferred choice. Having secured the office without U.S. backing, Insulza found it easier to distance himself from U.S. positions on some issues that came before the body, including the extent to which the Chávez government threatened regional security.

The next month, regional powers again employed entangling diplomacy to sink a high-priority OAS initiative sponsored by the United States. At the June 2005 meeting of the General Assembly in Fort Lauderdale, Florida, Washington proposed creating a mechanism within the OAS to monitor the democratic performance of member states and take action against those that failed to govern democratically. In a veiled reference to Venezuela during her opening address, U.S. Secretary of State Condoleezza Rice proclaimed that: "Together we must insist that leaders who are elected democratically have a responsibility to govern democratically . . . governments that fail to meet this crucial standard must be accountable to the OAS."[18] But Rice's proposal proved a tough sell. Brazilian foreign minister Celso Amorim's response typified the attitude of many delegates: "Madam Secretary, democracy cannot be imposed."[19]

Ultimately, over 80 percent of OAS members voted down the U.S. proposal to create a democracy monitoring mechanism. Some believed it violated the principle of nonintervention enshrined in the OAS charter; others feared it could eventually be turned against them. Many viewed it as a thinly disguised effort to weaken Venezuela's government and intervene in its domestic affairs, and most simply found U.S. insistence that it wasn't, unpersuasive: as an Argentine OAS delegate quipped, this proposition was "impossible to sell to any adult human being."[20] Venezuelan officials savored their victory. The OAS vote, claimed Vice President José Rangel, "was a defeat for Bush and Rice, who could not impose . . . this type of disguised intervention that they proposed and that was rejected by the majority."[21] These developments showcased the decline of U.S. influence in OAS operations, and underscored the efficacy of soft balancing tactics.

Just five months later, the same set of states (plus Paraguay) forged an informal alliance that torpedoed U.S. efforts to restart negotiations on hemispheric free trade at the November 2005 Summit of the Americas in Mar del Plata. Meaningful progress on the project had stalled since 2003. President George W. Bush traveled to the Summit hoping to revive it, but was met by tens of thousands of anti-FTAA protesters, and by other leaders with plans to scuttle it. Argentine President Néstor Kirschner, for example, publicly criticized the FTAA concept in his opening address,[22] while Hugo Chávez denounced it as a "colonialist project," declared he had come to the Summit to "bury" the FTAA, and pitched ALBA as the remedy to U.S. "imperialist" aspirations.[23] Although a large majority of states supported restarting negotiations, Summit rules required a consensus vote to proceed. The coordinated opposition of the South American soft balancers ensured there would be no consensus, however, and President Bush left the Summit early rather than suffer the humiliation of witnessing the final vote.

Summing up, in the first decade of the twenty-first century, various regional powers engaged in soft balancing to limit America's influence, resist U.S. initiatives, and constrain Washington's ability to realize its preferred outcomes. The short-term soft balancing strategies especially, proved highly effective. Depriving certain U.S. initiatives the support of international institutions not only prevented their formal adoption as multilateral policy, but also denied these proposals the international legitimacy they may otherwise have achieved.

It is worth noting the broader context in which these developments occurred. Governments that pursued soft balancing tactics did so not only out of concern for America's unilateralism (and its perceived quest for global unipolarity), but also in the context of declining American *soft power* and rising anti-U.S. public sentiments. As we learned in Chapter 2, soft power is the ability of state *A* to change *B*'s behavior by inducing it to prefer the same things that *A* does. Here, the exercise of power is indirect, and as political scientist Joseph Nye reminds us, soft power's efficacy turns on "the ability to attract others by the legitimacy of [a state's national] policies and the values that underlie them."[24] The Bush administration's unilateralism repelled much of the global community, thereby sapping America's soft power reserves. The more states questioned the legitimacy of U.S. actions, policies, and proposals, the greater the drain on American soft power. The more troubling or destabilizing some actions appeared (war, global unipolarity, support for coups, disguised intervention, or "Americanized" economic globalization), the stronger soft balancing incentives became.

The fact that many domestic climates in Latin American countries turned increasingly anti-U.S. in the 2000s, made it even easier for some governments to oppose U.S. initiatives. Between 1999 and 2002, the number of Latin Americans who viewed the United States favorably fell 14 percent in Argentina, 9 percent in Bolivia, 7 percent in Peru and Venezuela, and 4 percent in Brazil and Mexico.[25] Two months before the 2004 U.S. presidential election, a poll conducted by the firm GlobeScan and the University of Maryland's Program on International Policy Attitudes (PIPA), asked Latin Americans whether U.S. foreign policy under the Bush administration had made them feel better or worse about the United States. Large majorities responded "worse" in Argentina (65%), Brazil (66%), and Mexico (78%); a simple majority responded "worse" in Uruguay (51%); and pluralities responded "worse" in the Dominican Republic (49%) and Colombia (44%).[26] In a subsequent BBC World Service/ PIPA poll conducted after the elections, clear majorities in major Latin American states saw Bush's reelection as a negative for world peace and security: 79 percent of Argentines held this view, as did 78 percent of Brazilians, 62 percent of Chileans, and 58 percent of Mexicans.[27]

During the second Bush term, significant public opposition to U.S. foreign policy crystallized across most of Latin America. As shown in Table 10.2, large majorities in key states held a negative view of America's global influence and expressed sharp disapproval of U.S. policies respecting the Iraq War, treatment of detainees at the Guantánamo naval base in Cuba, Iran's nuclear program, and global climate change. The policies adopted early on by the Bush

Table 10.2 Public Attitudes (in percentage) toward the United States and U.S. Foreign Policies in Select Latin American Countries, 2007

	Global Influence		US Handling of Iraq War		Treatment of Guantánamo Detainees	Policy toward Iran's Nuclear Program	Policy toward Global Warming
	Mainly positive	Mainly negative	Approve	Disapprove	Disapprove	Disapprove	Disapprove
Argentina	13	64	3	92	78	85	78
Brazil	29	57	12	85	76	80	73
Chile	32	51	23	65	63	62	63
Mexico	12	53	13	80	70	51	67

Source: BBC World Service Poll, January 2007, http://news.bbc.co.uk/2/shared/bsp/hi/pdfs/23_01_07_us_poll.pdf, accessed January 6, 2011

administration yielded highly negative consequences for both the United States and its president. By 2007, not only had the administration become a "damaged brand" in much of the world, but as reflected in a 2007 Latinobarómetro poll conducted in 18 Latin American countries, Bush himself had become one of the hemisphere's least popular, least respected heads of state. On a 0–10 negative to positive scale, the president scored highest among tiny Panama (7), and lowest among the region's larger states, including Mexico (4.3), Brazil (3.4), and Argentina (1.9).[28]

Hemispheric Relations in Flux

Most regional powers may have had little use for U.S. foreign policy in the 2000s, but we should not confuse this displeasure—or the fact that some states coordinated soft balancing efforts against America—as a sign that Latin American states will forge an anti-U.S. bloc, or routinely define their interests in opposition to U.S. preferences in the future. One reason is that at the domestic level, several countries have become so politically polarized that their foreign policies could shift dramatically depending on domestic political dynamics. Ecuador, Honduras, Mexico, Nicaragua, Peru, and Venezuela all fall into this group. In some cases, extremely close elections in the 2000s made the difference between states adopting a more pro- or anti-U.S. foreign policy; in other instances, it was the failure or success of military coups.

Another reason is that states perceive their interests differently, have competing interests, and adopt foreign policies accordingly. This is true even for states that seem to share similar ideologies. For example, much has been made of left-of-center governments' recent ascendance in Argentina, Brazil, Ecuador, Honduras, Nicaragua, Uruguay, and Venezuela. But these states display somewhat different postures toward the United States and its trade policy preferences. Some, for example, are much more anti-American, and opposed to liberal free trade projects, than others. What's more, two of the "new Left" governments—Brazil and Venezuela—each aspire to the position of regional leader that only one can occupy, yet have pursued this objective through markedly different foreign policies. Brazil has sought the leadership post through policies that favor market-oriented regional economic development, evince periodic independence from Washington, yet sustain cordial bilateral relations overall; Venezuela has pursued the same position through policies that favor a more socialist model of regional development, and that are based on incendiary rhetoric, at times manufactured allegations, and deliberate antagonism that have damaged its bilateral relations with the United States.

In general, how states define their interests helps determine their foreign policy disposition. In the early twenty-first century, some Latin American states are defining their interests more globally, and others more regionally. The globalists tend to value closer ties with the United States, can be comfortable *within limits* with U.S. leadership, and prefer market-oriented free trade either throughout the hemisphere or at least with America. Chile, Central America (save Nicaragua), Colombia, Mexico, and Peru fall into this camp. By contrast, regionalists like Argentina, Bolivia, Cuba, Ecuador, Paraguay, and Venezuela are content to have "correct" but not close relations with Washington, are uncomfortable even with moderate U.S. leadership, and are less interested in market-oriented free trade schemes. Brazil—which values good ties with Washington, is comfortable with market policies, yet prefers regional over hemispheric economic integration—straddles these two categories. If these trend lines hold, future hemispheric relations will play out under diminished U.S. influence, but not in the context of a coherent, Latin American anti-U.S. monolith.

A Multipolar Western Hemisphere?

Does the decline of U.S. regional influence spell the end of hemispheric unipolarity? If so, might U.S.–Latin American relations of the twenty-first century take place within a multipolar system where power is distributed less asymmetrically? Latin American states have long desired a more multipolar order, and have even justified some of their recent soft balancing efforts on this basis. But multipolarity—at least in its classic sense—is not likely. First, the distribution of military power tilts far in America's favor. U.S. force-projection capacity knows no regional peer, and is unlikely to encounter one in the foreseeable future. America's economic prowess underpins its military power (advanced weaponry is expensive), and the distribution of economic power also tilts heavily America's way. Even in 2009—a year of global economic recession whose epicenter was the U.S. economy—America's gross domestic product was still twice as large as those of the hemisphere's nine other largest economies combined (Table 10.3).

Second, it's unlikely that the entrance of extra-hemispheric powers will give birth to classic multipolarity. Despite China's rise, Beijing understands that maintaining good bilateral relations with the United States requires it to follow a prudent foreign policy in the Western Hemisphere. Guided by the principle of "peaceful ascendance," China has been content to expand its economic relations with Latin American countries, but has eschewed establishing military

Table 10.3 Western Hemisphere's 10 Largest Economies ($), 2009

Rank	Country	GDP (Purchasing Parity Power)
1	United States	14.140 trillion
2	Brazil	2.013 trillion
3	Mexico	1.456 trillion
4	Canada	1.279 trillion
5	Argentina	549 billion
6	Colombia	402 billion
7	Venezuela	349 billion
8	Peru	251 billion
9	Chile	242 billion
10	Cuba	111 billion

Source: Central Intelligence Agency, *CIA World Factbook 2010*

ties or alliances there. Russia has inked arms sales with some regional powers like Bolivia and Venezuela, rekindled warmer diplomatic ties with Cuba, and engaged in joint maneuvers with Venezuela's navy. But by and large, like China, Russia has not sought a greater regional military presence and has more pressing strategic concerns closer to home. The European Union, meanwhile, is preoccupied with its own affairs.

The picture grows a bit murkier, however, when we consider U.S. soft power and regional states' increased diplomatic independence. For decades, even states that resented how America sometimes used its power were still drawn by the allure of its economic success, political values, and aspects of its culture. This attraction, along with U.S. influence in the Inter-American System and other multilateral institutions like the IMF, helped the United States influence other governments' behavior without relying on hard power alone. As we have learned, though, U.S. soft power fell dramatically in the 2000s. While the election of Barack Obama stopped this hemorrhage—thanks to the administration's renunciation of torture, its pledge to try and close the Guantánamo detention camp, and the fact that Obama simply is "not Bush"—it will take some time for the United States to replenish its once abundant soft power base.

Moreover, Latin American states have forged new institutional arrangements to coordinate their policies and address common concerns that the United States is not party to. MERCOSUR, the Rio Group, ALBA, and the Union of South American Nations (UNASUR) are prime examples. These arrangements could, potentially, increase the region's economic and political integration, while strengthening its independence; and a fully functional Union of South American Nations might provide a moderate political counterweight to the United States. Yet, UNASUR remains a work in progress. It also excludes Mexico, and Central American and Caribbean states, and its members lack sufficient unity to act as a single power vis-à-vis America. All these factors weigh against the prospects of a classic multipolar system of several relatively balanced states (or state groupings) replacing the hemisphere's traditional unipolar structure. The prospects for a classic bipolar structure (UNASUR vs. U.S.) are also slim.

On the other hand, fundamental aspects of the old unipolar order have clearly eroded. U.S. military power is unmatched. But the wars launched in 2001 (Afghanistan) and 2003 (Iraq) have stretched America's military to its limits: defeating the Afghan Taliban and Saddam Hussein's forces proved far easier than winning the peace. The residual conflict in each theater has dragged on much longer than the wars' architects ever envisioned, and have required a long-term commitment of U.S. military assets they never contemplated. Even if this were not the case, the hemisphere's strongest state cannot use its military might to achieve outcomes it prefers on key issues like free trade.

The old systemic "rules" have lapsed as well. The times when Latin American states showed almost automatic deference to U.S. policies, and Washington served as gatekeeper to extra-hemispheric powers' entrée into the Americas, are gone. Regional powers not only part company with Washington on matters like war, trade, drugs, or relations with Cuba and Hugo Chávez's Venezuela, but have expanded their economic and political ties with China, Russia, Spain, India, and even Iran. Finally, domestic-level factors also work against old-style unipolar leadership. As democracy has spread and gradually deepened across much of Latin America, leaders have become more beholden to their fellow citizens. Even governments that might want to follow the U.S. lead must consider the costs of doing so in contexts where anti-Americanism and frustrations with neoliberal market policies may run high.

All this is to say that while elements of unipolarity remain, classic unipolarity is gone, and classic multipolarity is unlikely. Applying these concepts unthinkingly to contemporary hemispheric relations will almost certainly mislead us. Looking ahead, the most likely scenario might be termed unipolarity "lite," in which economic and military power remains more concentrated in the North, while actual political influence in matters of regional concern is distributed more equally than in the past.

An Interdependent Future

Increasing interdependence will also characterize future relations. Geographic proximity, shared history, and commercial and human ties all bind the United States and its neighbors in complex ways. This interdependence will ensure that what happens in each America will, for good or ill, affect the other. The examples abound. Despite China's growing regional economic importance, for instance, Latin America still trades far more with the United States, and America exports much more extensively to the region than China does (in 2008, $216 billion versus $67 billion, according to the International Monetary Fund's *Direction of Trade Statistics*). Mutual trade dependence will endure for some time. So will America's energy dependence. The United States depends heavily on Latin America for its energy security, importing more oil from the region than from the Middle East. In turn, regional energy producers depend on U.S. consumers for an important source of revenue. Broader economic interdependence will remain a reality too. To cite a recent example, just as Mexico's 1995 peso crisis threatened the U.S. economy, many Latin American states could not escape the gravitational pull generated by the 2008 collapse of the U.S. sub-prime mortgage sector: as global recession set in, the aggregate growth for Latin America and the Caribbean fell from 5.8 percent in 2007—one year before the crash—to –1.9 percent in 2009, a year after. Although most regional economies recovered more rapidly than analysts expected, a strong U.S. economy still matters to America's neighbors.

Socially, immigration patterns and human ties also will continue to link the two Americas. Brazilians, Central Americans, Colombians, Cubans, Dominicans, Ecuadorians, Haitians, Mexicans, and Venezuelans have all established communities across the United States. According to the U.S. Census Bureau, in 2010 Latinos became America's largest ethnic minority (15.8 percent of the population). They contribute to its economy, enrich its culture and cuisine, and help transform (and complicate) its politics. Many immigrants maintain close ties with families abroad and funnel multiple billions of dollars in remittances to their countries of origin. Finally, transnational drug flows, which reflect the darker side of interdependence, will influence many states in areas ranging from security and political stability, to social and foreign policy. In the future, interdependence and broader globalization forces will not only present opportunities that invite inter-state collaboration, but generate complicated challenges whose resolution will require it.

Understanding U.S.–Latin American Relations Today

Given such complexity, how can we make sense of contemporary inter-American relations? Despite the many changes, even in the twenty-first century some traditional analytic frameworks will retain their utility. Although Dependency theory can yield inaccurate predictions, its underlying logic argues strongly for the adoption of policies that decrease external constraints on political autonomy and national development. In the early twenty-first century, Latin America's "regionalist" states all exhibit such policies, and are likely to continue them.

Realist theory, too, will continue to shed light on some aspects of U.S.–Latin American relations. Writing in 2008, political scientist Peter Smith suggested that "the global structure of power will determine the conduct and tone of inter-American relations for generations to come," and many realists would agree.[29] Realists' focus on security, the use of force, and the uncertainties of anarchy, for example, helps us understand why many Latin American governments strongly protested a 2009 bilateral accord that permits U.S. troops to operate out of seven Colombian military bases: in an anarchic environment, weaker states are naturally sensitive to encroachments by stronger powers.

But realism will prove much less helpful in understanding the international politics of other issues that American republics will confront, be they immigration, narcotics trafficking, establishing a non-coercive inter-state order, or the best ways to realize the benefits of transnational trade. Complex interdependence will certainly have bearing on the politics of these issues. So will the broader liberal conception of world politics—where institutions, regimes, and shared norms dampen anarchy's intensity, help create order, and nurture a broader sense of community. Future U.S.–Latin American relations might deviate some from the 1990s' vision of a united hemisphere composed of market democracies. But the institutions states have created since World War II still contribute to community development sub-regionally, and in some respects, throughout the hemisphere.

NAFTA, MERCOSUR, CARICOM, UNASUR, and ALBA are all sub-regional arrangements founded on certain norms adhered to by their members. These norms establish rules of behavior that regularize state interactions in certain policy domains and cultivate a sense of community identity; and sometimes, the institutions themselves can preserve community order in very practical terms. In August 2010, for example, UNASUR helped defuse a tense situation between Venezuela and Colombia (over Caracas' displeasure with the Colombian-U.S. basing rights treaty mentioned earlier, and Bogotá's allegations that Venezuela was aiding Colombian guerrilla insurgents). Even the

Organization of American States, which has seen good times and bad, continues to deepen the sense of hemispheric community among states. During the Cold War, the OAS lost credibility as an effective multilateral institution after its strongest member began pursuing security concerns unilaterally and surreptitiously. Even so, it still evolved certain norms that, in time, acquired increased influence.

Democracy promotion is a case in point. The 1948 OAS Charter specified promoting democracy as one of the organization's goals, as well as a condition for membership. Until the 1990s, however, the OAS rarely acted to enforce this norm and many members bore little resemblance to functioning democracies. Since 1990, though, its membership has been decidedly more democratic, and the OAS has responded—albeit, sometimes imperfectly—multiple times to democratic crises in countries ranging from the Caribbean and Central America (Haiti, Guatemala, Honduras), to the Andes (Peru and Venezuela), to the Southern Cone (Paraguay). Today, deviations from the democratic norm still occur, but are much less pervasive than in the past. Protecting human rights is another community norm that has gained more salience since states first enshrined it in the OAS Charter. In 1969, OAS members reaffirmed this norm through the American Convention on Human Rights (which addresses rights to life and liberty, freedom of assembly, expression, and religion); and in the 1990s, they passed a range of human rights declarations barring torture, forced disappearances, violence against women, and other abuses.

It's true that many Western Hemispheric governments sometimes conducted their internal affairs or foreign policies in ways that paid only lip-service to these democratic and human rights norms. But while states might flout them—at times, with apparent impunity—they almost always paid a price. Cuba was initially suspended from the OAS for embracing Communism and seeking to export its revolution to other countries. However, it also suffered years of diplomatic isolation due to its violations of OAS norms; the Argentine, Brazilian, and Chilean dictatorships found themselves increasingly ostracized for similar offenses; Honduras was also suspended after a 2009 coup removed its elected president; and by countenancing torture in its terrorist detention camps, the United States lost a great deal of legitimacy, prestige, support, and ultimately, influence in OAS operations. As these examples suggest, norms embedded within international institutions may not always be enforceable. But because they embody community values, they help distinguish acceptable from unacceptable community behavior, and thus, can legitimize or delegitimize a political action. The stronger shared norms become at the sub-regional or hemispheric levels, the greater their contribution to community building in these realms.

A formal, unified Western Hemispheric community might not be realized soon, and trade relations between some states may evolve along more market-friendly principles or less market-oriented ones. But sub-regional communities will likely endure and grow stronger, thanks to international institutions and norms. Some communities will be oriented more toward economics, some more toward politics, and not all states (including America) will be formal members of each. It is through these arrangements that states stand the best chance of realizing their common aspirations, structuring a more just political order, and managing some of the more pressing problems the future will bring.

Change and Continuity

Obviously, the future is not set in stone, and we should not be surprised if U.S.–Latin American relations take some unexpected turns. External shocks and economic crises, for example, could force regional powers back under IMF tutelage, and in the process, reduce their autonomy, impinge on their agency, and provide the United States greater indirect leverage over their economic policies. Insurrections could prompt some states to rely—as Colombia has— on U.S. military assistance for security, thereby moving them closer into the U.S. orbit. The violence spawned by drug cartel turf battles could so destabilize parts of the Mexico-U.S. border that some type of U.S. military intervention— unthinkable today—becomes less unthinkable down the line. And greater conflict is conceivable between the United States, Cuba, or Venezuela if governments somehow mismanage their relationships. Each contingency will alter the course of inter-American relations in different, unforeseen ways.

Yet, while some change is a near-certainty, continuity is too. Stark asymmetries will still mark relations between the United States and its neighbors; cooperation and conflict will continue, and regional anti-U.S. sentiments will not die out completely anytime soon. States will continue pursuing their varied interests, and will cooperate or compete based on them. Those that enjoy greater power resources and more skillful leadership will likely out-compete others. Because this competition might breed friction, the future, like the past, may also entail conflict, injustice, and disorder. The order that is required to obtain just outcomes for the many will come from the hard power and various balance of power strategies that realists stress, and the institutions and norms that liberals emphasize. However, states will not be acting inside a vacuum. Their foreign policies will still respond to the incentives generated by the self-help, anarchic international system, and by various domestic factors; they also will bear the marks of their individual leaders' ideas, strengths, and deficits.

In short, the future will resemble the past, but only so far. Some aspects of the future will be quite different. One difference is the extent to which U.S.–Latin American relations will unfold not within a relatively lawless international system, but an increasingly legalized one. Although the legal architecture of hemispheric international politics pales in comparison to the legal infrastructure of most domestic political systems, systemic legality—codified in treaties and institutions—is at an all-time high when set against historic standards of the eighteenth, nineteenth, and first half of the twentieth centuries. Some of this legality is the long-term fruit of Latin American labors. Like community norms, systemic legality will not eliminate injustice or the inappropriate use of state power. It will, however, dampen anarchy's intensity and modify the indiscriminate use of force. Because anarchy persists there is nothing inherent in the international system to "stop" the United States from intervening when it believes situations warrant it, and regional powers will remain sensitive to this possibility; but they also will breathe easier because increasing systemic legality means there are more impediments and costs to imperious behavior.

Another difference will be the extent to which some regional powers assume larger leadership roles within the hemisphere and beyond. There is nothing new about Latin American states desiring to strengthen their international position or exert more influence on the world stage. What's different today is the greater capacity that some powers—Brazil and Venezuela, for example—have to pursue these interests. Brazil's economic strength has already made it the de facto leader of MERCOSUR and the Southern Cone states. It took the lead in creating UNASUR, and further legitimized its regional leadership in 2004 by spearheading UN peacekeeping efforts in Haiti. Brazil also plays an increasingly significant role in venues outside Latin America. These include the World Trade Organization, international financial forums like the G-20 (a group of 19 states and the European Union that work to stabilize the international financial system), and multilateral partnerships with other emergent countries from the South, like China, India, and South Africa. Finally, Brazil has sought a broader role by explicitly calling for the UN Security Council to reflect the reality of states' power in the twenty-first century, instead of 1945: like Germany, India, and Japan, Brazil has made securing a permanent Security Council seat a high priority.

Venezuela, meanwhile, has used its oil revenues and reserves to reorganize much of Latin America's energy sector and promote regional integration via ALBA. It also proposed—and along with Argentina, Bolivia, Brazil, Ecuador, and Uruguay—helped capitalize a new Bank of the South in 2009, to fund development projects in Latin America and help states bypass the U.S.-led IMF and World Bank. Hugo Chávez critics argue that Venezuela's oil revenues could be better spent domestically on the Venezuelan people (the same could be said of the tax dollars other governments expend on their foreign policies).

Such critiques may have merit, but they miss a larger point about how Caracas increasingly plays the game of international politics. Under Chávez, Venezuela has used its resources to pursue a decidedly American-style foreign policy designed to advance its perceived national interests. Like the United States, for example, Venezuela has sought to promote its brand of regional integration and trade; and like the United States, it has worked (not always successfully) to ensure friendly governments take power in neighboring countries like Bolivia and Peru, and more distant ones like Mexico and Nicaragua. Also like the United States, Venezuela has employed international institutions (or created new institutional instruments) to pursue its interests; and, like the United States it has even deployed soft power resources (particularly its political values and anti-neoliberal ideology) to help set the international agenda and alter the behavior of other states in ways that can advance its interests. Such tactics have long been effective staples of U.S. foreign policy, and Venezuela has realized gains by taking a page out of the American foreign policy playbook. So long as global oil prices permit, it is likely to maintain a robust foreign policy.

Although Venezuela's agenda runs contrary to some U.S. interests, its foreign policy—like Brazil's—reflects its national ambitions and growing capacity to pursue them. In different ways, each state's foreign policies display a type of political maturity more commonly associated with regional powers of Europe or Asia, than Latin America. The more successful these policies are, the more influence both states are likely to obtain. Consequently, in the future the United States may find it has to compete more aggressively to maintain the hemisphere's center stage to itself.

Looking Ahead

If you had a say in the future of inter-American relations, what direction would you prefer they take? Should the United States become more engaged with its neighbors or less? Work primarily with those that share its economic and political philosophies or make reasonable accommodations with those whose philosophies differ? Accept the diminishment of its traditional preeminence or renew its drive to lead the hemisphere? Should Latin American states continue seeking greater autonomy even if it causes discord with Washington? Maintain the traditional U.S.-led Inter-American System (anchored by the OAS) or perfect a new set of institutions that are more "Latin American"? Embrace U.S.-style globalization and garner its benefits or resist globalization to avoid falling back under the U.S. shadow? Is greater harmony between the two Americas simply utopian? If not, how can the American republics get to this point? Answering these questions is not easy, since most options involve trade-offs that will redound to the benefit or detriment of individual states, and will affect hemispheric relations writ large.

As you ponder the future, how will you make sense of state interactions that unfold within a changing environment? Classic hemispheric unipolarity is over, but classic multipolarity will not replace it. America's soft power reserves have dwindled while those of some other states have grown. In 2001, political scientist Robert Keohane suggested that "Latin American countries are takers, instead of makers, of international policy."[30] This may have been true through the dawn of the twenty-first century, but given current trends, it may not hold in times to come. Can the United States accustom itself to such a scenario in a region long considered to be America's "backyard"? Will Latin American states accept anything less than such accommodation?

Today, increasing interdependence and globalization link the two Americas more closely than ever before, but this does not imply automatic harmony. These same forces have generated inter-state tensions over trade and economic policies, drug trafficking, and immigration. They have also empowered non-state actors, and eroded states' ability to control their borders, manage their economies, and regulate commerce. Globalization is unlikely to "Americanize" Latin America beyond recognition (its rich cultures have deep roots). On the other hand, by unleashing social changes that challenge local and national identities, globalization heightens anxiety among citizens and state leaders, and provides new hooks on which to hang traditional anti-U.S. sentiments. All these factors suggest that the future may bewilder casual observers and will not always be tidy.

To understand contemporary U.S.–Latin American relations we will need to draw upon both the realist and liberal perspectives of international politics, be mindful of dependency logic, and be able to conceptualize opposing ideal types simultaneously. Pure realism and complex interdependence are abstract heuristics that can assist our analysis, but do not exist in the real world. Realists perceive a world where states play the dominant political role, exist and compete in an anarchic environment, and employ power to safeguard their security. Relaxing these assumptions yields complex interdependence, wherein non-state actors influence outcomes, non-military power resources are more viable, and economic, environmental, or social welfare goals can have greater salience than military security. Most inter-state relationships lie in between these two extremes. Each approach is needed to make contemporary international politics more intelligible. We must also be alert that dependency logic colors states' political calculations south of the Rio Grande much more than to the north.

This book has sought to introduce you to a way of thinking about U.S.–Latin American relations (and international politics more generally), by providing you the analytic tools to help organize facts, think systematically about issues, untangle complexity, weigh competing explanations, and have confidence in your conclusions. It's my hope that the resulting discourse between theory and history will enrich your understanding of inter-American relations, unravel some of their riddles, and broaden your horizons as to their possibilities.

Study Questions

1. How might U.S.–Latin American relations of the twenty-first century resemble the relationship of the twentieth century? How might twenty-first century relations differ from the past? Will the future entail a hemispheric community of integrated, market democracies with the United States in the lead?

2. What is the relationship between neoliberal economic policies and the rise of Latin America's new Left? How might the Left's ascendance affect U.S. regional leadership, hemispheric free trade initiatives, and relations between Latin American states themselves?

3. What are the arguments for and against depicting the current Western Hemispheric order as unipolar?

4. Although the United States remains the world's sole superpower with unmatched economic, political, and military power resources, today it enjoys less regional influence than anytime within the last hundred years. How can we account for this apparent anomaly and what factors best explain the decline of U.S. influence?

5. What do analysts mean by "soft balancing"? To what extent is such state behavior similar to traditional hard balancing, and in what ways, if any, is it different?

6. Is Anti-Americanism diminishing in importance in U.S.–Latin American relations, or is it still a potent force? Cite examples.

7. Under President Hugo Chávez, does Venezuela's foreign policy exhibit a more realist stance or a more liberal one?

8. Is democratic governance becoming a more important community norm in the Western Hemisphere? What role do international institutions play in deepening the democratic norm?

9. In the twenty-first century, which theoretical perspective—realism, liberalism, or dependency—will offer the most assistance in explaining and understanding international politics in the Western Hemisphere?

Selected Readings

Burges, Sean W. "Building a Global Southern Coalition: The Competing Approaches of Brazil's Lula and Venezuela's Chávez." *Third World Quarterly* 28 (2007): 1343–1358.

Corrales, Javier and Richard Feinberg. "Regimes of Cooperation in the Western Hemisphere: Power, Interests, and Intellectual Traditions." *International Studies Quarterly* 43 (1999): 1–36.

Domínguez, Jorge I. "Free Politics and Free Markets in Latin America." *Journal of Democracy* 9 (1998): 70–84.

Hakim, Peter. "Is Washington Losing Latin America?" *Foreign Affairs* 85 (January/February 2006): 39–53.

Hakim, Peter and Michael Shifter. "United States-Latin American Relations: To the Summit and Beyond." *Current History* 94 (February 1995): 49–53.

Pape, Robert A. "Soft Balancing against the United States." *International Security* 30 (Summer 2005): 7–45.

Romero, Carlos A. and Javier Corrales. "Relations between the United States and Venezuela: 2001–2009: A Bridge in Need of Repairs." In *Contemporary U.S.–Latin American Relations: Cooperation or Conflict in the Twenty-first Century?* edited by Jorge I. Domínguez and Rafael Fernández de Castro, 218-246. New York: Routledge, 2010.

Sweig, Julia. *Friendly Fire: Losing Friends and Making Enemies in the Anti-American Century*, chs 13, 18, and Epilogue. New York: PublicAffairs, 2007.

Williams, Mark Eric. "The New Balancing Act: International Relations Theory and Venezuela's 'Soft Balancing' Foreign Policy." In *The Revolution in Venezuela: Social and Political Change Under Chávez*, edited by Jonathan Eastwood and Thomas Ponniah. Cambridge, MA: Harvard University Press, David Rockefeller Center for Latin American Studies, 2011.

Further Readings

Burges, Sean W. "Brazil as Regional Leader: Meeting the Chávez Challenge." *Current History* 109 (February 2010): 53-59.

Domínguez, Jorge I. and Rafael Fernández de Castro (eds). *Contemporary U.S.–Latin American Relations: Cooperation or Conflict in the 21st Century?* New York: Routledge 2010.

Hakim, Peter. "NAFTA . . . and After: A New Era for the US and Latin America?" *Current History* 93 (March 1994): 97–102.

Huntington, Samuel P. "The Lonely Superpower." *Foreign Affairs* 78 (March/April 1999): 35–49.

Hurrell, Andrew. "Lula's Brazil: A Rising Power, but Going Where?" *Current History* 107 (February 2008): 51–57.

Legler, Thomas, Sharon F. Lean, and Dexter S. Boniface (eds). *Promoting Democracy in the Americas*. Baltimore: Johns Hopkins University Press, 2007.

Prevost, Gary. "Contesting Free Trade: The Development of the Anti-FTAA Movement in the Streets and in the Corridors of State Power." *Journal of Developing Areas* 21 (2005): 369–387.

Sweig, Julia. *Friendly Fire: Losing Friends and Making Enemies in the Anti-American Century*. New York: PublicAffairs, 2007.

Waltz, Kenneth N. "The Emerging Structure of International Politics." *International Security* 18 (Fall 1993): 44–79.

Glossary

ALBA (Bolivarian Alternative for the Americas)   A regional integration arrangement established by Venezuela in 2005, that is designed around non-market principles and which excludes the United States.

Alliance for Progress   A collaborative, U.S.–Latin American initiative adopted during the Kennedy administration that was designed to spur economic development, democratization, and greater social equity in Latin America.

Andean Community   A trade bloc established in 1996 between Bolivia, Colombia, Ecuador, Peru, and Venezuela, which replaced the Andean Pact of 1969. Venezuela withdrew in 2006. *See* Andean Pact.

Andean Pact   A trade bloc established in 1969 between Bolivia, Chile, Colombia, Ecuador, and Peru. Venezuela joined in 1973; Chile withdrew in 1976. In 1996 it was renamed the Andean Community. *See* Andean Community.

Appeasement   A diplomatic tactic through which one state accommodates the demands of another to avoid unnecessary conflict.

Balance of power   A term that refers to (1) the distribution of power in the international system, (2) a conscious state policy (alliances or arms build-ups) to keep another state from gaining a preponderance of power, or (3) the balance of military capabilities between opposing states or alliance systems.

Bipolar   The structure of an international system in which power is concentrated in two strong states or alliance systems. The Cold War between the Soviet Union, United States, and their respective allies exemplified a bipolar system.

Blowback   A term that describes the adverse, unintended consequences of a foreign policy initiative.

Bracero **Program**   A bi-national program in effect from 1942 to 1964, that allowed Mexican migrants legal entry into the United States, where most found work in the agricultural sector.

Calvo Clause   A legal principle developed in 1868 by Argentine jurist Carlos Calvo, which sought to prevent foreign intervention in Latin American affairs. It argued that foreign nationals who invested in Latin America and suffered financial injury could not call upon their own governments to settle such claims, but must adjudicate them under domestic laws and courts.

Certification   A process required by an amendment to the 1961 U.S. Foreign Assistance Act that required the President to submit to Congress, on a yearly basis, a list of those countries which he determined were not cooperating sufficiently in the global war on drugs. Countries that were "de-certified" could be penalized by loss of some types of U.S. aid.

Cocalero   A Spanish term that refers to indigenous persons (especially in Bolivia and Peru) who make their livelihood by farming coca. Bolivian president Evo Morales was the leader of a *cocalero* union.

Cold War   The 45-year period of intense hostilities between the Soviet Union and United States which began at the close of World War II, and ended when the Berlin Wall was torn down in 1989.

Conditionality   The conditions attached to a loan from the IMF (International Monetary Fund). During the 1980s debt crisis, the IMF conditionality often required Latin American governments that received new loans to undertake specific economic policy reforms including austerity budgets, deregulation, the privatization of state-owned enterprises, and trade liberalization.

Contadora Group   A diplomatic initiative launched in 1983 by Colombia, Mexico, Panama, and Venezuela which sought (unsuccessfully) to negotiate an end to the military conflicts in El Salvador, Guatemala, Nicaragua, and Central America more generally.

Containment   A foreign policy that seeks to prevent the expansion of a potential aggressor. During the Cold War, containment was a key U.S. foreign policy toward the Soviet Union and Communism.

Contras   A proxy insurgent guerrilla force created, trained, and equipped by the CIA that engaged in low-intensity warfare and was used by the United States to seek the overthrow of Nicaragua's Sandinista revolutionary government in the 1980s. *See* Low-intensity warfare, *and* Sandinistas.

Coyote   A professional smuggler who, for a price, helps Latin American immigrants enter the United States illegally.

Cuban Missile Crisis   A dramatic Cold War confrontation in October 1962 between the United States and Soviet Union over the secret installation of Soviet nuclear missiles in Cuba. It brought the world to the brink of nuclear war and was resolved when Moscow agreed to remove its missiles (without consulting the Castro government) in exchange for a U.S. pledge not to invade Cuba and to remove American nuclear missiles in Turkey.

Dependency theory   A Marxist-derived theory of development that predicted rich states at the "center" of world capitalism would pursue policies that exploited developing states in the "periphery," and that exploited states could only experience true development by severing their ties with international capitalism. Although popular in the 1960s and 1970s, dependency theory could not explain the rapid development of newly industrializing Asian states in the 1980s and 1990s.

Détente   A term that connotes a "relaxing of tensions," and a policy the United States adopted toward the Soviet Union in the 1970s to better manage the Cold War and avoid conflict.

Dollar Diplomacy   A U.S. policy developed during the Taft administration that sought to ensure financial and political stability in the Caribbean as a way to fend off European efforts to collect debts from regional powers by force. It encouraged private U.S. banks to loan money to Caribbean and Central American states to service their external debts, and required U.S. operatives to oversee the repayment process and debtor countries' customs houses.

Dominance   The acquisition of military, political, and economic superiority by one state over others, and the exercise of this power through the routine use of force and a habitual disregard of weaker states' rights of equality, independence, and sovereignty. In the late nineteenth and early twentieth centuries, the United States behaved in a dominant fashion toward Caribbean and Central American states.

Domino theory   A belief among U.S. policymakers that gained currency during the Cold War, which held that if one state fell to Communism, surrounding states would soon fall too, like a line of cascading dominoes.

Drago Doctrine   A legal precept developed by Argentine diplomat Luis Drago in 1902, which sought to prevent foreign military intervention in Latin American affairs. It argued that international law provided lending states no authority to collect debts by force.

Economic interdependence   Situations in which two or more states or actors are in a mutually dependent economic relationship.

Economic nationalism   A doctrine that prioritizes increasing a country's national independence and promoting its prosperity and power, by nurturing and protecting domestic manufacturers, and limiting foreign economic and political influence through trade barriers and nationalizations. Latin American states that adopted ISI (import-substitution industrialization) often displayed a strong sense of economic nationalism. *See* ISI.

Esquipulas II   A 1987 peace accord championed and developed largely by Costa Rican president Óscar Árias, that helped end Central America's military conflicts, and for which Árias won the 1987 Nobel Peace Prize.

FTAA (Free Trade Agreement of the Americas)   A proposal to unite the national economies of Western Hemispheric states into a single, free trade zone, officially launched at the 1994 Summit of the Americas in Miami. Efforts to negotiate and implement an FTAA by 2005 failed.

GATT (General Agreement on Tariffs and Trade)   A multilateral agreement that reduced tariffs and expanded trade, which began in 1947 and was superseded in 1994 by the WTO (World Trade Organization).

Globalization   A process in which regional economies, societies, and cultures become increasingly integrated through global networks of interdependence. Globalization minimizes the effects of distance, reduces communication and transportation costs, and speeds the flow of capital, information, products, and people across borders. Globalization is not new; beginning in the sixteenth century, it left a defining imprint on the Western Hemisphere, especially Latin America.

Good Neighbor Policy   A U.S. policy adopted in 1933 during the Franklin D. Roosevelt administration, that renounced unilateral action and U.S. intervention in Latin America in exchange for "reciprocity" by Latin American governments (fair treatment of U.S. firms and citizens). The Good Neighbor Policy greatly improved America's image in the region and facilitated greater inter-American cooperation during World War II.

Hegemony   A condition in which one state gains a preponderance of power relative to others, and thus can exert control over them. Hegemonic states prefer to exercise influence nonviolently. They concede weaker states have rights of equality and sovereignty, but will still violate those rights when their vital interests appear threatened. The United States is said to have exercised hegemony in the Western Hemisphere through much of the twentieth century.

IADB (Inter-American Development Bank)   An international financial institution established in 1959 to provide loans for development projects, policy advice, and technical assistance in Latin American and Caribbean countries.

IAS (Inter-American System)   A system of regional, international treaties and institutions established in the late 1940s to provide collective security, help regulate inter-American relations, and resolve disputes peacefully. Initially, the IAS consisted of the Rio Treaty of Reciprocal Assistance (1947), Organization of American States (1948), and Treaty of Peaceful Settlements (1948). In 1959, the IADB (Inter-American Development Bank) was created and integrated into the IAS.

IMF (International Monetary Fund)   An international financial institution established after World War II to provide loans to (primarily) developing countries and help stabilize currencies. During the debt crisis of the 1980s, the IMF made loans to indebted Latin American countries that helped them weather the crisis, but attached conditions to those loans that required borrowing states to marketize their economies. *See* Conditionality.

Imperialism   The systematic attempts by one state to extend its dominion beyond its own borders to other populations that are culturally and ethnically distinct from its own. Genuine imperialism typically spawns formal empires like those established in the sixteenth and seventeenth centuries by Britain, France, and Spain. The United States is said to have acted in an imperial fashion toward Latin American states during parts of the nineteenth and twentieth centuries.

Interdependence   Situations of mutual dependence between states or other actors.

International institutions   Organizations established to facilitate inter-state political, economic, or military cooperation. The OAS (Organization of American States), UN (United Nations), IADB (Inter-American Development Bank), and IMF (International Monetary Fund) are all examples of international institutions.

International law   The body of laws—based on treaties and shared customs—that govern the conduct of sovereign states and their relationships.

International regime   A set of principles, norms, and decision-making procedures that govern the relations of sovereign states. Regimes reduce uncertainty among nations, establish mutually acceptable standards of action, and provide a context where conflicts can be avoided or resolved peacefully. Over time, the Good Neighbor Policy eventually took on the properties of an international regime.

Intervention   Any external action that influences the domestic affairs of another state. Historically, the United States intervened in the affairs of Latin American states both militarily and covertly. These interventions marred America's image in the region and stimulated persistent anti-U.S. sentiments.

ISI (import-substitution industrialization)   An economic development strategy adopted by many Latin American governments in which the state employs trade barriers to protect domestic industry from foreign competition, and allows domestic producers to manufacture goods that otherwise would be imported. Economic nationalist sentiments sometimes accompany ISI development projects. *See* Economic nationalism.

Isolationism   A foreign policy based on the notion that a state's national interest is best served by avoiding external military and political entanglements. Small or weak states sometimes adopt an isolationist policy to protect themselves. Under the 1823 Monroe Doctrine, the United States adopted an explicit isolationist policy toward Europe, but in time, it became much less isolationist toward Latin America.

League of Nations An international institution created after World War I with the backing of Woodrow Wilson. While the United States refused to join the organization, many Latin American states did in hopes that membership could ensure their sovereignty and legal equality, and prevent U.S. intervention in their affairs. When the League failed to provide an effective counterweight to U.S. regional influence, many regional powers eventually withdrew.

Liberalism An analytic approach to international politics which views states not solely as isolated actors within an anarchic context, but as units of a broader global society whose norms of sovereignty and nonintervention help regulate their interactions. The roots of Classical Liberalism go back to the writings of philosophers like Immanuel Kant, John Locke, John Stuart Mill, David Ricardo, and Adam Smith.

Lost decade The economic devastation Latin American countries endured in the 1980s that was sparked by the onset of the international debt crisis, and which resulted in drastic economic contraction, high unemployment, stagnant or declining wages, and deepening poverty.

Low-intensity warfare A type of warfare that entails a minimal commitment of U.S. forces and a low probability of U.S. casualties, and is fought to achieve limited, political objectives. During the 1980s, the United States—working with the *contra* guerrilla insurgents—used low-intensity warfare to try to topple Nicaragua's Sandinista government. *See* Contras, *and* Sandinistas.

Manifest destiny A nineteenth-century expansionist ideology that animated the American national conscience and U.S. leaders. It assumed America's society and political system were exceptional compared to others, that its Anglo-Saxon racial stock was naturally superior to other ethnic groups, and that the United States was predestined to increase in stature, prestige, and territory. Manifest destiny helped justify America's 1846–1848 war for territory against Mexico, as well as U.S. expansionism during and after the 1898 war with Spain.

Marxism An approach to international politics which argued that capitalist states would pursue imperialist foreign policies to secure access to markets and natural resources, and ensure continued capitalist expansion.

MERCOSUR (South American Common Market) A 1991 agreement among Argentina, Brazil, Paraguay, and Uruguay that created a common market in the Southern Cone.

Modernization   A cluster of social science theories advanced by scholars like Gabriel Almond, Seymour Martin Lipset, and Walt Rostow, that posited a strong correlation between economic modernization, social change, and political democratization. Modernization theory influenced U.S. policymakers who helped devise and advocate the Alliance for Progress.

Monroe Doctrine   An 1823 U.S. policy declaration that (1) warned European states against seeking to recolonize newly independent Latin American republics, (2) deemed any attempt to extend "their system" of politics (monarchy) into the Americas as dangerous to the U.S. national interest, and (3) pledged to remain isolationist respecting Europe's military and political affairs.

Multipolar   The structure of an international system in which power is concentrated in three or more strong states. In the Western Hemisphere, international politics occurred within a multipolar system until the latter part of the nineteenth century, when the growth of U.S. power enabled the United States to enforce the Monroe Doctrine, increasingly exclude European states from the hemisphere, and transform the system's structure from multipolar to unipolar.

NAFTA (North American Free Trade Agreement)   A 1994 agreement that lowered trade barriers, facilitated transnational capital investment, and established a free trade zone among Canada, Mexico, and the United States.

Nationalization   The process whereby a sovereign state assumes ownership of an asset, usually from private sector actors. Many Latin American states nationalized foreign corporate assets in an effort to diminish foreign economic penetration.

Neoliberalism   An analytic approach to international politics in which transnational trade, economic interdependence, and international institutions influence state actions and yield greater inter-state cooperation.

Neoliberal economics   A term often used in Latin America to describe economic policies that limit the role states play in the economy and prioritize the role played by free market dynamics. It is often associated with the Washington Consensus. *See* Washington Consensus.

NIEO (New International Economic Order)   A set of proposals formulated in the 1970s and set forth through the UN Conference on Trade and Development, which sought to improve the terms of trade between the industrialized North and developing South. The NIEO called for wealthy northern countries to provide poor states greater development aid and technology transfers, and adopt other measures to increase developing countries' exports.

Non-state actor   An actor in international politics that is not a state. International institutions such as the OAS (Organization of American States) or IMF (International Monetary Fund), multinational corporations such as United Fruit Company or Exxon-Mobil, and international terrorist networks like *al Qaeda* are all examples of non-state actors.

NSC-68   A secret, 1950 National Security Council document that sought to operationalize U.S. containment policy. By blurring the distinction between containing Soviet power and stopping the spread of communist ideology, NSC-68 helped lead the United States to seek the overthrow of leftist governments that had been elected democratically, and had little or no direct ties with the Soviet Union, such as those of Guatemala (1954) and Chile (1973).

OAS (Organization of American States)   An international organization created in 1948 as part of the IAS (Inter-American System) to promote diplomatic and political cooperation between the American republics. In 1962, Cuba was suspended from the OAS for embracing Communism and seeking to export its socialist revolution to neighboring states; in 2009, Honduras was suspended after a coup ousted its democratically elected president, Manuel Zelaya. *See* IAS.

OPEC (Organization of Petroleum Exporting Countries)   An international organization composed of the world's leading oil-producing states that tries to stabilize the world oil market, coordinate its members' production policies, and guarantee them sustained profits over the long term.

Operation Condor   A transnational terrorist network established in 1975 primarily by the Augusto Pinochet dictatorship in Chile. Its members included the military governments of Argentina, Bolivia, Brazil, Chile, Paraguay, and Uruguay, and its objectives were to hunt down, kidnap, and assassinate these governments' critics and opponents in combined operations across national borders.

Platt amendment   A 1902 amendment to Cuba's constitution that was imposed by the United States and which among other things, granted the United States the right to intervene in Cuba's internal affairs. The Platt Amendment institutionalized U.S. hegemony over Cuba, stirred anti-U.S. sentiments, and fueled Cuban nationalist aspirations. It was repealed under the Good Neighbor Policy in 1934. *See* Good Neighbor Policy.

Power   The ability to change the behavior of others and realize preferred outcomes.

Power conversion   The ability to transform potential power—as measured by power resources such as land, natural resources, or population—into actual power as measured by the ability to change others' behavior and realize preferred outcomes.

Primacy   A situation in which a strong state acquires a leadership position over others because weaker states voluntarily confer it, not because the stronger state has employed coercion or force. States that hold primacy typically exercise influence through multilateral arrangements, and generally observe the rights of lesser powers. Britain's position in the British Commonwealth illustrates primacy.

Prisoner's dilemma   A thought experiment in which two prisoners separated from each other and acting alone, try to devise the best strategy to realize optimal outcomes. The nature of the dilemma is that by acting independently, rationally, and doing what is best for himself, each prisoner can realize a bad outcome. In international politics, states can become entangled in a prisoner's dilemma and pursue policies that ultimately have negative consequences.

Protectorate   The status of a state or territory that is autonomous from a stronger state, but is protected diplomatically or militarily from third parties by it. Protectorates are typically established by treaty. In the late nineteenth and early twentieth centuries, the United States established various protectorates in the Caribbean and Central America.

Realism   An analytic approach to international politics in which states are the main actors; they operate under conditions of international anarchy, employ power and force as tools of choice, and view security as their greatest concern.

Remittance   Money earned by immigrant workers that is sent back to family members in their home states.

Revolution   A political process that entails a government's downfall followed by the rapid transformation of a country's basic economic, political, and social institutions. Revolutions can exert powerful influences on other states and international politics more generally. During the Cold War, the United States and other Latin American governments sought to prevent Marxist revolutions that might tip the balance of power between communist and non-communist blocs.

Roosevelt Corollary   A 1904 corollary to the Monroe Doctrine, under which the United States sought to preclude European military intervention in the Americas by unilaterally assuming an "international police power" that could justify U.S. intervention when countries fell behind in their debt payments. The Roosevelt Corollary led to extensive U.S. intervention in Central America and the Caribbean, and evoked intense anti-U.S. sentiments across Latin America.

Security dilemma   A paradoxical situation in which the rational actions one state takes to make itself more secure, leads to reciprocal actions by another state that ultimately leaves them both less secure. The security dilemma played an important role in Cuban, Soviet, and U.S. policy calculations that led to the 1962 Cuban Missile Crisis.

Sandinistas   The Marxist-oriented revolutionary guerrilla force that fought along with other elements of Nicaraguan society to topple dictator Anastasio Somoza Debayle during the 1979 Nicaraguan Revolution. The Sandinistas subsequently came to power, but faced relentless opposition from the United States, and low-intensity warfare from the U.S. proxy guerrilla force, the *contras*. *See* Low-intensity warfare, *and* Contras.

Security regime   A specific type of international regime focused on enhancing states' security. After the 1962 Cuban Missile Crisis, the United States and Soviet Union established a limited security regime in the Caribbean that enhanced their own security and Cuba's. *See* International regime.

Sensitivity   A state or actor's short-term susceptibility to the effects of interdependence. In general, sensitivity refers to how quickly changes in one part of the system produce changes in another.

Social Darwinism   A nineteenth-century ideology popularized by British intellectuals like Herbert Spencer and American thinkers like John Burgess, that attracted a broad following in European and American intellectual and policy circles. It proposed that just as animals had evolved over time, human societies did too, and that "civilized" societies had a moral obligation to help civilize less evolved societies. In Europe and the United States, social Darwinian ideology provided intellectual justification for expansionist and imperialist foreign policies.

Soft balancing   A foreign policy tactic whereby weaker states use nonmilitary means—informal ententes, the procedural constraints of international institutions, or economic arrangements—to limit a stronger state's ability to realize preferred outcomes. In the early 2000s, various Latin American states pursued soft balancing tactics against the United States.

Soft power   A state's ability to realize preferred outcomes and alter the behavior of other states by attracting them to its values, preferences, or point of view, rather than by employing coercion.

Sovereignty   The status of having supreme, legal authority over a given territory. State sovereignty is a key feature of international law and international politics. Much of the historical tension in U.S.–Latin American relations is linked to U.S. interventions that failed to respect the sovereignty of neighboring states.

Truman Doctrine   A 1947 policy doctrine articulated by U.S. President Harry Truman that envisioned a global campaign to protect free peoples anywhere in the world from communist encroachment. The Truman Doctrine became the basis for the U.S. Cold War policy of containment. *See* Containment.

UNASUR (Union of South American States)   An intergovernmental framework established in 2008 and modeled after the European Union. It seeks to integrate the states that comprise the Andean Community and MERCOSUR, and eventually provide them a common currency, parliament, and passport. *See* Andean Community, *and* MERCOSUR.

Unipolar The structure of an international system in which one state holds a preponderance of power. Throughout most of the twentieth century, the structure of the Western Hemisphere's international system was unipolar, with the United States serving as the main pole of power.

Vulnerability The long-term costs a state or actor must bear when seeking to change a situation of interdependence it is in.

Washington Consensus A term coined by economist John Williamson to denote the neoliberal economic policies advocated by prominent actors in Washington, DC (the IMF, World Bank, and U.S. Treasury). In the 1980s and 1990s, many Latin American governments adopted elements of the Washington Consensus. *See* Neoliberalism.

Wilsonianism A philosophy espoused by Woodrow Wilson that envisioned making domestic U.S. political values—democracy, constitutionalism, and self-determination—the bedrock of U.S. foreign policy, rather than base foreign policy solely on economic and strategic interests. Typically seen as a liberal approach to foreign affairs, Wilsonianism as practiced toward Latin America was a realist-liberal hybrid that sought to promote liberal democracy in the region through force projection.

World Bank An international financial institution created after World War II to provide loans, policy advice, and technical assistance to developing countries. During the debt crisis of the 1980s, the World Bank made "structural adjustment" loans to indebted Latin American countries whose governments assumed a commitment to move away from statist, inward-oriented policies toward more market friendly, neoliberal ones.

WTO (World Trade Organization) An international institution established in 1994, which replaced the GATT (General Agreement on Tariffs and Trade). Its main objectives are to help promote international trade and regulate tariffs among its members. *See* GATT.

Notes

Preface

1 Steven A. Camarota, "Immigrants in the United States, 2007: A Profile of America's Foreign-Born Population," Table 4 (La Jolla: Center for Immigration Studies, University of California, San Diego, November 2007).
2 David Bushnell and Lester D. Langley (eds), *Simón Bolívar: Essays on the Life and Legacy of the Liberator* (Lantham, MD: Rowman & Littlefield, 2008), 135.

1 International Politics and U.S.–Latin American Relations

1 Alan McPherson, *Yankee No! Anti-Americanism in U.S.–Latin American Relations* (Cambridge, MA: Harvard University Press, 2003), 11.
2 Theodore Roosevelt, quoted in personal letter of Carl Schurz to Charles Francis Adams, n.d., in Carl Schurz, *Reminiscences of Carl Schurz*, vol. 3 (London: John Murray, 1909), 446–447.
3 Robert N. Burr, "The Balance of Power in Nineteenth Century South America: An Exploratory Essay," *Hispanic American Historical Review* 35 (1955): 36–60.
4 Theotonio Dos Santos, "The Structure of Dependence," *American Economic Review* 60 (1970): 231.
5 Robert O. Keohane, *Neorealism and its Critics* (New York: Columbia University Press, 1986), 4.
6 Theodore H. Moran, *Multinational Corporations and the Politics of Dependence: Copper in Chile* (Princeton: Princeton University Press, 1974), 6.
7 Quoted in Robert F. Kennedy, *Thirteen Days: A Memoir of the Cuban Missile Crisis* (New York: W. W. Norton, 1971), 161–162.
8 Jorge I. Domíngeuz, *To Make a World Safe for Revolution: Cuba's Foreign Policy* (Cambridge, MA: Harvard University Press, 1989), 3.

2 U.S.–Latin American Relations and Political Theory

1 Robert O. Keohane and Joseph S. Nye, Jr., "Globalization: What's New? What's Not? (And So What?)," in Jon C. Pevehouse and Joshua S. Goldstein (eds) *Readings in International Relations* (New York: Pearson/Longman, 2008), 17.

2 Craig Arceneaux and David Pion-Berlin, "Issues, Threats, and Institutions: Explaining OAS Responses to Democratic Dilemmas in Latin America," *Latin American Politics and Society* 49 (Summer 2007): 5.

3 Robert G. Gilpin, *War and Change in World Politics* (Cambridge: Cambridge University Press, 1981), 211.

4 Bruce Russett, Harvey Starr, and David Kinsella, *World Politics: The Menu for Choice*, seventh edition (New York: Wadsworth, 2004), 99.

5 Mary M. Kritz and Douglas T. Gurak, "International Migration Trends in Latin America: Research and Data Survey," *International Migration Review* 13 (Autumn, 1979): 409–410.

6 Joseph S. Nye, Jr., "The Decline of America's Soft Power," *Foreign Affairs* 83 (2004): 16.

7 Gregory Treverton and Seth G. Jones, "Measuring Power: How to Predict Future Balances," *Harvard International Review* 27 (Summer 2005), http://hir.harvard.edu/defining-power/measuring-power, accessed January 20, 2011.

8 Quoted in Dexter Perkins, *The Monroe Doctrine, 1823–1826* (Cambridge, MA: Harvard University Press, 1927), 84–85.

9 Quoted in Thomas Schoonover, *Dollars over Dominion: The Triumph of Liberalism in Mexican-United States Relations, 1861–1867* (Baton Rouge and London: Louisiana State University Press, 1978), 141.

10 David R. Mares, "Mexico's Foreign Policy as a Middle Power: The Nicaragua Connection, 1884–1986," *Latin American Research Review* 23 (1988): 90.

11 Robert N. Burr, "The Balance of Power in Nineteenth Century South America: An Exploratory Essay," *Hispanic American Historical Review* 35 (1955): 36–60.

12 James Dunkerley, "The United States and Latin America in the Long Run (1800–1945)," in Victor Bulmer-Thomas and James Dunkerley (eds) *The United States and Latin America: The New Agenda* (London and Cambridge, MA: Institute of Latin American Studies, University of London, and David Rockefeller Center for Latin American Studies, Harvard University, 1999), 20.

13 Stephen M. Walt, "Taming American Power," *Foreign Affairs* 78 (September/October 2005): 105–120; and T. V. Paul, "Soft Balancing in the Age of U.S. Primacy," *International Security* 30, (Summer 2005): 58.

14 Tony Smith, *America's Mission: The United States and the Worldwide Struggle for Democracy in the Twentieth Century* (Princeton: Princeton University Press 1995), 3.

15 Heraldo Muñoz, "Chile: The Limits of 'Success,'" in Abraham F. Lowenthal (ed.) *Exporting Democracy: The United States and Latin America, Case Studies* (Baltimore: Johns Hopkins University Press, 1991), 39.

16 Lorenzo Meyer, "Mexico: The Exception and the Rule," in Abraham F. Lowenthal (ed.) *Exporting Democracy: The United States and Latin America, Case Studies* (Baltimore: Johns Hopkins University Press, 1991), 106.

17 Stephen D. Krasner, *Defending the National Interest* (Princeton: Princeton University Press 1978), 339; Jeanne Kirkpatrick, "Dictatorships and Double Standards," *Commentary* 68 (November 1979): 34–45.

18 Cynthia Arnson, *Crossroads: Congress, the President, and Central America, 1976–1993* (University Park: The Pennsylvania State University Press, 1993); Robert Pastor, *Whirlpool: U.S. Foreign Policy Toward Latin America and the Caribbean* (Princeton: Princeton University Press, 1992); and Robert Packenham, *Liberal America in the Third World: Political Development Ideas in Foreign Aid and Social Science* (Princeton: Princeton University Press, 1973).

19 Heraldo Muñoz, "Chile: The Limits of 'Success,'" in Abraham F. Lowenthal (ed.) *Exporting Democracy: The United States and Latin America, Case Studies* (Baltimore: Johns Hopkins University Press, 1991), 40.

3 Foreign Policy Fundamentals: International Systems and Levels of Analysis

1 John Quincy Adams, "Address to U.S. House of Representatives," July 4, 1821, http://www.fff.org/comment/AdamsPolicy.asp, accessed January 20, 2011.

2 J. David Singer, "The Level-of-Analysis Problem in International Relations," in Klaus Knorr and Sidney Verba (eds) *The International System: Theoretical Essays* (Princeton: Princeton University Press, 1961), 77–92; and Kenneth N. Waltz, *Man, the State and War* (New York: Columbia University Press, 1959).

3 Kenneth N. Waltz, "The Anarchic Structure of World Politics," in Robert J. Art and Robert Jervis (eds) *International Politics: Enduring Concepts and Contemporary Issues*, sixth edition (New York: Longman, 2003), 55.

4 Jeffry A. Frieden, "The Economics of Intervention: American Overseas Investments and Relations with Underdeveloped Areas, 1890–1950," *Comparative Studies in Society and History* 31 (1989): 70.

5 Frieden, "The Economics of Intervention," 65.

6 Douglass C. North, William Summerhill, and Barry R. Weingast, "Order, Disorder, and Economic Change: Latin America versus North America," in Bruce Bueno de Mesquita and Hilton L. Root (eds) *Governing for Prosperity* (New Haven, CT: Yale University Press, 2000), 17–56.

7 Alexander Hamilton, "Federalist #11," in Clinton Rossiter (ed.) *The Federalist Papers: Hamilton, Madison, Jay* (New York: Penguin, 1964), 87.

8 Hamilton, "Federalist #11," 86–87.

9 Hamilton, "Federalist #11," 90–91.

10 Samuel Guy Inman, "The Monroe Doctrine and Hispanic America," *The Hispanic American Historical Review* 4 (Nov. 1921): 640–643.

11 Mark T. Gilderhus, "The Monroe Doctrine: Meanings and Implications," *Presidential Studies Quarterly* 36 (March 2006): 8; Federico Gil, *Latin American-United States Relations* (New York: Harcourt Brace Jovanovich, 1971), 63.

12 Agricultural, economic, population, rail, and steel figures taken from Sean Dennis Cashman, *America in the Gilded Age* (New York: New York University Press), 29, 79, 118, 266, and 272.

13 Susan B. Carter, Scott Sigmund Gartner, Michael R. Haines, Alan L. Olmstead, Richard Sutch, and Gavin Wright (eds), *Historical Statistics of the United States* 5 (New York: Cambridge University Press, 2006), Table Ee362-375 and Table Ed26-47; and Paul Kennedy, *The Rise and Fall of the Great Powers* (New York: Random House, 1987), 203.

14 William L. Harris, "Venezuela: Wars, Claims, and the Cry for a Stronger Monroe Doctrine," in Thomas M. Leonard (ed.) *United States-Latin American Relations 1850–1903: Establishing a Relationship* (Tuscaloosa: University of Alabama Press, 1999), 119; and Fareed Zakaria, "The Myth of America's 'Free Security' (Reconsiderations)," *World Policy Journal* 14 (Summer 1997): 42.

15 Paul Kennedy, "The Tradition of Appeasement in British Foreign Policy, 1865–1939, in Paul Kennedy (ed.) *Strategy and Diplomacy 1870–1945* (London: Allen & Unwin, 1983), 16.

4 The Expansion of American Power

1 Lester D. Langley, *The Banana Wars: United States Intervention in the Caribbean, 1898–1934*, revised edition (Wilmington, DE: Scholarly Resources, 2002), xv.

2 Peter H. Smith, *Talons of the Eagle: Latin America, the United States, and the World*, third edition (New York: Oxford University Press, 2008), 41, 35.

3 Hedley Bull, *The Anarchical Society: A Study of Order in World Politics* (New York: Columbia University Press, 1977), 214.

4 Paul Kennedy, *The Rise and Fall of the Great Powers* (New York: Random House, 1987), 246.

5 Stephen Van Evera, "Offense, Defense, and the Causes of War," *International Security* 22 (Spring 1998): 5, 7.

6 Charles A. Conant, "The Economics of Imperialism," *North American Review* 167 (September 1898): 326–341.

7 Stanley Karnow, *In our Image: America's Empire in the Philippines* (New York: Random House, 1989), 97.

8 Karnow, *In our Image*, 84.

9 Quoted in Warren Zimmermann, "Jingoes, Goo-Goos, and the Rise of America's Empire," *The Wilson Quarterly* 22 (Spring 1998): 51.

10 Howard K. Beale, *Theodore Roosevelt and the Rise of America to World Power* (New York: Collier Books, 1956), 64.

11 Zimmermann, "Jingoes, Goo-Goos, and the Rise of America's Empire," 48.

12 Quoted in Alan McPherson, *Yankee No! Anti-Americanism in U.S.–Latin American Relations* (Cambridge, MA: Harvard University Press 2003), 40.

13 Louis A. Pérez, Jr., *Cuba: Between Reform and Revolution*, third edition (New York: Oxford University Press, 2006), 151.

14 Cited in Dana G. Munro, *"Intervention and Dollar Diplomacy in the Caribbean, 1900–1920* (Princeton: Princeton University Press, 1964), 113.

15 Theodore Roosevelt, "'International Peace,' Address before the Nobel Prize Committee, Delivered at Christiania, Norway, May 5, 1910," in Hermann Hagedorn (ed.) *The Works of Theodore Roosevelt, American Problems* (New York: Charles Scribner's Sons, 1926), 414–415.

16 Victor Bulmer-Thomas, *The Economic History of Latin America since Independence* (New York: Cambridge University Press, 1994), 161.

17 Emily S. Rosenberg and Norman L. Rosenberg, "From Colonialism to Professionalism: The Public-Private Dynamic in United States Foreign Financial Advising, 1898–1929," *Journal of American History* 74 (June 1987): 65.

18 Quoted in Jenny Pearce, *Under the Eagle: US Intervention in Central America and the Caribbean* (London: Latin American Bureau, 1982), 19.

5 Hemispheric Relations through World War II

1 Quoted in Sidney Bell, *Religious Conquest: Woodrow Wilson and the Evolution of the New Diplomacy* (Port Washington, NY: National University Publications, Kennikat Press, 1972), 98.

2 Woodrow Wilson, quoted in "President Wilson and Latin America," *The American Journal of International Law* 7 (April 1913): 331.

3 Bell, *Religious Conquest*, 97.

4 Bell, *Religious Conquest*, 95.

5 Wilson's chief advisor, Edward M. House, was especially concerned on this point. See Roland N. Stromberg, "Uncertainties and Obscurities about the League of Nations," *Journal of the History of Ideas* 33 (Jan.–Mar. 1972): 139–154.

6 Quoted in United States Congress, *Papers Relating to the Foreign Relations for the United States, 1918*, Serial Set Vol. No. 7470-1, Session Vol. No. 1, 65th Congress, 3rd Session, H. Doc. 188, pt. 1, 821, 820.

7 Samuel Guy Inman, quoted in Gordon Connell-Smith, *The Inter-American System* (New York: Oxford University Press, 1965), 69.

8 Connell-Smith, *The Inter-American System*, 89.

9 Connell-Smith, *The Inter-American System*, 88.

10 Stephen D. Krasner, "Structural Causes and Regime Consequences: Regimes as Intervening Variables," in Stephen D. Krasner (ed.) *International Regimes* (Ithaca: Cornell University Press, 1983), 2.

11 Franklin D. Roosevelt, *Public Papers and Addresses*, 1938 Volume (New York: Macmillan, 1941), 412.

12 Quoted in Bryce Wood, *The Dismantling of the Good Neighbor Policy* (Austin: University of Texas Press, 1985), 9.

13 Sumner Welles, quoted in Federico Gil, *Latin American-United States Relations* (New York: Harcourt Brace Jovanovich, 1971), 109.

14 Quoted in Lars Schoultz, *Beneath the United States: A History of U.S. Policy Toward Latin America* (Chapel Hill: University of North Carolina Press, 1998), 295.

6 The Cold War, Part I

1 Daniel Yergin, *The Shattered Peace* (Boston: Houghton Mifflin, 1977), 73, 75.

2 George Kennan, "Latin America as a Problem in United States Foreign Policy," in Michael LaRosa and Frank O. Mora (eds) *Neighborly Adversaries* (Latham, MD: Rowman & Littlefield, 1999), 180, 193.

3 Wayne S. Smith, "Introduction: An Overview of Soviet Policy in Latin America," in Wayne S. Smith (ed.) *The Russians Aren't Coming: New Soviet Policy in Latin America* (Boulder, CO: Lynne Rienner, 1992), 11.

4 Stephen G. Rabe, "The Johnson Doctrine," *Presidential Studies Quarterly* 36 (March 2006): 469–474.

5 Lyndon B. Johnson, quoted in Rabe, "The Johnson Doctrine," 55.

6 Heraldo Muñoz, "The Rise and Decline of the Inter-American System: A Latin American View," in Richard J. Bloomfield and Gregory F. Treverton (eds) *Alternative to Intervention: A New U.S.–Latin American Security Relationship* (Boulder, CO: Lynne Rienner, 1990), 29.

7 Michael Grow, *U.S. Presidents and Latin American Interventions: Pursuing Regime Change in the Cold War* (Lawrence: University of Kansas Press, 2008), 187.

8 On the Velasco government's anti-communist stance, see Cynthia McClintock, "Velasco, Officers, and Citizens: The Politics of Stealth," in Cynthia McClintock and Abraham F. Lowenthal (eds) *The Peruvian Experiment Reconsidered* (Princeton: Princeton University Press, 1983), 275–308.

9 Stephen D. Krasner, *Defending the National Interest: Raw Materials Investments and U.S. Foreign Policy* (Princeton: Princeton University Press, 1978), 277.

10 Jorge I. Domínguez, "US-Latin American Relations During the Cold War and its Aftermath," in Victor Bulmer-Thomas and James Dunkerley (eds) *The United States and Latin America: The New Agenda* (London and Cambridge, MA: Institute of Latin American Studies, University of London and David Rockefeller Center for Latin American Studies, Harvard University, 1999), 34.

7 The Cold War, Part II

1 Quoted in Jorge I. Domínguez, *To Make the World Safe for Revolution: Cuba's Foreign Policy* (Cambridge, MA: Harvard University Press, 1989), 25.

2 Louis A. Pérez, Jr., *Cuba: Between Reform and Revolution*, third edition (New York: Oxford University Press, 2006), 286–287.

3 Kevin Sullivan, "40 Years After Missile Crisis, Players Swap Stories in Cuba," *Washington Post*, October 13, 2002.

4 George F. Will, "Lessons of the Cuban Missile Crisis," *Newsweek*, October 11, 1982, 120.

5 Domínguez, *To Make the World Safe for Revolution*, 47.

6 Walter Lippmann, "Cuba and the Nuclear Risk," *The Atlantic Monthly*, February 1963, http://www.theatlantic.com/past/docs/issues/63feb/lippmann.htm, accessed January 20, 2011.

7 Lippmann, "Cuba and the Nuclear Risk."

8 Quoted in Michael A. Heilperin, *Studies in Economic Nationalism*, Publication de L' Institut Universitaire des Hautes Etudes Internationales (Paris: Librairie Minard, 1962), 18.

9 Robert Gilpin, *The Political Economy of International Relations* (Princeton: Princeton University Press, 1987), 31.

10 Michael Lind, *Hamilton's Republic* (New York: Simon & Schuster, 1997), 229–230.

11 Harry G. Johnson, *Economic Nationalism in Old and New States* (Chicago: University of Chicago Press, 1967), 14–15.

12 Raúl Prebisch, "Economic Aspects of the Alliance," in John C. Dreier (ed.) *The Alliance for Progress: Problems and Perspectives* (Baltimore: Johns Hopkins University Press, 1962), 25.

13 Howard J. Wiarda, "Did the Alliance 'Lose Its Way,' or Were Its Assumptions All Wrong from the Beginning and Are Those Assumptions Still with Us?" in Ronald L. Scheman (ed.) *The Alliance for Progress: A Retrospective* (New York: Praeger, 1988), 99; Arthur Schlesinger, Jr., "The Alliance for Progress: A Retrospective," in Ronald G. Hellman and

H. Jon Rosenbaum (eds) *Latin America: The Search for a New International Role* (New York: Sage, 1975), 63.

14 Prebisch, "Economic Aspects of the Alliance," 24–25.

15 Eduardo Frei Montalva, "The Alliance that Lost its Way," *Foreign Affairs* 45 (1967): 441.

16 Victor Bulmer-Thomas, *The Economic History of Latin America since Independence* (New York: Cambridge University Press, 1994), 259.

17 Richard M. Nixon, *Six Crises* (Garden City: Doubleday, 1962), 256–257.

18 "THE AMERICAS: Operation Pan America," *Time*, June 30, 1958, http://www.time.com/time/magazine/article/0,9171,891915,00.html, accessed January 20, 2011.

19 *Act of Bogotá*, September 13, 1960, http://avalon.law.yale.edu/20th_century/intam08.asp, accessed January 20, 2011.

20 Frei Montalva, "The Alliance that Lost its Way," 441.

21 Quoted in Stephen G. Rabe, *Eisenhower and Latin America: The Foreign Policy of Anticommunism* (Chapel Hill: The University of North Carolina Press, 1988), 109.

22 José Figueres, "The Problems of Democracy in Latin America," *Journal of International Affairs* 9 (1955): 11.

23 Arturo Morales Carrión, "A Special Relationship," in Ronald Scheman (ed.) *The Alliance for Progress: A Retrospective* (New York: Praeger, 1988), 197.

24 John J. Johnson, *Political Change in Latin America: The Emergence of the Middle Sectors* (Stanford, CA: Stanford University Press, 1958), 181.

25 John F. Kennedy, speech in Tampa, Florida, October 18, 1960, quoted in Arthur Schlesinger, Jr., "The Alliance for Progress: A Retrospective," in Ronald G. Hellman and H. Jon Rosenbaum (eds) *Latin America: The Search for a New International Role* (New York: Sage, 1975), 59.

26 Albert Lleras, "Report on the Alliance for Progress," submitted to the Organization of American States, Washington, DC, 1963.

27 Lincoln Gordon, "The Alliance at Birth: Hopes and Fears," in Ronald L. Scheman (ed.) *The Alliance for Progress, A Retrospective* (New York: Praeger, 1988), 74.

28 Susanne Bodenheimer, "Dependency and Imperialism: The Roots of Latin American Underdevelopment," *Politics and Society* 1 (May 1971): 358.

29 Abraham F. Lowenthal, " 'Liberal,' 'Radical,' and 'Bureaucratic' Perspectives on U.S. Latin American Policy: The Alliance for Progress in Retrospect," in Julio Cotler and Richard R. Fagen (eds) *Latin America and the United States* (Stanford, CA: Stanford University Press, 1974), 232.

30 Lowenthal, "'Liberal,' 'Radical,'' and 'Bureaucratic' Perspectives," 231; Schlesinger, "The Alliance for Progress: A Retrospective," 65; and Federico Gil, "The Kennedy–Johnson Years," in John D. Martz (ed.) *United States Policy in Latin America: A Quarter Century of Crisis and Challenge, 1961–1986* (Lincoln: University of Nebraska Press, 1988), 15.

31 CIA report "Survey of Latin America," April 1964, quoted in Walter Lafeber, *Inevitable Revolutions: The United States in Central America*, second edition (New York: W. W. Norton, 1993), 157.

32 Richard Goodwin, "Our stake in a big awakening," *Life*, April 14, 1967, 83.

33 Jean Daniel, "Unofficial Envoy: An Historic Report from Two Capitals," *The New Republic*, December 14, 1963, http://www.kenrahn.com/JFK/history/wc_period/Pre-WCR_reactions_to_assassination/Pre-WCR_reactions_by_the_left/TNR—Unofficial_envoy.html, accessed January 20, 2011.

34 Daniel, "Unofficial Envoy."

35 Jean Daniel, "When Castro Heard the News," *The New Republic*, December 7, 1963, http://www.kenrahn.com/jfk/history/WC_Period/pre-wcr_reactions_to_assassination/Pre-WCR_reactions_by_the_left/When_Castro_Heard_TNR.html, accessed January 20, 2011.

8 Cold War Challenges to U.S. Hegemony

1 Hedley Bull, *The Anarchical Society: A Study of Order in World Politics* (New York: Columbia University Press, 1977), 214.
2 David A. Lake, "Escape from the State of Nature: Authority and Hierarchy in World Politics," *International Security* 32 (Summer 2007): 71.
3 Paul Kennedy, *The Rise and Fall of the Great Powers* (New York: Random House, 1987).
4 Robert Gilpin, *War and Change in World Politics* (New York: Cambridge University Press, 1986), 157.
5 Quoted in Seymour M. Hersh, "The Price of Power: Kissinger, Nixon, and Chile," *The Atlantic Monthly*, December 1982, 40.
6 Quoted in Anthony Lewis, "The Kissinger Doctrine," *New York Times*, February 27, 1975, 35.
7 Gabriel García Márquez, "The Death of Salvador Allende," *Harper's*, March 1974, 46.
8 Fidel Castro, quoted in Bernard Weintraub, "Castro accuses the U.S.," *New York Times*, September 18, 1973.
9 Carol Cook, "Echeverria accuses U.S. of intervening in 1973 Chile coup," *The Bryan Times*, February 20, 1975.
10 William D. Rogers, "Mythmaking and Foreign Policy," *Foreign Affairs* 83 (January/February 2004): 150–163.
11 Peter Kornbluh, *The Pinochet File: A Declassified Dossier of Atrocity and Accountability* (New York: New Press, 2004).
12 Kenneth Maxwell, "Maxwell Replies," *Foreign Affairs* 83 (January/February 2004): 163–165.
13 Colin L. Powell, "Interview on Black Entertainment Television's Youth Town Hall," February 20, 2003, http://www.fas.org/irp/news/2003/02/dos022003.html, accessed January 20, 2011.
14 Quoted in Michael Blum, *Killing Hope: U.S. Military and CIA Interventions Since World War II* (London: Zed Books, 2003), 215.
15 Peter Kornbluh, "The Chile Coup: The U.S. Hand," *Third World Traveler* (reprinted from iF Magazine, Nov./Dec. 1998), http://www.thirdworldtraveler.com/Terrorism/Chile%20Coup_USHand.html, accessed January 20, 2011.
16 Stephen D. Krasner, *Defending the National Interest: Raw Materials Investments and U.S. Foreign Policy* (Princeton: Princeton University Press, 1979), 311.
17 Hal Brands, "Third World Politics in an Age of Global Turmoil: The Latin American Challenge to U.S. and Western Hegemony, 1965–1975," *Diplomatic History* 32 (January 2008): 111–112.
18 Paul E. Sigmund, *Multinationals in Latin America: The Politics of Nationalization* (Madison: University of Wisconsin Press, 1980), 37–38.
19 ECLA, *Economic Survey of Latin America, 1975* (ECLA: Santiago, 1976), 14–20.

20 Quoted in Carlos Osorio (ed.) *National Security Archive Electronic Briefing Book No. 71* (Washington, DC: National Security Archive, 2002), http://www.gwu.edu/~nsarchiv/NSAEBB/NSAEBB71, accessed July 9, 2010.

21 Quoted in Heraldo Muñoz, *The Dictator's Shadow: Life Under Augusto Pinochet* (New York: Basic Books, 2008), 83.

22 Alfred Stepan, "The New Professionalism," in Alfred Stepan (ed.) *Authoritarian Brazil: Origins, Policies, and Future* (New Haven, CT: Yale University Press, 1973), 50.

23 Thomas O. Enders, "The Central American Challenge," *AEI Foreign Policy and Defense Review* 4 (1982): 9.

24 President Ronald Reagan, speech at the Organization of American States, February 24, 1982, quoted in Robert Dallek, *The Politics of Symbolism* (Cambridge, MA: Harvard University Press, 1999), 177.

25 President Ronald Reagan, television address, quoted in Lars Schoultz, *Beneath the United States: A History of U.S. Policy Toward Latin America* (Cambridge, MA: Harvard University Press, 1998), 365.

26 Quoted in Robert A. Pastor, "A Question of U.S. National Interests in Central America," in Wolf Grabendorff, Heinrich-W. Krumwiede, and Jorg Todt (eds) *Political Change in Central America: Internal and External Dimensions* (Boulder, CO: Westview, 1984), 185.

27 Miguel de la Madrid H., "Mexico: The New Challenges," *Foreign Affairs* 63 (Fall 1984): 68, 70.

28 The Report of the President's National Bipartisan Commission on Central America (New York: Macmillan, 1984), 5.

29 Daniel Ortega, 1983 interview in *Barricada International*, published in Bruce Marcus (ed.) *Nicaragua: The Sandinista People's Revolution: Speeches by Sandinista Leaders* (New York: Pathfinder Press, 1985), 196.

30 Robert A. Pastor, *Condemned to Repetition: The United States and Nicaragua* (Princeton: Princeton University Press, 1987), 243.

9 Interdependence and Globalization

1 "Joint Presidential Statement calling to a meeting of Latin American Foreign Ministers and Financial Authorities to discuss the international debt crisis," quoted in Riordan Roett, "The Debt Crisis: Economic and Politics," in John D. Martz (ed.) *United States Policy in Latin America: A Quarter Century of Crisis and Challenge, 1961–1986* (Lincoln: University of Nebraska Press, 1988), 249.

2 "Plan of Action," Latin American Economic Conference, Quito, 9–13 January 1984, 1–2, published by the SELA Permanent Secretariat.

3 Thomas L. Friedman, *The Lexus and the Olive Tree* (New York: Anchor Books, 2000), 9.

4 Kenneth N. Waltz, "Globalization and Governance," *PS: Political Science and Politics* 32 (December 1999): 695.

5 Address by President Ricardo Lagos of Chile to the United Nations at the Millennium Summit of the UN, New York, September 6, 2000, http://www.un.org/millennium/webcast/statements/chile.htm, accessed January 20, 2011.

6 Néstor García Canclini, "A Modernization That Holds Us Back: Culture Under the Neoconservative Regression," in Anthony Geist and José B. Monle-n (eds) *Modernism*

and its Margins: Reinscribing Cultural Modernity from Spain and Latin America (New York: Garland Publishing, 1999), 39, 45.

7 *Constrained Internationalism: Adapting to New Realities, Results of a 2010 Survey of American Public Opinion* (Chicago: Chicago Council of Global Affairs, 2010), http://www.the chicagocouncil.org/UserFiles/File/POS_Topline%20Reports/POS%202010/Global% 20Views%202010.pdf, accessed January 20, 2011; El Barómetro Iberoamericano de Gobernabilidad 2009 (Madrid: Consorcio Iberoamericano de Investigaciones de Mercados y Asesoramiento, 2009), http://www.cimaiberoamerica.com, accessed January 20, 2011; and Iberoamericano de Gobernabilidad 2008 (Madrid: Consorcio Iberoamericano de Investigaciones de Mercados y Asesoramiento, 2009), http://www. cimaiberoamerica.com, accessed January 20, 2011.

8 "Remittances to Latin America stabilizing after 15% drop last year—MIF," News Release, *Inter-American Development Bank*, March 4, 2010, http://www.iadb.org/news-releases/ 2010-03/english/remittances-to-latin-america-stabilizing-after-15-drop-last-year-fomin-6671.html, accessed January 20, 2011.

9 Manuel Orozco, "Transnationalism and Development: Trends and Opportunities in Latin America," in Samuel Manzele Maimbo and Dilip Ratha (eds) *Remittances: Development Impact and Prospects* (New York: World Bank, 2005).

10 Saskia Sassen, "U.S. Immigration Policy Toward Mexico in a Global Economy," *Journal of International Affairs* 43 (Winter 1990): 374–377.

11 Wayne A. Cornelius, "Controlling 'Unwanted' Immigration: Lessons from the United States, 1993–2004," *Journal of Ethnic and Migration Studies* 31 (2005): 774–794.

12 "Tunnels beneath U.S. border proliferate," *SECRECY NEWS_from the FAS Project on Government Secrecy,* http://www.fas.org/sgp/news/secrecy/2009/02/022309.html, accessed January 20, 2011.

13 Vicente Fox, "Mensaje de Vicente Fox, durante la Sesión Solemne del H. Congreso del Unión," December 1, 2000, http://wayback.archive-it.org/176/20060818191623/ http://www.presidencia.gob.mx/actividades/?contenido=6&pagina=377, accessed January 20, 2011.

14 Ana Arana, "How the Street Gangs took Central America," *Foreign Affairs* 84 (May/June 2005): 98 *Academic OneFile*. Web. 20 January 2011.

15 James Brooke, "Fighting in Panama: Latin America; U.S. Denounced by Nations Touchy About Intervention," *New York Times*, December 21, 1989.

16 Douglas W. Payne, "Why Drug Traffickers Love Free Trade," *Dissent* 44 (Summer 1997), 60.

17 Vicente Fox Quesada, "Drug Addiction, Organized Crime, and Security: A Moment of Reflection and Proposals," http://blogvicentefox.blogspot.com/2010/08/drogadiccion-crimen-organizado-y.html, accessed November 17, 2010.

18 Andres Oppenheimer, "Has the time come to legalize drugs?" *Miami Herald*, August 12, 2010.

10 Hemispheric Relations in the Twenty-First Century

1 President George Bush, "Remarks Announcing the Enterprise for the Americas Initiative," June 27, 1990, http://www.presidency.ucsb.edu/ws/index.php?pid=18644, accessed January 20, 2011.

2 Osvaldo Hurtado, "Latin America: Decline and Responsibility," in Abraham F. Lowenthal and Gregory F. Treverton (eds) *Latin America in a New World* (Boulder, CO: Westview Press, 1994), 219.

3 Jorge G. Castañeda, "Latin America and the End of the Cold War: An Essay in Frustration," in Abraham F. Lowenthal and Gregory F. Treverton (eds) *Latin America in a New World* (Boulder, CO : Westview Press, 1994), 40.

4 Peter Hakim, "President Bush's Southern Strategy: The Enterprise for the Americas Initiative," *The Washington Quarterly* 15 (Spring 1992): 96.

5 Protocol of Amendments to the Charter of the Organization of American States (A-56) "Protocol of Washington," http://www.oas.org/dil/treaties_A-56_Protocol_of_ Washington.htm, accessed January 20, 2011.

6 David Scott Palmer, *U.S. Relations with Latin America during the Clinton Years: Opportunities Lost or Opportunities Squandered?* (Gainesville: University Press of Florida, 2006), 37.

7 George W. Bush, "George W. Bush's Speech on Latin America," *Newsmax.com*, April 25, 2000, http://archive.newsmax.com/articles/?a=2000/8/26/195405, accessed January 20, 2011; David E. Sanger, "Bush Links Trade with Democracy at Quebec Talks," *New York Times*, April 22, 2001.

8 Jorge I. Domínguez, "The Changes in the International System during the 2000s," in Jorge I. Domínguez and Rafael Fernández de Castro (eds) *Contemporary U.S.–Latin American Relations: Cooperation or Conflict in the 21st Century?* (New York: Routledge 2010), 8.

9 Bush, "George W. Bush's Speech on Latin America."

10 "A Conversation with Vicente Fox Quesada," Council on Foreign Relations, September 15, 2005, http://www.cfr.org/publication/8884/conversation_with_vicente_fox_ quesada_rush_transcript_federal_news_service_inc.html, accessed January 20, 2011.

11 Kenneth N. Waltz, "The Emerging Structure of International Politics," *International Security* 18 (Fall 1993): 74, 79.

12 Samuel P. Huntington, "The Lonely Superpower," *Foreign Affairs* 78 (March/April 1999): 37.

13 "Rendering Account," *The New PDVSA Contact* (Caracas: Ministério de Energía y Petróleo, August 2005), 5, http://www.pdvsa.com/interface.en/database/fichero/ publicacion/934/20.PDF, accessed November 17, 2010.

14 Quoted in Florencia Copley, "Telesur is Constructing Another View," http://www. venezuelasolidarity.org.uk/ven/web/articles/Telesur_another_view.html, accessed November 17, 2010.

15 Robert O. Keohane, "Between Vision and Reality: Variables in Latin American Foreign Policy," in Joseph S. Tulchin and Ralph H. Espach (eds) *Latin America in the New International System* (Boulder, CO: Lynne Rienner, 2001), 212.

16 Quoted in Flávio Américo dos Reis, "The Al Jazeera of the South," *World Press Organization*, August 22, 2005, http://www.worldpress.org/Americas/2136.cfm, accessed November 17, 2010.

17 "Rice, Chávez Clash as OAS Meeting Opens," *Financial Times*, June 7, 2005.

18 Quoted in Jona Gindin, "Whose Democracy? Venezuela Stymies U.S. (Again)," June 8, 2005, http://www.venezuelanalysis.com/articles.php?artno=1473, accessed November 17, 2010.

19 Cleto Sojo, "Venezuela, OAS Countries Reject US Proposal to Monitor Democracies," June 8, 2005, http://www.venezuelanalysis.com/news.php?newsno=1651, accessed November 17, 2010.

20 Joel Brinkley, "U.S. Proposal in the O.A.S. Draws Fire as an Attack on Venezuela," *New York Times*, May 22, 2005.

21 Gregory Wilpert, "Venezuela Hails OAS Meeting As Great Success," June 9, 2005, http://www.venezuelanalysis.com/news/php?newsno=1654, accessed November 17, 2010.

22 See "Palabras del presidente de la República Argentina, Dr. Néstor Kirchner durante la inauguración de la IV Cumbre de las Américas, en Mar del Plata," November 4, 2005, http://www.summit-americas.org/NextSummit_eng.htm, accessed November 17, 2010.

23 See "Capitalism is Savagery," excerpts from a speech by Hugo Chávez at 2005 World Social Forum, *Third World Traveler*, April 10, 2005, http://www.thirdworldtraveler.com/South_America/CapitalismSavagery_Chavez.html, accessed November 17, 2010.

24 Joseph S. Nye, Jr., "The Decline of America's Soft Power," *Foreign Affairs* 83 (2004): 16.

25 The Pew Research Center for the Press and the Public, "What the World Thinks in 2002. How Global Publics View: Their Lives, Their Countries, The World, America," December 4, 2002, http://people-press.org/report/165/what-the-world-thinks-in-2002, accessed January 6, 2011.

26 Steven Kull and Doug Miller, "Global Public Opinion on the US Presidential Election and US Foreign Policy," September 8, 2004, Program on International Policy Attitudes, University of Maryland, and GlobeScan, http://www.pipa.org/OnlineReports/Views_US/USElection_Sep04/USElection_Sep04_rpt.pdf, accessed January 6, 2011.

27 "In 18 of 21 Countries Polled, Most See Bush's Reelection as Negative for World Security," http://www.pipa.org/OnlineReports/Views_US/BushReelect_Jan05/Bush Reelect_Jan05_rpt.pdf, accessed January 6, 2011.

28 "World Public Opinion.org, "Latin American Publics are Skeptical about US—But Not About Democracy," March 4, 2007, http://www.worldpublicopinion.org/pipa/articles/brlatinamericara/328.php?lb=btvoc&pnt=328&nid=&id=, accessed January 20, 2011.

29 Peter H. Smith, *Talons of the Eagle: Latin America, the United States, and the World*, third edition (New York: Oxford University Press, 2008), 414.

30 Robert O. Keohane, "Between Vision and Reality: Variables in Latin American Foreign Policy," in Joseph S. Tulchin and Ralph H. Espach (eds) *Latin America in the New International System* (Boulder, CO: Lynne Rienner, 2001), 211.

Credits

Index